INSTRUCTOR'S GUIDE WITH TEST ITEM FILE FOR

Sexual Interactions

FOURTH EDITION

Albert Richard Allgeier
Elizabeth Rice Allgeier

Deborah McDonald Winters
New Mexico State University

Elizabeth Rice Allgeier
Bowling Green State University

D. C. HEATH AND COMPANY
Lexington, Massachusetts   Toronto

Address editorial correspondence to:
D. C. Heath and Company
125 Spring Street
Lexington, MA 02173

International Standard Book Number: 0-669-33339-5

10 9 8 7 6 5 4 3 2 1

Contents

Letter to Instructors

Dear Fellow Human Sexuality Instructors:

This Instructor's Guide is a collaborative effort between an instructor who has used *Sexual Interactions* in her courses, Deborah McDonald Winters (DMW), and one of the authors of *Sexual Interactions*, Elizabeth Rice Allgeier (ERA). It contains suggestions for lectures and classtime activities prepared by ERA, and a test item file prepared by DMW. We also provide a list of the names and addresses of film distributors to contact for their catalogs. We use relatively few films in our own courses and describe them in the relevant chapters on suggestions for use of classtime.

For instructors using *Sexual Interactions*, ERA periodically writes a newsletter, *The Allgeier Update*, reviewing emerging research findings. We welcome suggestions for classroom demonstrations as well as reports of results of recent research by users of *Sexual Interactions* for inclusion in *The Allgeier Update*.

To obtain *The Allgeier Update* newsletter or the D. C. Heath Exam (the computerized test item file, available in IBM-PC and Macintosh versions), please contact your local D. C. Heath representative or telephone D. C. Heath toll-free at 1-800-235-3565.

Sincerely,

Deborah McDonald Winters, Ph.D.
New Mexico State University
Las Cruces, New Mexico 88003-0001

Elizabeth Rice Allgeier, Ph.D.
Bowling Green State University
Bowling Green, OH 43403

Film Distributors

ffirmative Action Office, AD 301, SUNY-Albany, 1400 Washington Ave., Albany, NY 12222 (518/442-5415).

mbrose Video Publishing, 1290 6th Ave., Suite 2245, New York, NY 10104 (800/526-4663).

ambridge Documentary Films, Inc., P.O. Box 385, Cambridge, MA 02139 (617/354-3677).

inema Guild, 1697 Broadway, Room 506, New York, NY 10019 (212/246-5522).

ine Research Associates, 32 Fisher Ave., Boston, MA 02120 (617/442-9756).

dan Programs, Box 133, 2215R Market St., San Francisco, CA 94114 (415/863-3999).

anlight Productions, 47 Halifax St., Boston, MA 02130 (617/524-0980).

HS, Films for the Humanities & Sciences, P.O. Box 2053, Princeton, NJ 08543-2053 (800/257-5126).

lmaker's Library, Inc., 124 E. 40th St., New York, NY 10016 (212/808-4980).

ocus International Inc., 1160 East Jericho Turnpike, Huntington, NY 11743 (800/843-0305; in New York, 516/549-5320).

uman Relations Media, 175 Tomkins Ave., Pleasantville, NY 10570 (800/431-2050; in New York or Canada, call collect, 914/769-7496).

ino International, 333 W. 39th St., Suite 503, New York, NY 10018 (212/629-6880).

insey Institute for Sex Research, Indiana University, Bloomington, IN (812/855-7686).

he Media Guild, 11722 Sorrento Valley Rd., Suite E, San Diego, CA 92121 (619/755-9191).

Mercury Productions, 655 6th Ave., New York, NY 10010 (212/869-4073).

Multi-Focus, 1525 Franklin St., San Francisco, CA 94109 (800/821-0514 or in CA, call collect 415/673-5103).

Jational Film Board of Canada, 16th Floor, 1251 Avenue of the Americas, New York, NY 10020 (212/586-5131).

Jew Day Films, 22 D Hollywood Ave., Hohokus, NJ 07423 (201/652-6590).

erennial Education, 1560 Sherman Ave., Suite 100, Evanston, IL 60201 (800/323-9084; in IL, call collect 312/433-1610).

olymorph Films, 118 South St., Boston, MA 02111 (800/223-5107).

SU, Penn State Audio-Visual Services, Special Services Building, Pennsylvania State University, 1127 Fox Hill Rd., University Park, PA 16803-1824 (814/863-3102 for purchase; 800/826-0132 for rental).

Jniversity of California Extension Media Center, 2000 Center Street, Berkeley, CA 94704 (510/642-0460 or 510/642-0461 for rental, preview, or purchase).

PART I:
SUGGESTIONS FOR LECTURES AND CLASS ACTIVITIES

General Recommendations

The suggestions in Part I are offered for lectures and class activities to correspond to each chapter in *Sexual Interactions*. My own course is offered at the 300 level to more than two hundred university students each semester, and I generally use lecture time to update or expand material in the textbook rather than to reiterate what is in the book. There are a few exceptions, and I will note them chapter by chapter in this guide, but depending on the educational level and number of students in your course, it may be appropriate for you to do more or less reiteration of text material. Some of my colleagues and I have used *Sexual Interactions* as the basic textbook for graduate-level courses on sex research or on clinical aspects of research on human sexuality for clinical psychology or medical students. At that level, we assign additional readings based on the focus of the course.

Some of my recommendations may be useful throughout the course. These include names of publications that provide up-to-date sex research findings (see Appendix B in *Sexual Interactions*) and the Sexual Attitudes and Experiences Questionnaire (beginning on p. 4 of this manual), which may be administered anonymously at the beginning of the course so that the responses of students can be provided when relevant throughout the course. Depending on your own research interests, you may want to omit some items or areas and add other topics to the questionnaire.

The Sexual Knowledge Survey, beginning on p. xxvii of the textbook, may also be administered at the beginning of the semester. In addition, you may wish to skim the rest of Part I for suggestions for guest speakers, who generally need to be contacted well in advance.

If you administer the Sexual Knowledge Survey or the Sexual Attitudes and Experiences Questionnaire (as is, or with your own modification), I advise you to have it approved by the ethics committee on your campus. In addition, unless you have sufficient space in your classroom to permit students to complete it without concern that others may see their responses, consider distributing it in class for students to complete at home. They can return it to you through campus mail or by depositing it in a box or large envelope at subsequent class sessions.

You may wish to tape music to be played at the beginning of class. For instance, "I Can't Get No Satisfaction," by the Rolling Stones, could be played at the beginning of the class that deals with sexual dysfunction (Chapter 8). "Hanky-Panky," the Madonna song from the movie *Dick Tracy*, is about female masochism and could be played at the beginning of the class on atypical sexual behavior (Chapter 19). (This song is about preferring spanking to kissing for the purpose of sexual arousal; it amazes me that in this time of censorship, it is being played on the radio.) Bette Midler's "The Rose" is a good song to play at the beginning of the class that focuses on loving sexual interactions (Chapter 20).

I strongly recommend that instructors who are interested in giving their students the opportunity to conduct their own research obtain a copy of *Sexuality-Related Measures: A Compendium* (Davis, Yarber & Davis, 1988), the first collection of measures with known psychometric properties that are relevant to sexual attitudes and behavior. A former editor of the *Journal of Sex Research*, Clive Davis, was in a position to collect many of the questionnaires and measures that have been used in research on sexuality. To order copies, instructors should write to William Yarber, HPER, Indiana University, Bloomington, IN 47405 (812/335-7974).

Sexual Attitudes and Experiences Questionnaire

Instructions: Completion of this questionnaire is voluntary and anonymous. Please do not write your name or any identifying information (student number and so forth) on the questionnaire.

DEMOGRAPHIC BACKGROUND

Please place the letter corresponding to your answer to the left of the item.

_____ Gender: a. male; b. female

_____ Age (in years)

_____ Class: a. fr.; b. so.; c. jr.; d. sr.; e. other

_____ Religious training: a. Protestant; b. Catholic; c. Jewish; d. Atheist/Agnostic; e. Other (specify _____)

_____ Frequency of attendance at religious services per year.

_____ Political affiliation: a. Very liberal; b. Liberal; c. Middle of the road; d. Conservative; e. Very conservative.

_____ Approximate annual family income.

ATTITUDES

Instructions: Place the letter representing one of the following five responses to indicate how you feel about the following issues relevant to sexuality:

a. Strongly approve
b. Approve somewhat
c. Neutral
d. Disapprove somewhat
e. Strongly disapprove

_____ 1. Education about sexuality in grade school.

_____ 2. Education about sexuality in junior high.

_____ 3. Education about sexuality in high school.

_____ 4. Availability of nonprescription contraceptives (condoms, foams, contraceptive sponges) in vending machines in public restrooms.

_____ 5. Sexual intercourse between an engaged couple.

_____ 6. Sexual intercourse between a couple in love.

_____ 7. Sexual intercourse between a couple who has dated a couple of times.

_____ 8. Sexual intercourse by a woman with a man the same night she meets him.

_____ 9. Sexual intercourse by a man with a woman the same night he meets her.

_____ 10. Sexual relations between two women.

_____ 11. Sexual relations between two men.

_____ 12. Masturbation by a single person who has no sexual partner.

_____ 13. Masturbation by a person when his or her partner is unavailable for lengthy periods of time (lives out of town, is ill, etc.).

_____ 14. Masturbation by a married person.

_____ 15. Oral-genital sexual stimulation between a man and a woman.

_____ 16. Oral-genital sexual stimulation between two people of the same gender.

_____ 17. Anal sexual stimulation between a man and a woman.

_____ 18. Anal sexual stimulation between two people of the same gender.

_____ 19. Abortion when a woman is pregnant due to rape or incest or when her health is endangered.

_____ 20. Abortion when a woman requests it, for whatever reason.

_____ 21. Group sex (sexual relations between three or more consenting partners).

_____ 22. Mate exchange (couples' exchanging partners for purposes of sexual relations).

_____ 23. Wife's taking primary care of the children while husband is employed outside the home.

_____ 24. Husband's taking primary care of the children while wife is employed outside the home.

_____ 25. Legal availability of erotic materials (books, movies, magazines, etc.) for adults.

EXPERIENCES

For the following questions, please indicate the age at which you first had the following experiences. If you have not had the experience, please write N/A (not applicable) on the line.

_____ 1. Discussion with mother about names for genitals.

_____ 2. Discussion with father about names for genitals.

_____ 3. Discussion with mother about menstruation.

_____ 4. Discussion with father about menstruation.

_____ 5. Discussion with mother about nocturnal orgasm.

_____ 6. Discussion with father about nocturnal orgasm.

_____ 7. Discussion with mother about conception (how sperm meets egg).

_____ 8. Discussion with father about conception.

_____ 9. Discussion with mother about emotional aspects ("love") of sexual intimacy.

_____ 10. Discussion with father about emotional aspects of sexual intimacy.

_____ 11. Discussion with mother about passionate aspects (sexual arousal) of sexual intimacy.

_____ 12. Discussion with father about passionate aspects of sexual intimacy.

_____ 13. Discussion with friends of the same gender about sex.

_____ 14. Discussion with friends of the other gender about sex.

_____ 15. Playing "doctor" (looking at or touching each other's genitals) with friends of the same gender.

_____ 16. Playing "doctor" with friends of the other gender.

_____ 17. Age (in years and months) of first menstrual period.

_____ 18. Age (in years and months) of first nocturnal orgasm.

_____ 19. Awareness of feelings of sexual arousal toward someone of the same gender.

_____ 20. Awareness of feelings of sexual arousal toward someone of the other gender.

_____ 21. Erotically kissing someone of the same gender.

_____ 22. Erotically kissing someone of the other gender.

_____ 23. Genital stimulation with someone of the same gender.

_____ 24. Genital stimulation with someone of the other gender.

_____ 25. Orgasm with someone of the same gender.

_____ 26. Orgasm with someone of the other gender.

_____ 27. Sexual intercourse with someone of the other gender.

_____ 28. Receiving oral-genital stimulation.

_____ 29. Giving oral-genital stimulation.

_____ 30. Self-stimulation (masturbation).

_____ 31. Receiving anal stimulation.

_____ 32. Giving anal stimulation.

_____ 33. First used a method of contraception (specify method: _____).

_____ 34. Regularly used a method of contraception (specify method: _____).

_____ 35. Experienced an unwanted pregnancy (by self or partner).

_____ 36. Experienced a wanted pregnancy (by self or partner).

For the following, please fill in the blank:

_____ 1. Number of lifetime sexual partners of the other gender.

_____ 2. Number of lifetime sexual partners of the same gender.

_____ 3. Average frequency per month of masturbation during past year.

_____ 4. Average frequency per month of sexual relations with a partner during past year.

_____ 5. Number of unwanted pregnancies by self or partner.

_____ 6. Number of unwanted pregnancies by self or partner resolved by:

    ___ a. miscarriage.

    ___ b. abortion.

    ___ c. keeping baby.

    ___ d. giving baby up for adoption.

_____ 7. Age at which you would like, ideally, to marry or to make a long-term commitment to someone. If you don't wish to make a long-term commitment (marital or otherwise), write N/A.

_____ 8. Age at which you would like, ideally, to have a child.

_____ 9. Age at which you first saw erotic books or magazines.

_____ 10. Likelihood that you would force someone to have sex if you could be sure that you would not be caught.

    a. none; b. slightly likely; c. somewhat likely; d. likely; e. very likely.

_____ 11. Have you ever tried to force someone to have sex who didn't want to?

_____ 12. Have you ever forced someone to have sex who didn't want to?

_____ 13. Has anyone ever tried to force you to have sex when you didn't want to?

_____ 14. Has anyone ever forced you to have sex when you didn't want to?

First Class Session

Informed Consent and Syllabus.   Chapter 1 is not assigned until the second class session. Given the nature of the topic, students should be given thorough informed consent about the content of the course. I strongly advise the distribution of a syllabus so that students can examine the range of topics that will be covered during the course. In response to difficulties that several sexuality course instructors have had from their departments or university administrators, some instructors distribute a written informed-consent form to be signed by students who wish to remain in the course. I use a verbal informed-consent procedure to discuss the explicit nature of the language used in the course ("we'll be calling a penis a penis rather than a dicky-bird, a clitoris a clitoris rather than a magic button, and so forth"). I also describe the kinds of audiovisual materials that will be used during the course regarding the extent to which they contain nudity, depictions of sexual interactions, and so on. I tell students they are not required to see movies that they think they will find morally offensive and that they may close their eyes at any point during a film that they are uncomfortable. I tell students that unless they obtain my permission in advance, they are not to invite friends who are not enrolled in the course to come on the days that movies are shown because the movies are screened for educational purposes in the context of the discussion of particular topics. After describing the content of the course and the difficulties in mastering the topic ("This is not an easy course!"), I urge students to withdraw from the course if they believe their exposure to the material is inconsistent with their moral values.

Instructor's Background.   After giving informed consent, you may want to describe how you became interested in sexuality (professionally!) and your academic background that prepared you to teach the course. I point out that most human sexuality instructors have been trained in one of the traditional social or biological sciences because there are only a few doctoral programs available in North America for people who wish to obtain an advanced degree in human sexuality.

Scientific Evidence versus Moral Values.   A discussion of the difference between moral values and objective or quasi-objective empirical data is useful during the first class session. You may want to point out that the textbook (and probably your course) is not aimed at shaping students' moral, religious, or ethical values but rather on increasing their sophistication in understanding new findings about sexuality and on making sexuality-related decisions. The emphasis is not on sex education per se but on increasing their knowledge about the correlates of sexual attitudes and behaviors, the consequences or correlates of various choices, and their ability to evaluate sex-research reports that are published long after the course ends.

In 1990, one of Phil Donahue's shows was devoted to the concerns of some segments of society with the "immorality" of providing college students with courses on human sexuality. Two of the four guests on the show were a Nassau Community College human sexuality course instructor and Debra Haffner of Sex Information and Education Council of the United States. The other two guests were members of organizations that were highly critical of such courses. They attacked aspects of the course they were "investigating" and the textbook that was being used. It was clear that the attackers were confusing description with advocacy. For example, the fact that a course or a textbook includes a definition of necrophilia (as most do) does not imply that the instructors or authors are suggesting that students seek their nearest mortuary to have coitus with a corpse. Given the climate of the times, however, it is important to stress at the beginning of the course, and while covering certain topics in the course (e.g., abortion, atypical sexual behaviors), the distinction between description and advocacy.

Self-stimulation. As an example of the ways in which beliefs about particular sexual activities can vary across time and cultures and the differences between religious beliefs, moral values, and scientific evidence, I discuss masturbation. Up through the nineteenth century (and still, in some circles), self-stimulation—called by some "self-abuse"—was viewed as a sin, and its practice was thought to lead to horrendous mental and physical maladies. As Bullough (1976) has pointed out, the belief that touching one's genitals was a sin was replaced during the nineteenth century with the view that it was a sickness, but consequences of engaging in the activity were still believed to be dire, involving loss of memory and other forms of mental deterioration. The fact that numerous surveys conducted by the Kinsey group and subsequent researchers have found that the majority of people in our culture report having engaged in self-stimulation contradicts the belief that this practice leads automatically to illness. In fact, some sex therapists and researchers now advocate the use of masturbation as a way to learn how to respond more readily with a partner, and directed masturbation programs for nonorgasmic women have been reported to be very successful (LoPiccolo and Stock, 1986; see Chapter 8 in the textbook). Thus, if a person wants to masturbate but refrains because of the belief that self-stimulation will have negative mental or physical consequences, he or she needs to know that that belief is not supported by empirical evidence. On the other hand, if a person avoids self-stimulation because the activity is in conflict with his or her moral or religious values, that is fine.

Class Activity: Slang Terms for Masturbation. As a means of desensitizing the class to discussion of sexual issues and as a demonstration of the kinds of attitudes we hold toward sexual activity, I conclude the lecture on variations in beliefs about masturbation with a request for contemporary slang terms for self-stimulation. I put a transparency on the overhead projector and begin by noting that one time-honored term is "jacking off." At this point, students typically begin to laugh and generate their own terms. As I write each of their terms on the transparency, there are renewed waves of laughter.

After your students have listed about 10 terms, ask them if they notice any common themes in the slang. You will probably find that most of the terms involve acts that are aggressive rather than loving or pleasuring, are done to foods or animals, involve a phallic form, are performed by someone else, or are bereft of female imagery—for example, "bopping your baloney," "choking your chicken," "spanking your monkey," "whacking your carrot," "slamming your ham," and "beating the bishop." One of the most unusual is "rubbing the heat-seeking moisture missile"—an interesting allusion to the connection between sex and war! Never has someone volunteered the term "caressing my clit" (implying pleasuring, female self-stimulation, with the speaker describing the activity as something that she, rather than someone else, engages in), although females as well as males do volunteer terms.

Note: This exercise has always worked in my large classes, but when I am teaching a small (e.g., 20 to 35 students) section, I either ask the students to form small groups to report terms that they have heard from others and then have each group report the terms, or I ask them to collect terms from their friends and roommates and report them at the next class session. With a small group, the likelihood is reduced of having enough students who are extroverted enough to volunteer these terms on their own, so use of groups or terms from others may be less threatening.

The same general points about the link between aggression and sexuality would probably also emerge if slang terms for intercourse were used rather than those for self-stimulation. Aside from "making love," most of the terms have an aggressive or hostile flavor—"jumping your bones," "screwing," "fucking," "scoring," and so forth. Students can be asked what the themes shown in our slang for masturbation or sexual intercourse suggest about contemporary attitudes toward sexual activity, and the constructs of "sex-negative" versus "sex-positive" cultures can be introduced.

Sexual Attitudes, Behavior, and Knowledge Questionnaires.   Because normative data reported in textbooks and published in journals are usually based on studies conducted at least two years prior to their publication and because students may be interested in knowing about the attitudes and behaviors of their peers, you may want to distribute the Sexual Knowledge Survey printed at the beginning of the textbook and the Sexual Attitudes and Experiences Questionnaire on pp. 4–7 of this Instructor's Guide. I ask students if they would like to respond to these questionnaires anonymously. If the majority of students raise their hands (and they always have), the questionnaires are distributed at the end of the second class session, and a large envelope is passed around during subsequent class sessions to collect them. Students should be assured that participation is voluntary and that their responses will be kept confidential but that group results will be reported to the class as the particular topic is introduced during the course. For example, when sexual socialization and sex education are discussed in Chapters 6 and 12, students can be told the percentage of males and females in the class who received information from their parents, and the age at which they received it, or the percentage who played "doctor." When sexual assault is being discussed (Chapter 18), the extent of students' experience with coercive sexuality can be described.

Note: If enrollment in your course is very small, it may be unwise to administer the questionnaires because of the difficulty of ensuring anonymity. An alternative is to ask each class member to distribute the questionnaire to 10 friends, with the responses returned to you via campus mail. As noted earlier, this procedure should be cleared with the ethics review board on your campus.

References and Other Sources for Lectures

Davis, C. M., Yarber, W. L. and Davis, S. L. (Eds.) (1988) *Sexuality-related measures: A compendium.* Lake Mills, IA: Graphic Publishing Company.

Bullough, V. (1976) *Sexual variance in society and history.* New York: Wiley.

Chapter 1: Historical and Cross-Cultural Perspectives on Sexuality

Topics Covered in the Chapter

The main purpose of this chapter is to show the diversity in sexual attitudes, beliefs, and practices that have existed across cultures and time periods. In the first edition, we attempted to do this using a chronological account moving from Mesopotamian times to the twentieth century. In subsequent editions, we have chosen to use a topical approach instead.

We begin with a discussion of variations across groups in the rationales for engaging in particular practices and the difficulties of making interpretations of one culture's behavior from the context of another. We suggest that students write down and discuss their own beliefs regarding the six sexual questions that are addressed in Chapter 1.

The first topic that is addressed involves beliefs about the nature of female and male sexuality beginning with brief reference to the biblical story of Adam and Eve. The worship of the Great Mother is described, as are the variations in defining and responding to male versus female extramarital relations, rape, and prostitution. Several pages are devoted to the phenomenon of witchcraft, and Box 1.1 contains an excerpt from the *Malleus Maleficarum*, the fifteenth-century handbook for diagnosing witchcraft. The excerpt focuses on the reasons why females, who were supposedly sexually insatiable, are more likely to be possessed by the devil than are males.

We draw on religious, historical, and cross-cultural accounts regarding beliefs about the purposes and effects of engaging in sexual intercourse and beliefs about the purpose and effects of male circumcision. Box 1.4 describes the contemporary practice of pharaonic circumcision of females in the Sudan. Variations in beliefs about the morality of contraception and the relationship between sexual intercourse and health are described. Variations in the rationales for, and the meaning of, same-gender sexual relationships are given considerable coverage. Beliefs about the relationship among love, sex, and marriage are discussed, with emphasis on the fact that the contemporary expectation that love precedes marriage is relatively recent.

We conclude with a description of variations in marital and family forms historically and cross-culturally, and we point out that the Western contemporary practice of (serial) monogamy has been less prevalent in the world's cultures than has polygamy.

Ideas for Lecture and Use of Class Time

If students have indicated an interest in completing the questionnaires described earlier, I distribute them during this class session, again emphasizing that responding is voluntary and anonymous.

I use this lecture to contrast the sexual values, beliefs, and practices of the So of Uganda, with whom I lived and did sex research for a year, with contemporary values, beliefs, and practices in North America. You may find it useful to use your own research interests or activities to illustrate issues relevant to understanding variations in sexual behavior and differences in methodological approaches to sexual questions.

A topic that is likely to be very interesting to students concerns attitudes and beliefs about nudity historically and cross-culturally. Due to space limitations, we provide very little information on nudity in the textbook, but the various ideologies associated with it would fit nicely into the overall point that we are trying to make in the first chapter. The books by Parmelee (1931) and by Roe (1911) contain some good photographs that could be used as slides or transparencies.

Randolph's (1874) book contains some wonderful quotations that can be used in conjunction with this chapter to illustrate inaccurate historical beliefs or in conjunction with later chapters. For example, "masculine" females and "feminine" males are "human monstrosities, and were born wrong. If you ask me why and how, listen, and the story shall be fully, fairly, yet briefly told. . . . If a human monad, or 'zoosperm,' from the left side of the father, encounters a ripe ovum from the left side of the mother, that fact determines the gender. It will be male. . . . Reverse the case, and reverse results will follow invariably,—though how to do it on purpose is a somewhat difficult problem to solve; yet it *can* be done, and is far more easily accomplished than at first sight may appear" [emphasis in original, p. 33].

Randolph went on to suggest that the pairing of a sperm with an ovum "from opposite sides of the parents' bodies produces what we would call transsexuality (in which case the body of the child will be of one gender, its soul and spirit of the opposite one," p. 33).

Randolph also had statements on "Negro sexuality" (p. 39), abortion (p. 102), "feminine seduction" (p. 138), and cures for "impotence." He suggested the following for the impotent man:

1st. He should occupy his own chamber *solus*. 2d. Breathe deeply. 3d. Be much in the sunshine. 4th. Drink no liquors. 5th. Bathe often. 6th. Eat solid beef, and unsifted flour—no potatoes at all; and in four weeks he will recuperate all his lost energies and be a man again; for while he remains a weakling and a passional [*sic*] imbecile, he could not be happy with the best and fairest wife that ever was fashioned by the master hand of Omnipotence! (p. 151)

The book has no index, but Randolph discussed cross-gender identity, homosexuality, and conception.

Raymond Lawrence's (1989) book, *The Poisoning of Eros: Sexual Values in Conflict*, focuses on the persistent conflict in sexual values that has characterized Western history. He argues that religious and political leadership has often conspired to suppress any memory of positive attitudes toward sexuality. Lawrence explores a number of periods in Western history in which a basic affirmation of sexuality has flourished but subsequent written history neglected. Lawrence's book, which won the Biennial Book Award at the World Congress of Sexology in 1989, can provide the basis for a historical overview of the hostility of Christian attitudes toward sexuality that you could use for lecture to accompany either this or the next chapter.

Gordon's (1988) findings about basketball and football coaches' attitudes toward pregame sex fit nicely with the textbook's material on beliefs about sexual intercourse or about the relationship of sexual stimulation and health. Alternatively, you may wish to discuss his study in the context of Chapter 14. Discussion of his findings can be preceded by asking students how many of the males and females have been involved in sports in high school and college and then asking of that group how many of them were told to avoid pregame sex and what reasons they were given for such avoidance. Gordon sampled Division 1 basketball and baseball coaches, and asked, "Do you feel that having sexual relations the night or morning before a game negatively affects athletic performance?" Only 9 percent agreed, 50 percent said no, and 41 percent said they didn't know. Coaches were also asked about the ways in which they believed pregame sex could affect performance both negatively and positively. His article is quite relevant to issues raised in this chapter, and coverage of it can provide a gentle introduction to sexuality for classes who seem anxious about the topic.

We discuss beliefs about same-gender sexual relationships in this chapter. Berliner (1987) wrote an interesting article about the role of religion in beliefs about homosexual relationships that could be incorporated into lectures for this chapter or for Chapter 15 (Sexual Orientation).

Most contemporary students believe that "love" is very important in deciding whether to marry a particular person. To extend the section on Beliefs about the Relationships Among Love, Sex, and Marriage in Chapter 1, you could describe the rather dramatic change in the importance of love to college students in selecting a mate. In the mid-1960s, Kephart (1967) asked more than 1,000 college students, "If a person had all the other qualities that you desired, would you marry this person if you were not in love with him or her?" The majority of men but only about a quarter of the women answered no (see specific numbers below).

In replication of the Kephart study, Simpson, Campbell, and Berscheid (1986) asked the question again in 1976 and in 1984. Although an increasing majority of men answered no, the more dramatic change occurred with women: by 1984, 85 percent of the women answered no. The authors suggested that the dramatic change might stem from changes in women's status that occurred between the mid-1960s and the 1980s. In early 1990, one of my students and I conducted a replication and extension of this research with more than 1,000 students (Allgeier and Wiederman, 1990). Based on the Simpson et al. speculation, we included a rough measure of women's expected status using anticipated income as a variable. Following are the proportions of men and women indicating they would not marry a person they did not love, even if that person had all the qualities they desired in a potential mate from the four samples:

Percentage of students answering "No" when asked if they would marry a person they did not love if that person had all the other qualities they desired in a marital partner:

	Kephart mid-1960s	Simpson et al. 1976	Simpson et al. 1984	Allgeier & Wiederman 1990
Males	65%	86%	86%	86%
Females	24%	80%	85%	91%

Although Mike Wiederman and I had hypothesized that women who expected larger incomes would rate love as more important in selecting marital partners, our data produced precisely the opposite finding: the more women expected to earn, the less important was their rating of love in making marital decisions.

I am including the one-page measure that we administered to college students if you wish to administer it (or a variation of it) to your students. We distributed it in large classes, but you could ask each student to distribute 10 copies of your measure to friends, to be returned anonymously. You might want to substitute the anticipated-income variable for other variables that you think might be responsible for the dramatic changes in the proportion of women willing to marry someone even if they were not in love with him. For a copy of our conference paper with a more complete reporting of our procedures and findings, please write to me. Also, we included a test of some evolutionarily derived hypotheses in the questionnaire for which the 18 characteristics potentially desired in a mate were listed. For a description of this, see the discussion in Chapter 3 of the Instructor's Guide.

Dear College Student,

The high divorce rate in this society suggests that marriage is a complex, and sometimes disappointing, experience. Please help us to increase understanding of what people look for in a marriage partner by filling out this questionnaire. Please do not write any information that might identify you, such as your name or social security number. If you are interested in obtaining a copy of the results of this project, you may contact Dr. Allgeier or Michael Wiederman at the Psychology Department. Thank you for your participation.

Male _____   Female _____   Age _____

Please indicate approximately what you expect your personal annual income will be 3 to 4 years after graduating from college: $_____ per year.

1. If a (man/woman) had all the other qualities you desired, would you marry this person if you were not in love with him/her? (Please circle a number.)

1	2	3	4	5	6	7
Strongly No	Moderately No		Undecided		Moderately Yes	Strongly Yes

2. If love has completely disappeared from a marriage, I think it is probably best for the couple to make a clean break and start new lives. (Please circle a number.)

1	2	3	4	5	6	7
Strongly Disagree	Moderately Disagree		Neutral		Moderately Agree	Strongly Agree

3. In my opinion, the disappearance of love is not a sufficient reason for ending a marriage, and should not be viewed as such. (Please circle a number.)

1	2	3	4	5	6	7
Strongly Disagree	Moderately Disagree		Neutral		Moderately Agree	Strongly Agree

4. Please rate each of the following characteristics on their importance to you in the selection of a marriage partner, using the following scale as a guide (the higher the number you assign to a particular item, the more important that quality is in a mate).

1	2	3	4	5	6	7
Extremely Unimportant	Moderately Unimportant		Neutral		Moderately Important	Extremely Important

_____ Dependable Character   _____ Emotional Stability

_____ Pleasing Disposition   _____ Mutual Attraction

_____ Good Health   _____ Desire for Home/Children

_____ Refinement/Neatness   _____ Good Cook/Housekeeper

_____ Ambition/Industriousness   _____ Sexual Chastity

_____ Education/Intelligence   _____ Sociability

_____ Similar Religious Background   _____ Good Looks

_____ Similar Educational Background   _____ Favorable Social Status

_____ Good Financial Prospect   _____ Similar Political Background

Please check all of the following that apply to you at the current time:

Not Dating _____   Casually Dating _____   Steadily Dating _____

Living with Boyfriend/Girlfriend _____   Engaged _____   Married _____

Separated _____   Divorced _____   Widowed _____

At what age would you ideally like to marry? (Write N/A if this doesn't apply) _____

Pollis (1987) has provided an intriguing review and discussion of Michel Foucault's perspective on sexuality. If you are teaching the sexuality course to beginning college students, some of the issues she raises may be a bit advanced for them. On the other hand, if you are using the textbook with advanced undergraduates or with graduate students, I highly recommend her article.

Smith's (1986) article is about parthenogenesis in various species.

References and Other Sources for Lectures

Allgeier, E. R., & Wiederman, M. W. (1990, June). *The Association Between Love and Marriage: Kephart (1967) Thrice Revisited.* Paper presented at the Annual Meeting of the Midcontinent Region of the Society for the Scientific Study of Sex, Toledo, OH.

Berliner, A. K. (1987). Sex, sin, and the church: The dilemma of homosexuality. *Journal of Religion and Health, 26,* 137–142.

Gordon, M. (1988). College coaches' attitudes toward pregame sex. *Journal of Sex Research, 24,* 256–261.

Haller, J. S., Jr., & Haller, R. M. (1974). *The physician and sexuality in Victorian America.* Urbana, IL: University of Illinois Press.

Kephart, W. M. (1967). Some correlates of romantic love. *Journal of Marriage and the Family, 29,* 470–474.

La Barre, W. (1984). *Muelos: A Stone Age superstition about sexuality.* New York: Columbia University Press. Reviewed in *Journal of Sex Research, 22,* 1986, 271–274.

Lawrence, R. J. (1989). *The poisoning of eros: Sexual values in conflict.* Roanoke, VA: Augustine Moore Press (217 Mountain Ave., #11, Roanoke, VA 24016, 703/343-8203).

Parmelee, M. (1931). *Nudism in modern life: The new gymnosophy* (Rev. ed.). New York: Alfred A. Knopf.

Pollis, C. A. (1987). The apparatus of sexuality: Reflections on Foucault's contributions to the study of sex in history. *Journal of Sex Research, 23,* 401–408.

Randolph, P. B. (1874). *Eulis! The history of love: Its wondrous magic, chemistry, rules, laws, modes, moods and rational; being the third revelation of soul and sex. Also reply to "why is man immortal?" The solution of the Darwin problem. An entirely new theory.* Toledo, OH: Randolph Publishing Company.

Roe, C. G. (1911). *Horrors of the white slave trade: The mighty crusade to protect the purity of our homes.* London, n. p.

Sears, H. D. (1977). *The sex radicals: Free love in high Victorian America.* Lawrence, KS: Regents Press of Kansas.

Simpson, J. A., Campbell, B., & Berscheid, E. (1986). The association between romantic love and marriage: Kephart (1967) twice revisited. *Personality and Social Psychology Bulletin, 12,* 363–372.

Smith, J. M. (1986). Contemplating life without sex. *Nature, 324,* 300–301.

Story, M. D. (1987). A comparison of social nudists and non-nudists on experience with various sexual outlets. *Journal of Sex Research, 23,* 197–211.

Waugh, A. C. (1986). Autocastration and biblical delusions in schizophrenia. *British Journal of Psychiatry, 149,* 656–659.

Chapter 2: Research on Sexuality

Topics Covered in the Chapter

Chapter 2 has two basic purposes: to provide a historical account of efforts to obtain accurate information about sexuality and to discuss the methods and measures that sex researchers use. The general focus is on becoming competent in evaluating findings from sex research.

We begin this chapter with a discussion of the movement from reliance on religious teachings and cultural beliefs to the movement toward obtaining empirical evidence. We discuss the relatively negative perspective taken by Krafft-Ebing, the relatively positive point of view held by Havelock Ellis, and the impact of Freud's models of the development of male and female sexuality. In Box 2.1, we discuss "psychological circumcision," the vaginal-clitoral orgasm debate, and you may want to expand on that issue in lecture. We then discuss the ways in which societal beliefs, political issues, and ethical values interact to have an impact on the kinds of questions that can be studied. Three examples are given of the difficulties experienced by pioneers in sexual science: the Kinsey group, Masters and Johnson, and historian Vern Bullough. Bonnie Bullough is also shown in the photo of Vern Bullough, and they collaborated on many studies of sexuality, but her primary focus has been in nursing. For a description of ways in which sex researchers still encounter problems related to their field of inquiry, see Box 2.2 on the initial approval and subsequent rejection of two major studies aimed at understanding contemporary sexual habits, with the goal of altering behaviors that may lead to contracting HIV, and "Ideas for Lecture and Use of Class Time" below for lecture material. The Tuskegee study of syphilis is used (Box 2.3) as an example of abuse of ethical standards regarding the conduct of research.

The second part of the chapter focuses on the sex research process. We provide basic definitions of research terms ("hypothesis," "operational definitions of variables," etc.) and describe problems of generalization resulting from sampling bias, volunteer bias, and self-report bias. Advantages and disadvantages of correlational versus experimental methods, observation in the field versus the lab, and cross-sectional versus longitudinal research are discussed. Six different approaches to sex research are described: self-administered questionnaires, surveys, and scales; interviews; direct observation in lab and field settings; physiological response measures; biochemical response measures; and the case study and focus group approaches. This overview is followed by a discussion of the advantages and disadvantages of these measurement methods. The chapter concludes with a discussion of the evaluation of conclusions from sex research, including limits on generalizability, temporary versus lasting effects, and an emphasis on the importance of replication of findings with different samples in different settings before accepting conclusions from research on sexuality.

Ideas for Lecture and Use of Class Time

Because there are no prerequisites for enrollment in this class at my university, I provide a basic "scientific method" lecture during this session. Coverage of methods used in sex research may help to sensitize students (even those who have had a course that discusses scientific methods) to issues raised in Chapter 2. A lecture of this sort, using sexual examples, also increases students' understanding of the difference between beliefs, values, and attitudes versus scientific observation. Issues that can be covered include:

1. The difference between correlation and causation (e.g., beliefs about penis size being correlated to foot size or nose size or beliefs about breast size being correlated to women's capacity for sexual arousal).

2. The advantages and disadvantages of different methods and measures of collecting data relevant to sexuality.

3. Ways in which government bodies and the popular press have presented conclusions without understanding basic issues regarding scientific methodology (e.g., the Hite Reports or the conclusions of the Meese Commission regarding the "effects" of exposure to erotic materials).

4. An overview of the search for the causes of death in previously healthy young men, which began in the early 1980s with correlational studies before the causal virus (HIV) was isolated. Such a lecture can illustrate the usefulness of correlational approaches even though such research cannot by itself conclusively demonstrate causal relationships.

5. In the third edition, we briefly reviewed the study by Masters et al. that resulted in the publication of *CRISIS: Heterosexual Behavior in the Age of AIDS* (1988) as an example of problems in inference that can occur from nonrepresentative samples, inappropriate generalization, and the like. We have taken it out of the fourth edition, but I expand on the issues in lecture material.

Class Demonstration.   As a demonstration of experimental methods and the conditions under which causal inferences may be drawn, Rich Zeller and I (1989) have used the following exercise in our classes. It serves a second purpose of stimulating discussion about the potential for harassment that can occur when faculty have sexual relations with their students. We call the exercise "Causal Inference and Sexual Harassment: Hands-on Experience to Illustrate a Hands-off Policy."

We distribute one of eight versions of a vignette to students. The vignettes describe a situation in which a student (aged 19 or 27) desired an A in a course and met with her professor to receive extra help. Following the review session, an affair is initiated (by the student or professor). At the end of the semester, the student receives the grade earned (B) or desired (A). Thus, this demonstration involves a 2x2x2 factorial design. Students are then asked to indicate on two nine-point scales the extent of their agreement that the professor should be dismissed and that the student should be expelled. After completing their ratings, one student is asked to read the vignette to the class. As it is read, other students realize that they have different versions. When the independent variables became clear to the students, the design is drawn on the chalkboard. Students are then asked to indicate the conditions under which they believe that judgments about the student and professor would be most harsh, and their hypotheses are written on the chalkboard. Common hypotheses are that judgments would be harsher on the professor when the student is 19 (versus 27), on the initiator of the affair, and on both the professor and the student when a grade of A is ultimately assigned. Their hypotheses are listed on the chalkboard, and then their ratings are tabulated in class.

A comparison of mean ratings with hypotheses illustrates how observations are used to confirm or disconfirm hypotheses. Specifically, in our classes the hypothesis is consistently confirmed that the student and professor would be judged more harshly when an A is assigned. However, the hypotheses that the judgment will be more harsh on the initiator of the affair and on the professor when the student is age 19 is not confirmed. The process of creating research designs, generating hypotheses, obtaining data to test the hypotheses, and interpreting the results demonstrates how experimental research is carried out.

We address the second goal by asking students what other variables they think might influence judgments of the student and professor who become romantically/sexually involved. Our past hypothesis was that an affair that occurs without a "sex-for-grade" or "grade-for-sex" verbal contract would be judged less harshly than when such a contract is made explicit. We subsequently tested and confirmed that hypothesis, and we have heard from colleagues who have successfully used this exercise. When these discussions take place, the vulnerability of students and evaluators who engage in sexual relations becomes apparent. Thus, the hands-on experience with causal inference pedagogy can be used to illustrate a hands-off policy. As pointed out spontaneously by our students, a romantic/sexual relationship between a student and or evaluator severely threatens academic integrity. I think that it is interesting that the difference in power between the professor and the student was not raised as an issue by students in any of our classes.

Here is the vignette that we used in one of these demonstrations. Our variations are in brackets. (You can, of course, vary the factors being manipulated to suit your purposes.) We use eight different letters in the upper-right-hand corner for each of the eight vignettes so that the people who receive the same version can gather together to figure out their mean ratings.

Bob and Mary

Last semester, Mary J was a student in Dr. Bob B's Chemistry 101 course. At that time, Mary was 19 [27] years old; Bob was 37. Mary was working hard in Bob's course; after the midterm, she was earning a B in the course. She wanted to finish the course with an A. She sought assistance from Bob during his office hours.

While working on course material, Bob [Mary] adjusted his [her] position such that Mary's breast was exposed nude to his view. Upon noticing Mary's nude breast, Bob continued [did not continue] to look at it. Bob continued to instruct Mary in the course material. Upon realizing that her nude breast was exposed to Bob's view, Mary adjusted [did not adjust] her position so that her breast was no longer [continued to be] exposed to Bob's view. Both Mary and Bob continued to concentrate on the coursework; both were sexually aroused and stimulated by the situation.

When the allocated time had elapsed, Mary needed more work and asked Bob for another work session before the exam. A check of their schedules indicated that the only time that was available for both of them was the following evening. Bob [Mary] proposed that they meet at his [her] apartment at 7 P.M.; Mary [Bob] agreed. Mary [Bob] arrived promptly at Bob's [Mary's] apartment at 7 P.M. that evening. They began to work, and accomplished a great deal during the next hour. Upon completion of the work, Bob [Mary] caressed Mary's [Bob's] hand, put his [her] arms around her [him], and began kissing her [him].

Over the next two months, the relationship between Mary and Bob became more intense, and they engaged in sexual intercourse on a number of occasions.

On the final, Mary's performance was such that she earned a B in the course. After the final, they discussed Mary's grade in Bob's course; Bob thought she should receive a B. Each held his or her own position firmly, and they quarreled. Bob assigned Mary an A [a B] in the course.

Please circle the number that most closely matches your opinion:

	Definitely no		No opinion		Definitely yes			

1. Should Mary be expelled
   from the university?   1   2   3   4   5   6   7   8   9

2. Should Bob be dismissed
   from the university?   1   2   3   4   5   6   7   8   9

Here are the results from one of our classes:

Students' Judgments of Student/Professor Sexual Involvement: Mean Responses*

Item 1: Judgments of student (1 = nonexpulsion, 9 = expulsion)

Initiator	Professor	Student (Age 19)	Professor	Student (Age 27)
Grade				
A	4.6	3.9	4.6	4.4
B	2.5	3.5	3.3	3.5

Main Effects

Student's age: 19 = 3.6; 27 = 4.0
Initiator: Professor = 3.8; Student = 3.8
Final grade: A = 4.4; B = 3.2

Item 2: Judgments of professor (1 = nondismissal, 9 = dismissal)

Initiator	Professor	Student (Age 19)	Professor	Student (Age 27)
Grade				
A	5.9	5.5	5.3	5.3
B	3.7	4.0	4.3	3.3

Main Effects

Student's age: 19 = 4.8; 27 = 4.6
Initiator: Professor = 4.8; Student = 4.5
Final grade: A = 5.5; B = 3.8
* With this exercise we do not perform inferential statistics, because it is beyond the level of introductory courses. We inform students that differences equal to or less than one full scale point are usually due to chance factors and are thus not reliable, whereas differences greater than one full scale point (e.g., the ratings of 5.5 versus 3.8 indicating greater approval for dismissal of the instructor who gives an A versus a B) are probably statistically significant.

In Chapter 2, we describe some of the difficulties that the Kinsey group, Masters and Johnson, and Bullough faced as they tried to conduct sex research. Students are regularly amazed at the problems these twentieth-century people had to overcome to get information on sexuality from the 1930s to the 1960s. For example, in the mid-1950s, the FBI had attempted to get Kinsey and Wardell Pomeroy to reveal their sources of sexually explicit materials. Kinsey and Pomeroy resisted and asked the FBI to share its holdings with the Kinsey Institute,

> causing great indignation at the Bureau. Internal memos indicate that the FBI continued to monitor Kinsey's "intrepid band" (as the agency referred to them), particularly because they were afraid the research would lead to an increase in "permissiveness" and "sexual deviancy." Further the FBI condemned the Rockefeller Foundation's funding of the Institute, feeling that continued research in Kinsey's direction would corrupt and endanger the nation's children. A May 19, 1959 memo says that the foundations have "a stranglehold on the training ground of youth," but goes on to say that "no better instance of a reputable name being lent to enhance an unsavory cause can be found than that offered by the Rockefeller Foundation's support of the Kinsey sex studies" (Sonenschein 1987, p. 409).

The same author asserts that "it appears that 30 years after Kinsey's day, we are again in the midst of a renewed effort to discredit and damage critical sex research" (p. 409). He describes a number of instances in the 1980s of sex researchers' having a variety of difficulties, including loss of jobs, entrapment and arrest, and seizure of data. In 1984, Sonenschein's own four-year accumulation of research on pedophilia and children's sexuality was seized. The arresting officer said, "Your research is through. Your research is over. I have finished your research for you. You can research anything but this" (p. 411). Sonenschein says that it was over seven months before he and American Civil Liberties Union lawyers were able to inventory the documents. The project was an ethnographic study of child-adult sexual relationships, but his content analysis was not complete, and the materials were destroyed. Additionally, he was fined $5,000 and sentenced to ten years in prison. I suggest reading Sonenschein's article and using it as the basis of a good lecture. Your students (and perhaps you) are likely to find some of the positions that Sonenschein takes controversial, stimulating considerable class discussion.

In the context of discussion of direct observation of sexual behavior in lab settings of the sort done by Masters and Johnson, Alzate and Londono's (1987) study of reactions to participation in this kind of research is useful. It is also appropriate for discussion of the issue of generalizability of findings obtained in this research approach to the behavior of individuals in their usual settings for sexual activity.

Burg's (1988) report is relevant to the discussion in the textbook (pp. 32–33) of assumptions about the effects of masturbation. He describes the records kept by a U.S. Marine, Philip Van Buskirk, from 1852 to 1858 of his frequency of masturbation and nocturnal emission between the ages of nineteen and twenty-five, and compares this man's behavior to findings from the Kinsey group's (1948).

Finally, Vern Bullough's (1994) new book, *Science in the Bedroom*, provides good lecture material for this and subsequent chapters in the textbook. (It was published after we had finished writing the book, so we have no citations to it.) He includes chapters on sex research and assumptions: from the Greeks to the nineteenth century; homosexuality; Hirschfeld, Ellis, and Freud; endocrinology; from Freud to biology and Kinsey; from statistics to sexology; the matter of gender; and problems of an emerging science.

References and Other Sources for Lectures

Alzate, H., & Londono, M. L. (1987). Subjects' reactions to a sexual experimental situation. *Journal of Sex Research, 23,* 362–367.

Bernhard, L. (1986). Methodology issues in studies of sexuality and hysterectomy. *Journal of Sex Research, 22,* 108–128.

Brecher, E. M., & Brecher, J. (1986). Extracting valid sexological findings from severely flawed and biased population samples. *Journal of Sex Research, 22,* 6–20.

Bullough, V. L. (1994). *Science in the bedroom: The history of sex research.* New York: Basic Books.

Burg, B. R. (1988). Nocturnal emission and masturbatory frequency relationships: A 19th century account. *Journal of Sex Research, 24,* 216–219.

Catania, J. A., McDermott, L. J., & Pollack, L.M. (1986). Questionnaire response bias and face-to-face interview sample bias in sexuality research. *Journal of Sex Research, 22,* 52–72.

Earls, C. M., Quinsey, V. L., & Castonguay, G. (1987). A comparison of three methods of scoring penile circumference changes. *Archives of Sexual Behavior, 16,* 493–500.

Kilpatrick, A. C. (1987). Childhood sexual experiences: Problems and issues in studying long range effects. *Journal of Sex Research, 23,* 173–196.

Minton, H. L. (1988). American psychology and the study of human sexuality. *Journal of Psychology and Human Sexuality, 1,* 17–34.

Money, J. (1988). Commentary: Current status of sex research. *Journal of Psychology and Human Sexuality, 1,* 5–15.

Pollis, C. A. (1988). An assessment of the impacts of feminism on sexual science. *Journal of Sex Research, 25*, 85–105.

Sonenschein, D. (1987). On having one's research seized. *Journal of Sex Research, 23*, 408–414.

Wheeler, D., & Rubin, H. B. (1987). A comparison of volumetric and circumferential measures of penile erection. *Archives of Sexual Behavior, 16*, 289–299.

Winer, G. A., Makowski, D., Alpert, R. H., & Collins, F. J. (1988). An analysis of experimenter effects on responses to a sex questionnaire. *Archives of Sexual Behavior, 17*, 257–263.

Chapter 3: Contemporary Explanations of Human Sexuality

Topics Covered in the Chapter

In this chapter, we provide an overview of the theoretical models and explanations that have been advanced to account for various aspects of our sexual attitudes and behavior. We begin with a discussion of the fact that attempts to understand how particular variables are related to one another is not just a behavior peculiar to scientists and scholars. We list a series of questions on textbook page 66 and suggest that all of us have attempted to understand and explain various aspects of sexuality in our own lives. Scientists and scholars also do so, but they devote more time to verification or refutation of formal statements (hypotheses) than most of us do in our personal lives.

Four major theories are explored in this chapter: evolutionary, psychoanalytic, learning, and sociological approaches. The section on evolutionary theory gives a broad overview of the concepts of natural selection, reproductive success, and fitness and relates the relationships of these variables to observed gender differences in sexual behavior. We describe the remarkable research by David Buss (1989, 1994) on characteristics desired in a mate that was conducted in 33 societies with more than 10,000 respondents. His findings are consistent with evolutionarily based predictions.

Psychoanalytic approaches are then described, with an emphasis on Freud's theory of personality development and psychosexual stages. This section concludes with an examination of more recent psychoanalytic ideas and an introduction to Erikson's perspective, which is later used as the organizational framework in Chapters 12 and 13 on life span.

The learning approaches section encompasses both the basic paradigms (classical versus operant) and social learning theory, in which cognitions as well as behavior are considered valid sources of data. Social learning theory is applied (briefly) to the issue of exposure to violent erotic and sexually coercive behavior, a subject that could be readily expanded in lecture.

Sociological approaches deal with the theories advanced by Gagnon and Simon (1973) and by Reiss (1986). We examine the ways in which societal norms are related to sexual beliefs and behaviors. We then discuss scripted behavior, kinship and jealousy, power and gender, and the ways in which ideologies are related to societal perceptions of normality.

We conclude the chapter with a discussion of the relationship of scientific theories, political ideologies, and beliefs about morality, emphasizing that theories are models of how particular variables are related or how specific beliefs or behaviors came to exist. Such models are *not* meant to *advocate* gender differences or similarities or any specific pattern of sexual behavior.

Ideas for Lecture and Use of Class Time

To reinforce the idea presented in the textbook that we all attempt to understand and explain various aspects of sexuality, you might think of some of the explanations that were popular in your own peer group in junior high or high school and then ask for some of the beliefs about sexuality that your students encountered. For example, when I was in junior high, I was told by my peers that you could tell whether a "girl" had begun menstruating by looking at the inside corners of her eyes. If there were little holes (in reality, tear ducts), she had begun menstruating. Stated more formally, the belief was that menarche causes the development of little holes in the corner of the eyes. I didn't hear about this until after I had experienced menarche, but I studied my eyes, and, sure enough, there were those telltale little holes! It never dawned on me to test this hypothesis by looking closely at men's eyes. Other common beliefs or "theories" are that kissing causes pregnancy, showering during menstruation causes sickness, women cannot become pregnant the first time they engage in intercourse, and so on. You can point out that the difference between the models or theories advanced by scientists versus those advanced by laypeople is that scientists seek to obtain objective evidence that supports or refutes hypotheses, and they use scientific methods to test the theories.

Bixler (1986) examines evolutionary explanations of rapid ejaculation, synchronization of ovulation, possessiveness, courtship, and woman's pleasure as an enhancer of man's excitement. His article can provide the basis for an interesting lecture.

If you administered the questionnaire employing the Kephart question about the importance of love in marital decisions and the characteristics desired in a mate (see Chapter 1 of this guide), you can provide students with the results of their responses to the 18 characteristics in the context of discussing evolutionary theory and the results of the Buss research to see if their patterns match those obtained by Buss.

Gender differences in selectivity about potential mates (Townsend, 1987) can also be discussed in the context of evolutionary theory. Townsend pointed out that research has consistently shown that women are more cautious and selective than men in entering and maintaining sexual relationships. This difference has been explained as due to status differentials between men and women or, in contrast, as due to a basic gender difference between men and women in the extent of disassociation between sexual activity and emotional attachment. On the basis of interviews with 20 male and 20 female medical students, Townsend concluded that high female socioeconomic status does not appear to eliminate or substantially reduce the basic gender difference (favoring the latter explanation). Townsend's article contains some good quotations that could be used in lecture on men's and women's decisions about sexual intimacy. (See also Townsend and Levy, 1990.)

In the textbook, we stress that theories are meant to provide models of ways in which variables are related rather than to advocate particular relationships. It is important in lecture to reiterate this point, and I expand on it by discussing the inappropriateness of using the word "proof" when describing theories and research findings. Instead, we have varying levels of support—strong, moderate, weak, preliminary, and so on—for various theoretical models and research conclusions.

I like to use the example of causes of sexual orientation. Students can be asked what they believe causes a person to be erotically attracted to someone of the same gender. They typically come up with various hypotheses, such as the triangular family system (although they do not use that phrase), hormone irregularity, or a history of childhood sexual abuse. I point out that research comparing large groups of people with homosexual versus heterosexual orientations does not find significant differences in these variables between the two groups and that we do not know the cause of individual orientation—homosexual, bisexual, or heterosexual. I emphasize the importance of testing various cultural beliefs or theories before using them as the basis for policy decisions. The attempt to pass legislation to quarantine HIV-positive people on the basis of the erroneous belief that AIDS can be spread by casual contact is a good example for this issue.

Students tend to dismiss psychoanalytic (Freudian) ideas out of hand. If you are teaching a clinically oriented course to advanced undergraduates or graduate students, I strongly recommend reading Seymour Epstein's article (1994) on the reconceptualization of notions of unconscious (experiential) and conscious (rational) thoughts and behaviors. He provides ample examples of the differences between the two ways that may motivate our behavior, and Table 1 in his article could be put on a transparency for students and applied to sexual behavior. For example, experiential responding is pleasure-pain oriented (what feels good), whereas rational responding is reason oriented (what is sensible). Epstein maintains that irrational fears stem from nonrational processing of information. Although material in the experiential system may be unconscious, it can also be brought to consciousness. If you provide a brief introduction to his article, you may want to return to his ideas in the context of Chapter 8, on dysfunctions and therapy. As a gentle introduction to Epstein's ideas, I ask students to raise their arms if they have moved since coming to college. Most have, I then ask if they have found themselves walking or driving toward their former residence for a short period of time after moving. Most have (experiential versus rational behavior). I then ask them to apply concepts from Epstein's Table 1 to their own responses to potential sexual partners or sexual situations.

To illustrate the phallocentric (versus gynocentric) nature of traditional psychoanalytic theory, I tell the following story, which I originally heard from David Bullard in a slightly different form at a meeting of the Society for the Scientific Study of Sex:

> A little girl is brushing her teeth in the bathroom while her father is taking a shower. He gets out of the shower to dry himself off with a towel, and the little girl notices for the first time that her father has a penis. She leaves the bathroom to seek her mother in her study and says, "Mommy, Daddy has something hanging down between his legs." Her mother gulps and while worrying about the concept of "penis envy" tries to think of something to say. She ends up by simply acknowledging her daughter's statement: "Yes, dear, he does." The daughter says, "And we don't." Her mother, still trying to think about what to say, acknowledges her daughter's statement: "No, we don't." And the little girl says with great solemnity, "And we mustn't laugh at him, right?"

I present this story after asking for questions about traditional psychoanalytic approaches. After the students have finished laughing, I go into how Freud's theories about human sexuality and personality development might have differed had he been female instead of male.

References and Other Sources for Lectures

Bixler, R. H. (1986). Of apes and men (including females). *Journal of Sex Research, 22,* 255–267.

Buss, D. M. (1989). Sex differences in human mate preferences: Evolutionary hypotheses tested in 37 cultures. *Behavioral and Brain Sciences, 12,* 1–49.

Buss, D. M. (1994). *The evolution of desire: Strategies of human mating*. New York: Basic Books.

Epstein, S. (1994). Integration of the cognitive and the psychodynamic unconscious. *American Psychologist, 49*, 709–724.

Gagnon, J. H., and Simon, W. (1987). The sexual scripting of oral genital contacts. *Archives of Sexual Behavior, 16*, 1–25.

Reiss, I. L. (1986). *Journey into sexuality: An exploratory voyage*. Englewood Cliffs, N. J.: Prentice-Hall.

Townsend, J. M. (1987). Sex differences in sexuality among medical students: Effects of increasing socioeconomic status. *Archives of Sexual Behavior, 16*, 425–444.

Townsend, J. M., & Levy, G. D. (1990). Effects of potential partners' physical attractiveness and socioeconomic status on sexuality and partner selection. *Archives of Sexual Behavior, 19*, 149–164.

Chapter 4: Development and Sexual Differentiation

Topics Covered in the Chapter

Those of you who used the third edition of Allgeier and Allgeier should note that in this fourth edition, we have moved the material on transsexuality from Chapter 4 to Chapter 19.

In this chapter, we describe the process of fertilization, normal and atypical gender differentiation, and prenatal development. The discussion of fertilization includes a description of the process of cell division, the difference between germ cells and body cells, and the difference between mitosis and meiosis. Chromosomes, genes, genetic inheritance, and genetic gender are described, along with methods of determining genetic gender. The effects of dominant versus recessive genes are presented, and reasons that males have more X-linked disorders than females do are discussed.

The process of normal gender differentiation at the genetic, gonadal, hormonal, and genital levels is described. Box 4.1 contains a discussion of the effects of sex hormones on prenatal brain development.

Table 4.1 contains a chronology of sexual differentiation during the prenatal and pubescent development periods. Common sex chromosome abnormalities (Klinefelter's, XYY, Turner's, and Triple X syndromes) are listed in Table 4.2, along with information about incidence, characteristics, and treatments. Box 4.2 contains a discussion of the early link made between XYY and aggressiveness by Jacobs et al. (1965) and the subsequent failure to find a consistent relationship. Inconsistencies in prenatal gender differentiation (hermaphroditism and pseudo-hermaphroditism) are discussed, along with androgen insensitivity syndrome and the effects of prenatal exposure to excess levels of androgen. The phenomenon of DHT deficiency syndrome (the subject of Imperato-McGinley's Dominican Republic study) is presented. Coverage of atypical differentiation in genetic females includes adrenogenital syndrome, exposure to excess androgen from the mother, and hormone administration to the mother during pregnancy. This section concludes with a discussion of the relationship between sexual differentiation and gender identity.

Ideas for Lecture and Use of Class Time

Reinisch, Rosenblum, and Sanders's (1987) edited book, *Masculinity/Femininity*, contains 21 chapters on various aspects of the topic that can provide useful lecture material for both this chapter and Chapter 12.

Money's famous twin study (not described in the textbook) in which one of two monozygotic twins had his penis damaged during circumcision and was subsequently raised as a girl (apparently successfully, at least prior to puberty) has sometimes been used to support the conclusion that gender of assignment and rearing are more important than biological variables of gender in determining gender identity. Diamond (1982) reported, however, that the XY male twin raised as a female has been described by psychiatric evaluators as experiencing considerable difficulty in adolescence. A description of Diamond's controversial short report, along with discussion of the DHT deficiency syndrome, described on pages 114–115 of the textbook, can provide the basis for a lecture that stimulates a lot of questions from students. Interestingly, most males born with ambiguous or female-appearing genitalia stemming from the absence of 5-alpha reductase and who at puberty began to masculinize physically appear to have adjusted successfully to the male role during puberty. In contrast, the male twin raised as a female did not adjust successfully to the female role. I have been seeking recent information on that twin, who would now (1994) be about 30 years old. According to Diamond (1994), the twin raised as a girl ultimately sought reconstructive surgery for a penis, now lives as a man and seeks women for erotic partners.

Material from the Pillard and Weinrich (1987) and Weinrich (1988) papers is probably a bit advanced for an introductory-level sexuality class but would be appropriate for an upper-level undergraduate or graduate class.

The film *Miracle of Life* (57 minutes, color; check with your D. C. Heath representative about getting a copy) is the all-time favorite of my students. Using animation and Lars Nilsson's photography, it shows the voyage of the sperm and the egg from the testicles and ovary, their union, and subsequent prenatal development. I use it every semester in the contexts of Chapters 4 and 5 because it beautifully caps the biological coverage of prenatal gender differentiation, fertilization, and sexual anatomy and physiology.

References and Other Sources for Lectures

Cundy, T. F., et al. (1986). Mild androgen insensitivity presenting with sexual dysfunction. *Fertility and Sterility, 46,* 721–723.

Diamond, M. (1982). Sexual identity, monozygotic twins reared in discordant sex roles, and a BBC follow-up. *Archives of Sexual Behavior, 11,* 181–186.

Diamond, M. (1994). Sexuality: Orientation and identity. In R. J. Corsini (Ed.), *Encyclopedia of Psychology* (Vol. 3, pp. 399–402). New York: Wiley.

Hurtig, A. L., & Rosenthal, I. M. (1987). Psychological findings in early treated cases of female pseudohermaphroditism caused by virilizing congenital adrenal hyperplasia. *Archives of Sexual Behavior, 16,* 209–223.

Jacobs, P. A., Brunton, M., Melville, M. M., Britain, R. P. and McClement, W. F. (1965) Aggressive behavior, mental subnormality, and the XYY male. *Nature, 208,* 1351–1352.

Pillard, R. C., & Weinrich, J. D. (1987). The periodic table model of the gender transpositions: Part I. A theory based on masculinization and defeminization of the brain. *Journal of Sex Research*, 23, 425–454.

Reinisch, J. M., Rosenblum, L. A., & Sanders, S. A. (1987). *Masculinity/femininity: Basic perspectives.* New York: Oxford University Press.

Weinrich, J. D. (1988). The periodic table model of the gender transpositions: Part II. Limerent and lusty sexual attractions and the nature of bisexuality. *Journal of Sex Research*, 24, 113–129.

Chapter 5: Sexual Anatomy and Physiology

Topics Covered in the Chapter

This chapter describes sexual anatomy and the endocrine system. The section on male sexual anatomy covers the testes, genital ducts, semen-producing glands (seminal vesicles, prostate, and Cowper's glands), and penis. Concerns about penis size are addressed, and we note that because the clitoris is more important for sexual arousal and response of most women than is the vagina, penis length is relatively irrelevant to female sexual pleasure. The section on female sexual anatomy covers the ovaries, fallopian tubes, uterus, vagina, Gräfenberg spot, vulva, clitoris, pelvic muscles, breasts, and lips. Directions on finding the Gräfenberg spot are given in Box 5.1.

The next section focuses on hormones, the endocrine system, and the nervous system's role in sexual arousal and response. The location and functions of the adrenal glands, the pituitary gland, and the hypothalamus are presented. The major sex hormones are described in Box 5.2, and the effects of hormones on males and females are discussed. Box 5.3 contains one woman's positive reactions to menarche. The section ends with a description of menstrual cycle phases.

The final section of the chapter reviews research on the impact of illness and disease on sexual expression (a topic contained in Chapter 14 in the third edition of the textbook). We devote a considerable amount of space to sexuality and cancers of the breast and reproductive organs of women and men. Box 5.4 describes sexual issues that emerge following mastectomy. Boxes 5.5 and 5.6 provide directions for breast and testes self-exams. We consider as well the relationship of hysterectomy to sexual feelings, essentially concluding that changes in the experience of arousal stem not only from psychological reactions but also from physical changes and the subsequent reduction in sensation during arousal and orgasm stemming from the missing uterus. We also review research on sexuality and cardiovascular illness and diabetes.

Ideas for Lecture and Use of Class Time

I generally use this class to review the genital anatomy of males and females, pronouncing names of genital structures, and reiterating much of what is in the textbook. Although students are generally familiar with female internal anatomy, they tend to be relatively unaware of the extent of male internal anatomy. Transparencies or slides of male and female anatomy are helpful in taking students on the voyage from the testes to the penis and from the ovaries to the vaginal entrance and the clitoris. Coverage of the subject of male anatomy first may help in discussing the hypothesis that the Gräfenberg spot may be a rudimentary prostate gland (Sevely & Bennett,

1978). The film *Orgasmic Expulsions in the Sexually Stimulated Female* (Focus International, 9 minutes, color) can be shown during this class. It shows how to locate the Gräfenberg spot and discusses lab analyses comparing the fluid to urine. The coverage of the expulsion of fluid from the urethra in several women in response to Gräfenberg spot stimulation is graphic. The embarrassment and concern of women who think they may be urinating when they ejaculate during orgasm is addressed. Beverly Whipple, one of the primary researchers in the area, plays the role of the counselor in the film. My students report some discomfort over the explicitness of the genital responses, and I have some question about the sheer amount of ejaculate that is shown being expelled in that the amount is considerably greater than that ejaculated by the average male. You may find Zaviacic and Whipple's (1993) short article useful for providing a background and updated lecture material on female ejaculation.

Martha Cornog (1986) has been carrying on a delightful line of research, interviewing people about their names for their genitals and breasts; a description of her findings can provide comic relief during the "organ recital" involved in covering this material. You could ask students anonymously to indicate whether they have given their genitals a name and, if so, what they named them, when they did so, and why they selected the name they did, and then report findings back to the class.

References and Other Sources for Lectures

Chen, V. W., et al. (1994). Histological characteristics of breast carcinoma in blacks and whites. *Cancer Epidemiology, 3*, 127–135.

Cornog, M. (1986). Naming sexual parts: Preliminary patterns and implications. *Journal of Sex Research, 22*, 393–398.

Elledge, R. M., Clark, G. M., Channess, G. C., & Osborne, C. K. (1994). Tumor biologic factors and breast cancer prognosis among white, Hispanic, and black women in the United States. *Journal of the National Cancer Institute, 86*, 705–712.

Filsinger, E. E., & Monte, W. C. (1986). Sex history, menstrual cycle, and psychophysical ratings of alpha androtenone, a possible human sex pheromone. *Journal of Sex Research, 22*, 243–248.

Morris, N. M., Udry, J. R., Khan-Dawood, F., & Dawood, M. Y. (1987). Marital sex frequency and midcycle female testosterone. *Archives of Sexual Behavior, 16*, 27–37.

Prather, R. C. (1988). Sexual dysfunction in the diabetic female: A review. *Archives of Sexual Behavior, 17*, 277–284.

Rosen, R. C., Kostis, J. B., & Jekelis, A. W. (1988). Beta-blocker effects on sexual function in normal males. *Archives of Sexual Behavior, 17*, 241–255.

Rousseau, L., Dupont, A., Labrie, F., & Couture, M. (1988). Sexuality changes in prostrate cancer patients receiving antihormonal therapy combining the antiandrogen flutamide with medical (LHRH agonist) or surgical castration. *Archives of Sexual Behavior, 17*, 87–98.

Schover, L. R., Evans, R. B., & von Eschenbach, A. C. (1987). Sexual rehabilitation in a cancer center: Diagnosis and outcome in 384 consultations. *Archives of Sexual Behavior, 16*, 445–461.

Sevely, J. L., & Bennett, J. W. (1978). Concerning female ejaculation and the female prostate. *Journal of Sex Research, 14*, 1–20.

Stanislaw, H., & Rice, F. J. (1988). Correlation between sexual desire and menstrual cycle characteristics. *Archives of Sexual Behavior, 17,* 499–508.

Zaviacic, M., & Whipple, B. (1993). Update on the female prostate and the phenomenon of female ejaculation. *Journal of Sex Research, 30,* 148–151.

Chapter 6: Arousal and Communication

Topics Covered in the Chapter

In Chapter 6, we describe models and sources of arousal, variations in response to feelings of arousal, the relationship between fantasies and sexual arousal, and ways of managing sexual feelings. We begin with the point that the capacity for arousal is inborn, but the specific objects that we find arousing appear to be learned.

Our discussion of models of arousal contrasts classical and operant conditioning and focuses on Berscheid and Walster's (1974) two-stage model of love. We review research on sources of arousal—touch, smell, sight, hearing, and kissing—and discuss variations in response to feelings of arousal, the purposes of sexual arousal, and the relationship between sexual socialization and reactions to arousal. The role of fantasy in sexual arousal, and the controversy regarding the health or deviance of sexual fantasies, is discussed, and we describe the possible functions of fantasy, including rehearsal of potential future behaviors, relief from boredom, entertainment, enhancement of excitement in a relationship of long duration, and indulgence in an activity that we would not, in reality, wish to carry out.

The second half of the chapter deals with various aspects of communication about sexuality: socialization for communicating about sex, gender differences in the communication of feelings, and methods of improving interpersonal communication. The relationship of sex guilt and erotophobia versus erotophilia to communication and to positive sexual experiences is discussed. Box 6.1 contains some sample items from Mosher's (1966) measure of sex guilt.

The chapter concludes with a description of ways to manage sexual feelings and behavior. We note the difference between feelings and actual behavior and stress that to make satisfying behavioral decisions, it is helpful to be aware of one's feelings and to form sexual policies. Specifically, we advocate identifying the conditions that a person believes are important in order to act on his or her sexual feelings. We also review the kinds of relationship agreements that couples may make, ranging from total monogamy to open marriage (or relationship). We then describe strategies that can be used to help a person honor his or her agreements, whatever they may be, when that person experiences attraction to a third person.

Ideas for Lecture and Use of Class Time

To highlight the similarities between emotional disturbance and initial sexual attraction, I begin this class by asking students to raise their hands if they have ever known anyone they consider to be emotionally disturbed. Almost all of them indicate that they have. I then put a transparency on the overhead projector with the title "Characteristics of People Who Are Mentally or Emotionally Disturbed," with the numbers 1 to 10 down the left-side. I ask the students to tell me what the person did that made them think that he or she was disturbed, and I write down the responses. Students suggest things like "large swings in mood," "talking to self," "obsession with another person," "strange sleeping and eating habits," "behavior discrepant with usual lifestyle," "bizarre behavior," and so forth. I then cross out the portion of the title reading "Mentally or Emotionally Disturbed" and write "in Love" in place of the deleted words. There are waves of laughter as they read through the list that they have generated. The responses don't always fit both categories perfectly, but enough of them do to demonstrate the relationship between extreme arousal and the characteristics associated with deviation from typical behavior.

This exercise serves as a lead-in to explaining Berscheid and Walster's two-stage model of love (or lust). Students often have difficulty comprehending their model, and the exercise seems to help them to understand that initial feelings of attraction and arousal aren't a matter of romantic caring and commitment to another person. I also discuss the phenomenon of liking and respecting a particularly nice and considerate person but falling in love ("lust") with someone else who may be less reliable and less considerate, and be potentially less of a rewarding partner than the particularly nice person. I ask how many people have either experienced or observed this phenomenon in others, and more than half the class members raise their arms. I then speculate that greater attraction to the second person may stem from the greater arousal (misattributed as "love") associated with the anxiety caused by the second person's behavior. This exercise can be used instead in conjunction with Chapter 20, on loving sexual interactions, if you have other material that you prefer to use when students are reading this chapter.

Although we have considerable material in the textbook (pp. 180–182) on women's signaling and men's subsequent approaches, usually students haven't read this chapter when I begin covering it because they have just taken an exam on the first five chapters. I ask them to pay attention to the behavior of women entering a singles or dating bar or party who are not accompanied by a partner. After obtaining informed consent from a male student in the front of the class to serve as my target, I then mimic the behaviors described in Monica Moore's (1985) article in more detail than that provided in the textbook, and the students generally laugh uproariously. Supportive of Perper's (1985) contention that women are far more aware of the process of signaling and approach than are men, the women in my classes show expressions of recognition. Further anecdotal evidence of women's greater conscious awareness of signaling can be seen in their reactions to signaling behaviors to a woman's partner by an interloper. Women sometimes ask their partners about the behavior of the interloper, only to be told, "I didn't notice anything." I also note that we are lacking parallel research on same-gender signaling, approach, and courtship behavior. This lecture generates a lot of class discussion and typically takes up two class sessions.

The Sexual Orientation Survey, a 21-item measure of erotophilia and erotophobia, could be distributed to your students. A copy of it is available in Byrne and Fisher's (1983) book. The major review by William Fisher and his colleagues (1988) of the work on erotophobia and erotophilia and the variety of aspects of sexual and reproductive life to which scores on the SOS are related can provide a good basis for a lecture.

A set of color photographs at the end of the chapter illustrate variations in perceptions of beauty through the ages. Last semester, I asked students to write down anonymously the names of public figures or media stars whom they thought were the most sexually appealing. Tom Cruise and Sharon Stone were the overwhelming winners. In providing them with feedback about their responses, ask them what it is about these people that makes them sexy. This exercise can be used as a lead-in to Mazur's (1986) article, which can provide the basis for a lecture dealing with variations in standards of beauty. In addition to providing a short historical and cross-cultural discussion of ideals of beauty in females, he analyzes ideals of beauty during the twentieth century using body measurements of Miss America contestants from 1940 through 1985 and ties the variations in ideals of beauty into sociobiological approaches and the contemporary concern over eating disorders. The photos, drawings, and graphs in the article could provide good audio-visual material for your lecture.

Finally, we introduce the issues of developing sexual policies for oneself in this chapter, a concept discussed again in the context of sexually transmitted diseases (Chapter 17) and sexual assault (Chapter 18). In the ideas for the lecture section of Chapter 17 of this manual, I suggest an exercise that you may prefer to introduce in conjunction with Chapter 6.

References and Other Sources for Lectures

Beggs, V. E., Calhoun, K. S., & Wolchik, S. A. (1987). Sexual anxiety and female sexual arousal: A comparison of arousal during sexual anxiety stimuli and sexual pleasure stimuli. *Archives of Sexual Behavior, 16,* 311–319.

Berscheid, E. and Walster, E. (1974). Physical attractiveness. In L. Berkowitz (Ed.). *Advances in experimental social psychology* (pp. 157–215). N.Y.: Academic Press.

Byrne, D. and Fisher, W. A. (Eds.) (1983). *Adolescents, sex, and contraception.* Hillsdale, N.J.: Lawrence Erlbaum Associates.

Fisher, W. A., Byrne, D., White, L. A., & Kelley, K. (1988). Erotophobia-erotophilia as a dimension of personality. *Journal of Sex Research, 25,* 123–151.

Follingstad, D. R., & Kimbrell, C. D. (1986). Sex fantasies revisited: An expansion and further clarification of variables affecting sex fantasy production. *Archives of Sexual Behavior, 15,* 475–486.

Garcia, L. T., & Kushnier, K. (1987). Sexual inferences about female targets: The use of sexual experience correlates. *Journal of Sex Research, 23,* 252–256.

Hatfield, E., et al. (1988). Gender differences in what is desired in the sexual relationship. *Journal of Psychology and Human Sexuality, 1,* 39–52.

Loren, R. E. A., & Weeks, G. R. (1986). Sexual fantasies of undergraduates and their perceptions of the sexual fantasies of the opposite sex. *Journal of Sex Education and Therapy, 12* (2), 31–36.

Mazur, A. (1986). U.S. trends in feminine beauty and overadaptation. *Journal of Sex Research, 22,* 281–303.

Mosher, D. L. (1966). The development and multitrait-multimethod matrix analysis of three measures of three aspects of guilt. *Journal of Consulting and Clinical Psychology, 30,* 25–29.

Moore, M. M. (1985). Nonverbal courtship patterns in women: Context and consequences. *Ethology and Sociobiology, 6,* 201–212.

Perper, T. (1985). *Sex signals: The biology of love.* Philadelphia, PA: ISI Press.

Rubinsky, H. J., Eckerman, D. A., Rubinsky, E. W., & Hoover, C. R. (1987). Early-phase physiological response patterns to psychosexual stimuli: Comparison of male and female patterns. *Archives of Sexual Behavior, 16,* 45–56.

Smith, D., & Over, R. (1987). Correlates of fantasy-induced and film-induced male sexual arousal. *Archives of Sexual Behavior, 16,* 395–409.

Chapter 7: Sexual Behavior

Topics Covered in the Chapter

In Chapter 7, we discuss the various sources of sexual stimulation, the sexual response cycle, and controversies surrounding orgasm. The section on sexual behaviors describes normative data on nocturnal orgasm, solitary and mutual masturbation, oral sex, variations in coital positions, and anal sex. We have added material on frequency of coitus (Table 7.5) and number of sexual partners based on recent studies (Billy et al., 1993; Smith, 1991). In the section on anal sex, we note that a decline in the incidence of this activity may be expected because of the risk of contracting AIDS, and we suggest that couples who choose to engage in anal sex should use lubricated condoms. We end this section by suggesting that variations in appetites and desires for particular activities are normal and that simultaneous orgasm may be a goal that can interfere with the sexual pleasure of partners.

In our description of the sexual response cycle in the next part of the chapter, which relies on Masters and Johnson's (1966) model, we summarize the changes that occur in the male and the female during the four phases (Boxes 7.3 and 7.4). Box 7.5 contains descriptions of orgasm given by males and females from the Vance and Wagner (1976) study. We also discuss Kaplan's (1974, 1979) three-phase model (desire, excitement, orgasm), suggesting that it may be subjectively more meaningful to people than the Masters and Johnson's model.

The section on controversies about orgasm deals with hypotheses regarding three kinds of female orgasm, with Box 7.6 presenting the controversy over the evolution of female orgasm. Research on female ejaculation is discussed, but because there has been relatively little work done in this area since the early 1980s, we reduced the amount of space from the previous edition devoted to the topic. We discuss possible reasons for differences in the consistency of male versus female orgasm and describe the research on multiple orgasms in males and in females.

Ideas for Lecture and Use of Class Time

Because I usually devote several class sessions to Chapter 6 and because the material in Chapter 7 is quite straightforward, I spend relatively little time in class on lecture relevant to Chapter 7.

The Society for the Scientific Study of Sex (SSSS) issued a policy statement on the Supreme Court's decision (set out in Box 7.2) upholding the state of Georgia's sodomy statute in Bowers v. Hardwick: "The decision of the Supreme Court to uphold Georgia's Sodomy Statue threatens sexual freedom of choice and intrudes into extremely intimate and private aspects of human life and personality. The Georgia Statute criminalizes the acts of oral and anal sex occurring between consenting adults, whether married or not, in the privacy of the home by transforming such common and noninjurious acts into felonies, punishable by 20 years in prison" (p. 284). For the full text, see the *Journal of Sex Research* (1987), 23, 284. You may want to reiterate the issue of the relationship between anal sex and the risk of contracting AIDS, stressing the importance of using a condom with a lubricant containing nonoxynol-9.

Loos, Bridges, and Critelli's (1987) article provides useful lecture material on the consistency of female orgasm. The Singer and Toates (1987) article deals with the "sex-as-drive-or-appetite" controversy and attempts to integrate sexual motivation under a theory of motivational systems that is similar to contemporary incentive motivation theories. Singer and Toates suggest that, like hunger and thirst, sexual motivation emerges from an interaction of external incentives and internal states. They provide hypotheses about why orgasm and sexual motivation can be separated, how female sexual motivation arises and is similar to males' motivation, and how novel stimulation affects sexual motivation. Material from the article is probably more appropriate for advanced than for beginning students. It could also be introduced in lecture in conjunction with Chapter 8 on fantasies, feelings, and communication.

Depending on the demographics of your class members, you may want to use Weinberg and Williams's (1988) article on black sexuality and Wyatt et al.'s (1988) two articles on the sexual socialization and behavior of black and white women as the bases for lecture.

Hartman and Fithian's (1984) book, *Any Man Can*, cited in the textbook, describes these authors' approach to training men to have multiple orgasms. We don't give details in the textbook, so more information on the techniques could be used for lecture material.

Orgasmic Responses of the Sexually Stimulated Female, the film described in Chapter 4 of this manual, could be shown in conjunction with the material on female ejaculation. Its explicit subject matter makes some students uncomfortable, so you should request informed consent during the previous class session. Because it is the visual close-ups of the vulva (rather than the soundtrack) that appear to be embarrassing to some students, I suggest that they close their eyes if they feel uncomfortable.

References and Other Sources for Lectures

Billy, J. O. G., Tanfer, K., Grady, W. R. and Klepinger, D. H. (1993). The sexual behavior of men in the United States. *Family Planning Perspectives, 25,* 52–60.

Kaplan, H. S. (1974). *The new sex therapy.* New York: Bruner/Mazel.

Kaplan, H. S. (1979). *Disorders of sexual desire.* New York: Bruner/Mazel.

Loos, V. E., Bridges, C. F., & Critelli, J. W. (1987). *Journal of Sex Research, 23,* 348–361.

Mosher, D. L., et al. (1988). Subjective sexual arousal and involvement: Development of multiple indicators. *Journal of Sex Research, 25,* 412–425.

Pinney, E. M., Gerrard, M., & Denney, N. W. (1987). The Pinney Sexual Satisfaction Inventory. *Journal of Sex Research, 23,* 233–251.

Singer, B., & Toates, F. M. (1987). Sexual motivation. *Journal of Sex Research, 23,* 481–501.

Weinberg, M. S., & Williams, C. J. (1988). Black sexuality: A test of two theories. *Journal of Sex Research, 25,* 197–218.

Wells, B. L. (1986). Predictors of female nocturnal orgasms: A multivariate analysis. *Journal of Sex Research, 22,* 421–437.

Wyatt, G. E., et al. (1988). Kinsey revisited, Part I: Comparisons of the sexual socialization and sexual behavior of white women over 33 years. *Archives of Sexual Behavior, 17,* 201–239.

Wyatt, G. E., et al. (1988). Kinsey revisited, Part II: Comparisons of the sexual socialization and sexual behavior of black women over 33 years. *Archives of Sexual Behavior, 17,* 289–332.

Chapter 8: Sexual Dysfunctions and Therapy

Topics Covered in the Chapter

Chapter 8 begins with a vignette involving potential sexual dysfunctions in a heterosexual and a homosexual couple and then moves on to a discussion of biological and psychological factors associated with sexual dysfunctions. We review types of dysfunction and contemporary therapeutic approaches.

Box 8.1 contains Kaplan's categories of organic factors related to dysfunctions. Under psychological factors, we include past (traumatic) experiences and current sources of dysfunction. Box 8.2 describes a case of incest, which was followed by sexual anesthesia and subsequently successful therapy. We discuss the problems of miscommunication and stress as possible contributors to unsatisfying sexual relationships.

Problems with desire include hyperactive and inhibited sexual desire, and Box 8.3 gives a case history of a man diagnosed with compulsive sexual behavior. In describing the types of dysfunctions, we have used Kaplan's model of sexual response (described in Chapter 7) as the organizational basis. Problems during the excitement phase are described, and we discuss the pejorative nature of the terms "impotence" and "frigidity" that clinicians and the public sometimes still use. Orgasm/ejaculation dysfunctions include premature ejaculation, inhibited male orgasm, and inhibited female orgasm. In the discussion of premature ejaculation, we note that the definition of this dysfunction is the subject of controversy in that it is sometimes tied to the speed of response of one's partner. Under the heading "Sexual Pain Disorders," we include a discussion of dyspareunia and vaginismus, and priapism.

The second half of the chapter is devoted to sex therapy, beginning with a description of Masters and Johnson's (1970) approach. The controversy over their reported success rates is discussed, along with possible reasons for the discrepancy between their rates and those reported more recently in the literature by other therapists. Kaplan's approach is then presented, followed by a description of specific interventions: systematic desensitization, nondemand pleasuring and sensate focus, masturbation training, and the start-stop and squeeze techniques. Boxes 8.4 through 8.6 contain, respectively, a case history of the treatment of inhibited ejaculation in a man who until treatment was unable to impregnate his wife, a description of a systematic desensitization hierarchy for the treatment of inhibited ejaculation, and a detailed description of the masturbation training program developed by LoPiccolo and his colleagues. Group therapy and hypnosis are briefly discussed, and the controversies surrounding the employment of sexual surrogates in sex therapy are described. Other treatment approaches are presented as well: the use of prosthetic penile implants, microsurgery to improve blood flow into the penis, and anxiety-reducing drugs. The chapter concludes with a discussion of qualifications and ethical issues raised in selecting a therapist when experiencing sexual difficulties.

Ideas for Lecture and Use of Class Time

The topic of sexual dysfunction appears to be one of the big three anxiety-causing topics among my students (sexual orientation and masturbation are the other two). Although the chapter begins by noting that occasional discrepancies between how you respond and how you want to respond do not indicate a sexual dysfunction or a need for sex therapy, frequently students stop by my office to express concern about their patterns of sexual response. Thus, I think that it is important to reinforce the idea in discussing each of the dysfunctions that just as we humans experience normal variations in our appetite for food, no matter how tasty it is, we also experience normal variations in our response to opportunities for sexual intimacy.

Based on a random sample of undergraduate and graduate students, Spencer and Zeiss (1987) found that sexual pressures from a partner are more positively related to manifest sexual dysfunction among masculine (as measured by the Bem Sex Role Inventory) than among non-masculine men. Contrary to the authors' expectations, androgynous respondents did not report lower levels of sexual dysfunction or concern than did nonandrogynous students.

Before his death, Ed Brecher led a discussion at one of the summer Kinsey Institute courses several years ago on the injection of papavarine into the corpus cavernosum of men with erectile dysfunction to produce tumescence. According to Brecher, who used papavarine himself, the injections produced only minor momentary discomfort. Following tumescence, erection could be produced by manual stimulation by oneself or a partner and these erections could last for three or four hours. Szasz et al. (1987) compared the injection of three solutions (phenoxybenzamine, papavarine-phentolamine, and saline) and found that the first two did result in penile swelling, whereas saline alone produced no effect. Their procedures, findings, and conclusions provide good lecture material.

Students taking your class because of a potential interest in becoming clinical psychologists competent to provide sex therapy will be interested in Nathan's (1986) report on the results of a questionnaire study of the directors of each of the 113 American Psychological Association–approved clinical psychology doctoral programs (56 percent return rate). Only 37 percent of the directors reported that their programs offered a graduate-level course on human sexuality, sexual disorders, or sex therapy. Another 41 percent reported that part (5 to 15 percent) of a more general course on psychopathology, psychotherapy, or behavior modification was devoted to sexual topics, but only 5 percent of the programs had any plans to develop new courses. Nathan's report also refers to studies of the sexuality content in graduate programs in other areas, such as medicine, nursing, and social work. This article may be particularly useful to those of you who are offering a graduate-level human sexuality course. On this same topic, a colleague and I (Yarris & Allgeier, 1988) wrote an article for a special double issue of *Women and Therapy* devoted to sex therapy. Yarris and I focused on the issue of training (or absence thereof) of clinicians to deal with "transference" and "countertransference" and rates of sexual involvement of therapists with clients. Pope and his colleagues (1993) have published an excellent book on sexual feelings during therapy that can serve as a good source of lecture material or an additional book to assign to advanced students. This topic could be handled either in this chapter or in the context of sexual harassment (Chapter 18).

References and Other Sources for Lectures

Assalian, P. (1988). Colmipramine in the treatment of premature ejaculation. *Journal of Sex Research, 24,* 213–215.

Fahrner, E. M. (1987). Sexual dysfunction in male alcohol addicts: Prevalence and treatment. *Archives of Sexual Behavior, 16,* 247–257.

Gooren, L. J. G. (1987). Androgen levels and sex functions in testosterone-treated hypogonadal men. *Archives of Sexual Behavior, 16,* 463–473.

Levin, R. J., & Wagner, G. (1987). Self-reported central sexual arousal without vaginal arousal—duplicity or veracity revealed by objective measurement? *Journal of Sex Research, 23,* 540–544.

Masters, W. H. and Johnson, V. E. (1970). *Human sexual inadequacy.* Boston, MA: Little, Brown.

Milan, R. J., et al. (1988). Treatment outcome of secondary orgasmic dysfunction: A two- to six-year follow-up. *Archives of Sexual Behavior, 17,* 463–480.

Nathan, S. G. (1986). Are clinical psychology graduate students being taught enough about sexuality? A survey of doctoral programs. *Journal of Sex Research, 22,* 520–524.

Pope, K. S., Sonne, J. L., & Holroyd, J. (1993). *Sexual feelings in psychotherapy: Explorations for therapists and therapists in training.* Washington, D. C.: American Psychological Association.

Rosen, R. C., & Leiblum, S. R. (1987). Current approaches to the evaluation of sexual desire disorders. *Journal of Sex Research, 23,* 141–162.

Segraves, K. A., Segraves, R. T., & Schoenberg, H. W. (1987). Use of sexual history to differentiate organic from psychogenic impotence. *Archives of Sexual Behavior, 16,* 125–137.

Spencer, S. L., & Zeiss, A. M. (1987). Sex roles and sexual dysfunction in college students. *Journal of Sex Research, 23,* 338–347.

Strassberg, D. S., Kelly, M. P., Carroll, C., & Kircher, J. C. (1987). The psychophysiological nature of premature ejaculation. *Archives of Sexual Behavior, 16,* 327–336.

Stuart, F. M., Hammond, D. C., & Pett, M. A. (1987). Inhibited sexual desire in women. *Archives of Sexual Behavior, 16,* 91–106.

Szasz, G., Stevenson, R. W. D., Lee, L., & Sanders, H. D. (1987). Induction of penile erection by intracavernosal injection: A double-blind comparison of phenoxybenzamine versus papavarine-phentolamine versus saline. *Archives of Sexual Behavior, 16,* 371–378.

Tiefer, L., & Melman, A. (1987). Adherence to recommendations and improvement over time in men with erectile dysfunction. *Archives of Sexual Behavior, 16,* 301–309.

Wakefield, J. (1988). Female primary orgasmic dysfunction: Masters and Johnson versus DSM III on diagnosis and incidence. *Journal of Sex Research, 24,* 363–377.

Wilensky, M., & Myers, M. F. (1987). Retarded ejaculation in homosexual patients: A report of nine cases. *Journal of Sex Research, 23,* 85–91.

Yarris, E., & Allgeier, E. R. (1988). Sexual socialization for therapists: Training and clinical applications. *Women and Therapy, 7,* (2/3), 57–75.

Chapter 9: Pregnancy and Birth

Topics Covered in the Chapter

Chapter 9 covers conception, pregnancy, labor and birth, postpartum decisions and events, and postpartum sexual expression. The second part of the chapter focuses on problems with pregnancy and childbirth. The topic of infertility, in this chapter in the third edition, has been moved to Chapter 14.

The material on conception includes methods for increasing the chances of conception; it also describes gender-selection methods and notes the debate over the use of these techniques. Early symptoms of pregnancy are described, and substances that may affect the fetus (drugs, medications, maternal diseases, and the like) are listed in Table 9.1. Pregnancy tests are discussed along with factors that may adversely affect test results. We describe tests used for detecting fetal abnormalities in Box 9.1. The stages of pregnancy are presented, covering the physiological and psychological changes in pregnant women. Feelings about sexual intimacy during pregnancy are discussed along with reasons that expectant mothers and fathers report a decline in intercourse frequency.

The section on labor and birth begins with an overview of contemporary childbirth preparation programs. The location of birth (home, hospital, or birthing center) and the issue of family involvement during labor and delivery are discussed. Material on birth in other species from the first edition has been deleted, and descriptions of birth in other cultures have been shortened. The onset and stages of labor are described, and some of the controversies involving the routine shaving of pubic hair, administration of enemas, use of anesthesia, administration of an episiotomy, and the use of forceps are reviewed.

The material on postpartum decisions and events includes a comparison of breast-feeding versus bottle-feeding and a description of the pros and cons of routine circumcision of male infants. Postpartum adjustment issues are discussed, along with brief coverage of postpartum depression. Factors related to the length of time following birth before a woman can comfortably engage in sexual intercourse are reviewed, and some of the issues that arise for new parents (role changes, fatigue, loss of freedom, and so forth) are described, along with suggestions for reducing the impact of these factors on the parents' relationship.

The final part of this chapter focuses on reproductive problems. It examines sources of fetal and maternal difficulties during pregnancy, including environmental threats to fetal development, maternal alcohol use, and infection with STDs. Threats to pregnant women that we describe include ectopic pregnancy, spontaneous abortion, toxemia, and eclampsia. We conclude with a description of complications that can occur during childbirth, such as problematic birth position of the fetus, the need for (and controversies surrounding overuse of) cesarean sections, multiple births, variations in length of gestation, and problems associated with low birth weight.

Ideas for Lecture and Use of Class Time

I show the movie *Birth of a Family* (Perennial # 1051, 24 minutes, color) at the beginning of this class because it emphasizes the importance of participation by the father in childbirth preparation and provides a good description of generic prepared childbirth and a realistic depiction of the process of labor and birth. The strongest student reaction typically is to the episiotomy and cutting of the umbilical cord. Students should be told ahead of time that both are painless at the time that they are performed. Although I generally plan to lecture after this brief movie, it provokes so much curiosity in students that the rest of the 75-minute class is frequently taken up with questions and class discussion.

Although chorionic-villus sampling (CVS) for genetic screening is described in the textbook, most of the students may not have heard of it, although some are aware of amniocentesis. CVS provides a number of advantages over amniocentesis: it is less invasive and can be performed during the first trimester, eliminating the need for a second-trimester abortion if the mother decides to terminate the pregnancy. In addition, with the advances in prenatal medical interventions, presumably the earlier that problems are detected, the more likely it is that solutions can be found. We also acknowledge the opposition of some antiabortion groups to genetic counseling based on their belief that such counseling encourages abortion.

We provide no examples of instances in which genetic counseling can lead to prenatal treatment to eliminate a problem that would be nontreatable if not detected in utero. One example is retinoblastoma, a tumor that forms in the eyes of children up to 4 years old, causing blindness and sometimes death. About 300 to 400 children a year develop retinoblastoma. As more people survive the disease and pass it on to their children, the number of cases is likely to rise. Although normal cells each have two sets of genes (one from each parent), the tumor cells have lost a segment of one set. To identify the cancer-causing genes, samples of the parents' blood, a sibling's eye tumor, and the fetus's amniotic fluid or blood are taken. If the fetus carries the defective gene, doctors can readily treat the resultant disease in its early stages with radiotherapy. A first child with the tumor is needed in order to assess the second child's risk, but in the next generation, it will be possible to identify the first child's risk because samples of parents' tumors will be saved.

In our textbook description of cesarean section, we note that one C-section doesn't necessarily mean that future babies need to be delivered via C-section as well. In 1988 the American College of Obstetricians and Gynecologists (ACOG) issued guidelines to the medical profession to end the practice of "once a C-section, always a C-section," which it said had been the general rule since 1916. Of the approximately 3.7 million babies born in the United States each year, about 24 percent are delivered by C-section, and a third of these are repeat operations. Almost all C-sections involve a low transverse incision, in which a horizontal cut is made across the lower abdomen and uterus. Essentially, ACOG took the position that regardless of a woman's previous C-section history (except in the 1 or 2 percent of C-sections that involved classical incisions with the abdominal incision made vertically), women should attempt vaginal birth with subsequent pregnancies unless there are medical reasons for the particular pregnancy that require the use of C-sections.

Reamy and White's (1987) well-organized review of research on sexual interactions during the period before and after childbirth can provide good lecture material.

References and Other Sources for Lectures

Dunn, P. C., Ryan, I. J., & O'Brien, K. (1988). College students' acceptance of adoption and five alternative fertilization techniques. *Journal of Sex Research, 24,* 282–286.

Fisher, W. A., & Gray, J. (1988). Erotophobia-erotophilia and sexual behavior during pregnancy and postpartum. *Journal of Sex Research, 25,* 379–396.

Reamy, K. J., & White, S. E. (1987). Sexuality in the puerperium: A review. *Archives of Sexual Behavior, 16,* 165–186.

Smith, P. B. (1986). Sociologic aspects of adolescent fertility and childbearing among Hispanics. *Developmental and Behavioral Pediatrics, 7,* 346–349.

Werner, P. D. (1988). Personality correlates of reproductive knowledge. *Journal of Sex Research, 25,* 219–234.

Chapter 10: Contraception

Topics Covered in the Chapter

This chapter begins with a description of the development and use of modern contraceptives, then reviews the currently available methods of contraception including sterilization procedures, and concludes with a discussion of research on future methods of birth control.

The first section is devoted to the political, legal, and social obstacles faced by those pioneers—notably Margaret Sanger—who tried to support the development of reliable contraceptive methods. Among the controversies discussed are the issue of greater allocation of resources to the development of female than of male methods and the greater support for sexual and contraceptive education in response to AIDS than was available in response to unwanted pregnancy among adolescent females. Technological and medical issues are described regarding the effectiveness of various methods, and the difference between the theoretical and actual failure rates of particular methods is noted.

Material on adolescents and contraceptive use covers data on sexual behavior and contraceptive use, contraceptive education, legal access to contraceptives, motivation to use contraception, and the relationship of sexual attitudes to contraceptive use. Table 10.2, new for this edition, compares the relative risks of mortality from a variety of lifestyle choices (e.g., smoking, playing football) and various reproductive and contraceptive choices. In Box 10.1, we examines research on the cross-cultural correlation between the provision of sexual and contraceptive education with birth, abortion, and miscarriage rates, demonstrating that cultures that are more open about sexuality have fewer unwanted pregnancies. Males' roles and responsibilities regarding contraception are discussed, and the section ends with an examination of the risks for females of contraceptive use versus unprotected intercourse. Figure 10.3, showing the mortality rates associated with various methods of contraception, illustrates that the riskiest option is engaging in unprotected intercourse. Box 10.2 features a discussion of the myth of spontaneous sex in an attempt to dispel the idea that sex somehow just happens without any prior intentions or opportunities to engage in plans to enhance the pleasure and reduce the risks associated with sexual intimacy.

Major contraceptive methods are the focus of the next section. We begin with a brief discussion of the "rhythm method" and then provide a detailed description of the sympto-thermal method to pinpoint the date of ovulation, noting that use of this method may help to increase the effectiveness of other methods or to increase the likelihood of conceiving at a particular time. The diaphragm and spermicide are described, followed by the contraceptive sponge, cervical cap, male and female condoms, foams and suppositories, oral contraceptives, and IUDs. We devote extensive coverage to the varieties of pills available and to the findings that pill use is associated with lower risks of some cancers and a slowed growth rate for breast cancer. We treat the IUD in a quasi-historical fashion, noting that most authorities are recommending removal of the IUD from single nulliparous women who are still wearing it (particularly those with multiple partners) because the risks outweigh the benefits of its use. We turn then to a description of relatively ineffective methods of contraception: withdrawal, postcoital douching, and breast-feeding.

The section on sterilization covers the vasectomy, several methods of tubal ligation, and the latest findings on success rates of vasovasectomy and reversal of tubal ligations. The final section of the chapter is devoted to descriptions of research on the development of new methods of birth control for men and for women.

Ideas for Lecture and Use of Class Time

I typically devote two class sessions to this chapter. In the first class, I discuss variables correlated with reliable contraceptive use. Milan and Kilmann's (1987) article, an extensive review of research on psychological, social, and situational correlates of contraceptive use among young men and women, provides a useful adjunct to the discussion at the beginning of the chapter on variables related to the consistent use of effective contraceptives. They present a seven-page table summarizing sampling procedures, samples, type of research, primary data collection methods, and relevant dependent variables from 52 studies published between 1972 and 1984. See also Strassberg and Mahoney (1988) and Tanner and Pollack (1988).

The latest edition of *Contraceptive Technology* (Hatcher et al., 1994) is an excellent resource for this chapter, as well as Chapter 11, on resolving unwanted pregnancy, and Chapter 17, on sexually transmitted diseases. The book contains a large number of tables and figures, which you may want to put on transparencies for lecture.

In the second class session, I use a transparency of a variation of Figure 10.8 in the textbook on the use of the sympto-thermal method to pinpoint the date of ovulation. Because of the data indicating that reluctance to touch one's own genitals (or to report masturbation) is associated with nonuse of barrier methods of contraception, I try to reinforce the health benefits of knowing the phases of one's own cycle, inspecting the changing characteristics of healthy cervical mucus, knowing what one's cervix feels like, and so on.

In the remainder of the lectures devoted to contraception, I pass around each of the contraceptive devices in class and always notice that many of the students pass the unrolled condom to the next student as if it were a hot potato! I note that for those who claim that latex condoms interfere with the amount of sensation they experience, the more expensive cecum condoms permit more "natural" sensation. It is important to emphasize, however, that the *cecum condoms provide less protection against AIDS and herpes viruses.* The pores in these condoms are smaller than a sperm or some gonorrhea bacteria but more than 10 times the size of the AIDS virus and more than 25 times the size of hepatitis B virus. *Consumer Reports'* study of condoms in 1989 might be recommended to students who want a consumer-based comparison of the advantages and disadvantages of different brands of these devices.

As reported in the textbook, the Mentor Corporation markets male condoms in plastic cups for sale to women to carry in their purses. You might reiterate this point in class to reinforce the idea that women can purchase and encourage the use of condoms. The female condom, approved by the FDA in 1992, is not widely available yet. Before lecturing on this chapter you might check your local Planned Parenthood or pharmacies to see if it can be purchased in your area.

In the textbook, we stress the problems that have been associated with the use of the IUD in the past. Before you lecture on contraceptives, you may want to call the local Planned Parenthood or family planning clinic to get the latest information on the IUD.

Some branches of Planned Parenthood have well-developed educational programs and send representatives to classes to present material on contraceptives. If you are just beginning to teach the human sexuality course, you might invite Planned Parenthood representatives to provide an overview of the programs, services, and the methods that they prescribe.

I showed the award winning *Condom Sense* (Perennial, 1117, 25 minutes, color), which through the use of humor and examination of myths encourages male contraceptive responsibility. Although it was produced in 1981. I first saw it in the late 1980s and thought that it was surprisingly undated. On the other hand, my students didn't particularly like it. Although there was a considerable amount of laughter during the movie, their mean rating of the film was 2.8 on the 7-point scale I use (1 = Do not show in future semesters). The written comments indicated that the students felt that the film would be appropriate for high school students. If you choose to show it, you may want to reinforce the benefits of the use of spermicidal lubricants with condoms for contraception, as the film does not deal with spermicidal lubricants.

References and Other Sources for Lectures

Consumer Reports (1989, March). Can you rely on condoms? *Consumer Reports*, pp. 135–141.

Djerassi, C. (1994). A new look at male contraception. *Nature, 370* (6484) 11–12.

Hatcher, R. A., et al. (1994). *Contraceptive technology, 1994–1996* (16th rev. ed.). New York: Irvington Publishers.

Marsiglio, W., & Menaghan, E. G. (1987). Couples and the male birth control pill: A future alternative in contraceptive selection. *Journal of Sex Research, 23,* 34–49.

Milan, R. J., Jr., & Kilmann, P. R. (1987). Interpersonal factors in premarital contraception. *Journal of Sex Research, 23,* 289–321.

Strassberg, D. L., & Mahoney, J. M. (1988). Correlates of the contraceptive behavior of adolescents/young adults. *Journal of Sex Research, 25,* 531–536.

Tanner, W. M., & Pollack, R. H. (1988). The effect of condom use and erotic instructions on attitudes toward condoms. *Journal of Sex Research, 25,* 537–541.

Chapter 11: Resolving Unwanted Pregnancy

Topics Covered in the Chapter

In this chapter, we discuss unwanted pregnancy, abortion, and unplanned parenthood. We begin the section on unwanted pregnancy noting that unplanned and unwanted pregnancies are not necessarily the same thing. Noting the controversial aspects of abortion, in Box 11.1 we describe its legal status, the Hyde Amendment, and the Supreme Court decisions on abortion rendered between 1973 and 1992. Legal and moral arguments against and favoring abortion are presented, and Box 11.2 contains several descriptions of abortion applicants from the Allgeier et al. research on public policies toward abortion. Table 11.2 provides a listing of the reasons given by women for obtaining abortions from Russo et al.'s (1992) report. This section concludes with a review of data that fail to support the "abortion as birth control" hypothesis.

We turn next to a description of early, first-trimester, and second-trimester abortion methods. Box 11.3 describes one college woman's experience with abortion. We discuss the male role in abortion and the conflicting rights of women and men in making decisions when a woman has an unwanted pregnancy. Research on psychological responses to unwanted pregnancy and abortion is presented.

The chapter concludes with a review of research on outcomes of unplanned parenthood. The difficulties of single motherhood are described along with factors that can reduce some of the negative aspects for both the mother and her offspring. We discuss single fatherhood and the small amount of research on men's reactions to this role. We end by advocating methods that parents and schools could use to provide more adequate sexual socialization to reduce the likelihood that adolescents and young adults will have to face the dilemma of unwanted pregnancy.

Ideas for Lecture and Use of Class Time

The legal availability of abortion is a particularly sensitive area on which to lecture. Few of us are neutral on the subject, yet as instructors, we should attempt to provide balanced coverage. In the past few years, I have provided lectures on the history of the so-called gag rule, initially upheld by the U.S. Supreme Court, that prohibited health providers, including physicians, in any health care facility receiving federal funds from discussing abortion with their patients even if the patient requested information. This legislation placed physicians in a conflict of interest with their ethical standards and state licensing boards requiring the provision of information and informed consent about the range of options available to patients. The legislation was subsequently modified to exclude medical doctors, but other health care providers (who make up the vast majority of clinic personnel) continued to be governed by the law. One of the first things that President Clinton did after his inauguration was to overturn the law. Although the gag rule is no longer in effect, coverage of the very recent history of attempts to erode women's (particularly poor women's) legal right to abortion is important. The gag rule legislation is no doubt familiar to most of us who teach, but many college students may be unaware of that legislation and the debates about it that occurred during the late 1980s and early 1990s, when they were in their early to mid-teens.

The Hatcher et al. (1994) book and Planned Parenthood can provide excellent resources for lecture and class presentations, respectively. Our local Planned Parenthood headquarters has a panel of adolescent women who have experienced unplanned pregnancies and have resolved them through abortion, becoming single parents, or placing their babies for adoption. Sometimes the panel includes parents of these young women, and all members of the panel have typically spoken candidly and movingly.

Representatives from pro-life and pro-choice groups can be invited to class to discuss their positions on the issue of abortion and the conditions, if any, under which they would support pregnancy termination. (See Table 11.1 in the textbook for a description of such positions taken by members of NARAL, NRLC, and national samples of adults.) Questions regarding the morality of in-vitro fertilization, the freezing of sperm, and fertilized embryos can also be raised.

For a third possible panel (I'm not suggesting that you have all three in a single semester) you could invite males and females from your class to debate the issues on men's and women's rights regarding decisions about unwanted pregnancy. If you opt for this kind of a panel, it is important to set up ground rules in which the students are instructed to focus on issues and to avoid attacking one another at a personal level.

Another possible class activity is to have students form small groups and to assume that they are advisory panels to judges in the various states regarding the legal right of women to obtain abortion versus the rights of Americans (in this case, antiabortion protesters) to freedom of speech and assembly. What would they recommend to resolve the current conflicts between these two sets of rights? According to Sydell (1993), attacks on abortion clinics and providers have been accompanied by a 10 percent decline in the number of abortion providers in the past 12 years. You can then have a spokesperson for each group report their recommendations.

The legal status of abortion, particularly with respect to parental notification, consent, and judicial bypass, changes quickly. I recommend that you call the toll-free Planned Parenthood hot line, 800/230-7526, to obtain information on status of laws relating to contraception and abortion.

References and Other Sources for Lectures

Allgeier, A. R., Allgeier, E. R. and Rywick, T. (1982). Response to requests for abortion: The influence of guilt and knowledge. *Journal of Applied Social Psychology, 12*, 282–292.

Grimes, D. A. (1992). Clinicians who provide abortions: The thinning ranks. *Obstetrics and Gynecology, 80*, 719–723.

Rosenwasser, S. M., Wright, L. S., & Barber, R. B. (1987). The rights and responsibilities of men in abortion situations. *Journal of Sex Research, 23*, 97–105.

Russo, N. F., Horn, J. D. and Schwartz, R. (1992). U.S. abortion in context: Selected characteristics and motivations of women seeking abortion. *Journal of Social Issues, 48* (3), 183–202.

Sydell, L. L. (1993, August). The right-to-life rampage: Anti-abortion groups step up the terror. *Progressive, 57* (8), 24–28.

Chapter 12: Gender and Sexuality in Childhood and Adolescence

Topics Covered in the Chapter

Chapters 12 and 13 cover the development of gender identity and sexuality over the life span. Although we consider various theoretical approaches to life-span development in these two chapters, we rely primarily on Erikson's model of the crises and opportunities that emerge during the eight stages of life. In this chapter we focus on the period from infancy into adolescence.

We begin with a discussion of the problems researchers have encountered in attempting to get information about infant and childhood sexuality because of taboos and assumptions that children are not sexual. There has been more research on the acquisition of gender identity. We review parent-child attachment (and gender differences in the behaviors associated with attachment); discuss the interactions of language development, gender role expectations, and sexuality; and describe the issue of real gender differences versus stereotypic ones, introducing the concept of overlapping distributions and noting that various stereotypes may or may not be accurate. Sex education, sexual rehearsal, and homosociality are considered, and the process of sexual and reproductive maturation is described. Since the previous edition, major comparisons have been made on the outcomes of exposure to "abstinence-only" versus "postponement and protection" approaches to sex education. We have introduced a major new section, "Formal Sex Education," that reviews the surprising findings from these studies (see the textbook, pp. 397–402).

Coverage of the entrance into adolescence includes gender-role identification and traditional versus contemporary (i.e., androgynous) conceptualizations of identification, the development of a sexual repertoire, and societal attitudes about appropriate roles for males and females in signaling potential partners and engaging in courtship. We review research on gender differences and similarities in seducing and rejecting potential sexual partners and end the chapter with women's reactions to their first experience of sexual intimacy.

Ideas for Lecture and Use of Class Time

If you administered the questionnaire at the beginning of Part I of this guide, now is an appropriate time to present class results on the ages at which your students first experienced various sexual feelings and activities, their experiences with parental reactions to their sexual questions, and so on. You can also solicit students' reports of erroneous sexual beliefs that they or their friends held during late childhood and early adolescence, such as their early ideas about how babies were conceived.

The Goldmans' (1982) book is a gold mine of fascinating information concerning childhood ideas about a variety of aspects of reproduction and sexuality. We had space in the textbook to cover only a small number of their findings, so you may want to examine the book for information on topics of particular relevance for your class. Their book includes many delightful quotations from children and children's beliefs about appropriate male and female roles.

Terri Fisher (1987, 1988, 1989; Fisher and Hall, 1988) has done a series of studies on sexual socialization in the family and subsequent sexual attitudes and behaviors of college students that should be very interesting (and, in most cases, familiar) to your students. Remarkably, she has been able to get students and both their parents to complete questionnaires about sexual socialization in the family. She found that in high-communication families, sexual attitudes of parents and offspring were correlated, whereas in low-communication families, they were generally uncorrelated. Her results support the idea that students who choose to become parents in the future may find their own offspring more responsive to their values and attitudes if they provide sex education than if they attempt to avoid the topic.

The paperback *The First Time* (Fleming and Fleming, 1975) describes the reactions of various celebrities to their first experience of sexual intercourse. The piece by a young Victoria Principal provides a superb illustration of female selection and seduction attempts (as described in Chapter 6 of the textbook).

The short film *A Real Naked Lady* is good for illustrating the confusion that young boys can experience about the meaning of sexuality and erotica at an age when they reject friendships with girls.

References and Other Sources for Lectures

Fisher, T. D. (1987). Family communication and the sexual behavior and attitudes of college students. *Journal of Youth and Adolescence, 16,* 481–495.

Fisher, T. D. (1988). The relationship between parent-child communication about sexuality and college students' sexual behavior and attitudes as a function of parental proximity. *Journal of Sex Research, 24,* 305–311.

Fisher, T. D. (1989). An extension of the findings of Moore, Peterson, and Furstenberg (1986) regarding family sexual communication and adolescent sexual behavior. *Journal of Marriage and the Family, 51*, 637–639.

Fisher, T. D., & Hall, R. G. (1988). A scale for the comparison of the sexual attitudes of adolescents and their parents. *Journal of Sex Research, 24*, 90–100.

Fleming, K., & Fleming, A. T. (1975). *The first time.* New York: Berkeley.

McCabe, M. P. (1987). Desired and experienced levels of premarital affection and sexual intercourse during dating. *Journal of Sex Research, 23*, 23–33.

Money, J. (1988). Longitudinal outcome research and strategies: Career support in pediatric sexology and psychoendocrinology. *Journal of Psychology and Human Sexuality, 1*, 105–114.

Chapter 13: Gender and Sexuality in Adulthood

Topics Covered in the Chapter

In this chapter, we review research on sexuality from early adulthood through the rest of the life span. At the outset, we acknowledge that the age of the division between adolescence and adulthood varies from one person to another but is generally associated with relative independence from parents. We rely again on Erikson's model of life stages and begin in this chapter with the challenge of intimacy versus isolation, which typically occurs around the end of the second decade of life.

We describe Roche's model of five dating stages which starts with dating without affection and culminates in the couple's becoming engaged to marry, and we examine attitudes toward sexual intimacy at each of the stages. We have updated the section on the relationship between sexual and emotional intimacy based on the longitudinal Boston couples study (Peplau et al., 1993). Lifestyle choices—remaining single, cohabiting, or marrying—are discussed, and we consider relationship contracts. Box 13.1 examines questions that couples may want to consider before deciding whether to cohabit or marry.

The section on love and marriage presents data on the increasing age at first marriage, and Table 13.2 from previous editions of the textbook, "Contemporary American Families: Dreams and Reality," has been updated with data from 1993. Family formation and the division of labor is covered, and we focus on the impact of children on availability of time and energy for sexual intimacy. Long-term relationships are described in terms of the frequency of arguments versus sexual pleasure, and we retain the discussion of attraction versus attachment from the previous edition.

Extramarital sex is discussed, although we have shortened the description of its different forms to make room for coverage of the recent research by Glass and Wright (1992), Smith (1991), and Billy et al. (1993) on the decline in frequency of such relationships (Box 13.2). Research on gender differences in reactions to separation and divorce is presented. Finally we examine issues related to aging and sexual expression: the double standard of aging, midlife changes and assessments, menopause, midlife challenges, and the physiological changes of aging that interact with sexual expression. We review research indicating that declining estrogen levels in women are not necessarily related to declining sexual arousal and responsiveness; socioeconomic status may be a moderating variable, with those of higher SES showing less decline in sexual interest and activity than those of lower SES.

As people become elderly, they face the Eriksonian challenge of integrity versus despair. The potential impact of social stereotypes about the elderly on self-image is addressed. Based on available research, we question the notion that aging alone is responsible for the decrease in or elimination of sexual expression. In this section, we also discuss changes in gender roles among couples as they age and retire from paid work, reviewing studies that suggest that people holding more flexible gender role identities adjust more readily to the aging process than do those holding more rigid gender role identities and attitudes. Further, retirement affords couples more leisure to engage in sexual intimacy. The loss of one's partner through death or institutionalization, however, can be emotionally traumatic. As noted earlier, men generally have more difficulty coping with this loss than do women, but (heterosexual) women are more likely to outlive their partners than are men.

Ideas for Lecture and Use of Class Time

The Strouse (1987) article focuses on motives for going to college bars versus perceptions of others' motives. The data provide an interesting adjunct to the studies by Tim Perper, Naomi McCormick, and Monica Moore that are described in the textbook. Strouse collected his data from 637 students in a human sexuality course and from 260 bar patrons. If your students are interested in comparing the results from Strouse's sample to their own self-reported motivations and perceptions of others' motives, they could collect similar data.

In my experience, student interest in flirtation behaviors in bars is high, and if you have a relatively small class, you might suggest a field trip to a bar to observe seduction and rejection behaviors. If the class is too large, students might want to do some observations on their own. If you choose to set up a class field trip, I advise that you clear it with the ethics review board on your campus, making it clear that participation is entirely voluntary, and avoid offering extra credit for the experience, as that can be perceived as coercive for those students whose grades are borderline.

We cited the Perper and Weis (1987) article in the textbook but didn't delve into it. For those of you who are interested in the issues of courtship, female proceptivity, incomplete rejection strategies, and so forth that we discussed in the textbook, their article provides a good update of related research.

David Weis's research on females' affective responses to first coitus is reported in the textbook. Now he is collecting data on males' reactions to first coitus. When his results are available, I will report them in *The Allgeier Update*. You may also write to him to request a report of his results (Department of Applied Human Ecology, Bowling Green State University, Bowling Green, OH 43403).

Data from Hansen (1987) are likely to be highly interesting and relevant to college students. Hansen collected responses from 244 college students (only one refused to participate) via questionnaires and found that the majority of men (71 percent) and women (57 percent) had experienced some sort of extradyadic relationship. As with studies of extramarital relations, students in Hansen's study were more likely to engage in the behavior than to approve of it. The article contains a number of other interesting findings, and if students in your class are interested, they could anonymously complete questionnaires relevant to the issue.

Students in my classes tend to equate the decision to marry with an agreement for monogamy. After they have read the material on variations in agreements between spouses about extrarelationship involvements, you could ask for volunteers for a panel to discuss the various options. As noted in Chapter 11 in this guide on class panels regarding unwanted pregnancy, it is important to caution students to deal with the issues and to avoid attacks on other students' morality.

Another possibility for an enlightening panel is to obtain volunteers from a senior citizens' center or from colleagues close to retirement age in your college to participate in a discussion of their perceptions of the role that sexual intimacy has played at different points in their lives. If you announce such a panel in advance, you can ask students to write down questions anonymously and provide them to panel members prior to the class session in which aging and sexuality is discussed.

References and Other Sources for Lectures

Billy, J. O. G., Tanfer, K., Grady, W. R. and Klepinger, D. H. (1993). The sexual behavior of men in the United States. *Family Planning Perspectives, 25,* 52–60.

Eisen, M., & Zellman, G. L. (1987). Changes in incidence of sexual intercourse of unmarried teenagers following a community-based sex education program. *Journal of Sex Research, 23,* 527–532.

Fabes, R. A., & Strouse, J. (1987). Perceptions of responsible and irresponsible models of sexuality: A correlational study. *Journal of Sex Research, 23,* 70–84.

Glass, S. P. and Wright, T. L. (1992). Justifications for extramarital relationships: The association between attitudes, behaviors, and gender. *Journal of Sex Research, 29,* 361–387.

Goldman, R. and Goldman, J. (1982). *Children's sexual thinking: A comparative study of children aged 5 to 15 years in Australia, North America, Britain and Sweden.* London: Routledge and Kegan Paul.

Hansen, G. L. (1987). Extradyadic relations during courtship. *Journal of Sex Research, 23,* 382–390.

Kurdek, L. A., & Schmitt, J. P. (1987). Partner homogamy in married, heterosexual cohabiting, gay, and lesbian couples. *Journal of Sex Research, 23,* 212–232.

Newcomb, M. D. (1986). Sexual behavior of cohabitors: A comparison of three independent samples. *Journal of Sex Research, 22,* 494–513.

Peplau, L. A., Hill, C. T. and Rubin, Z. (1993). Sex role attitudes in dating and marriage: A 15-year follow-up of the Boston couples study. *Journal of Social Issues, 49* (3), 3–52.

Perper, T., & Weis, D. L. (1987). Proceptive and rejective strategies of U.S. and Canadian college women. *Journal of Sex Research, 23,* 455–480.

Smith, T. W. (1991). Adult sexual behavior in 1989: Number of partners, frequency of intercourse, and risk of AIDS. *Family Planning Perspectives, 23,* 102–107.

Strouse, J. S. (1987). College bars as social settings for heterosexual contacts. *Journal of Sex Research, 23,* 374–382.

Turner, B. F., & Adams, C. G. (1988). Reported change in preferred sexual activity over the adult years. *Journal of Sex Research, 25,* 289–303.

Weizman, R., & Hart, J. (1987). Sexual behavior in healthy married elderly men. *Archives of Sexual Behavior, 16*, 39–44.

Chapter 14: Enhancing Sexual Health

Topics Covered in the Chapter

We begin this chapter by briefly mentioning Ornstein and Sobel's book *Healthy Pleasures* (1989), in which they contend that in addition to being fun, 20 minutes of sexual activity can burn 110 calories. We discuss the interactions of psychological and physical health and sexual functioning and point out that although health is often treated as a dichotomous variable, it is more accurate to describe health as existing along a continuum. Information on infertility and its treatment, formerly in Chapter 9, has been updated and moved to this chapter. The relationship of the use of various substances and drugs ("aphrodisiacs" and "anaphrodisiacs") to sexual functioning is reviewed. We suggest that the impact of disabilities and injuries on sexuality may vary depending on the age and stage at which the problem arises, the acute or chronic nature of the disability, and the individual's sexual attitudes and experiences prior to the emergence of the health threat. Material on illnesses (cancers, cardiovascular problems, and diabetes) has been moved to Chapter 5 in this edition.

We introduce the construct of sexual self-esteem and describe two measures relevant to this construct by Snell & Papini (1989) and Winter (1988), as well as Wiederman and Allgeier's (1993) short form (see Box 14.1) of the Snell and Papini sexual self-esteem measure. Body image and sexuality and variations in beliefs about attractiveness (slenderness versus plumpness, etc.) across time periods are considered. We review research on anorexia nervosa and bulimia and the relationship of these eating disorders to sexual attitudes and behaviors.

In the section on menstruation and health, we discuss cultural attitudes toward menstruation and premenstrual syndrome. Box 14.3 describes the reactions of several young women to menarche. Box 14.2, "Menstruation and the Marketplace," which deals with toxic shock syndrome, is retained from the previous edition. The second part of this section is devoted to menopause and an examination of the risks and benefits of hormone-replacement therapy (HRT). Although the current research suggests that the benefits outweigh the risks, we recommend that menopausal women seek detailed information from their physicians before making a decision about obtaining HRT.

Sources and treatments for infertility in men, women, and couples are described. Our coverage looks at alternative avenues to parenthood, including adoption, artificial insemination by the partner or a donor, and surrogate motherhood.

Injuries and impairments are the subject of the next major section of this chapter. Our culture is not notably competent in providing adequate sex education for "normal" people, and people with sensory impairments (sight, hearing) and development disabilities experience additional difficulties in acquiring accurate information about sexuality. We focus on the dilemma that caretakers face in protecting the 6 million Americans with developmental disabilities from exploitation and unwanted (and, in some cases, inappropriate) conception. The second part of this section, spinal-cord injuries, reports research indicating a range in the capacity of those with such injuries to respond to sexual stimulation and to reproduce.

The material on so-called aphrodisiacs and anaphrodisiacs begins by considering the kind of research needed to demonstrate that a particular substance or practice does or does not have a direct effect on sexual arousal and performance. Box 14.5 provides students with instructions for engaging in Kegel exercises. Box 14.6 is a description of the media's distortion of the work of Davidson and his colleagues on yohimbine. The section also refers to research on cantharides, yohimbine, alcohol, barbiturates, sedatives, amphetamines, amyl nitrate, marijuana, LSD, and opiates; the administration of testosterone and the impact of some drugs prescribed for medical or psychological conditions (e.g., thorazine, antihypertensives, antidepressants) on sexual desire; saltpeter as an example of a reputed, but not demonstrated, anaphrodisiac; and the use of estrogen administration and other antiandrogenic substances to reduce sexual (and other) activity.

We conclude the chapter with a discussion of epilepsy as an exemplar of a disability stereotypically thought to interfere with sexual expression, noting that it was some of the traditional medications used to control the disorder (e.g., phenobarbital) rather than epilepsy itself that depressed sexual interest. The point is that we need to be cautious in accepting stereotypes about the relationship between sexual interest and functioning, and infirmities and disabilities.

Ideas for Lecture and Use of Class Time

In the context of the discussion of the newly developed measures of sexual self-esteem, we suggest several hypotheses about the possible relationship of sexual esteem to experience with sexual coercion, sexual dysfunction, and so on, that your students might want to test.

Our review of the literature on hormone-replacement therapy (estrogen plus progesterone) for menopausal women led us to conclude that it provides sexual and general health benefits that far outweigh the risks of estrogen exposure. Walling et al.'s (1990) review reaches the same general conclusions.

We discuss the controversy about the provision of contraception to people with developmental disabilities and mention the issue of the ability to obtain informed consent from those with low IQs before providing contraception or sterilization. You can expand on this point, noting that sometimes a person may be assessed as having a developmental disability stemming from genetic causes when, in fact, the source of his or her low performance is emotional disturbance, which may be amenable to treatment. You may be able to invite several people from local schools or institutions for developmentally disabled adolescents to provide a guest lecture or panel on the policies about sexual intimacy and contraception in their institutions. By this point in the course, my students have tended to be fairly sympathetic to the plight and needs of people stigmatized in our culture, but you should caution them to be polite in their questions and comments, questioning policies without attacking the guest describing the policies.

The Schover et al. (1988) article on patients with multiple sclerosis may be too specialized for beginning undergraduates, but, depending on the focus of your course, it could be used as lecture material for more advanced students. In addition to describing orgasmic dysfunctions, the authors list techniques that can be used to help treat multiple sclerosis patients experiencing these dysfunctions.

References and Other Sources for Lectures

Cooley, M. E., et al. (1986). Sexual and reproductive issues for women with Hodgkin's disease. *Cancer Nursing, 9*, 248–255.

Cutler, W. B., Garcia, C. R., & McCoy, N. (1987). Perimenopausal sexuality. *Archives of Sexual Behavior, 16*, 225–234.

DeHaan, C. B., & Wallander, J. L. (1988). Self-concept, sexual knowledge and attitudes, and parental support in the sexual adjustment of women with early- and late-onset physical disability. *Archives of Sexual Behavior, 17*, 145–161.

Glass, C. A., Fielding, D. M., Evans, C., & Ashcroft, J. B. (1987). Factors related to sexual functioning in male patients undergoing hemodialysis and with kidney transplants. *Archives of Sexual Behavior, 16*, 189–207.

Malloy, G. L., & Herold, E. S. (1988). Factors related to sexual counseling of physically disabled adults. *Journal of Sex Research, 24*, 220–226.

Ornstein, R. and Sobel, D. (1989). *Healthy Pleasures*. Reading, MA: Addison-Wesley.

Schover, L. R., et al. (1988). Orgasm phase dysfunctions in multiple sclerosis. *Journal of Sex Research, 25*, 548–554.

Walling, M., Anderson, B. L., and Johnson, S. B. (1990). Hormone replacement therapy for post-menopausal women: A review of sexual outcomes and related gynecologic effects. *Archives of Sexual Behavior, 19*, 119–137.

Warner, H., et al. (1986). Electrostimulation of erection and ejaculation and collection of semen in spinal cord injured humans. *Journal of Rehabilitation Research and Development, 23* (3), 21–31.

White, J. R., et al. (1990). Enhanced sexual behavior in exercising men. *Archives of Sexual Behavior, 19*, 193–209.

Chapter 15: Sexual Orientation

Topics Covered in the Chapter

Our coverage of variations in sexual orientation begins with the problems of defining a person's orientation. We deal with same-gender sexual interaction across species and cultures and describe the legal and social status of homosexuality. The formation of a gay identity is discussed, and we review the five major theoretical hypotheses regarding the cause or etiology of sexual orientation. Issues of adjustment and homophobia are discussed, and the chapter concludes with a review of research on bisexuality.

Determining how to define a person as heterosexual, homosexual, or bisexual presents some problems. We discuss several different definitions that have been used, including the Kinsey group's seven-point continuum and Anna Freud's hypothesis that the content of fantasies should be the basis of defining orientation. Because students commonly confuse homosexual orientation with gender-role identity variations, Box 15.1 provides definitions of heterosexuals, homosexuals, bisexuals, transsexuals, and transvestites. We point out that homosexual behavior is fairly common among various nonhuman animals. Material on homosexual contacts across cultures is presented to stress the point that beliefs about the meaning of same-gender sexual contacts vary considerably across cultures and appear to be related to some extent to traditional versus egalitarian gender-role norms.

The removal of homosexuality by the American Psychiatric Association of homosexuality in 1974 from its list of psychological disorders is reported. We attribute this change to the results of research over three decades showing that sexual orientation appears to be unrelated to one's mental or emotional status.

The prosecution of homosexuals under sodomy laws is discussed, and we allude to the upholding of Georgia's sodomy law by the Supreme Court (discussed more thoroughly in Chapter 7). The start of the gay liberation movement is described, but we point out that despite the movement's efforts toward civil rights for gays, no state or federal laws prohibit discrimination against homosexuals in employment, housing, immigration, military service, child custody, or marriage. Box 15.2 describes the difficulty experienced by a German man who, when attempting to visit the United States, acknowledged that he was bisexual when asked about his sexual orientation.

In the second section, the problem of determining the proportion of people who are homosexual or bisexual is discussed. The process involved in the acquisition of a gay identity, and the problems associated with coming out versus keeping one's homosexual orientation secret, are described. Research on variations in gay lifestyles and on sexual expression between men and between women is presented. We examine the research by Masters and Johnson (1979), who conclude that although sexual response is physiologically the same for heterosexual and homosexual lovers, the latter appear to be more relaxed and less goal-oriented than are many heterosexual couples.

Research on gender differences in homosexual behavior indicates that lesbians tend to have fewer partners and to place greater value on commitment and exclusivity than do gay men. The process of aging among gays is discussed, and this section ends with coverage of the phenomenon of situational homosexuality.

The major hypotheses regarding the cause of sexual orientation are then reviewed: heredity, hormones, family influences, gender-role nonconformity, and early sexual experience. In this edition, we have described the preliminary research by LeVay and by Hamer and his associates on hypothalamic, chromosomal, and pedigree patterns in gays versus heterosexuals, noting that lesbians are not represented in these studies. Research on the adjustment of gays is presented, and we note that early results were flawed by the use of inappropriate comparison groups. Box 15.3 contains a humorous parallel to early conclusions about the pathology of homosexuals by reporting stories of aggressive behavior by heterosexuals under the headline, "Is Heterosexuality an Illness?" Therapeutic interventions with homosexuals are described along with the biases that have accompanied some of these attempts to "cure" homosexuals of their attraction to people of the same gender.

In discussing antigay prejudice, we review research on contemporary attitudes toward homosexuality. Box 15.4 contains an account of former California superintendent of public instruction Max Rafferty's view that homosexuals are not morally fit to teach. We review research relevant to some of the myths about homosexuals and conclude this section by expressing the hope that homosexuals will someday be treated as ordinary people. Regarding bisexuality, we discuss problems involved in obtaining estimates of prevalence rates, and bisexual lifestyles are described. We report the findings of several new studies relevant to attitudes toward bisexuals (Rust, 1993) and to stability in bisexual orientation over time (Stokes et al., 1993).

Ideas for Lecture and Use of Class Time

I typically devote two class sessions to the topic of orientation, the first to lecture and the second to a guest panel. In the first edition, we devoted considerable coverage to Storms's (1981) triadic model of the development of orientation. In subsequent editions, we reduced the amount of space for his model because there has been little research on it. However, during lecture, I review his model because I particularly like his attempt to explain the development of sexual orientation rather than just homosexual orientation (typical of earlier theories) and because it is a multivariate rather than a unidimensional model. For those of you who also like his model, the extensive coverage of it in the first edition (pp. 507–508) could be readily adapted for lecture material. If you don't have a copy of the first edition, your D. C. Heath sales representative may be able to provide you with one.

I then review other attempted explanations for variations in orientation, briefly reviewing most of them but devoting more time to the LeVay (1991; 1993, cited in the textbook) and the Hamer et al. (1993) research. Figure 15.7 shows family trees of families containing gay men. You might want to enlarge the figure and put it on a transparency, as students may tend to skip over the rather remarkable suggestion of potential transmission through the maternal line. I think that it is also important to point out that this research is preliminary and needs replication by other independent research teams before any firm conclusions can be drawn. Further, I do not believe (and say so) that any one explanation is likely to explain the etiology of all cases of homosexuality (or, for that matter, bi- or heterosexuality).

Results suggestive of a relationship between a history of gender-role nonconformity in childhood, as described in the textbook, and the development of a homosexual orientation (at least for some gays) continue to accumulate. Billingham and Hockenberry (1987) distributed questionnaires to members of men's homophile organizations. They concluded from the responses (219, or 53%, were returned) that early childhood gender conformity or nonconformity and masturbatory fantasies were significantly related to adult sexual orientation. See also Green's (1987) work on gender-role nonconformity cited in the textbook. I think this material has been handled carefully, and I stress the difference between correlational and causal evidence in discussion. Students should be reminded that although there is a relationship, many gay men were masculine identified during childhood and continue to have masculine or androgynous gender-role identities, and many lesbians were and are, feminine or androgynous.

Herek's (1988) article contains a 20-item scale, Attitudes Toward Lesbians and Gay Men (p. 477), that could be administered in your class prior to your lecture on orientation to examine the extent to which your students' responses are similar to those found in Herek's samples. The Stevenson (1988) article reviews attempts to increase college students' tolerance of an alternative orientation (homosexual attraction) and is a good companion piece to the Herek article.

Wells (1990) examined the terminology found erotic by male and female heterosexuals and homosexuals. He found that gay men and women used erotic or arousing vocabulary with their partners more often than did heterosexuals.

If you have a lesbian and gay support group on campus or in your community, its members are usually happy to help form a sexual-orientation panel, which can be extremely valuable in dispelling myths about gays. My major goal is to demonstrate that as much diversity prevails among homosexuals as among heterosexuals. I generally try to have a group of about six to eight, including a heterosexual and a bisexual person. We begin the session by having each person on the panel give his or her first name and major in school (or occupation). Students in the course are asked to write down the names of the panel members and then to indicate what they think their orientation is. Panel members may be willing to code the class members' responses for you to tell students about their accuracy (or relative inaccuracy) in "being able to tell one when you see one". After the students have guessed the orientation of each panel member, the panel members again give their names, now adding their orientation and their current relationship status (celibate, dating, involved in a committed relationship, etc.). At that point, we open up the session to questions from the class, with the heterosexual members of the panel responding to all questions asked of the gay members of the panel (e.g., "How old were you when you were first aware of your orientation?" "Do your parents know your orientation?"). A number of times I have administered a before-after seven-point attitude scale measuring the acceptance of homosexual orientation for others, and in every case, the mean moves from less to more accepting.

Note: With one exception, hostility from my students to panel members has been minimal. The main concern seems to be from some men that a homosexual man might see them in the locker room, get aroused, and come on to them. I point out that this is possible but unlikely because most gays do not seek uninterested heterosexual men. I also suggest that they might want to approach their women friends for tips on how to handle unwanted approaches because most women have had plenty of experience with this from men.

Several years ago, though, one student lost no opportunity to make disparaging comments about gays beginning the first day of the course, even wearing a t-shirt labeled "militant heterosexual." During the panel's visit, he was openly hostile, which they handled very well. When members of the panel remained after class to talk with students who had additional questions, the hostile young man came down and whipped out a knife to demonstrate how he cuts up "queers" who come on to him. He was apparently not intending to cut members of the panel, but because of his litany of all the times that he perceived that gays had approached him, he scared members of the panel with the knife waving. I had him removed from the class and taped my lectures so that he could complete the course without returning to class. Since that experience, I have begun the class with the panel by describing that incident as an example of antigay prejudice, saying that students are not allowed to carry weapons on campus, and anyone who happens to have one should keep it out of sight.

References and Other Sources for Lectures

Billingham, R. E., & Hockenberry, S. L. (1987). Gender conformity, masturbation fantasy, infatuation, and sexual orientation: A discriminant analysis investigation. *Journal of Sex Research, 23,* 368–374.

Ellis, L., Burke, D., & Ames, M. A. (1987). Sexual orientation as a continuous variable: A comparison between the sexes. *Archives of Sexual Behavior, 16,* 523–529.

Ernulf, K. E., & Innala, S. M. (1987). The relationship between affective and cognitive components of homophobic reaction. *Archives of Sexual Behavior, 16,* 501–509.

Freund, K., Watson, R., & Rienzo, D. (1989). Heterosexuality, homosexuality, and erotic age preference. *Journal of Sex Research, 26,* 107–117.

Herek, G. M. (1988). Heterosexuals' attitudes toward lesbians and gay men: Correlates and gender differences. *Journal of Sex Research, 25,* 451–477.

Herek, G. M. (1989). Hate crimes against lesbians and gay men: Issues for research and policy. *American Psychologist, 44*, 948–955.

Hockenberry, S. L., & Billingham, R. E. (1987). Sexual orientation and boyhood gender conformity: Development of the Boyhood Gender Conformity Scale (BGCS). *Archives of Sexual Behavior, 16*, 475–492.

Hutchins, L., & Kaahumanu, L. (Eds.) (1991). *Any other name: Bisexual people speak out.* Boston: Alyson Publications.

Leigh, B. C. (1989). Reasons for having and avoiding sex: Gender, sexual orientation, and relationship to sexual behavior. *Journal of Sex Research, 26*, 199–209.

Rust, P. C. (1993). Neutralizing the political threat of the marginal woman: Lesbians' beliefs about bisexual women. *Journal of Sex Research, 30*, 214–228.

Schneider, M. S. (1986). The relationships of cohabiting and heterosexual couples: A comparison. *Psychology of Women Quarterly, 10*, 234–239.

Stevenson, M. R. (1988). Promoting tolerance for homosexuality: An evaluation of intervention strategies. *Journal of Sex Research, 25*, 500–511.

Stokes, J. P., McKirnan, D. J., & Burzette, R. G. (1993). Sexual behavior, condom use, disclosure of sexuality, and stability of sexual orientation in bisexual men. *Journal of Sex Research, 30*, 203–213.

Storms, M. D. (1981). A theory of erotic orientation development. *Psychological Review, 88*, 340–353.

Testa, R. J., Kinder, B. N., & Ironson, G. (1987). Heterosexual bias in the perception of loving relationships of gay males and lesbians. *Journal of Sex Research, 23*, 163–172.

Weinburg, M. S., Williams, C. J., & Pryor, D. W. (1994). *Dual attraction: Understanding bisexuality.* New York: Oxford University Press.

Wells, J. W. (1990). The sexual vocabularies of heterosexual and homosexual males and females for communicating with a sexual partner. *Archives of Sexual Behavior, 19*, 139–147.

Chapter 16: Sex for Profit

Topics Covered in the Chapter

We begin with a review of erotic products, discuss erotica and the law, review research on the correlates and effects of exposure to erotica, and consider public policy on the availability of erotic materials. Differentiating erotica from violent pornography, we have a major section on the latter topic, describing research on prolonged exposure, cultural variation, child pornography, and the issue of protection from pornography. The last section focuses on prostitution.

We discuss the terms "erotica" and "pornography" and then describe ways in which sexuality is used in magazines and newspapers, advertisements, television programs, erotic movies and videotapes, adult bookstores, telephone sex, computer sex, stripping, and promoting sexual toys and aids. We note that as erotic home videos have become available, sales of erotic magazines and profits of adult theaters have dropped. Box 16.1 contains a graduate student's description of the kinds of erotic movies that she and her fiancé enjoy. We describe the relationship between traditional ideas about male and female sexuality and the plots of erotic media, indicating that X-rated films generally seem to reflect male fantasies, whereas romance novels (discussed in Box 16.2) appear to be designed to appeal to females' fantasies. Potential uses of various forms of erotica are described at the end of this section.

The second section focuses on legal issues involving erotic materials and definitions of obscenity. We describe the 1987 change in the Supreme Court's criteria for obscenity. The attempt by feminists to differentiate between erotica and pornography is also described, and Box 16.4 contains a description of the Canadian Supreme Court's 1992 ruling on obscenity, which employs a harm-based approach. Box 16.3 contains my reactions to testifying for the defense as an expert witness in a trial in which 11 adult bookstores in Toledo, Ohio, were charged with obscenity.

The third section focuses on the effects and correlates of exposure to erotica. We describe the differing conclusions emerging from the 1970 and 1986 U. S. Commissions on Obscenity and Pornography, and those of the 1979 British and 1985 Canadian commissions, and report the results of Smith and Hand's (1987) interesting field research, which found no differences in levels of sexual aggression before and after screening of a nonviolent erotic film on a southern campus.

Research on viewers' reactions to romanticized versus realistic violent erotica is then considered, as are the differing arousal responses of force-oriented versus nonforce-oriented males to rape depictions. Material on the relative amount of violence in X-rated, compared to PG- or R-rated, movies is presented, and characteristics of people who attend X-rated movies are described, which indicate that viewers tend to hold more gender-egalitarian attitudes than do nonviewers. Experimental research on the effects on attitudes of prolonged exposure to erotica is reviewed. The phenomenon of using children as erotic stimuli in print and film media is considered, as are the correlates of such experiences for children. We discuss the legal responses to such abuse of children and report the Supreme Court's 1982 decision that publishers and sellers of child erotica may be prosecuted under child abuse laws.

In the concluding section, we discuss prostitution, historically and in contemporary society. The status hierarchy of prostitution (streetwalkers, bar prostitutes, massage parlors, call girls) is described, and Box 16.5 contains an account of training for massage parlor employment. Box 16.6 raises issues regarding the definition of prostitution. Male prostitution is described. We review data suggesting that laws regulating or forbidding prostitution tend to be differentially applied as a function of the prostitute's economic status and that customers and pimps are arrested relatively rarely. To protect themselves, many prostitutes have formed local and national unions that lobby for decriminalization and provision of services for prostitutes, and the advantages of decriminalization are described. Research on the factors associated with becoming a prostitute and feelings of prostitutes about their work is reviewed, and the characteristics of clients are described. We end this chapter with a discussion of the possible reasons for the existence of prostitution.

Ideas for Lecture and Use of Class Time

Before students read this chapter, you might want to ask them to list the criteria they would use in defining material as obscene. Coding the variations in their criteria can illustrate the difficulties in determining community standards between acceptable and nonacceptable erotic material.

The film *Still Killing Us Softly: Advertising's Image of Women* (1987, Cambridge, 30 minutes, color) is an update of the 1980 film *Killing Us Softly*, which documents a presentation by Jean Kilbourne at Harvard University and the audience's reaction to her narration in the context of a series of slides of ads that appear harmless. She deals effectively with the sexism in these ads in a humorous, nonvindictive manner and progresses toward the more damaging ads, which involve violence against women, toward the end. This is a very good film, and although some of my students complain that Kilbourne seems "feminist" (as if this were an epithet), most of them are enthusiastic about the film, giving it an overall rating of 5.5 on a 7-point scale. Personally, I think that the earlier version, which employed more humor and less rhetoric, was more effective with students.

The Society for the Scientific Study of Sex (SSSS) issued a policy statement disputing the scientific accuracy of the conclusions of the U.S. Attorney General's Commission on Pornography. (For the SSSS policy statement, see pp. 284–285 of *Journal of Sex Research* (1987), 23, 284–287.) The photograph of the news conference in which Meese released the commission's report in the summer of 1986 against a backdrop of a nude statue appeared in a number of places and can be put on a slide or transparency to introduce discussion of the scientific and public policy issues raised by the commission's conclusions. I found a copy of the photograph in an issue of *Mother Jones* that had the subtitle, "Meese Makes Guinness Book of Records by Viewing 2 Million Dirty Pictures in One Year." The photograph (without the *Mother Jones* caption) is in the textbook.

You may be able to provide personal experiences regarding differing definitions of pornography based on your experience in teaching the human sexuality course. For example, regarding the textbook, an instructor in a prison in the Midwest was offering a course of human sexuality and wanted to use our book. However, the course was delayed because prison officials wanted to have the state board of education determine whether the book was "pornographic." I was alerted to this situation by a prison inmate, who wrote to me about it. We corresponded over a number of months, and he was the author of the gruesome description of prison rape in Chapter 18 (Box 18.2). The board of education decided that our textbook was not "pornographic."

Very recently a colleague at another university called me because several persons in the community had charged that the textbook that they used for the human sexuality course was "pornographic," and they wanted to eliminate the course. Additionally, one member of the board of trustees of the university had been swayed by the arguments of the anti–sex education persons. The colleague asked me to write a letter. The textbook in question was based on empirical data and most definitely was not pornographic (or, legally speaking, *obscene*), whether based on U. S. or Canadian definitions of the term. I wrote a letter of support for the instructor regarding her choice of textbook (even though it was not our own). I would like to hear from those of you who have experienced similar attacks on your choice of textbooks and attempts to eliminate your course. Such experiences could provide the basis for an eye-opening panel for a future symposium of a meeting of the SSSS.

Linz (1989) reviewed the data on experimental studies conducted since 1970 on the effects of exposure to sexually explicit materials on attitudes and perceptions about rape. His review distinguishes between exposure to sexually violent materials and nonaggressive erotic materials and is useful for lecture material.

For a sort of point/counterpoint discussion of the issues raised by Malamuth and Donnerstein (1984) in their book, *Pornography and Sexual Aggression*, see Mosher's (1986) review and Malamuth and Donnerstein's (1987) subsequent letter to the editor in which they describe the Mosher review as "inaccurate and unfair. It is by and large, not a book review but his viewpoint regarding the dangers of censorship" (p. 281). For additional lecture material on this issue, see

Mould (1988a, 1988b), Malamuth (1988), Donnerstein and Linz (1988), and O'Grady (1988). You might want to outline the various opinions on a transparency and then ask students to give their opinions.

The textbook cites data indicating that attitudes toward women and toward the sentencing of rapists are altered by exposure to violent erotica. Because I share Mosher's concerns about the dangers of censorship, however, I support educational approaches aimed at sensitizing students to ways in which their sexual arousal can be conditioned through association of sexual stimuli to particular themes. To heighten students' sensitivity to themes that are currently being linked to sexuality, you could encourage them to conduct research based on Armstrong's approach (1986). He analyzed country music themes and found that more of the songs contained references to prostitution (16) and extramarital sex (15) than to other themes. Similarly, small groups of students within the class could conduct analyses of themes in (1) top 40 hits; (2) MTV videos, differentiating between the visual and audio themes; (3) heavy metal music; and (4) new wave music. Each group could generate possible themes with the help of the class as a whole—for example, men use women, women use men, love makes people crazy, passion can't be controlled, or the use of nonparallel language or language that suggests a power differential. Each group could then listen to or watch material from their category and make independent ratings of the presence of the themes, examine the correlations among their ratings, and report their findings to the class. This exercise could begin in the context of Chapter 6, in which we discuss the conditioning of arousal, and the results could be reported in the context of Chapter 16. A similar project could involve themes in print and photo media using Scott and Cuvelier's (1987a, 1987b) method.

Naomi McCormick's (1994) book, *Sexual Salvation*, contains well-balanced chapters on erotica and commercial sex workers that can provide excellent bases for lectures. If a chapter of one of the unions for prostitutes, such as COYOTE or Scapegoat, is in your area, you could invite several of the members to provide a panel for your class to discuss how they got into the business, the risks they face, and the potential benefits they see in unionization and decriminalization.

References and Other Sources for Lectures

Armstrong, E. G. (1986). Country music songs: An ethnomusicological account. *Journal of Sex Research*, 22, 370–378.

Donnerstein, E. E., & Linz, D. (1988). A critical analysis of "A critical analysis of recent research on violent erotica." *Journal of Sex Research*, 24, 348–352.

Gibson-Ainyette, I., Templer, D. I., Brown, R., & Veaco, L. (1988). Adolescent female prostitutes. *Archives of Sexual Behavior*, 17, 431–438.

Laan, E., Everaed, W., van Bellen, G., & Hanewald, G. (1994). Women's sexual and emotional responses to male- and female-produced erotica. *Archives of Sexual Behavior*, 23, 153–169.

Linz, D. (1989). Exposure to sexually explicit materials and attitudes toward rape: A comparison of study results. *Journal of Sex Research*, 26, 50–84.

McCormick, N. B. (1994). *Sexual salvation*. Westport, CT: Greenwood.

Malamuth, N. M. (1988). Research on "violent erotica": A reply. *Journal of Sex Research*, 24, 340–348.

Malamuth, N. M., & Donnerstein, E. (Eds.) (1984). *Pornography and sexual aggression.* Orlando, FL: Academic Press.

Malamuth, N. M., & Donnerstein, E. (1987). Letter to the book review editor. *Journal of Sex Research, 23,* 281–283.

Mosher, D. L. (1986). Review of Malamuth and Donnerstein's book. *Journal of Sex Research, 22,* 532–536.

Mould, D. E. (1988a). A critical analysis of recent research on violent erotica. *Journal of Sex Research, 24,* 326–340.

Mould, D. E. (1988b). A reply to Malamuth and Donnerstein and Linz. *Journal of Sex Research, 24,* 353–358.

O'Grady, K. E. (1988). Donnerstein, Malamuth, and Mould: The conduct of research and the nature of inquiry. *Journal of Sex Research, 24,* 358–362.

Scott, J. E., & Cuvelier, S. J. (1987a). Sexual violence in *Playboy* magazine: A longitudinal content analysis. *Journal of Sex Research, 23,* 534–539.

Scott, J. E., & Cuvelier, S. J. (1987b). Violence in *Playboy* magazine: A longitudinal analysis. *Archives of Sexual Behavior, 16,* 279–288.

Scott, J. E., & Schwalm, L. A. (1988). Rape rates and the circulation rates of adult magazines. *Journal of Sex Research, 24,* 241–249.

Smith, M. D. and Hand, C. (1987). The pornography/aggression linkage: Results from a field study. *Deviant Behavior, 8,* 389–399.

Chapter 17: Sexually Transmitted Diseases

Topics Covered in the Chapter

This chapter begins with a discussion of the interaction between psychosocial attitudes and the spread of STDs. The symptoms, causes, and available cures for bacterial infections, AIDS, and other viral and parasitic infections are then described. We conclude with a discussion of safer-sex practices.

In the first section, we examine attitudes held by members of the general public and by public and private health deliverers that may impede the likelihood of screening, diagnosis, treatment, and follow-up for reduction of the incidence of STDs. We also address the problem of ignorance about STDs, the reactions of people to positive test results for an STD, and attitudes toward people who contract STDs. Box 17.1 contains a test of AIDS knowledge.

To help students group the large amount of information about STDs, we have organized coverage into bacterial, viral, and parasitic infections, with their symptoms presented in Table 17.1. In the section on bacterial infections, we describe gonorrhea, syphilis, chlamydia and nongonococcal urethritis, cystitis, prostatitis, gardnerella vaginalis, shigellosis, and pelvic inflammatory disease.

AIDS is the topic of the next major section. Figure 17.1 displays a worldwide map of predicted future sites of HIV infection. Box 17.2, "An Epidemic of Stigma," describes episodes of discrimination against people who have contracted AIDS. We review research on the origins, prevalence, and risk factors for AIDS, and Figure 17.5 depicts the percentages of AIDS patients from various risk groups (e.g., gay and bisexual males, intravenous drug users, heterosexuals). We describe the ways HIV infiltrates the immune system, and Box 17.3 focuses on Randy Shilts's (1987) description of the sluggish response of the U. S. government to AIDS and the scientific infighting that accompanied the search for its cause. Shilts died from AIDS-related causes on February 17, 1994. Background on his life is presented in a memorium written by William Darrow and published in *The Journal of Sex Research* (1994), Issue #3. (As I write this, the memorium is in press, so I cannot provide page numbers). Symptoms of AIDS are listed, and Box 17.4 contains a first-person account of being tested for HIV. Attempts to treat AIDS and opportunistic infections that attack AIDS patients are reviewed, and we discuss the infection of children with HIV. A two-page color feature, "Living with AIDS," depicts people from various groups who are afflicted with HIV. Finally, we conclude this section with a description of practices that may reduce the likelihood of contracting HIV.

Other viral infections reviewed are genital herpes, genital warts, and hepatitis B; the characteristics, treatment, and long-term complications of each are described. Parasitic infections and their symptoms are described, including candidiasis, trichomoniasis, amebiasis, scabies, and pediculosis pubis.

We conclude the chapter with a section on safer-sex practices, beginning with suggestions for relationship negotiation. Specifically, we suggest that individuals determine their own sexual policies, communicate their policies to a potential partner, give and receive informed consent regarding the extent to which past sexual behaviors may put one at risk of transmitting an STD, and, if at risk, postponing any physical intimacy involving body fluid exchange until lab tests verify freedom from STDs. In addition, we suggest taking a shower or bath together before becoming sexually intimate, learning about each other's bodies, and using a condom and spermicide during all sexual acts, avoiding anal contact (or using condoms and spermicide lubricant if one chooses to have anal sex despite the risks) and urinating and washing the genitals after sex. Finally, we list other practices to reduce risk, including avoidance of intravenous drug use, needle sharing, use of belongings of others that could contain body fluids, and sexual intimacy with people in high-risk groups (intravenous drug users, for example) or others until there is confidence that sexual activity will not pose health risks.

Ideas for Lecture and Use of Class Time

In my experience, many of my (heterosexual, sexually active) students do not believe that they are at risk of contracting *any* STD, let alone one of the incurable viral infections, such as AIDS or herpes. Therefore, I devote most of my energy in conjunction with this chapter to disabusing them of their apparent belief in their own invulnerability. One of the students who was in my class several years ago obtained a positive-HIV antibody test and has volunteered to appear in my class to talk about his feelings and experiences with the onset of symptoms, relatively minor so far. If you know someone who has tested positive for HIV or for genital herpes who is willing to speak to your class, that may be a particularly powerful method of increasing students' awareness of their own risks.

If any of you have come up with other effective strategies for communicating the risk of contracting STDs, please let me know so that I can include your ideas in *The Allgeier Update*.

Professor Lyman Gilmore, who heard a presentation about my research group's findings from our studies of sexual policies and coercion, has his students write an essay examining their own sexual policies regarding situations that they have encountered or are likely to encounter in the future. (This assignment is relevant to a number of chapters in the textbook.) He asks student to begin with their opinions and their own behavior, and then to address three major questions: (1) What is good for me? (2) What is good for those with whom I am in relationships? and (3) What is good for society? The students are required to develop reasoned and documented statements of their positions, citing references clearly indicating the basis of their assertions. Gilmore tells them that the topics they examine within this framework are up to them but provides them with a list of potential topics:

What is my position on virginity and celibacy?

How do I decide what I want in a relationship?

How do I decide what I am willing to do in a relationship?

How do I get what I want?

How honest should a relationship be?

What are my criteria for having intercourse?

Contraception: What type and why?

Would I participate in an abortion? Why? Why not (male and female)?

How can I avoid acquaintance rape (male and female)?

How do I feel about having consensual or clandestine extramarital or extrarelationship sexual relations?

What is my position on the availability of erotica?

What is my position on mandatory and voluntary AIDS testing?

How do I feel about seduction?

What about sex without love and one-night stands?

How do drugs (including alcohol) affect my sexuality?

How do I feel about homosexuality and bisexuality?

How do I feel about masturbation?

I don't know if Gilmore uses a code number system or some other method of protecting students' anonymity, but I suggest doing so. Students can be asked to put the last four digits of their social security number or a parent's birthday on a separate card, and the instructor can promise to separate the card from the essays after placing the grade on the card so that the instructor can grade these essays blindly. In the context of this chapter, students could be asked to write a dialogue or script of a conversation indicating how they would go about trying to give and receive informed consent to physical intimacy with a new (potential) partner, what steps they would take to reduce their risk of contracting an STD, and what conditions they might impose on the relationship if they were to enter it or to continue in it.

Shilts's (1987) book, *And the Band Played On*, can provide the basis for a good lecture on political and cross-cultural responses to AIDS. The videotape based on his book is too long for the average class session of 50 or 75 minutes, but you could come up with another way to show it. I have occasionally scheduled an extra nonrequired session to show particular movies.

In the mid-1980s, I began to put annual rates of new AIDS cases and cumulative deaths, such as are reported in Table 17.2, onto a transparency, and I add the latest figures to it each semester. For my lectures for second semester 1995, I will photocopy Table 17.2, enlarge it, make a transparency of it, and add the figures from 1994 using a transparency pen. I will then add the latest figures each semester until a new edition of our textbook comes out. These figures can be obtained from the Centers for Disease Control's *Mortality and Morbidity Reports*, or you can call 800/342/AIDS to get the latest statistics.

References and Other Sources for Lectures

Abramson, P. R., & Herdt, G. (1990). The assessment of sexual practices relevant to the transmission of AIDS: A global perspective. *Journal of Sex Research, 27*, 215–232.

Centers for Disease Control. (1989). *Behaviorally bisexual men and AIDS*. Executive summary of a workshop sponsored by the Centers for Disease Control. Washington, D.C.: American Institutes for Research.

Jedlicka, D., & Robinson, I. E. (1987). Fear of venereal disease and other perceived restraints on the occurrence of premarital coitus. *Journal of Sex Research, 23*, 391–396.

Kane, S. (1990). AIDS, addiction and condom use: Sources of sexual risk for heterosexual women. *Journal of Sex Research, 27*, 427–444.

Leigh, B. C. (1990). The relationship of substance use during sex to high-risk sexual behavior. *Journal of Sex Research, 27*, 199–213.

Mirotznik, J., Shapiro, R. D., Steinhart, J. E., & Gillespie, O. (1987). Genital herpes: An investigation of its attitudinal and behavioral correlates. *Journal of Sex Research, 23*, 266–272.

Shilts, R. (1987). *And the band played on*. New York: St. Martin's Press.

Warren, N. (1993). Out of the question: Obstacles to research on HIV and women who engage in sexual behaviors with women. *SIECUS Reports, 22* (1) 13–17.

Chapter 18: Sexual Coercion

Topics Covered in the Chapter

This chapter examines assault, harassment, and child sexual abuse. We begin by describing official incidence rates for sexual assault and discussing the problems of obtaining accurate incidence and prevalence rates because most victims do not report their assaults to legal authorities. Box 18.1 lists 20 common stereotypes about sexual assault victims and perpetrators to which students can respond true or false.

The section on characteristics of assailants distinguishes between convicted rapists and assailants who are unidentified primarily because their victims did not report them to authorities or they have not been located and arrested. The socialization experiences of sex offenders are described, and we review research on their attitudes, personality traits, and sexual characteristics.

We begin the coverage of victims of assault by describing male rape victims, partially because we believe that this may make males and females who have not been sexually coerced more sensitive to the problems experienced by female victims and may reduce the "blame the victim" phenomenon. Box 18.2 provides a graphic description of a male victim's rape experience in prison (see Chapter 16 in this guide regarding charges that sexuality textbooks are pornographic). We then review research on female assault victims and devote considerable space to the difference in incidence rates as a function of the source of data—FBI statistics versus victimology studies. We emphasize acquaintance assault because it is much more common than assault by strangers.

We review research relevant to contemporary hypotheses regarding the causes of sexual assault—victim precipitation, uncontrolled lust, uncontrolled aggression, and exaggerated gender-role identity—generally concluding that there is little support for the first two beliefs. The hypothesis that exposure to violent erotica leads to rape was discussed in Chapter 16.

The aftermath of sexual assault for victims is described using Burgess and Holmstrom's rape trauma syndrome as an organizing strategy. We then describe the potential helpfulness of rape crisis centers in dealing with emergency rooms, the police, and the courts. Box 18.3 contains a fictitious account of "John's" experience with mugging in which I have confronted John with the kinds of questions that female rape victims have encountered by police and the courts.

We turn next to sexual assault and the law, discussing changes in the rules of evidence regarding consent. Box 18.4 sets out false rape allegations, based on Kanin's (1994) article. We deliberated about including this material because we do not want to minimize the plight of women who have been sexually assaulted; however, because of our strong commitment to balanced coverage, we chose to discuss the issue of false allegations. I believe that it is important to emphasize in lecture, as we do in the textbook, that most people who believe they have been assaulted, harassed, or abused struggle with making the allegation. They suffer additional losses in time, money, and (potentially) reputation in making such charges, which should be taken very seriously. On the other hand, occasionally the alleged perpetrator is innocent, so it is important to emphasize that we adhere to an "innocent until proved guilty" code. In my lecture on the topic, I point out that because sexual coercion (assault, harassment, and abuse) is generally a recidivist crime, such experiences should be reported.

In the final section on assault, methods of reducing personal vulnerability are presented. We begin with the issue of politics and research on sexual assault, because some have taken the position that examination of victim variables is tantamount to holding the victim responsible for rape, a position with which I ardently disagree. We then review research on factors associated with being sexually assaulted, and end with steps that may reduce (but cannot eliminate) rape risk: determining one's sexual policies, discussing these policies with potential partners in public settings, avoiding intoxication with a person with whom one does not wish to become intimate, and making one's desires to have or to avoid physical intimacy known both verbally and nonverbally.

The next major section deals with sexual harassment in three different settings: occupational, educational, and therapeutic. Variations in definitions of sexual harassment are discussed, and research on the incidence and forms of this phenomenon is reviewed. Box 18.5 describes the sequelae of experiences of harassment on the job. The results of a questionnaire study we conducted with a stratified random sample of undergraduate and graduate student males and females are presented in Box 18.6. Perhaps the most interesting finding was that male students were as likely to report having had sexual relations with their female instructors as female students were to report having had sex with their male instructors. The description of harassment in educational settings ends with advice for students on what to do if they experience inappropriate sexual approaches by faculty or graduate students. We end this section with a discussion of sexual harassment of clients or patients by mental-health professionals or medical doctors.

Coverage of the sexual coercion of children begins with a discussion of the issue of the inability of children to give informed consent to sexual contact. Difficulties in obtaining accurate estimates of the prevalence of child sexual abuse are described, and Finkelhor's (1990) telephone survey of a representative sample of Americans on their experiences with sexual abuse is presented in Table 18.4. Risk factors for sexual abuse during childhood are presented, followed by a review of research on the characteristics of adult-child sexual contacts and the long-term correlates of children's sexual experiences with adults. Researchers in this area have been puzzled by the consistent finding that the overwhelming majority of known abuse situations involve male adults and female children. A number of hypotheses have been advanced to explain this finding, and we end the chapter with a description of these hypotheses along with relevant data that support or refute them.

Ideas for Lecture and Use of Class Time

I generally devote several class sessions to this chapter. In an attempt to sensitize men and women in the class to the varieties of physical and psychological coercion without raising their defensiveness to a level at which they cannot take in the information, I begin by being self-disclosive about my own experiences with both attempts to coerce me and my own psychological coerciveness. Regarding the latter, I point out that women, including myself, may make demands on someone they genuinely like for a level of relationship, including sexual intimacy or long-term commitment, beyond that with which the other person is comfortable, threatening to terminate the entire friendship if their specific demands are not met. I ask my students if they can recall engaging in any sort of psychological coercion, but I generally limit class discussion and disclosure to part of one class session to cover other material that is important about this topic.

Another strategy for organizing lectures to accompany this chapter is to use Box 18.1 on sexual assault stereotypes. You might distribute the 20 items to students early in a true-false format and then discuss each one during lecture for this chapter. For those items for which I provide no commentary, I believe that there is sufficient coverage in the chapter for the student to be able to provide an accurate answer.

Stereotypes About Rapists

1. *Only a male can be a rapist (F).* Females are far less likely to engage in physical coercion than are males, but females do engage in psychological coercion or take advantage of intoxicated males who subsequently feel degraded and used. See the description of Struckman-Johnson's (1988) article in the textbook for quotations by victimized males, in addition to those appearing on pages 635 and 637 of the textbook.

2. *Men rape because they are unable to obtain sexual release in any other way (F).* Kanin's (1985) article, cited in the textbook, shows greater numbers of consensual partners and frequency of sexual activity among males who anonymously report sexual coercion than among those who don't. His article contains a number of good tables that you can put on transparencies for lecture dealing with methods of coercion, expectation of peer approval for coercion of certain "types" of women, and so forth.

3. *Men rape because of hormonally caused excessive sexual drives (F).*

4. *Castration is an effective treatment for preventing a rapist from attacking more victims (F).* Material on this issue is presented in Chapter 19 when we deal with treatment approaches for sex offenders.

5. *After a man reaches a certain level of sexual arousal, he is unable to control his impulse to engage in intercourse (F).* The key issue here is intercourse with a nonconsenting partner. If one's partner doesn't want to have intercourse, one can always masturbate.

6. *Pornographic material containing rape scenes provokes men to commit sexual assault (F).* We deal with the issue of the ethical and methodological problems that do not permit such a causal assertion in Chapter 16. Sexual aggression as a result of exposure to violent erotica has not been demonstrated, although rape-myth-supportive attitudes do appear to be increased by exposure to violent erotica.

7. *The majority of rapes occur when the attacker has been drinking (T).*

8. *The vast majority of men rape women they have never met before (F).*

9. *The average convicted rapist spends at least ten years in prison (F).*

10. *The majority of men who are brought to trial for rape are convicted of that charge (?).* I know of no recent analysis relevant to this question. Schram's (1978) work, cited in the textbook, indicates that 5 percent of alleged assailants are arrested, and less than 3 percent are convicted. Because of plea-bargaining to lesser charges, my inclination is to suggest that the answer to this question is false. If you are aware of data on this issue, I would appreciate references.

Stereotypes About Victims

1. *The majority of women who are raped secretly want to be forced to have sex (F).*

2. *A woman cannot be raped against her will (F).*

3. *A man cannot be raped by a woman (F).*

4. *A man cannot be raped by another man (F).*

5. *The majority of women who charge rape actually consent to the act and then change their minds later (F).*

6. *The majority of women who are raped by acquaintances consent to the act and then charge rape when the relationship breaks up (F).*

7. *A married woman cannot be raped by her husband (F).* From a behavioral standpoint, the answer to this question has always been false. From a legal standpoint, it was true when we wrote

the first edition, but during the 1980s, a majority of states removed the spousal-exception clause.

8. *The majority of rape victims are highly attractive women who are assaulted while walking alone at night (F).*

9. *A brutal, violent sexual attack is much more traumatic for the victim than a sexual attack not involving physical violence (F).*

10. *Attack by a total stranger is more traumatic than attack by an acquaintance (F).* The answers to both 9 and 10 are false because of the problem of self-blame by victims; that is, victims may feel less blameworthy in a rape involving physical violence or attack by a stranger, whereas they may feel more shame and blame if they were physically coerced or if they knew the assailant, and they may feel (and get) less support from friends in the latter situations.

The final description in Box 18.2 was sent to me as part of a series of letters from a prison inmate who took a human sexuality course in which our textbook was used. In addition to noting that many inmates engaged in consensual sexual activity, he also wrote that sexual coercion was common among inmates and that he had experienced or heard about sexual coercion of inmates by guards and prison counselors.

I included the "likelihood to rape" (LR) item in the questionnaire at the beginning of Part I of this guide; if you administered it, you could provide results to the students at this point. Responses to LR were the basis for categorizing men as force or nonforce oriented in the research by Malamuth and his colleagues, described in the textbook in Chapter 16. I have administered this measure to my own classes in human sexuality and have been astounded that the responses of males were consistent with the general findings from a variety of difference samples: about one-third indicated some likelihood of raping if assured of not getting caught. To decrease defensiveness during lectures on the topic, I emphasize that two-thirds of the males indicated *no* likelihood of raping.

Katie Roiphe's (1993) book, *The Morning After: Sex, Fear, and Feminism on Campus,* cited in the textbook, has stimulated heated debate. She suggested that a number of programs on college campuses are encouraging women to identify themselves as victims rather than as powerful and effective persons. In my role as editor of the *Journal of Sex Research (JSR),* I invited psychologist Charlene Muehlenhard to select a group of people holding diverse attitudes toward the book to write commentaries. The resulting symposium was published in *JSR* (1994), pp. 143–154, and you might find the authors' contributions useful for lecture material. Although I don't agree with everything that Roiphe wrote, her message about helping people to realize their power is important for those dealing with potential date rape and harassment. In that regard, I think it is valuable to provide information, including addresses and phone numbers, on community and campus resources for students who are confronted with attempted assaults or harassment.

A representative of the Affirmative Action Office can be invited to class to discuss the prevalence of harassment on your campus and to tell students the procedures they should use in the event that they believe they are being harassed. Before the representative comes, you may want to give students the (anonymous) opportunity to write questions or to describe their own experiences to be given to your guest.

If there is a child-abuse survivors group in your area, you can invite members to provide a panel for presentation in your class. Another possibility for a panel is to ask representatives from recovered-memory syndrome and from false-memory syndrome groups to visit your class.

Kilpatrick's (1992) book on findings regarding child-adult sexual contacts can provide a good basis for lecture on the long-term correlates of these contacts.

References and Other Sources for Lectures

Alexander, P. C., & Lupfer, S. L. (1987). Family characteristics and long-term consequences associated with sexual abuse. *Archives of Sexual Behavior, 16,* 235–245.

Amick, A. E., & Calhoun, K. S. (1987). Resistance to sexual aggression: Personality, attitudinal, and situational factors. *Archives of Sexual Behavior, 16,* 153–163.

Condy, S. R., Templer, D. I., Brown, R., & Veaco, L. (1987). Parameters of sexual contact of boys with women. *Archives of Sexual Behavior, 16,* 379–394.

Gilbert, B., & Cunningham, J. (1986). Women's postrape sexual functioning: Review and implications for counseling. *Journal of Counseling and Development, 65* (2), 71–73.

Hucker, S., Langevin, R., Wortzman, G., Bain, J., Handy, L., & Wright, S. (1986). Neuropsychological impairment in pedophiles. *Canadian Journal of Behavioural Science, 18,* 440–448.

Jackson, J. L., et al. (1990). Young adult women who report childhood intrafamilial sexual abuse: Subsequent adjustment. *Archives of Sexual Behavior, 19,* 211–221.

Jaffe, D., & Straus, M. A. (1987). Sexual climate and reported rape: A state-level analysis. *Archives of Sexual Behavior, 16,* 107–123.

Kanin, E. J. (1994). False rape allegations. *Archives of Sexual Behavior, 23,* 81–92.

Kilpatrick, A. C. (1992). *Long-range effects of childhood and adolescent sexual experiences: Myths, mores, and menaces.* Hillsdale, NJ: Lawrence Erlbaum Associates.

McCarty, L. M. (1986). Mother-child incest: Characteristics of the offender. *Child Welfare, 65,* 447–458.

Pope, K. S. (1986). Research and laws regarding therapist-patient sexual involvement: Implications for therapists. *American Journal of Psychotherapy, 40,* 564–567.

Reilly, M. E., Lott, B., & Gallogly, S. M. (1986). Sexual harassment of university students. *Sex Roles, 15,* 333–358.

Roipe, K. (1993). *The morning after: Sex, fear, and feminism on campus.* Boston, MA: Little, Brown.

Sell, J. M., Gottlieb, M. C., & Schoenfeld, L. (1986). Ethical considerations of social/romantic relationships with present and former clients. *Professional Psychology: Research and Practice, 17,* 504–508.

Struckman-Johnson, C. (1988). Forced sex on dates: It happens to men, too. *Journal of Sex Research, 24,* 234–241.

Chapter 19: Atypical Sexual Activity

Topics Covered in the Chapter

This chapter has undergone considerable reorganization since the previous edition: we moved and updated material on transsexuality from Chapter 4 to this chapter, and made a major distinction between paraphilias that are noninvasive (fetishes, transvestism, transsexuality, and consensual sexual sadism and masochism) and those that invade the rights of others (voyeurism, exhibitionism, frotteurism, pedophilia, zoophilia, and other miscellaneous "philias"). We also discuss compulsive sexual behavior, which is under the section on invasive paraphilias, but students should be reminded that if the behavior does not interfere with others' rights (e.g., compulsive solitary masturbation), then it qualifies as a noninvasive paraphilia. The final section of this chapter focuses on available treatments of invasive paraphilias.

In the first section, we set out the problems with definitions of fetishes and define the term "paraphilia." In covering transvestism, we have retained Table 19.1 on a nonclinical sample of transvestites. Despite its age, we are aware of no more recent large study of this population. Our description of transvestism, and the next topic, transsexuality, includes reviews of attempts to explain these paraphilias. We end the section on the noninvasive paraphilias with a description of sexual sadism and masochism and include material on beliefs versus empirical data on gender differences in these paraphilias.

In the second section, on invasive paraphilias, we begin with voyeurism and consider characteristics of voyeurs. Exhibitionism is covered next, followed by obscene phone calls. Frotteurism is covered briefly, and we note that research has indicated that the majority of men arrested for that activity have also been arrested for other invasive paraphilias, including voyeurism, exhibitionism, and rape. Pedophilia is described next, and we contrast the typical characteristics of these people with characteristics associated with other sex offenders. Zoophilia is then discussed, as are other paraphilias, including necrophilia and asphyxiophilia (although strictly speaking, this last paraphilia does not invade others' rights). We end with a discussion of compulsive sexual behavior and consider the controversy between those who argue that such behaviors result from sexual addiction versus those who reject the disease model implied by the use of the term "addiction."

In the last section of this chapter, we review attempts to treat the paraphilias: psychotherapy, surgical castration, hormone administration, psychosurgery, and cognitive-behavior therapies.

Ideas for Lecture and Use of Class Time

In the textbook, we attempt to make the point that to a greater or lesser extent, most of us have fetishes (although not necessarily in the clinical sense that a particular object *must* be present for us to experience arousal). It is a good idea to reiterate this point, giving examples and suggesting that we can view the phenomenon as a continuum ranging from *preferences* for particular hair colors, body types, sexual toys, and so forth, to the *necessity* of having the particular object available for arousal to occur.

In making the distinction between paraphilias or fetishes that are invasive versus noninvasive of others' rights to privacy, choice, and so forth, you might list the paraphilias on a hand-out. Ask students to indicate which they find acceptable for others and which they think should be prohibited, and then ask them the basis for their judgments. Some may decide on the basis of what they find acceptable for themselves (that is, making judgments for others on the basis of their own value system), but some will make judgments based on the issue of invasiveness of others' rights. The process can provide a good values clarification exercise. If you have a large class, you may be able to ask students to respond orally with their lists and their reasons. With a small class, it may be more appropriate to have them respond in writing. You can then provide them with their (anonymous) responses at the next class session.

If there are any bars featuring female impersonators, you may be able to invite several of these men to be on a panel. These men may or may not fit the clinical description for transvestism; that is, some of them may engage in the activity solely for economic reasons, whereas others may have begun cross-dressing because of erotic arousal. You could ask the panel members to identify their motives for engaging in female impersonation to illustrate the range of reasons men give for cross-dressing.

Depending on where you live, you may also be able to find transsexuals who are willing to give a guest lecture or participate in a panel. If you are inviting guests for the first time, it may be helpful to ask students to write out questions that can be given to your guests in advance so that they can let you know about any topics or issues that they would prefer not to discuss in class.

The Moser and Levitt (1987) article contains a good review of research on sadomasochism plus questionnaire data from a sample of 178 men and 47 women attending S&M support groups who defined at least part of their sexual activity as sadomasochistic. Table 2 in the article provides an extensive list of sexual behaviors, some of them quite novel, showing the percentage of their sample who had tried the activity and the percentage who had enjoyed it. This table would make a good transparency for lecture. If students are interested, you could distribute a list of the behaviors for their anonymous responses. If you choose to do this and want to send me the results, I can include them in a future edition of *The Allgeier Update*.

The Rosen (1986) book contains photographs of and essays written by people engaging in sadomasochistic activities.

Because moving the material on transsexuality to this chapter increased the chapter's length, we deleted Figure 19.1, which appeared in the third edition. However, I believe that it is important to emphasize the work of Freund and his colleagues and others that show a concordance rate between the various invasive paraphilias, and I use that material in my own lectures. The major point that I emphasize is that research indicates that people engaging in one paraphilia (e.g., exhibitionism) may also engage in others (e.g., preferential rape, using just enough force to coerce a woman to have sex). Thus, a person encountering an exhibitionist or voyeur should notify authorities of the invasive behavior.

We have not dealt with stalkers in either Chapter 18 or 19 because of the paucity of empirical data on the phenomenon. However, a number of my students and their friends have been stalked. You might give your students a questionnaire to report anonymously their personal or second-hand knowledge of episodes of stalking. You could check with your local police to find out how they respond to people who report that they are being stalked.

If you have psychologists in your community who reject or adhere to Carnes's sexual addiction model, you could invite them to provide a debate for your class.

References and Other Sources for Lectures

Money, J. (1987). Masochism: On the childhood origin of paraphilia, opponent-process theory, and antiandrogen therapy. *Journal of Sex Research, 23*, 273–275.

Moser, C., & Levitt, E. E. (1987). An exploratory-descriptive study of a sadomasochistically oriented sample. *Journal of Sex Research, 23*, 322–337.

Rosen, M. (1986). *Sexual magic: The S/M photographs*. San Francisco: Shayview Press.

Weinberg, T. S. (1987). Sadomasochism in the United States: A review of recent sociological literature. *Journal of Sex Research, 23*, 50–69.

Chapter 20: Loving Sexual Interactions

Topics Covered in the Chapter

In this chapter, we broadly summarize some of the relationship themes that occur throughout the book, using a quasi-life-span approach. We begin by reviewing research from three different areas (the Harlow group's primate studies, studies of neglected children, and cross-cultural observations) that support the conclusion that experience with contact and affection during infancy and childhood is associated with the ability to give and receive love throughout life.

The second section is a brief essay dealing with the difference between loving or valuing oneself versus selfishness.

The theme of the third section is loving others. After providing quotations and poems that have been written about love, we describe systematic attempts that have been made to measure it. We discuss Cancian's (1986) contention that many scales employed to measure love reflect a stereotypically feminine perspective that emphasizes emotional expression and shared feelings. Our coverage of attachment has increased in this edition, and we focus on the work of Sternberg on forms of love. Figure 20.5 provides the eight possibilities he has described based on the presence or absence of intimacy, passion, and commitment in a relationship. In this section, we discuss friendship, infatuation, limerence, romantic love, empty love, fatuous love, companionate love, and consummate love. Under the topic of love versus lust, we consider differences between feelings and behavior and the ways in which lust can be confused with love.

The fourth section is entitled "Love as Dependency, Jealousy, and Other Unlovely Feelings." Throughout the book, we have generally taken the position that love and sexual intimacy is most possible and satisfying between independent adults who are in a position of relative equality to one another. In the discussion of the confusion of love with dependency of one adult on another, Box 20.2 contains Liebowitz's suggestion that phenylethylamine (a chemical in chocolate) may be involved in extreme reactions to the end of love affairs. Box 20.3 describes a couple who are overly dependent on and possessive of one another. We turn next to a consideration of jealousy cross-culturally and a description of characteristics of those people most likely to experience and to provoke jealousy. Box 20.3 focuses on potential tensions that can exist in couples as a function of differences in their fears of abandonment and fears of engulfment by the relationship. Box 20.4, which describes research on dating "infidelity," is likely to be of high interest to most students.

"Loving Sexual Interactions" is the final section in the chapter (and book). We provide a set of five issues in question form for couples to consider as they try to create a satisfying love relationship with one another. Vitality in long-term relationships is discussed. We end the book by stressing the importance of self-esteem and of setting time aside to share feelings and experiences in order to develop satisfying and loving sexual relationships.

Ideas for Lecture and Use of Class Time

Hendrick and Hendrick (1986) describe their work with measures of sexual attitudes and love. They have developed a 42-item measure based on six major love styles: *eros* (passionate, romantic love), *ludus* (game-playing love), *storge* (companionate love), *pragma* (logical, computer-dating love), *mania* (dependent, possessive love), and *agape* (selfless, all-giving love). If your students are interested, you might want to administer the measures to them and report back to them group findings, gender similarities and differences, and relationship of scores to level of sexual experience.

If you did not do the exercise described in this guide for Chapter 6, involving the similarities between emotional disturbance and falling in love, the demonstration can be used effectively in the context of this chapter.

Jealousy is a provocative topic. When I have asked my students whether they believe jealousy is learned or an innate response to situations in which their partners are sexually attentive to a third person, they tend to favor the genetic explanation. The Buunk and Hupka article (1987) can provide a good basis for lecture on the topic. They administered questionnaires to 2,079 students in seven countries (Ireland, Hungary, the United States, Yugoslavia, Mexico, the U.S.S.R., and the Netherlands) on the extent of jealousy elicited by various behaviors and obtained some interesting gender differences, and differences (and similarities) between nations. The six behaviors that they measured are listed in the article, and you could administer the measure in a previous class and compare your students' responses to those found by Buunk and Hupka. The article addresses some of the methodological difficulties of collecting data and thus can provide a reminder of issues of interpretation and generalization that were discussed in Chapter 2 of the textbook, giving you a final opportunity to remind students to evaluate critically generalizations from research that is reported in the popular press.

We have deleted coverage of Rubin's (1970, 1973) love scale from this edition of the textbook, but you might want to administer his short scales to your students to see if his findings still appear. Rubin found no difference in love scores between couples but noted a tendency for women, compared to men, to give higher liking scores. We think that this difference might be due to status differences between men and women and gender-role attitudes. You might ask for volunteers who have partners to take Rubin's 10-item love scale and 10-item liking scale, and Spence & Helmreich's Attitudes Toward Women Scale (cited in the textbook). If our hypothesis is correct, the males in each couple with egalitarian attitudes should have liking scores for their partners similar to those of females, whereas the males with traditional attitudes should have lower liking scores.

References and Other Sources for Lectures

Buunk, B., & Hupka, R. B. (1987). Cross-cultural differences in the elicitation of sexual jealousy. *Journal of Sex Research, 23*, 12–22.

Cancian, F. M. (1986). The feminization of love. *Signs: Journal of Women in Culture and Society, 11*, 692–709.

Hatfield, E., & Rapson, R. L. (1987). Passionate love/sexual desire: Can the same paradigm explain both? *Archives of Sexual Behavior, 16*, 259–278.

Hendrick, C., & Hendrick, S. (1986). A theory and method of love. *Journal of Personality and Social Psychology, 50*, 392–402.

Hendrick, S., & Hendrick, C. (1987). Multidimensionality of sexual attitudes. *Journal of Sex Research, 23*, 502–526.

Rubin, Z. (1970). Measurement of romantic love. *Journal of Personality and Social Psychology, 16*, 265–273.

Rubin, Z. (1973). *Liking and loving: An invitation to social psychology.* New York: Holt, Rinehart & Winston.

PART II: TEST ITEM FILE

CHAPTER 1

Historical and Cross-Cultural Perspectives on Sexuality

Multiple-Choice Questions

1. Asceticism is defined as (p. 3):

   a. interest in worldly pleasures.
   b. the belief that procreation is the sole purpose of sexual contact.
   c. penetration of the vagina by the penis.
   *d. the practice of extreme self-denial.

2. Early historical writings regarding sexuality may be misleading because (p. 4):

   a. they may reflect the views of only a select group of individuals.
   b. they may be distorted by the requirements of the ruling authorities.
   c. there is a tendency to read one's own thoughts and values into them.
   *d. all of the above.

3. Ethnocentrism is (p. 4):

   *a. the tendency to read one's own values into the sexual practices of other cultures and historical times.
   b. a bias to fund only those archaeological projects that do not collect sexual artifacts.
   c. the belief that frequency of sexual intercourse declines with age.
   d. seen primarily in matriarchies.

4. Early historical writings regarding sexuality may be misleading for all the following reasons except (p. 4):

   a. They may reflect the views of only a select group of individuals.
   b. The gathering of information has been hindered by the paucity of documents.
   c. Ethnocentrism is evident.
   *d. None of the above.

5. The perception that females are sexually insatiable and dangerously seductive is (p. 5):

   a. common to all cultures.
   *b. true mainly of Western cultures until a couple of centuries ago.
   c. characteristic of the So of Uganda.
   d. supported by modern research.

6. Earlier in this century, it was believed that females were (p. 5):

   *a. passive and uninterested in sex.
   b. aggressive and interested in sex.
   c. relatively deviant in sexual appetite.
   d. more sexual than males.

7. The biblical story of Eve's disastrous influence on Adam in the Garden of Eden represents a belief about the nature of female and male sexuality that has been more prevalent throughout our history (p. 5):

    *a. than is the current stereotype of men as having more sexual appetite than women have.
    b. since it was scientifically supported by Masters and Johnson's research.
    c. as times passes.
    d. none of the above.

8. The *vagina dentata* is (p. 5):

    *a. a mythical toothed vagina.
    b. the technical name for impairments of the vagina caused by drug use.
    c. a mythical poison-secreting vagina.
    d. an ancient religious doctrine about feminine hygiene.

9. Historically, in the patriarchies that are characteristic of Western civilization, females have been viewed as (p. 5):

    *a. insatiably seductive and powerful sexual temptresses.
    b. holding most of the actual economic, political, and social power.
    c. having few sexual desires.
    d. highly spiritual beings.

10. Although males have generally held the economic, political, and social power throughout the history of Western civilization, the dominant view has been that females are (p. 5):

    *a. sexual temptresses who pose danger to males.
    b. childlike and somewhat ignorant about sex.
    c. of no threat to males.
    d. none of the above.

11. In Mesopotamian culture, husbands and fathers believed that women (p. 6):

    *a. were low-status creatures.
    b. ovulated irregularly.
    c. were evil.
    d. should sometimes be sacrificed to the high priest.

12. In Mesopotamian culture, most of the gods (p. 6):

    *a. symbolized the belief that life was dependent on fertility.
    b. represented movements of the sun.
    c. were worshipped in the form of children.
    d. were appeased through rituals involving animal sacrifice.

13. In Mesopotamian culture, the Great Mother was (p. 6):

    *a. worshipped by cults.
    b. thought of as an evil spirit.
    c. the goddess of sexual fantasy.
    d. the name of the first queen.

14. In ancient _____ culture, women were permitted to own property, initiate lawsuits, and pay taxes (p. 6).

    a. Mesopotamian.
    b. Hebrew
    *c. Egyptian
    d. Greek

15. Temples built to honor the Great Mother provided the setting for (pp. 6–7):

    *a. sexual rituals.
    b. human sacrifices.
    c. farmers' markets.
    d. sexual acts performed by animals.

16. In ancient Hebrew culture, adultery (p. 7):

    a. by men was punished more severely than by women.
    b. by women was punished more severely than by men.
    c. was considered to be a violation of the husband's property rights.
    *d. both b and c.

17. In ancient Hebrew culture, adultery (p. 7):

    a. was defined similarly to how it is today.
    *b. by women was punishable by death.
    c. by men was punishable by death.
    d. was legal.

18. Some Hebrew sexual laws may have derived from competition between (p. 7):

    a. male and female prostitutes.
    b. the Great Father and the Great Son.
    c. the incubus and the succubus.
    *d. Jehovah and the Great Mother.

19. In the 4th century A.D., the Christian church _____ that women were sexual temptresses (p. 7):

    a. first introduced the idea
    *b. continued earlier historical patterns insisting
    c. reversed its earlier position
    d. denied

20. It was believed in medieval Europe that for the purpose of sexual intercourse, demons could take the form of either a(n) (p. 7):

    *a. incubus or a succubus.
     b. basilisk or a mandrake.
     c. monstrance or a ciborium.
     d. meridian or a cumeridian.

21. The book *Malleus Maleficarum* describes (p. 7):

     a. accepted seventeenth-century sexual techniques.
    *b. procedures for diagnosing witchcraft.
     c. how a civilized husband should treat his wife.
     d. a Latin translation of the Old Testament.

22. Early medieval clergymen helped to strengthen the idea that female witches (p. 7):

     a. were superior beings.
     b. contained all the potential for good in the world.
    *c. were the cause of ailments such as impotence and memory loss.
     d. had souls superior to those of men.

23. After the publication of *Malleus Maleficarum,* many Church leaders considered it heresy to (p. 7):

     a. discuss birth control.
     b. burn witches at the stake.
     c. buy herbs from the clergy.
    *d. question the existence of witches.

24. So-called witches were persecuted for _____ reasons (p. 8).

     a. religious
     b. economic
    *c. both a and b
     d. none of the above

25. Although the reasons given to justify witch hunts were religious and sexual, another motivation was the desire to (p. 8):

    *a. eliminate competition with village healers.
     b. encourage women to have many male children.
     c. secretly reduce the female population.
     d. prevent women from working as anything other than housekeepers.

26. The last executions for witchcraft in Europe took place in (p. 8):

    *a. 1782 A.D.
     b. 1382 A.D.
     c. 1082 A.D.
     d. 800 A.D.

27. Chastity belts, which were used widely in the fifteenth century, were designed to (p. 10):

    *a. control women's sexuality.
    b. control the sexuality of adolescent men.
    c. protect the wearer from potential rapists.
    d. make women's waists smaller for purposes of fashion.

28. In the nineteenth century, when the Industrial Revolution created an expanded _____ class, male and female roles became _____ differentiated (p. 10).

    *a. middle; increasingly
    b. middle; less
    c. upper; less
    d. lower; increasingly

29. The dominant sexual ideology of the Victorian era was that men were expected to be _____ and women were expected to be _____ (p. 10).

    *a. aggressive; passive
    b. passive; aggressive
    c. gentlemanly; lustful
    d. passive; passive

30. In Victorian society, prostitutes were (p. 10):

    *a. social outcasts but tolerated anyway.
    b. of high status.
    c. few in number.
    d. generally from the middle class.

31. In Victorian society, prostitutes were tolerated by society because they provided (p. 10):

    *a. an outlet for proper Victorian husbands.
    b. an outlet for unmarried men.
    c. cocaine to the many addicts.
    d. a benefit to the economy of England.

32. Results of a study conducted by Dr. Clelia Mosher in the United States in the late 1800s, designed to find whether Victorian morality influenced women's private lives, revealed that (p. 11):

    a. most women were reluctant to engage in sexual behaviors.
    b. very few women used birth-control methods.
    *c. some women defied the Victorian stereotype.
    d. only the very wealthy could afford sex-education courses.

33. The legacy of the Victorian era was so influential that until recently (p. 11):

    *a. many women attempted to hide their sexual interests.
    b. many churches promoted birth control.
    c. many men believed that it was easy to convince a woman to have sex.
    d. the British government did not have laws against prostitution.

34. The idea that procreation is the sole justification for having sexual relations is known as (p. 12):

    *a. reproductive bias.
     b. reactivism.
     c. clerical dogma.
     d. none of the above.

35. Although Jesus is reported to have said relatively little about sex, he reportedly condemned (p. 12):

    *a. lust.
     b. coitus.
     c. marriage.
     d. none of the above.

36. _____ stated that a man who looks at a woman with lust is committing adultery (pp. 12–13).

     a. Jesus
     b. Pope John Paul II
     c. St. Jerome
    *d. all of the above

37. St. Augustine and St. Thomas Aquinas believed in (p. 13):

     a. sexual austerity.
     b. the condemnation of sexual activity that did not have reproduction as its main purpose.
     c. sex as a necessary evil.
    *d. all of the above.

38. Historically, the Christian tradition has (p. 13):

    *a. emphasized that one may incur personal guilt for having "lustful" thoughts.
     b. been comparable to the Hindu tradition in its repressive attitudes toward sexuality.
     c. been deeply influenced by Greek attitudes toward sexuality.
     d. none of the above.

39. In what society is it believed that young girls are incapable of developing breasts or beginning to menstruate unless they experience sexual intercourse (p. 15)?

    *a. Tiwi
     b. Mehinaku
     c. Batista
     d. Sambia

40. The Mehinaku of central Brazil believe that as boys approach puberty, they need to (p. 14):

    *a. practice sexual abstinence.
    b. have contact with sexually mature women.
    c. rub menstrual blood on their bodies.
    d. avoid eating cooked meat.

41. The Tiwi and Sambia cultures (p. 14):

    a. failed to teach their offspring about sexual intercourse and did not survive.
    *b. encourage their offspring to engage in sexual activities during childhood.
    c. have an abnormally high number of twins and triplets.
    d. were the first primitive cultures to practice effective contraception.

42. The Mehinaku of central Brazil think of fathering children through sexual intercourse as (p. 14):

    *a. a collective project by the males.
    b. a privilege of the tribal leader alone.
    c. unnecessary, because conception results from an act of God.
    d. an evil but necessary event.

43. The tradition of performing circumcision on both males and females appears to have (p. 15):

    *a. existed long before Christianity and Islam.
    b. begun at about the same time that Christianity did.
    c. begun during the sixth century.
    d. existed as of the Victorian era.

44. In the So tribe of Uganda (p. 16):

    a. married women who are not multiorgasmic are considered ill.
    b. homosexual contact is common.
    *c. women have sex primarily for reproduction, rather than enjoyment.
    d. effective contraception has been practiced since the mid-1700s.

45. In ancient Egypt, circumcision of both males and females was perceived as (p. 15):

    *a. eliminating any barriers to having adult sexual lives.
    b. necessary for hygiene.
    c. aesthetically pleasing in a cosmetic way.
    d. undesirable.

46. The most likely reason that circumcision on males was practiced in ancient Egypt was (p. 15):

    a. that it was believed to reduce sexual desire.
    b. that it was believed to reduce or prevent genital disease or infection.
    *c. to eliminate any feminine characteristics of the body.
    d. as a punishment for those who were discovered masturbating.

47. The possession of both masculine and feminine characteristics is called (p. 17):

    *a. androgyny.
    b. acronymy.
    c. synchrony.
    d. parsimony.

48. Circumcision of male infants (p. 17):

    a. reduces the risk of getting AIDS.
    b. is practiced in all known industrialized nations.
    c. is highly recommended by the American Academy of Pediatrics.
    *d. none of the above.

49. Today female circumcision (p. 17):

    *a. is carried out in about 40 nations.
    b. is considered barbaric everywhere in the world.
    c. is performed only when required due to disease.
    d. has banned by the World Health Organization.

50. Birth control (p. 19):

    a. has been practiced only in the twentieth century.
    *b. was attempted through the use of contraceptives as early as ancient Egypt.
    c. by means of abortion was strictly illegal under Anglo-American law until the twentieth century.
    d. was tolerated by the medieval church as a concession to "lust."

51. Sylvester Graham developed the graham cracker and John Harvey Kellogg invented Kellogg's Corn Flakes for the similar purpose of (p. 20):

    a. curing infertility in males and females.
    b. promoting healthy bowels and improving sexual functioning.
    *c. reducing sexual desire or responsiveness.
    d. none of the above.

52. In which of the following ancient cultures was pederasty relatively common (p. 21)?

    a. Egyptian
    *b. Greek
    c. Roman
    d. Mesopotamian

53. From about 650 B.C. to 150 B.C., Greek men found their most profound intellectual relationships with _____ and their most profound emotional and erotic relationships with _____ (p. 21).

    *a. adolescent boys; adolescent boys.
    b. adolescent boys; adolescent girls.
    c. adolescent boys; adult women.
    d. adult men; adult women.

54. The ancient Greeks believed that manliness could be symbolically transferred to boys through (p. 21):

    *a. the adult male's penis and semen.
    b. rites of passage involving physical stamina and pain.
    c. discussions with their fathers.
    d. ceremonies conducted by females.

55. Information regarding sexual relationships between women in ancient times is (p. 21):

    *a. scarce.
    b. abundantly depicted in art.
    c. found primarily in the Bible.
    d. available from the World Health Organization.

56. The term *lesbian* comes from the name of (p. 21):

    *a. a Greek island.
    b. an African tribe.
    c. a prison in Russia.
    d. the first known female homosexual.

57. Male homosexuality was condemned and punished in ancient _____ culture, but lesbianism there was not illegal (p. 21).

    *a. Hebrew.
    b. Greek.
    c. Roman.
    d. Chinese.

58. The ancient Hebrews made male homosexuality _____ and female homosexuality _____ (p. 21).

    *a. illegal; legal.
    b. illegal; illegal.
    c. legal; illegal.
    d. legal; legal.

59. During which historical period was homosexuality most positive (p. 22)?

    a. Roman
    b. early Christian
    *c. Greek
    d. Middle Ages

60. Based on studies of Sambian society, as well as research on ancient Greek society, it can be argued that (p. 22):

    *a. people are capable of responding sexually to both genders at different times in the life span.
    b. sexual orientation is innate.
    c. sexual orientation is relatively unchangeable.
    d. homosexuality is associated with mental illness.

61. Among the early Romans, marriages (p. 23):

    *a. were arranged by parents to strengthen economic and political alliances.
    b. usually occurred between couples who chose to be together because they were in love.
    c. often occurred between second cousins.
    d. sometimes occurred between men.

62. The early-medieval church regarded the minimum age for matrimony as _____ years for girls and _____ years for boys (p. 23).

    *a. 11½; 13½
    b. 9½; 11½
    c. 13½; 15½
    d. 15½; 17½

63. Courtly love (p. 23):

    *a. was a true love, not to be consummated by sexual intercourse.
    b. was a true lust, to be consummated by sexual intercourse.
    c. occurred only between nobility who were married to each other.
    d. was the name given to marriages between the elderly.

64. Most cultures and past societies have generally regarded marriage as (pp. 22–23):

    a. the culmination of lovers' sexual attraction to each other.
    *b. primarily a social and economic relationship out of which love and affection might develop.
    c. an institution that could be adapted to the couple's chosen lifestyle.
    d. a religious ceremony.

65. Romantic love (p. 24):

    a. is strongly rooted in Western cultural traditions, although it became the preferred basis of marriage only in relatively recent times.
    b. was characteristic of ancient Greek and Roman society but was later condemned by the Christian church.
    c. has been shown in the past few decades to be an increasingly important motive for North American men (but not women) to marry.
    *d. none of the above.

66. Both Martin Luther and John Calvin (p. 24):

    *a. advocated marriage for the clergy.
     b. thought that marriage should not be a sacrament.
     c. belonged to the Cult of the Virgin Mary.
     d. advocated courtly love.

67. Among the So people (p. 24):

    *a. pregnancy before marriage is desirable.
     b. premarital sex is discouraged.
     c. women are expected to have jobs before marriage.
     d. the father of the bride receives gold as part of the betrothal.

68. Among the Mehinaku people (p. 24):

    *a. romance between spouses borders on bad taste.
     b. pregnancy before marriage is desirable.
     c. spouses spend a great deal of time alone together.
     d. married couples generally do not respect each other.

69. Historically, it is suggested that female circumcision arose among groups in Somalia because circumcision (p. 17):

     a. made them more beautiful.
     b. prevented some STDs.
     c. was also done on males.
    *d. rendered them odorless.

70. Within Western civilization, most groups have practiced (p. 25):

    *a. monogamy.
     b. polygamy.
     c. polygyny.
     d. pederasty.

71. The characteristic pattern of modern American relationship is (p. 25):

    *a. serial monogamy.
     b. parallel monogamy.
     c. serial polygyny.
     d. parallel polyandry.

72. Of all the marital forms, which has been normative in more human cultures than any other form (p. 25)?

    *a. polygamy
     b. monogamy
     c. sororates
     d. pederasty

73. Monogamy (p. 25):

    a. has been normative in more human cultures than polygamy.
    *b. has been normative in fewer human cultures than polygamy.
    c. is related to the practice of tracing inheritance through the mother's line.
    d. is associated primarily with agricultural societies.

74. Which culture thinks of fathering children as a collective project done by the males (p. 14)?

    a. So
    b. Sambia
    c. Tiwi
    *d. Mehinaku

75. If a man is married to two or more women, the relationship is called (p. 25):

    a. monogamy.
    b. polyandry.
    c. misogamy.
    *d. polygyny.

76. Which form of relationship is characteristic of industrialized and complex cultures (p. 25)?

    a. misogamy
    *b. monogamy
    c. polygyny
    d. polyandry

77. _____ is strongly correlated with a patrilineal social organization (p. 25).

    *a. Polygyny
    b. Polygamy
    c. Monogamy
    d. Serial polygamy

78. Which marital form is usually found in cultures with agricultural economies (p. 26)?

    *a. polygyny
    b. polyandry
    c. monogamy
    d. misogyny

79. Which of these types of relationships has been the least frequent among world cultures (p. 26)?

    a. monogamy
    b. homosexual
    *c. polyandry
    d. polygyny

80. In patrilineal societies (p. 26):

   *a. offspring are considered to belong to the father's social group.
   b. the gender of female offspring is not considered important.
   c. offspring are considered to belong to the mother's social group.
   d. none of the above.

81. A sororate is (p. 26):

   *a. the practice of the marriage of a widowed man to his former wife's sister.
   b. a fertility ritual in matrilineal societies.
   c. the practice of the marriage of a widow to her brother-in-law.
   d. another name for *purdah*.

82. Which of the following describes the practice of the levirate (p. 26)?

   *a. When a woman's husband dies, her brother-in-law may marry her.
   b. When a man's wife dies, his sister-in-law may marry him.
   c. When a man's wife dies, his sister may marry him.
   d. When a woman's husband dies, she may never marry again.

83. The early Egyptians, Hawaiians, and Peruvians accepted (p. 26):

   a. purdah.
   b. courtly love.
   *c. marriage between brothers and sisters.
   d. the levirate.

84. Purdah is the practice of (p. 26):

   a. removing the penis from the vagina before ejaculation.
   *b. secluding women from men.
   c. loving a person intensely without engaging in intercourse.
   d. forming marriages by means of contractual arrangements.

Essay Questions

85. Describe potential sources of inaccuracy in contemporary interpretations of historical records of sexual attitudes and behavior (pp. 4–5).

86. Compare and contrast perceptions of the nature of male and female sexuality from the beginnings of Christianity to the period just prior to the Victorian era (pp. 3–10).

87. How did the dominant views of the nature of male and female sexuality during the Victorian era differ from beliefs prior to that period (pp. 10–11)?

88. What is reproductive bias (p. 12)?

89. Sexual activity has been viewed as having a variety of different functions across different cultures and time periods. Briefly describe four of these (p. 4–12).

90. Describe variations in beliefs about the purpose of circumcision for males and females. What are your views (pp. 15–17)?

91. Describe variations in historical beliefs about the use of birth control (p. 19).

92. Discuss the work of Sylvester Graham and John Harvey Kellogg (p. 20).

93. Describe variations in the way same-gender sexual relationships have been viewed historically (pp. 21–22).

94. At some point you may make a long-term commitment to another person. What factors do you think will be important to you in making such a commitment (or what factors were important to you if you have already done so)? Compare these factors with those that were considered important in forming relationships in other cultures and time periods (pp. 23–25).

95. Describe the different views toward love and marriage that have existed historically. Which do you find most appealing and why (pp. 22–24)?

96. Describe the variations in marital and family forms that exist cross-culturally. Which do you find most appealing, and why (pp. 25–27)?

97. Compare and contrast the sororate and levirate systems (p. 26).

CHAPTER 2

Research on Sexuality

Multiple-Choice Questions

1. For several centuries prior to 1900, religious interpretation of phenomena was _____, as scientific explanations of human behavior became _____ influential (p. 32).

    *a. on the decline; more
    b. on the increase; less
    c. holding steady; more
    d. holding steady; less

2. Prior to the twentieth century, scientists' views on sexuality were (p. 32):

    *a. slightly more tolerant than clergymen's.
    b. much more tolerant than clergymen's.
    c. much more tolerant than politicians'.
    d. of almost the same opinion as farmers'.

3. As the devil was held less accountable for the world's misfortunes, a new scapegoat was found. That scapegoat was _____, and it was supposedly caused by _____ (p. 32).

    a. insanity; adultery
    *b. insanity; masturbation
    c. depression; sexually transmitted disease
    d. depression; premarital intercourse

4. From the eighteenth century until the end of the nineteenth century, masturbatory insanity was (p. 32):

    a. a mental illness found primarily in Europe.
    *b. a scapegoat used to account for otherwise unexplainable problems.
    c. a term used by the military.
    d. a myth held by most scientists at the time.

5. In 1758 Tissot published by a book on (p. 32):

    a. homosexuality.
    b. pregnancy and childbirth.
    *c. masturbation.
    d. adultery.

6. Consumption, poor eyesight, digestive problems, and impotence were some of the disorders that _____ claimed could be caused by masturbation (p. 32).

    a. Michael Bergson
    b. Dr. Sigmund Freud
    c. Florence Nightingale
    *d. Dr. Benjamin Rush

7. The "secret sin" that medical authorities in Europe during the 1700s and 1800s referred to was (p. 32):

    *a. masturbation.
    b. prostitution.
    c. premarital intercourse.
    d. sexually transmitted diseases.

8. The book published by Tissot in 1758 provided (p. 32):

    a. psychiatrists with incorrect information about sexual disorders.
    b. the layperson with accurate information on the childbirth process.
    c. the medical community with accurate information about sexually transmitted diseases.
    *d. medical backing to the supposed role of self-stimulation as a cause of madness.

9. The father of American psychiatry, Dr. Benjamin Rush, claimed that masturbation could produce (p. 32):

    a. pulmonary consumption.
    b. vertigo.
    c. epilepsy.
    *d. all of the above.

10. In the 1700s and 1800s, treatments for _____ included castration (p. 32).

    *a. disorders rooted in masturbation
    b. disorders involving sexual crimes
    c. tumors in the groin
    d. none of the above

11. An eighteenth-century English physician, J. L. Milton, recommended that young men (p. 32):

    *a. wear locked chastity belts during the day to prevent masturbation.
    b. engage in physical sports to increase sexual stamina.
    c. get married before age 20 to ensure the chances of fertility.
    d. wear what is now called a "jock strap" for protection of the genitals.

12. Physicians such as Tissot and Rush claimed that masturbation caused (p. 32):

    a. poor eyesight and vertigo.
    b. impotence.
    c. epilepsy.
    *d. all of the above.

13. Past treatments for disorders assumed to be caused by masturbation include (p. 32):

    *a. castration or removal of the clitoris.
    b. hormone replacement therapy.
    c. burning at the stake.
    d. removal of the liver.

14. The connection between masturbation and various physical maladies (p. 32):

    a. is well documented in primitive societies today.
    *b. was once widely supported by physicians.
    c. was popularized by medieval church authorities.
    d. is the subject of current scientific research.

15. Krafft-Ebing's major book reflected the dominant theme of the 1800s as (p. 32):

    a. sex as a scientific field of study.
    b. sex as producing health.
    *c. sex as disease.
    d. none of the above.

16. In his major work, Krafft-Ebing emphasized (p. 32):

    *a. bizarre cases of sexual expression.
    b. intelligence test scores of child molesters.
    c. therapeutic techniques for premature ejaculation.
    d. the period of prenatal development.

17. Krafft-Ebing's work reflected the concern of the times about sexual acts (p. 33):

    *a. that did not have reproduction as their goal.
    b. in terms of physiological response.
    c. such as soixante neuf.
    d. all of the above.

18. The leading figure in the pseudoscientific linkage of nonreproductive sexual activity with disease was (p. 33):

    a. McDowell.
    *b. Krafft-Ebing.
    c. von Zilbergeld.
    d. Havelock Ellis.

19. The leading figure in the emergence of the modern study of sexuality who attempted to broaden the spectrum of normal sexual behavior to include homosexuality and masturbation was (p. 33):

    *a. Ellis.
    b. Freud.
    c. Krafft-Ebing.
    d. Robinson.

20. The book *Auto-Eroticism* (p. 33):

    a. helped to spread fear about sex that did not have reproduction as a goal.
    b. described deviation as congenital or inborn.
    c. was the first to use the term "masturbation."
    *d. attacked theories that linked masturbation with insanity.

21. In his initial book, *Sexual Inversion*, Henry Havelock Ellis attempted to broaden the spectrum of normal sexual behavior to include (p. 33):

    *a. homosexuality.
    b. oral-genital sex.
    c. masturbation.
    d. none of the above.

22. Ellis held the view that homosexuality was (p. 33):

    *a. congenital.
    b. curable.
    c. abnormal.
    d. a moral choice.

23. According to Ellis, most major forms of sexual deviation (p. 33):

    a. should be viewed as grounds for imprisonment.
    *b. are related to some aspect of normal sexual life.
    c. should be viewed as grounds for insanity.
    d. are learned during adolescence.

24. Sigmund Freud emphasized sex as (p. 34):

    *a. the central aspect of human development.
    b. the main cause of psychological disorders.
    c. a sin.
    d. all of the above.

25. Sex research with _____ may be contrary to the ethical values held by the scientific community because it is likely to violate the principle of informed consent (p. 35).

    a. senior citizens
    b. the clergy
    c. government officials
    *d. children

26. Freud contributed enormously to the understanding of human sexuality, but his theories also led to some major misunderstandings, particularly regarding (p. 35):

    a. male sexuality.
    *b. female sexuality.
    c. sexuality during late old age.
    d. sexuality in other cultures.

27. According to Byrne (1977), until the mid-twentieth century most of our knowledge about sexual behavior was based on systematic observations of (p. 35):

    a. animal sex.
    b. native sex.
    c. crazy sex.
    *d. all of the above.

28. In the 1800s, the majority of physicians believed it was improper for (p. 35):

    a. them to see a woman's genitals during labor and delivery.
    b. medical students to do vaginal exams on consenting pregnant women.
    c. them to present research on sexually transmitted diseases at professional meetings.
    *d. all of the above.

29. Dr. James Platt White was expelled from the American Medical Association for (p. 35):

    a. engaging in research on child sexuality.
    *b. allowing his medical students to perform a vaginal exam on a consenting pregnant woman.
    c. asking his patients about their sexual behavior.
    d. opening a sex-therapy unit in his large metropolitan hospital.

30. Which of the following researchers was the first to use interview techniques to learn about sexual experiences of Americans (p. 35)?

    a. Wolfe
    b. Hefner
    c. Clifford
    *d. Kinsey

31. When the Kinsey group published *Sexual Behavior in the Human Female,* (p. 36):

    *a. the United States was going through the McCarthy era.
    b. the administration at Indiana University refused to stand behind it.
    c. Kinsey was arrested.
    d. over a million copies were sold the first year.

32. Rockefeller Foundation funds to support _____ work were withdrawn when the interview research was attacked (p. 36).

    *a. Kinsey's
    b. Bullough's
    c. Masters's
    d. Hite's

33. The first major book on sexuality by Masters and Johnson was (p. 37):

    a. *Masturbatory Responsiveness.*
    b. *The Joy of Sex.*
    c. *Enlightened Sexuality.*
    *d. *Human Sexual Response.*

34. Masters and Johnson studied sexual responsiveness by (p. 37):

    *a. direct observation.
    b. means of questionnaires.
    c. means of interviews.
    d. observing animals.

35. The first large-scale sex-research project to employ direct observation and physiological measurement was conducted by (p. 37):

    *a. Masters and Johnson.
    b. Kinsey and colleagues.
    c. Tissot and Rush.
    d. Bullough.

36. Masters and Johnson's research differed from previous studies in that they (p. 37):

    a. used people from around the world as their subjects.
    *b. measured sexual response with physiological instruments.
    c. had very little institutional resistance to their research proposals due to the acceptance of sex research by others before them.
    d. none of the above.

37. Which of the following, who was awarded a Fulbright Award to conduct research in Egypt, was also classified as a "dangerous subversive" by the FBI (p. 38)?

    a. A. Kinsey
    *b. V. Bullough
    c. W. Masters
    d. S. Hite

38. Which of the following factors have influenced sexuality research (p. 42)?

    a. availability of research funds
    b. societal complaints that such research is inappropriate or immoral
    c. rights, safety, and well-being of the research participants
    *d. all of the above

39. The principle of informed consent requires (p. 42):

    a. informing the person's friends, family, and local news media of the results of the sex research in which the person participated.
    b. telling the people of potentially embarrassing or damaging aspects of research before they agree to participate.
    c. permitting the person the opportunity to refuse to participate.
    *d. both b and c.

40. As to research on sexuality, prisoners, mental patients, developmentally disabled people, and children are (p. 42):

    *a. considered incapable of giving informed consent.
    b. considered to be prime candidates for experimentation.
    c. used in experiments as long as they sign release forms.
    d. frequently used in experiments today in the Deep South.

41. The principle of _____ requires that potential volunteers be free from undue pressure to participate in research (p. 42).

    *a. freedom from coercion
    b. informed consent
    c. risk-benefit
    d. anonymity

42. According to the principle of protection from physical or psychological harm, volunteers (p. 42):

    *a. should encounter no more risk during an experiment than they would in normal daily life.
    b. can experience risk as long as they are told what it will be prior to the experiment.
    c. should be given the option to end participation at any time during the experiment.
    d. must sign a release form.

43. The duty of a researcher to keep a participant's responses confidential is one of the responsibilities implied by the ethical principle of (p. 42):

    a. informed consent.
    b. freedom from coercion.
    *c. protection from physical or psychological harm.
    d. risk-benefit.

44. In evaluating the ethical acceptability of research procedures, ethnical committees generally rely on the major principle of (pp. 42–43):

    a. informed consent.
    b. freedom from coercion.
    c. risk-benefit.
    d. protection from physical or psychological harm.
    *e. all of the above.

45. Scientists who do funded research in the area of human sexuality (p. 43):

    a. are subject to political harassment even today.
    *b. must demonstrate that their research is relevant to the solution of a societal problem.
    c. are free to use whatever procedures they choose.
    d. have been working primarily at Harvard University.

46. The Tuskegee study on the long-term effects of syphilis demonstrates the violation of which of the following ethical principles (p. 44)?

    a. informed consent
    b. freedom from coercion
    c. risk-benefit
    d. protection from physical or psychological harm
    *e. all of the above

47. A hypothesis is a(n) (p. 45):

    *a. educated guess that can be proved or rejected on the basis of research results.
    b. set of principles that explains new facts.
    c. assumption that cannot be proved.
    d. one type of independent variable.

48. A(n) _____ involves describing each variable so that it can be measured and so that people can agree on what is meant (p. 45).

    *a. operational definition
    b. correlational definition
    c. brief report
    d. replication factor

49. Levels of hunger, happiness, sexual arousal, and time spent studying can all change; thus, they are (p. 46):

    *a. variables.
    b. hypotheses.
    c. theories.
    d. operational definitions.

50. In a psychology experiment, the _____ variable is manipulated by the experimenter (p. 46).

    a. dependent
    *b. independent
    c. control
    d. experimental

51. In a psychology experiment, the dependent variable is the one that (p. 46):

    *a. is measured.
    b. causes the behavior being studied.
    c. is manipulated by the experimenter.
    d. changes randomly.

52. In an experimental study, we measure the _____ variable after manipulating the _____ variable and holding the _____ variables constant (p. 46).

    a. independent; dependent; control
    b. control; independent; dependent
    c. control; dependent; independent
  *d. dependent; independent; control

53. *Note:* The question should be answered after reading this sentence: "In a study designed to measure the effect of erotic material on sexual arousal in males, the type of erotic material was varied." The type of erotic material is (pp. 46–47):

  *a. an independent variable.
    b. a dependent variable.
    c. a control variable.
    d. extraneous.

54. *Note:* The question should be answered after reading this sentence: "In a study designed to measure the effect of erotic material on sexual arousal in males, the type of erotic material was varied." The gender of the subjects is (pp. 46–47):

    a. an independent variable.
    b. a dependent variable.
  *c. a control variable.
    d. an ordinal variable.

55. *Note:* The question should be answered after reading this sentence: "In a study designed to measure the effect of erotic material on sexual arousal in males, the type of erotic material was varied." The amount of sexual arousal is (pp. 46–47):

    a. an independent variable.
  *b. a dependent variable.
    c. a control variable.
    d. a sampling variable.

56. _____ variables are factors that could vary but are held constant (p. 47).

    a. Consistency
    b. Conjoint
  *c. Control
    d. Constant

57. In most research we take a (p. 48):

    a. population and generalize to the sample.
  *b. sample and generalize to a population.
    c. population and avoid generalizing.
    d. sample and avoid generalizing.

58. In a research project, sampling involves (p. 48):

    a. separating volunteers from nonvolunteers.
    b. obtaining complete data from every possible source.
    c. measuring the presence of self-report bias.
    *d. none of the above.

59. Because volunteer bias is a problem in sexuality research, researchers should (p. 49):

    a. be careful to choose subjects who have a minimum of bias.
    b. understand that the usefulness of their research is seriously limited.
    *c. be cautious when generalizing results of studies.
    d. advertise for research volunteers but perform the experimental manipulation only on those who are open-minded.

60. Which of the following is true based on a review of studies on volunteer bias (p. 49)?

    a. Volunteers score higher than nonvolunteers on neuroticism scales.
    b. Volunteers are older than nonvolunteers.
    c. Nonvolunteers masturbate more frequently than volunteers.
    *d. Males are more likely to volunteer than females are.

61. _____ bias can result from a reluctance to provide honest answers or from an inability to give accurate answers (p. 50).

    *a. Self-report
    b. Volunteer
    c. Generalization
    d. Informed-consent

62. Guaranteeing _____ is one way of reducing self-report bias (p. 50).

    *a. anonymity
    b. payment
    c. the credibility of the research project
    d. All of the above are essential.

63. Masters and Johnson used direct observation to reduce the problem of (p. 50):

    *a. self-report bias.
    b. volunteer bias.
    c. artificiality.
    d. reactivity.

64. If we could enlist the cooperation of people who have tested positive for the AIDS virus and who have taken varying levels of AZT, we could then examine the relationship between dosage levels and the extent of the AIDS symptoms. This would be an example of a(n) _____ study (p. 50).

    *a. correlational
    b. longitudinal
    c. experimental
    d. focus group

65. If we were to assemble a large group of people who tested positive for the AIDS virus, control for length of time of infection, and randomly assign these people to one of four treatment groups receiving high AZT dosages, medium AZT dosages, no treatment, or a placebo, it would be example of a(n) _____ study (p. 50).

    a. correlational
    b. longitudinal
    *c. experimental
    d. case

66. When an association between two variables is found using correlational methods, (p. 50):

    *a. the variables are related.
    b. a causal relationship exists between the variables.
    c. there was some degree of artificiality involved.
    d. reactivity was produced.

67. If you want to infer a cause-effect relationship between variables, it is necessary to use the _____ method (p. 51).

    a. correlational
    b. compositional
    *c. experimental
    d. case study

68. An advantage of experimental over correlational methods is that (p. 51):

    a. results are less reactive.
    b. results are less artificial.
    *c. cause and effect can be established.
    d. both b and c.

69. Research by Perper and Moore on flirting in singles' bars has been conducted using (p. 52):

    a. the experimental method.
    *b. field research.
    c. longitudinal studies.
    d. all of the above.

70. _____ research involves comparisons of different groups over the same time period, when the groups are similar in almost every way other than in the variable of interest (p. 53).

     *a. Cross-sectional
      b. Longitudinal
      c. Survey
      d. Direct-observation

71. A researcher who tests the same people when they are 20, 25, 30, 35, and 40 years old is conducting _____ research (p. 54):

     *a. longitudinal
      b. cross-sectional
      c. cohort
      d. relocation

72. Relatively few researchers rely on _____ approaches because they are very time-consuming and more expensive than _____ research (p. 54).

     *a. longitudinal; cross-sectional
      b. cross-sectional; longitudinal
      c. cohort; relocation
      d. correlational; longitudinal

73. A large group of people receive roughly the same score on a measure of sex guilt when they retake the same scale six months later. This result indicates that the sex guilt scale is most likely (p. 55):

      a. valid.
      b. ethical.
      c. generalizable.
     *d. reliable.

74. A measurement is valid to the extent that scores on it (p. 55):

     *a. accurately reflect the variable in question.
      b. provide significant differences.
      c. stay the same over time.
      d. are generalizable.

75. Which of the following methods did Kinsey use to determine the reliability of volunteers' responses (p. 55)?

      a. They were reinterviewed.
      b. Husbands' and wives' responses to the same questions were compared.
      c. A variety of investigators coded responses.
     *d. All of the above.

76. Which of the following populations was underrepresented in the Kinsey studies (p. 55)?

    a. the middle class
    b. the well educated
    c. the sexually active
  *d. ethnic minorities

77. Which of the following research methods represents the preferred way to test the hypothesis that there is a biological distinction between clitoral and vaginal orgasms (p. 56)?

    a. self-administered surveys
    b. interviews
    c. direct observation
  *d. physiological measures

78. The most frequently used scientific measure of female genital response is (p. 57):

    a. the mercury-in-rubber strain gauge.
    b. the metal band gauge.
  *c. the photoplethysmograph.
    d. position emission scanning.

79. Both case-study and focus-group research methods are aimed at (p. 59):

  *a. hypothesis generation.
    b. hypothesis testing.
    c. theory testing.
    d. generalizing findings from the sample to the population.

80. _____, a drug that has been used to maintain pregnancy, has been linked with cancer in daughters of the women who used it (p. 60).

    a. FDA
  *b. DES
    c. Testosterone
    d. Androgen

Essay Questions

81. Define "masturbatory insanity," and describe some of the treatments used to try to cure it (p. 33).

82. Compare the basic beliefs about sexuality held by Richard von Krafft-Ebing and Havelock Ellis (pp. 32–33).

83. Describe Freudian ideas about the nature of female sexual responding (pp. 33–34).

84. How have political and social issues interacted with the collection of data about sexuality? Cite some examples from the Kinsey group, Masters and Johnson, or Bullough (pp. 35–39).

85. Compare the methods the Kinsey group and Masters and Johnson used to obtain information about sexuality (pp. 35–38).

86. Describe the ethical issues with which researchers should be concerned when conducting sex research (pp. 43–45).

87. What ethical principles were violated during the Tuskegee experiment on syphilis (pp. 43–44)?

88. What is volunteer bias? How can it affect conclusions about findings from sex research (p. 48)?

89. What is self-report bias? How can it affect conclusions about findings from sex research (p. 50)?

90. Pose a question or hypothesis about some aspect of sexual behavior. Then describe how you would test it using a correlational versus experimental approach (pp. 51–52).

91. Pose a question or hypothesis about some aspect of sexual behavior. Then indicate how you would test it using a cross-sectional versus longitudinal approach (pp. 51–52).

92. Sex research may be conducted using self-administered measures, interviews, direct observation, physiological response measures, biochemical response measures, and case studies. Choose two of these methods of measurement, and compare them, noting their advantages and disadvantages for yielding information about sexual behavior (pp. 54–58).

93. A researcher has just published the results of a study in which she concluded that tea made from a mixture of pansies and maple leaves increases sexual desire and performance. Describe three factors that you should consider before accepting her conclusions as accurate (pp. 60–61).

94. Discuss the issue of generalizability and side effects. Refer to both the birth control pill and DES (pp. 60–61).

Multiple-Choice Questions

1. In Western societies couples spend approximately _____ per week copulating (p. 65).

    *a. 15 minutes
    b. 30 minutes
    c. 65 minutes
    d. 100 minutes

2. Thoughts and fantasies are an attempt to _____ sexual events to ourselves (p. 66).

    a. rationalize
    b. distort
    c. deny
    *d. understand and explain

3. A _____ is a tentative explanation that has been tested empirically but is not accepted as fact (p. 66).

    *a. theory
    b. hypothesis
    c. law
    d. postulate

4. The origins of _____ theory can be traced to the work of Mendel and Darwin (p. 66).

    a. biological
    *b. evolutionary
    c. psychoanalytic
    d. social-learning

5. _____ discovered that biological inheritance is based on the transfer of genetic material (p. 67).

    *a. Mendel
    b. Galton
    c. Darwin
    d. Thorton

6. Genetic material is _____ over the course of successive generations (p. 67).

    a. lost
    b. changed somewhat
    c. changed radically
    *d. relatively unchanged

7. Darwin proposed that organisms evolve from more simple life forms through a process called (p. 67):

    a. responsive transmission.
    b. inclusive fitness.
   *c. natural selection.
    d. reproductive success.

8. _____, in which adaptive characteristics are selected for continuation, is a crucial concept in natural selection (p. 67).

    a. Maximal odds
  *b. Reproductive success
    c. Prehominid awareness
    d. Environmental extension

9. Individuals who produce a large number of children are _____ to have their genes transmitted to future generations (p. 68).

  *a. more likely
    b. less likely
    c. not likely
    d. no more likely than those who produce a small number of children

10.. Offspring inherit characteristics from their parents that may be (p. 68):

    a. primarily moderated.
    b. slightly demographic.
    c. inherently attenuated.
  *d. more or less adaptive.

11. About _____ years elapsed between the appearance of the first creatures with grasping hands and the ability to hold their bodies upright and the appearance of a humanlike creature (p. 68).

    a. 5 billion
    b. 20 million
  *c. 65 million
    d. 100,000

12. Organisms having greater reproductive success are considered to have greater (p. 68):

  *a. fitness.
    b. genes.
    c. variation.
    d. adaptation.

13. _____ involves both an individual's reproductive contribution to the gene pool of the next generation and that individual's contribution in aiding survival of kin (p. 68).

    a. Natural selection
    b. Adaptation
    c. Reproductive success
    *d. Inclusive fitness

14. To try to determine how a particular behavior came to exist is to seek its _____ cause (p. 68).

    *a. proximate
    b. ultimate
    c. distal
    d. relevant

15. To try to determine why a particular behavior exists is to seek its _____ cause (p. 68).

    a. proximate
    *b. ultimate
    c. distal
    d. relevant

16. In McCormick's study of contemporary courtship strategies, men reported using _____ strategies than women to _____ sexual activity (pp. 69–70).

    *a. more; initiate
    b. fewer; initiate
    c. more; limit
    d. fewer; limit

17. A pattern of _____ investment in offspring by _____ characterizes the behavior of humans and most other species (p. 70).

    *a. greater; females
    b. greater; males
    c. reduced; females
    d. reduced; siblings

18. How do evolutionary theorists explain observed gender differences in courtship behavior (p. 70)?

    a. differences in the extent to which each gender is rewarded for taking the initiative
    b. contemporary roles and scripts that label a sexually assertive man as "healthy" and a sexually assertive woman as "easy"
    c. fundamental biological/psychological aspects of male and female sexuality
    *d. amount of investment of resources and time in their offspring made by males versus females

19. Which of the following is *not* a way that parental investment influences sexual behavior in humans, according to Trivers (p. 70)?

    *a. Females are less endangered by an absence of commitment in a relationship.
    b. Male-male competition for female mates is greater than female-female competition for male mates.
    c. There is greater variation in reproductive success among males than females.
    d. Selective pressure will be greater on males than on females.

20. Evolutionary theorists assume that many current sexual behaviors (p. 70):

    a. are due to greater selective pressure on human females than on males.
    b. can be explained by psychoanalytic views.
    c. are a result of social learning.
    *d. can be traced to behaviors that existed in early hunting and gathering groups.

21. According to Trivers, in species where there is female-female competition to mate with males, females are (p. 70):

    a. more selective of mates.
    b. likely to form a monogamous relationship.
    *c. larger and more aggressive.
    d. genetic carriers of altruistic impulses.

22. Evolutionary theorists view male and female sex differences as the result of different (p. 71):

    a. modeling.
    b. social learning.
    *c. reproductive strategies.
    d. operant conditioning.

23. A large cross-cultural study by Buss found that women place a higher value on the
    _____ of potential partners than men do (p. 72):

    a. body appearance
    b. age
    *c. financial prospects
    d. facial appearance

24. In a contemporary study among college students by Wiederman and Allgeier on selection of a potential mate, the results (p. 73):

    *a. were consistent with predictions based on evolutionary theory.
    b. did not match the cross-cultural findings of Buss.
    c. supported Freudian views of the Oedipus complex.
    d. showed identical concerns for both men and women.

25. Which of the following does the textbook mention as a criticism of evolutionary theory (p. 73)?

   a. *a. reductionism
        b. allegory
        c. covert ovulation
        d. jealousy among women

26. _____ theory emphasizes the influence of an individual's early experiences on his or her development (p. 73).

   *a. Psychoanalytic
    b. Evolutionary
    c. Social-learning
    d. Information-processing

27. _____, or sexual energy, is the source of all human endeavors in Freud's view (p. 74).

   *a. Libido
    b. Altruism
    c. Egoism
    d. Theology

28. Freud argued that sexual experiences during _____ influence the development of _____ personality (p. 74).

   *a. infancy; adult
    b. middle adulthood; adolescent
    c. adolescence; adult
    d. adult; late adulthood

29. Freud's assertions _____ the prevailing view that children are _____ (p. 74).

   *a. challenged; pure and asexual
    b. challenged; sexually impulsive
    c. supported; pure and asexual
    d. supported; sexually impulsive

30. Freud's theory of _____ was a revolutionary idea (p. 74).

   *a. infantile sexuality
    b. preteen morality
    c. adolescent sexuality
    b. female morality

31. According to Freud, because social prohibitions prevent humans from acting freely on their sexual impulses (p. 75):

   *a. sexual energy is diverted into other activities.
    b. people repress sexual energy.
    c. people behave prudently, for the most part.
    d. internal control is established.

32. In Freud's view, Victorian society _____ childhood sexuality (p. 75).

    a. neglected
    b. overly encouraged
    *c. too severely repressed
    d. exploited

33. Freud's major contribution was that he (p. 75):

    a. performed many systematic experiments to test his theories.
    b. wrote that the mature female orgasm results from clitoral stimulation.
    *c. recognized the importance of early childhood experiences for human development.
    d. developed an excellent explanation of homosexuality employing the oedipal conflict.

34. In psychoanalytic theory, the subsystem of the mind that seeks only to gratify instinctual drives is the (p. 75):

    *a. id.
    b. ego.
    c. libido.
    d. superego.

35. Freud believed that humans have two basic kinds of instincts (p. 75):

    *a. eros and thanatos.
    b. phantasmal and maternal.
    c. sorcerer and saint.
    d. collective and individual.

36. Freud developed his theory of personality development around the (p. 75):

    *a. fate of the libido.
    b. death instinct.
    c. instinctive need for food and water.
    d. appearance of altruism.

37. In psychoanalytic theory, the subsystem of the personality that includes the conscience is the (p. 75):

    a. libido.
    b. id.
    c. ego.
    *d. superego.

38. According to Freud, the _____ is present at birth (p. 75).

    *a. id
    b. ego
    c. superego
    d. Oedipus complex

39. In psychoanalytic theory, the id operates on the (p. 75):

    a. simplicity principle.
    b. perfection principle.
    c. reality principle.
    *d. none of the above.

40. The attempt to satisfy instinctual demands by producing a mental image is called (p. 75):

    *a. wish fulfillment.
    b. the reality principle.
    c. critical examination.
    d. projection.

41. The ego must try to satisfy _____ "masters" (p. 75).

    a. two
    *b. three
    c. four
    d. five

42. In psychoanalytic theory, the superego operates on the (p. 75):

    a. defense mechanism.
    b. libido enhancer.
    *c. conscience.
    d. mediator between the id and ego.

43. In psychoanalytic theory, the ego attempts to compromise the demands of sexual instincts and societal values by employing the (pp. 75–76):

    *a. the demands of societal instinct and societal values.
    b. unconscious conflicts.
    c. the phallic and latency stages.
    d. all of the above.

44. Freud placed greatest emphasis on the _____, where he believed that all our thoughts originate (pp. 75 –76).

    a. conscious
    b. preconscious
    *c. unconscious
    d. postconscious

45. Most of Freud's theorizing on human sexuality was based on (p. 75):

    a. interviews with medical students.
    b. experimental studies.
    *c. the experiences of emotionally disturbed patients and self-analysis.
    d. surveys of the inhabitants of Vienna.

46. According to Freud, preference for same-gender playmates occurs during the _____ psychosexual stage (p. 76).

    a. oral
    b. phallic
    c. genital
    *d. latency

47. According to Freud, the young boy represses his sexual desire for his mother because he (p. 77):

    a. envies his father's penis.
    b. isn't able to perform sexually.
    c. prefers girls of his own age more.
    *d. fears his father will castrate him.

48. Freud's theory has been sharply criticized because (p. 77):

    a. of its masculine bias.
    b. it is too pessimistic about human nature.
    c. he supplied inadequate scientific evidence to support his assumptions.
    *d. all of the above

49. Psychoanalytic theorists, including Reich, Marcuse, and Roheim, have (p. 78):

    *a. stressed the importance of sex even more than Freud did.
    b. disagreed completely with Freud about the importance of sex.
    c. agreed with Freud about penis envy.
    d. stressed the power of experiences throughout life less than Freud did.

50. For Reich, _____ was a measure of _____ (p. 78).

    a. the degree of penis envy; deviance
    *b. the extent of orgasmic release; health
    c. a positive experience in later life; positive development
    d. observable behavior; scientific evidence

51. Early proponents of behaviorism maintained that sex researchers must focus on (p. 78):

    a. sexual thoughts and desires.
    b. early childhood experiences.
    *c. observable sexual behavior.
    d. sexual fantasies.

52. Which of the following scientists was instrumental in initiating a school of research that has yielded several important principles of learning theory used to study sexual responses (p. 79)?

    a. Freud
    *b. Watson
    c. Symons
    d. Rogers

53. John Watson maintained that (p. 79):

    *a. researchers must focus on what is measurable.
    b. thoughts and fantasies need to be studied.
    c. psychology cannot be studied scientifically.
    d. psychoanalysis is important in understanding fantasies.

54. In Pavlov's classic experiment, the dog's salivation to the sound of the buzzer was a(n) (p. 79):

    *a. conditioned response.
    b. conditioned stimulus.
    c. unconditioned response.
    d. unconditioned stimulus.

55. In Pavlov's classic experiment, the dog's salivation to food was a(n) (p. 79):

    *a. unconditioned response.
    b. unconditioned stimulus.
    c. conditioned response.
    d. conditioned stimulus.

56. In the classical conditioning experiment used to demonstrate how people can come to be sexually aroused by a wide range of stimuli, male students were shown slides of women's black boots, followed by slides of nude women they had previously rated as attractive. After repeated pairings of the nudes and the boots, the students were shown the boots alone, and it was found that the males then (p. 79):

    *a. were aroused by the boots alone.
    b. were aroused by nudes alone.
    c. showed increased heart rates but no penile changes.
    d. showed more arousal to bikinis than to shoes.

57. Which of the following best explains physiological arousal upon seeing a particular kind of car or smelling a certain perfume (p. 79)?

    *a. classical conditioning
    b. instrumental learning
    c. sociobiology
    d. social cognition

58. What theory maintains that behavior is influenced by its consequences (p. 80)?

    *a. operant conditioning
    b. classical conditioning
    c. social learning
    d. social contracts

59. According to principles of operant conditioning, theorists have suggested that pleasurable experiences with people of the same gender will _____ the likelihood that a person will seek sexual partners of the _____ in the future (p. 80).

    *a. increase; same gender
    b. increase; opposite gender
    c. decrease; same gender
    d. not affect; same gender

60. Punishment tends to work best when it is (p. 80):

    *a. immediate.
    b. avoidable.
    c. unpredictable.
    d. frequent.

61. Which of the following statements regarding the therapeutic use of punishment is correct (p. 80)?

    a. In general, punishment is not a very effective training strategy.
    b. The negative effects of punishment usually outweigh the positive effects.
    c. Punishment may produce aggressive behavior.
    *d. All of the above.

62. Punishment has been found to be highly effective in eliminating (p. 80):

    a. rape.
    b. masturbation.
    c. premarital sex.
    *d. none of the above.

63. Research has shown that punishment reduces the frequency of undesirable sexual behavior but also that (p. 80):

    *a. harmful side effects may occur.
    b. it decreases aggression.
    c. it eliminates a rapist's tendency to assault others.
    d. all of the above.

64. The individual most closely associated with social learning theory is (p. 81):

    a. Watson.
    *b. Bandura.
    c. Erikson.
    d. White.

65. _____ would be predicted to influence sexual behavior according to social learning theorists, but not according to Freudian theorists, or to classical or operant conditioning (p. 81).

    a. Early childhood experiences
    b. One's religious orientation regarding sexuality
    c. Direct reinforcement of a sexual behavior of one's own
   *d. Observation of reinforcement of someone else's sexual behavior

66. According to social learning theory, a person who observed someone being punished for practicing premarital sex would be (p. 81):

   *a. less likely to have sex before marriage.
    b. more likely to have sex before marriage.
    c. less likely to have extramarital affairs.
    d. more likely to feel guilt about premarital sex.

67. In social learning approaches, most significance is placed on (p. 81):

    a. cognitions.
    b. past experience.
    c. social norms.
   *d. all of the above.

68. Gagnon and Simon believe that we can better understand human sexual behavior by primarily examining _____ processes (p. 82).

   *a. socialization
    b. biological
    c. cognitive
    d. theta

69. Reiss devised a theory of human sexuality that emphasizes (p. 82):

    a. early childhood experiences.
    b. biological factors.
   *c. societal norms.
    d. the importance of conditioning and reinforcement.

70. The concept of scripts is employed by (p. 83):

    a. evolutionary theorists.
    b. social learning theorists.
    c. Freudian theorists.
   *d. sociological theorists.

71. On the individual level, _____ are cognitive plans that enable us to behave in an organized and predictable fashion (p. 83).

    *a. scripts
    b. schemas
    c. schedules
    d. psychodramas

72. Those who interpret behavior using the concept of scripts believe that sexual orientation (p. 83):

    *a. is based on a loosely defined set of behaviors that a person employs in dealing with others.
    b. involves permanent traits.
    c. involves genetic influences.
    d. is determined by socially accepted behaviors that a person is familiar with.

73. Most people do not perceive a gynecological or urological exam as sexual, because of the power of (p. 83):

    a. ethics.
    *b. scripts.
    c. hormones.
    d. psychosexual stages.

74. The _____ phenomenon for scripts can sometimes lead to difficulty in ambiguous situations, such as when you are following a friendship script but your friend is following a romantic script (p. 84).

    a. homogeneity
    b. novelty
    c. resolution
    *d. gap-filling

75. From the standpoint of script theory, there is _____ sexual interaction that can truly be called _____ (p. 84).

    *a. little; spontaneous
    b. much; spontaneous
    c. little; planned
    d. much; planned

76. When asked to arrange a series of 25 statements about activities ranging from kissing to orgasm in the order in which they would be most likely to occur, males and females were _____ in their sequences (p. 84).

    *a. very close
    b. somewhat close
    c. very different
    d. extremely different

77. According to Reiss's theory, powerful males seek to control sexual access to (p. 85):

    *a. those who are important to them.
    b. almost everyone they know.
    c. their co-workers.
    d. their offspring.

78. According to Reiss's theory, differences between the roles of men and women stem from (p. 85):

    *a. social learning.
    b. innate differences.
    c. the degree of male control of key societal institutions.
    d. all of the above.

79. In Reiss's view, a premature ejaculator in this culture is (p. 86):

    *a. a nonconformist.
    b. dysfunctional.
    c. abnormal.
    d. a man who probably dislikes women.

Essay Questions

80. Define parental investment theory, and explain how sociobiologists use it to explain gender differences in sexual behavior (p. 70).

81. Explain how evolutionary theory views modern courtship patterns (pp. 70–71).

82. What is the Oedipus complex, and how is it resolved, according to Freud? Compare it to the Electra complex (pp. 76–77).

83. Explain several aspects of Freud's theory that are not accepted by more recent psychoanalytic thinkers, being sure to identify these thinkers in your answer (p. 78).

84. You smell the odor of the cologne used by your romantic partner on someone else, and you momentarily feel aroused. Explain how your arousal would be explained by classical conditioning (pp. 78–79).

85. Your young son masturbates frequently when the two of you are in public (at the grocery store, and so forth). You don't object to his masturbation but don't want him to do so in public. Based on what you have learned about the principles of operant conditioning, how would you deal with this situation (other than keeping him out of public forever) (pp. 79–80)?

86. Compare learning theorists' and social learning theorists' explanations of the acquisition and maintenance of particular sexual behaviors (pp. 78–82).

87. What is sociologist Ira Reiss's basic disagreement with the positions taken by psychoanalytic, sociobiological, and social learning theorists in explaining sexual behavior (p. 82)?

88. What do sociologists mean by the concept of scripts? How are these scripts related to sexual interactions between people (pp. 83–85)?

89. What is a theory? How are theories different from advocacy (pp. 86–87)?

90. Do you think a person can hold religious and scientific beliefs simultaneously? How is religious and moral thinking different from scientific reasoning? How could scientific research affect religious and moral thinking (pp. 86–87)?

91. Describe the theory of natural selection (p. 67).

92. Describe parental-investment theory. List and discuss the three ways that the average parental investment of males versus females in a species influences sexual behavior, according to Trivers (p. 70).

93. Describe and discuss the id, ego, and superego. How do they develop? Include a discussion of the pleasure principle and the reality principle (pp. 75–76).

94. Explain classical conditioning. Include a description of Pavlov's classic experiment (pp. 78–79).

95. Explain operant conditioning. Include a description of reinforcement and punishment. What are the pros and cons of the use of punishment (pp. 79–80)?

96. Discuss kinship and its relationship to jealousy (p. 85).

CHAPTER 4

Development and Sexual Differentiation

Multiple-Choice Questions

1. Sperm are (p. 92):

    a. miniature, preformed human beings that need to be united with an ovum in order to survive and develop.
    b. among the largest cells in the human body.
    c. produced by the endometrium.
    *d. none of the above

2. The semen of fertile men who have not ejaculated in the previous 24 hours or so contains _____ sperm (p. 92).

    a. 50–100
    b. 500–1000
    c. 50,000–100,000
    *d. 100 million–500 million

3. The ovum (p. 92):

    a. is about the same size as a sperm cell.
    b. has a tail.
    *c. is about one-fourth the size of this dot (.).
    d. is normally released from an ovary about once every three months.

4. About 50 to 60 percent of the average man's sperm are _____; some of these may be destroyed by the normally _____ secretions of the vagina (p. 92).

    a. viscous; alkaline
    b. somatic; acidic
    c. motile; alkaline
    *d. motile; acidic

5. For fertilization to take place, the meeting of the egg and sperm generally must occur between _____ after sexual intercourse (p. 93).

    a. 1 and 2 hours
    *b. 2 and 48 hours
    c. 2 and 4 days
    d. 5 and 6 days

6. By the process known as mitosis, (p. 94):

    a. the zygote is formed.
    b. it is determined whether an embryo will be male or female.
    *c. body cells divide, creating two new, identical cells.
    d. genes are arranged on chromosomes.

7. Germ cells differ from body cells in (p. 94):

    a. how they divide.
    b. number of chromosomes.
    c. the presence of a nucleus.
    *d. both a and b.

8. The number of chromosomes in the cells of the human body (p. 94):

    a. is 23.
    *b. is 46.
    c. is 92.
    d. varies from person to person.

9. Cell division in body cells occurs by (p. 94):

    a. meiosis.
    *b. mitosis.
    c. kertosis.
    d. symbiosis.

10. In meiosis, cells are produced that have _____ chromosomes as in the parent cell (p. 94).

    *a. half the number of
    b. the same number of
    c. twice as many
    d. ten times the number of

11. _____ are the basic units of hereditary transmission and are made up of the chemical called (p. 95).

    *a. Genes; DNA
    b. Chromosomes; keratin
    c. Zygotes; neoprotein
    d. Autosomes; chromatin

12. DNA (p. 95):

    a. is found only in humans.
    b. is a messenger that transmits RNA instructions.
    *c. acts as a blueprint for cellular activity.
    d. both a and b.

13. The basic unit of hereditary transmission is the (p. 95):

    a. sperm.
    b. egg cell.
   *c. gene.
    d. mitochondria.

14. The genetic sex of a child is determined by the _____, due to the contribution of a(n) _____ chromosome (p. 96).

   *a. father; Y
    b. mother; X
    c. father; X
    d. mother; Y

15. The X chromosome is _____ the Y chromosome (p. 96).

   *a. 5 times larger than
    b. 50 times larger than
    c. the same size as
    d. half as big as

16. In every cell of her body, a normal female has (p. 96):

    a. two Y chromosomes.
   *b. two X chromosomes.
    c. X and Y chromosomes.
    d. an A and a B chromosome.

17. X and Y chromosomes are known as (p. 96):

    a. autosomes.
   *b. sex chromosomes.
    c. genes.
    d. both a and b.

18. Sperm carry (p. 96):

    a. only an X chromosome.
   *b. either an X or a Y chromosome.
    c. only a Y chromosome.
    d. a B chromosome.

19. The _____ pair of chromosomes is composed of the sex chromosomes (p. 96).

    a. twenty-ninth
   *b. twenty-third
    c. forty-sixth
    d. one hundredth

20. The average female has _____ Barr body (bodies) (p. 96).

    a. 0
    *b. 1
    c. 2
    d. 23

21. The average male has _____ Barr body (bodies) (p. 96).

    *a. 0
    b. 1
    c. 2
    d. 23

22. Barr and Bertram (1949) reported that the substance _____ is seen in the nuclei of developing females but not in those of developing males (p. 96).

    a. RNA
    b. DNA
    c. gendarmerie
    *d. chromatin

23. Dominant genes are those that (p. 97):

    *a. determine a person's inherited characteristics.
    b. are located on the male Y chromosome.
    c. are located on the female Y chromosome.
    d. survive the perilous journey down the fallopian tubes.

24. In order for _____ genes to determine an individual's characteristics, the person must have two of them—one from each parent (p. 97).

    a. dominant
    *b. recessive
    c. passive
    d. chromatin

25. A male whose single X chromosome carries the recessive genes for a trait (p. 97):

    a. will be a carrier of the trait.
    *b. will manifest the trait.
    c. both a and b.
    d. neither a nor b.

26. The transmitters of sex-linked disorders are (p. 97):

    *a. females.
    b. males.
    c. equally likely to be either males or females.
    d. more likely to be males, but females can transmit.

27. The stage of development encompassing the first two weeks following conception is the (p. 98):

   a. period of the zygote.
   b. embryonic period.
   *c. germinal period.
   d. period of the fetus.

28. The external genitals of the fetus are distinguishable by the end of the _____ week of pregnancy (p. 99).

   a. first
   b. third
   c. seventh
   *d. twelfth

29. If born prematurely, a fetus of this age could live, but its chances for survival are low (p. 99).

   a. 4 months
   b. 5 months
   c. 6 months
   *d. 7 months

30. The outer layer of the embryo is called the (p. 99):

   a. mesoderm.
   b. gonad.
   c. placenta.
   *d. ectoderm.

31. The mesoderm layer of the embryo will develop into the (p. 99):

   *a. heart, blood vessels, muscles, and skeleton.
   b. amniotic sac and umbilical cord.
   c. respiratory and digestive systems.
   d. genitals.

32. The placenta and embryo remain connected by the (p. 99):

   a. seminal vesicles.
   *b. umbilical cord.
   c. digestive system.
   d. fallopian tubes.

33. The _____ absorbs oxygen and nourishment from the mother's bloodstream and transfers body wastes from the embryo to the mother (p. 99).

   a. amniotic sac
   *b. placenta
   c. endocrine system
   d. stomach

34. The _____ sac is a fluid-filled space that encases the developing organism (p. 99).

    a. phylogenous
    *b. amniotic
    c. skeletal
    d. congestive

35. The rule that _____ repeats _____ is the idea that during prenatal development we briefly display characteristics of our species' evolutionary past (p. 99).

    a. progesterone; lanugo
    b. colostrum; denigration
    c. ancestres; sapience
    *d. ontogeny; phylogeny

36. The developing fetus is nourished via the (p. 99):

    *a. umbilical cord.
    b. Barr body.
    c. autosomes.
    d. blastocyst.

37. At the beginning of the ninth week of pregnancy, bone cells appear, and the _____ stage begins (p. 99).

    a. inception
    b. generative
    c. embryonic
    *d. fetal

38. The placenta (p. 99):

    a. allows the blood of the mother and developing organism to mix with each other.
    *b. produces the hormones that support pregnancy and later assist in preparation of the breasts for lactation.
    c. often leads to malnourishment in the mother, due to the removal of nutrients from her blood.
    d. completely protects the developing organism from all harmful substances by means of filtration.

39. In the correct order, the three stages of development in the uterus are (p. 99):

    a. fetal, germinal, embryonic.
    b. fetal, embryonic, germinal.
    *c. germinal, embryonic, fetal.
    d. germinal, neurula, blastocyst.

40. A major source of hormones during pregnancy is the (p. 99):

    *a. placenta.
    b. zygote.
    c. amniotic fluid.
    d. ovotestes.

41. By the end of the eighth week of pregnancy, it is likely that the fetus's (p. 100):

    a. legs are well developed.
    b. external genitals are distinguishable.
    *c. head constitutes about half the length of the fetus.
    d. basic reflexes have developed.

42. A fetus born prematurely is most likely to have problems with which of the following systems (p. 100)?

    a. excretory
    b. limbic
    c. circulatory
    *d. respiratory

43. Which of the following statements about the ninth month of pregnancy is false (p. 101)?

    a. The average fetus weights between 5 and 7 pounds.
    b. The testes have descended from the abdomen to the scrotum.
    *c. Lanugo and vernix begin to form.
    d. The fetus acquires some antibodies from the mother.

44. A greasy substance called _____ is held on the skin of the fetus by a fine, downy hair called _____ (p. 101).

    a. Cowper's; frenum
    b. tubercle; Wolffian substance
    *c. varix; lanugo
    d. varimax; cecum

45. Two substances secreted by the testes important for the sexual differentiation of males are (p. 103):

    a. estrogen and progesterone.
    b. estrogen and testosterone.
    c. testosterone and progesterone.
    *d. testosterone and Mullerian inhibiting substance (MIS).

46. The basic human form is (p. 103):

    a. asexual.
    *b. female.
    c. male.
    d. chropodal.

47. Two crucial factors associated with male prenatal development are (p. 103):

    a. an X chromosome and testosterone.
    b. a Y chromosome and estrogen.
    c. an X chromosome and estrogen.
    *d. a Y chromosome and androgens.

48. During the period of prenatal development from fertilization to implantation, the developing organism is called a(n) (p. 103):

    a. embryo.
    b. egg.
    c. fetus.
    *d. zygote.

49. Which of the following statements about Mullerian-inhibiting substance is false (p. 103)?

    a. MIS is responsible for curbing the growth of the Mullerian-duct system.
    b. In the absence of testosterone or MIS, the fetus differentiates in a female direction, regardless of genetic gender.
    c. MIS inhibits the development of female reproductive structures.
    *d. MIS is secreted by the ovaries.

50. Which of the following statements about sex hormones is true (p. 103)?

    a. Turner's syndrome is the result of exposure to excessive progesterone levels in the womb.
    b. Females secrete only estrogens.
    c. Males secrete only androgens.
    *d. Both males and females secrete the same three kinds of sex hormones.

51. External genitals are created from a bud of tissue called a (p. 106):

    *a. genital tubercle.
    b. deferens.
    c. genro.
    d. gamete bud.

52. The _____ develops into the urethral tube in males or the inner vaginal lips in females (p. 106).

    a. labioscrotal swelling
    b. labial sacs
    *c. urogenital folds
    d. prostate gland

53. Dihydrotestosterone (DHT) (p. 106):

    a. neutralizes the effect of testosterone in females.
    *b. causes the elongation of the genital tubercle into the phallus.
    c. causes androgen insensitivity syndrome.
    d. blocks the usual effect of testosterone in males.

54. At the time of puberty for males (p. 108):

    a. the testes and penis begin to grow.
    b. the larynx grows.
    c. skin eruptions are common.
    *d. all of the above.

55. Spermarche is (p. 109):

    *a. the onset of sperm emission.
    b. an event that first occurs at age 15 for most males.
    c. an event that often occurs during urination.
    d. all of the above.

56. The most common chromosomal defect affects about 1 in every 1,000 live births. It is (p. 109):

    a. Turner's syndrome.
    b. XYY syndrome.
    *c. Down's syndrome.
    d. androgen insensitivity syndrome.

57. Most children with Down's syndrome (p. 109):

    a. have physical defects but no psychological ones.
    b. live until the age of 60.
    c. have 41 chromosomes in the fertilized egg instead of 46.
    *d. are born to women older than 34.

58. Hermaphrodites (p. 109):

    a. have been prenatally exposed to excessive levels of androgen.
    b. have hemophilia.
    c. have no uterus.
    *d. are genetic females, despite the presence of testes.

59. Which of the following statements about chromosomal defects is false (p. 109)?

    a. The number of babies born with visible chromosome-related abnormalities has remained relatively constant since the United States began recording such data in the 1960s.
    b. A visible chromosome-related abnormality is present in more than 8 out of every 1,000 live births.
    c. Chromosomal abnormalities are present in about 50 percent of all spontaneous abortions.
    *d. Chromosomal defects are always a result of inheritance.

60. Which chromosome abnormality is least likely to be apparent in one's physical appearance (p. 110)?

    a. Down's syndrome
    b. Turner's syndrome
    *c. XYY syndrome
    d. androgen insensitivity syndrome

61. Most forms of atypical gender differentiation fall in the category of (p. 111):

    a. true hermaphroditism.
    b. transsexualism.
    *c. pseudohermaphroditism.
    d. intersexualism.

62. Which of the following statements about true hermaphroditism is false (p. 111)?

    a. True hermaphroditism is exceedingly rare.
    b. True hermaphrodites possess an ovary on one side and a testis on the other.
    c. The term comes from the names of the Greek god and goddess of love.
    *d. The cause of true hermaphroditism is well understood.

63. Most hermaphrodites are genetic _____ and usually are raised as _____ (p. 111):

    a. females; females.
    *b. females; males.
    c. males; females.
    d. males; males.

64. Most true hermaphrodites are characterized by (p. 111):

    a. an enlarged phallus.
    b. a uterus.
    c. developments of breasts at puberty.
    *d. all of the above.

65. This chromosome abnormality has been publicized due to a supposed association with criminal potential (p. 112).

    a. Down's syndrome
    b. androgen insensitivity syndrome
    *c. XYY syndrome.
    d. Turner's syndrome.

66. Research on the XYY syndrome (p. 112):

    a. suggests that aggressive males also tend to have higher IQs.
    b. has established that an extra Y chromosome causes extra aggression.
    c. has called into question older theories of gender differentiation.
    *d. demonstrates the dangers of jumping to conclusions on the basis of a single study.

67. Having an extra X or an extra Y chromosome seems to be related to the incidence of (p. 112):

    *a. mental retardation.
    b. transsexualism.
    c. homosexualism.
    d. infertility.

68. Which of the following statements is true about prenatal exposure to elevated levels of estrogen and progesterone (p. 113)?

    a. The elevated levels affect the anatomical development of human males.
    b. The elevated levels affect the gender-related behavior of human males.
    *c. In mammals, exposure results in demasculinization of the genitals.
    d. In mammals, exposure results in stereotypic masculine behaviors.

69. In androgen insensitivity syndrome (p. 113):

    a. the fetus is born with a complete set of female internal genital organs.
    b. the body secretes abnormally low levels of androgen.
    c. there are severe psychological disturbances.
    *d. target cells are unresponsive to androgen.

70. A condition sometimes called testicular feminization is also called (p. 113):

    a. Down's syndrome.
    *b. Androgen insensitivity syndrome.
    c. Turner's syndrome.
    d. XYY syndrome.

71. Genetic males with AIS (p. 113):

    a. secrete too much androgen.
    b. secrete too much estrogen.
    *c. are unresponsive to androgen.
    d. usually die within five years after birth.

72. Dihydrotestosterone (DHT) deficiency syndrome is a genetic disorder that prevents the prenatal conversion of _____ into _____ (p. 114).

    a. testosterone; estrogen
    *b. testosterone; DHT
    c. hydrotestosterone; DHT
    d. DHT; testosterone

73. Most of the individuals studied who have DHT deficiency syndrome were raised as (p. 114):

    a. females until puberty and continued to maintain a feminine gender-role identity despite the appearance of male secondary sex characteristics.
    *b. females until puberty, but with the appearance of male secondary sex characteristics, they gradually adopted a masculine gender-role identity.
    c. males until puberty, at which point they adopted a feminine gender-role identity.
    d. males until puberty, at which point they continued to display a masculine gender-role identity.

74. DHT deficiency syndrome is (p. 114):

   a. produced by exposure to too much testosterone during prenatal differentiation.
   b. produced by exposure to too much estrogen during prenatal differentiation.
   *c. a genetic disorder that prevents the conversion of testosterone into DHT.
   d. found only in genetic females.

75. Studies of baby girls born to women who took progestins during their pregnancies have shown that (p. 115):

   *a. the masculinizing effects of the hormones were limited to the prenatal period.
   b. the babies all looked female in appearance.
   c. the effects are biochemically similar to those of estrogens.
   d. none of the above.

76. Genetic females with congenital adrenal hyperplaxia (CAH) (p. 115):

   *a. secrete too much androgen.
   b. secrete too much estrogen.
   c. are unresponsive to androgen.
   d. secrete too much progesterone.

77. Which of the following statements about puberty is false (p. 115)?

   a. Hormonal processes stimulate the changes associated with puberty.
   b. The most obvious sign of a boy's maturation is nocturnal emission.
   c. The most obvious sign of a girl's maturation is menarche.
   *d. Males generally enter puberty at an earlier age than do females.

78. Ehrhardt (1975) found that genetic males exposed to excess androgen had (p. 116):

   a. an enlarged phallus.
   *b. a greater interest in sports and rough outdoor activity.
   c. dysfunctional testes.
   d. all of the above.

79. Prenatal exposure to excess androgen has the effect of masculinizing genetic females. A source of this masculinization is (p. 116):

   a. a malfunction of fetal adrenal glands.
   b. ovarian tumors during pregnancy.
   c. drinking alcohol during pregnancy.
   *d. both a and b.

80. Administration of progesterone to maintain pregnancy has resulted in (p. 116):

   a. masculinizing of the external genitals of genetic females through puberty.
   b. dysfunction of internal reproductive organs in females.
   *c. masculinizing of the external genitals of genetic females in the prenatal period only.
   d. dysfunction of internal reproductive organs in males.

81. Money and Ehrhardt (1972) found that normal girls displayed fewer masculine stereotyped interests and behaviors than (p. 116):

    a. prenatally masculinized girls.
    b. girls with CAH.
    c. neither a nor b.
  *d. both a and b.

82. In experiments with monkeys, testosterone administered to a pregnant mother has been observed to do which of the following to her offspring (p. 117)?

    a. have a masculinizing effect on the females
    b. lead to a small but well-formed penis in genetically female monkeys
    c. lead to more aggressive behavior in the infant female monkeys
  *d. all of the above

83. Which of the following general statements can be made concerning exposure of humans to atypical hormones during prenatal development (p. 117)?

    a. Sex hormones (e.g., androgens) have little influence on anatomical differentiation in a male or a female during prenatal development.
  *b. Gender assignment has more of an impact on gender identity than one's genetic (XX or XY) gender.
    c. Damage usually results, which leads to poor gender identity even if the problem is corrected during infancy.
    d. The benefits far outweigh the negative effects.

84. Probably the most important determinant of one's gender self-concept is one's _____ gender identity (p. 118).

  *a. psychological
    b. hormonal
    c. genital
    d. genetic

Essay Questions

85. Describe two differences between germ cells and body cells (p. 94).

86. What are chromosomes, and how many do humans have (p. 96)?

87. Does the father or the mother determine the genetic gender of their offspring? What is the chromosomal pattern of a normal genetic male and a normal genetic female (p. 96)?

88. Describe the phases of normal prenatal gender differentiation in the order in which they occur, starting with conception. (pp. 98–101).

89. Identify one of the sex chromosomal abnormalities, and describe the characteristics of a person with that abnormality (pp. 109–116).

90. An early study concluded that XYY males are more aggressive than XY males. Describe the problems with that study and the current conclusion about the relationship between having an XYY chromosomal pattern and engaging in violent criminal behavior (p. 112).

91. Assume that you and your mate have produced a male with androgen insensitivity syndrome. What treatments would you allow, how would you raise the child (as a male or female), and what is the basis of your decisions (p. 113)?

92. Describe the findings from research on individuals with DHT deficiency syndrome. What is the genetic gender of these people, what is their appearance at birth, what happens at puberty, and what gender identity do most of them have in adulthood (p. 114)?

93. Assume that you and your mate have produced a female with congenital adrenal hyperplasia. What treatments would you allow, how would you raise the child (as a male or female), and what is the basis of your decisions (p. 115)?

94. Discuss the ways in which gender identity is related to genetic gender, atypical hormone exposure during prenatal development, and gender of rearing (pp. 117–118).

CHAPTER 5

Sexual Anatomy and Physiology

Multiple-Choice Questions

1. The word *testes* comes from the Latin word meaning (p. 124):

   *a. to witness.
   b. to surround.
   c. to reproduce.
   d. to protect.

2. The term *balls* is slang for the (p. 124):

   *a. testes.
   b. spermatic cords.
   c. seminal vesicles.
   d. tunica dartos.

3. When the early Romans took an oath, it was customary for them to (p. 124):

   a. place their right hand over the left breast.
   b. place their hands on a Bible.
   c. raise their right hand.
   *d. place their hands over their testes.

4. Each testis is located in a saclike structure called the (p. 124):

   a. tunicum.
   *b. scrotum.
   c. inguinal pouch.
   d. endometrium.

5. Normal scrotal temperature is about _____ than normal core body temperature (p. 124).

   *a. 5½ degrees F lower
   b. 5½ degrees F higher
   c. 9½ degrees F lower
   d. 9½ degrees F higher

6. The production of sperm and of sex hormones is a major function of the (p. 124):

   a. prostate gland.
   b. seminal vesicles.
   *c. testes.
   d. Cowper's glands.

7. What body part contains blood vessels, nerves, a sperm duct, and a thin muscle (p. 124)?

    *a. spermatic cord
     b. cremasteric sac
     c. bulbourethral gland
     d. seminal vesicle

8. Each of the testes is suspended at the end of (p. 124):

     a. an ejaculatory duct.
     b. the seminiferous tubes.
     c. the vas deferens.
    *d. a spermatic cord.

9. The _____ encircles the testes and raises them closer to the body in response to cold, fear, anger, and sexual arousal (p. 124).

     a. prostate gland
    *b. cremaster muscle
     c. epididymis
     d. corpora cavernosa

10. Sperm are produced in the (p. 124):

    *a. seminiferous tubules.
     b. vas deferens.
     c. spermatic cord.
     d. ejaculatory ducts.

11. The purpose of the epididymis is to (p. 125):

     a. transport sperm in the penis.
    *b. store sperm.
     c. produce sperm.
     d. contribute fluid to semen.

12. Semen is composed of (p. 125):

     a. fluid from the seminal vesicles.
     b. fluid from the prostate gland.
     c. sperm.
    *d. all of the above.

13. The _____, which synthesize and secrete sex hormones, are located in the connective tissue between the seminiferous tubules (p. 125).

     a. morphus glands
     b. seminal vesicles
     c. epididymal tubules
    *d. interstitial cells

14. The term *seminiferous* means (p. 125):

    a. life giving.
    *b. seed bearing.
    c. life supporting.
    d. tightly coiled.

15. Contractions during ejaculation move sperm out of the epididymis and into the _____, which empty into the ejaculatory ducts (p. 125).

    a. seminal vesicles
    b. seminiferous tubules
    *c. vasa deferentia
    d. Cowper's glands

16. Which of the following is (are) part of male anatomy (p. 125)?

    a. Bartholin's gland
    b. mons pubis
    c. cervix
    *d. vas deferens

17. The acidity of the vagina (p. 125):

    a. is neutralized by a combination of urine mixed with semen.
    *b. can be fatal to sperm.
    c. can lead to infections if it is too high.
    d. all of the above.

18. Sperm account for about _____ of the total volume of semen (p. 125).

    *a. 1 percent
    b. 20 percent
    c. 50 percent
    d. 90 percent

19. Women may become impregnated from sperm in fluid from the _____, prior to male ejaculation (p. 125).

    a. prostate gland
    *b. Cowper's gland
    c. epididymis
    d. seminal vesicles

20. The seminal vesicles are located (p. 126):

    a. directly beneath the glans.
    *b. on either side of the bladder.
    c. inside the scrotum at the base of the testes.
    d. on either side of the spermatic cord.

21. In the _____, fluid combines with sperm to produce semen, which enters the urethra (p. 126).

    *a. prostate gland
    b. Bartholin's gland
    c. frenulum
    d. corpus cavernosa

22. The prostate gland (p. 126):

    a. is about the size of a large pea.
    b. consists of three layers of spongy tissue.
    *c. surrounds the urethra at the base of the bladder.
    d. none of the above.

23. What structure is at the base of the bladder and expels its alkaline fluid into the urethra at the moment of ejaculation (p. 126)?

    a. Cowper's glands
    b. seminal vesicle
    c. prepuce
    *d. prostate gland

24. The primary function of the prostate gland is to (p. 126):

    a. store sperm.
    b. supply fluid to increase acidity in the urethra.
    *c. supply much of the seminal fluid.
    d. supply male sex hormones.

25. The Cowper's gland secretes a fluid that (p. 126):

    a. regulates the temperature in the urethra.
    b. may increase the ability of sperm to swim when deposited in the vagina.
    *c. may help neutralize the acidic effect of urine in the urethra.
    d. all of the above.

26. The seminal vesicles secrete a fluid that provides sperm with _____ and _____ acidity in the vagina (pp. 125–126).

    *a. energy; neutralizes
    b. the ability to coagulate; neutralizes
    c. energy; increases
    d. the ability to coagulate; increases

27. The function of the urethra in the male is to (p. 127):

    a. convey urine.
    b. convey semen.
    c. store sperm.
    *d. both a and b.

28. The human penis consists of _____ that provide it with the ability to become erect (p. 127).

    *a. three cylinders of spongy tissue
    b. flexible cartilage
    c. an intricate series of bones
    d. five bulbous glands

29. The _____ is a strip of skin on the underside where the glans meets the body of the penis (p. 127).

    a. corona
    b. glans
    *c. frenulum
    d. shaft

30. During male circumcision, the _____ is surgically removed (p. 127).

    *a. foreskin
    b. corona
    c. inguinal fold
    d. all of the above

31. The urethra of the human male is contained in the (p. 127):

    a. corpus cavernosum.
    b. ancillary cavity.
    c. coronal cytoplasm.
    *d. corpus spongiosum.

32. The rigidity and stiffness of the penis when erect is due to (p. 127):

    a. tightening of the cremaster muscle.
    b. tightening of muscles in the groin.
    *c. dilation of blood vessels, which become filled with blood.
    d. an intricate series of bones.

33. The foreskin of the penis is also called the (p. 127):

    a. corona.
    b. frenulum.
    c. glans.
    *d. prepuce.

34. The penis is most sensitive (p. 127):

    a. along the shaft.
    b. at the base near the scrotum.
    *c. at the glans.
    d. along the underside of the shaft.

35. On the average, an erect penis is _____ inches long (p. 128).

   a. 2.5
   b. 4.8
   *c. 6.3
   d. 7.9

36. Penis size is highly related to the (p. 128):

   a. length of the man's nose.
   b. height of the man.
   c. diameter of the man's thumb.
   *d. none of the above.

37. The ovaries are similar to the testes in that both (p. 128):

   a. develop from the same tissue.
   b. produce reproductive cells.
   c. secrete hormones.
   *d. all of the above.

38. The ovaries of the human female primarily secrete (p. 128):

   *a. estrogens and progesterone.
   b. testosterone.
   c. enzymes.
   d. luteinizing hormone.

39. The bundles that consist of an ovum, nutrients, and hormone-secreting cells are called ovarian (p. 129):

   *a. follicles.
   b. cysts.
   c. tubules.
   d. fimbria.

40. Each fallopian tube is about _____ inches long (p. 129).

   a. two
   *b. four
   c. six
   d. eight

41. After the ovum moves into the fallopian tube, tiny hairlike structures called _____ help transport it toward the uterus (p. 129).

   *a. cilia
   b. fimbria
   c. whorfs
   d. none of the above

42. When fertilization occurs, it usually takes place in the (p. 129):

    a. uterus.
  *b. upper third of the fallopian tubes.
    c. space between the ovaries and the fallopian tubes.
    d. ovary.

43. The ovum is transported through the fallopian tubes by (p. 129):

    a. tiny muscles in the fallopian tubes.
    b. a fluid secreted by the fallopian tubes.
  *c. hairlike structures in the fallopian tubes.
    d. none of the above.

44. The uterus is (p. 130):

  *a. suspended in the pelvic cavity by ligaments.
    b. composed of striated muscle.
    c. a thin-walled muscular tube.
    d. located between the vagina and the cervix.

45. Womb is another name for the (p. 130):

    a. vulva.
    b. cervix.
  *c. uterus.
    d. vagina.

46. Which of the following is the most internal layer that lines the uterine cavity (p. 130)?

    a. myometrium
    b. perimetrium
    c. mucosal layer
  *d. endometrium

47. The portion of the uterus that is called the _____ contains glands that secrete varying amounts of mucus (p. 130).

  *a. cervix
    b. Gräfenberg spot
    c. perimetrium
    d. clitoral hood

48. The vagina is (p. 131):

  *a. a thin-walled muscular tube.
    b. a sphincter muscle.
    c. composed of thick tissue layers.
    d. lined with an endometrium.

49. Particularly the _____ of the vagina contain(s) few touch and pressure receptors (p. 131).

    *a. inner two-thirds
    b. outer two-thirds
    c. inner one-third
    d. outer one-third

50. According to Perry and Whipple, the Gräfenberg spot is (p. 131):

    *a. located about halfway between the pubic bone and cervix.
    b. sensitive only to very soft stroking.
    c. very near the cervix.
    d. present only in some women.

51. Which of the following statements about the Gräfenberg spot is true (p. 131)?

    a. Stimulation of the spot leads to ejaculation in most women.
    *b. Perry and Whipple located the spot in every woman they tested.
    c. The spot can usually be readily stimulated by intercourse in the missionary position.
    d. all of the above.

52. It is hypothesized that some women ejaculate a fluid that originates in a rudimentary female _____ upon stimulation of the Gräfenberg spot (p. 131).

    a. Bartholin's gland
    b. Cowper's gland
    c. seminal vesicle
    *d. prostate gland

53. The term *vulva* refers to _____ of the female (p. 133).

    *a. all the external genitals
    b. all the internal genitals
    c. the perineum
    d. the labia majora and minora

54. The mons pubis (p. 133):

    *a. is a cushion of fatty tissue.
    b. is hairless.
    c. has more touch receptors than the clitoris.
    d. is found in both males and females.

55. The outer lips of the vulva are called the (p. 133):

    a. labia minora.
    *b. labia majora.
    c. mons pubis.
    d. Bartholin's folds.

56. The inner lips of the vulva are (p. 133):

    *a. hairless.
     b. more concentrated with sensory receptors than the clitoris.
     c. thicker than the outer lips.
     d. none of the above.

57. In general, the _____ is most erotically sensitive of the following body parts in the female (p. 134).

     a. labia majora
    *b. clitoris
     c. vaginal introitus
     d. mons pubis

58. The clitoris is similar to the penis in that both (p. 134):

     a. contain the urethra.
    *b. develop from the same tissue during prenatal growth.
     c. contain the corpus spongiosum.
     d. all of the above.

59. The _____ is a ring or fold of connective tissue at the vaginal opening in most new-born girls (p. 134).

    *a. hymen
     b. perineum
     c. clitoris
     d. introitus

60. The slang term for the hymen is (p. 134):

     a. pussy.
    *b. cherry.
     c. bearded clam.
     d. Georgia peach.

61. Which of the following statements about the hymen is true (p. 135)?

     a. First intercourse for a woman is usually painful because of rupture of the hymen.
     b. The presence of the hymen is usually a reliable indicator of virginity.
     c. Its purpose is partially to block the entrance of the vagina to retain menstrual fluid.
    *d. none of the above.

62. It has been suggested that when exercised, the pubococcygeus muscle can (p. 135):

     a. increase sexual responsiveness.
     b. help prevent urinary incontinence.
     c. produce pleasurable sensations.
    *d. all of the above.

63. The main purpose of Kegel exercises is to (p. 135):

    a. reduce anxiety during sexual arousal.
    b. decrease the incidence of urinary infection.
  *c. improve genital muscle tone.
    d. none of the above.

64. The breasts are composed primarily of (p. 135):

    a. smooth muscle.
    b. striated muscle.
  *c. fatty tissue.
    d. touch and pressure receptors.

65. Responsiveness to stimulation of the breasts is influenced primarily by (p. 135):

  *a. learning.
    b. the number of touch and pressure receptors in the breast.
    c. the size of the breasts.
    d. whether or not the woman has had a child.

66. The practice of touching mouths together for erotic pleasure is (p. 136):

    a. found primarily in sexually permissive societies.
    b. done purely for erotic reasons.
  *c. not universal.
    d. a custom that originated in France.

67. The body has _____ main types of glands (p. 136).

  *a. two
    b. four
    c. six
    d. eight

68. Sweat glands, salivary glands, mammary glands, and digestive glands are examples of _____ glands (p. 136).

    a. endocrine
    b. hormonal
  *c. exocrine
    d. parasympathetic

69. The _____ lie(s) on top of the kidneys (p. 136).

  *a. adrenal glands
    b. bladder
    c. pituitary gland
    d. testes

70. The pituitary gland is largely controlled by the (p. 136):

    a. thalamus.
  *b. hypothalamus.
    c. medulla.
    d. limbic system.

71. Which of the following are endocrine glands (p. 137)?

    a. prostate gland
  *b. testes
    c. Cowper's gland
    d. sweat glands

72. Luteinizing hormone stimulates (p. 137):

  *a. ovulation.
    b. the ovarian follicles to mature.
    c. sperm production in the testes.
    d. lactation.

73. Prolactin and oxytocin are hormones from the pituitary gland that are important in (p. 137):

  *a. the production of breast milk.
    b. stimulation of sperm production.
    c. inducing ovarian follicles to mature.
    d. causing breast size to change.

74. _____ stimulates sperm production (p. 137).

    a. Vasoactive Intestinal Peptite (VIP)
  *b. Follicle Stimulating Hormone (FSH)
    c. Dopamine
    d. Prolactine

75. Excessive estrogen seems to _____ sexual desire in men _____ in women (p. 138).

  *a. reduce; and
    b. reduce; but not
    c. increase; and
    d. increase; but not

76. The major difference between male and female sex-hormone secretion lies in the _____ of secretion (p. 139).

    a. amount
  *b. pattern
    c. relative proportion
    d. none of the above

77. Sexual desire in females is correlated with levels of (p. 139):

    a. androgen.
    *b. testosterone.
    c. estrogen.
    d. progesterone.

78. Which of the following sequences in the menstrual cycle is in the correct order (p. 140)?

    a. ovulation, follicular phase, luteal phase, premenstrual phase, menstruation
    b. ovulation, follicular phase, premenstrual phase, luteal phase, menstruation
    c. follicular phase, ovulation, premenstrual phase, luteal phase, menstruation
    *d. follicular phase, ovulation, luteal phase, premenstrual phase, menstruation

79. The initial onset of the menstrual cycle is called (p. 140):

    a. menopause.
    b. mittelschmerz.
    c. dysmenorrhea.
    *d. menarche.

80. The menstrual cycle can be conceptualized as a series of _____ processes (p. 140).

    a. three separate
    b. four separate
    *c. five overlapping
    d. six overlapping

81. The complete menstrual cycle generally ranges from _____ to _____ days (p. 140).

    a. 21; 29
    *b. 21; 35
    c. 25; 39
    d. 25; 45

82. A woman produces about _____ of estrogen and progesterone over her entire life span (p. 140).

    a. one teaspoonful
    *b. two tablespoonsful
    c. one pint
    d. two pints

83. Which phase in the menstrual cycle is characterized by an increase in the level of progesterone (p. 140)?

    a. ovulation
    b. premenstrual phase
    *c. luteal phase
    d. follicular phase

84. About 18 hours after the LH surge, the mature follicle in the ovary ruptures and releases the developing ovum, a process called (p. 142):

     *a. ovulation.
     b. the luteal moment.
     c. premenstruation.
     d. menstruation.

85. The sharp twinge some women feel when the ovum ruptures from the ovary is called (p. 142):

     a. corpus luteum.
     b. PMS.
     *c. mittelschmerz.
     d. FSH surging.

86. Day 1 of the menstrual cycle refers to the (p. 142):

     a. onset of the growth of a new follicle.
     b. release of an egg from the ovary.
     *c. first day in which menstrual blood appears.
     d. none of the above.

87. The brain and the spinal cord make up the _____ nervous system (p. 143).

     *a. central
     b. peripheral
     c. autonomic
     d. sympathetic

88. The process of becoming sexually aroused is predominated by the _____ nervous system (p. 143).

     *a. parasympathetic
     b. sympathetic
     c. central
     d. parallel

89. Ejaculation is carried out primarily by the _____ nervous system (p. 143).

     a. parasympathetic
     b. central
     c. parallel
     *d. sympathetic

90. The technical name for the experience of the "point of no return" in male sexual response is (p. 144):

     *a. emission.
     b. ejaculation.
     c. vesticulation.
     d. activation.

91. Human sexual responses such as ejaculation, erection, and vaginal lubrication are influenced by _____ centers in the brain (p. 144).

    *a. lower
    b. central
    c. higher
    d. uppermost

92. The _____, although only the size of a marble, appears to be the motivational and emotional control center in the brain (p. 144).

    a. thalamus
    *b. hypothalamus
    c. cerebellum
    d. forebrain

93. Experiments with the _____ centers in the brain were first described by Olds and Milner (p. 147).

    a. pain
    b. masochism
    c. stress
    *d. pleasure

94. The _____ is involved in the sense of smell in most species (p. 148).

    a. reticular activating system
    *b. limbic system
    c. hypothalamus
    d. cerebrum

95. Which of the following statements about breast cancer is true (p. 149)?

    a. Fear of breast loss often outweighs fear of remaining malignancy or death.
    b. It is one of the more common forms of cancer.
    c. It primarily afflicts women rather than men.
    *d. All of the above.

96. Routine breast self-examination (p. 151):

    a. should be supplemented with mammograms after age 35.
    b. results in the diagnosis of over 90 percent of all breast cancers.
    c. increases early detection and the chances of survival.
    *d. all of the above.

97. The most common treatment for breast cancer is _____, followed by chemotherapy and/or radiation treatment (p. 152).

    a. radical mastectomy
    *b. modified radical mastectomy
    c. mammography
    d. breastectomy

98. Which of the following is false about mammography (p. 152)?

     a. It is an X-ray technique.
    *b. The procedure is quite painful.
     c. Most women in their 40s should have one every other year.
     d. It involves placing the breast between sheets of clear plastic.

99. Witkin, a sex therapist who has had two mastectomies, recommends that (p. 153):

     a. husbands should deal with a spouse's mastectomy in a matter-of-fact way.
     b. husbands should avoid displays of concern so as to discourage dependency.
    *c. sexual relations resume within a week after surgery or as soon as the patient feels
        physically able.
     d. mastectomy patients use a prosthesis (false breast) during intercourse.

100. Breast cancer is more likely for women who (p. 153):

     *a. are from families with a history of breast cancer.
     b. have their first child before the age of 30.
     c. begin menstruation relatively late.
     d. are thin.

101. If there is no evidence that the breast cancer has spread beyond the tumor, the surgical
     operation called _____ may be performed, in which the malignant tumor and some
     surrounding tissue is removed (p. 153).

     a. radical mastectomy
     b. modified radical mastectomy
    *c. lumpectomy
     d. mammography

102. Annual PAP tests are advised for women (p. 153):

     a. beginning in their late teens or when they become sexually active.
     b. at least once a year.
     c. only if they have a family history of cervical cancer.
    *d. both a and b.

103. Cervical cancer is more likely to strike women who (p. 153):

     a. begin having sexual intercourse at a young age.
     b. have a large number of sexual partners.
     c. have certain STDs.
    *d. all of the above.

104. Cervical cancer (p. 153):

     a. has a fairly high five-year survival rate for women if diagnosed and treated early.
     b. may be related to the presence of genital herpes and the papilloma virus.
     c. can be detected with a PAP test.
    *d. all of the above.

105. Which of the following is true about hysterectomy (p. 154)?

    a. Intercourse is impossible after a hysterectomy.
    b. After a hysterectomy, multiple orgasms are more likely to occur.
    c. Hysterectomy affects a woman's sexual response only in a psychological way.
   *d. As long as the ovaries remain intact, a woman's hormone levels are not affected.

106. Cancer of the prostate gland (p. 155):

    a. is much more likely in black American than white American men.
    b. is the second leading cause of cancer deaths in men.
    c. often leads to the symptom of frequent urination, particularly at night.
   *d. all of the above.

107. Annual prostate exams are recommended for men (p. 155):

    a. from the time they reach their late teens.
    b. who are sexually active.
   *c. over 40 years old.
    d. none of the above.

108. _____ cancer strikes at a younger age than most other cancers, usually afflicting men between the ages of 20 and 35 (p. 156).

    a. Lung
    b. Rectal
    c. Prostate
   *d. Testicular

109. Which of the following is true about diabetes (p. 157)?

   *a. Many diabetic men eventually develop erectile difficulties.
    b. Women with insulin-dependent diabetes report major problems with their sexuality.
    c. Type I diabetes begins in adulthood.
    d. All of the above.

Essay Questions

110. Briefly describe the functions of the seminiferous tubules, the epididymis, the seminal vesicles, and the prostate gland (pp. 125–126).

111. Summarize the anatomy and physiological functioning of the penis (p. 127).

112. What is the relationship between penis length and women's sexual arousal (p. 128)?

113. Describe the functions of the ovaries, fallopian tubes, uterus, vagina, and clitoris (pp. 128–131).

114. Discuss the Gräfenberg spot. How can the Gräfenberg spot be located in a woman? Is there scientific support for its existence (p. 131)?

115. Discuss the hymen. What are some myths associated with it (pp. 134–135)?

116. What are the PC muscles? How can they be strengthened? Why would anyone want to strengthen the PC muscles (p. 135)?

117. List and describe the phases of the menstrual cycle (pp. 139–142).

118. Explain the relationship of the nervous system to sexual responsiveness (pp. 143–145).

119. Discuss the effect of a hysterectomy on a woman's sexual responding (p. 154).

Identification

For the figures that follow, write the name of each lettered structure on the correspondingly lettered blank line following each figure.

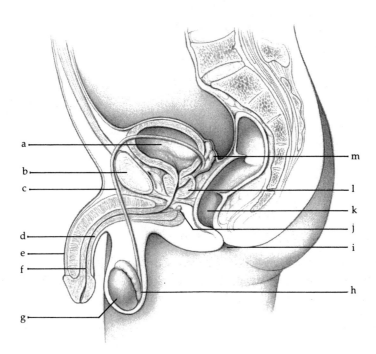

The Male Genital System

a. _____   h. _____

b. _____   i. _____

c. _____   j. _____

d. _____   k. _____

e. _____   l. _____

f. _____   m. _____

g. _____

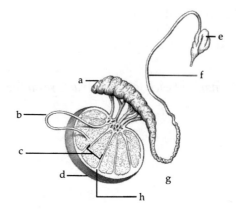

**Cross-Section of the Internal Structure
of a Testis**

a. _____   e. _____

b. _____   f. _____

c. _____   g. _____

d. _____   h. _____

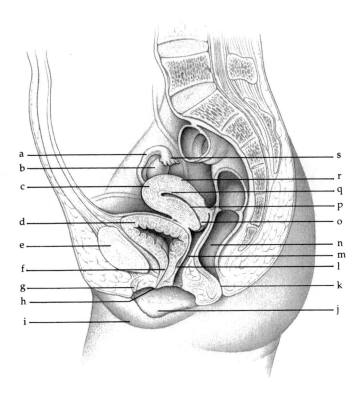

The Female Genital System

a. _____

b. _____

c. _____

d. _____

e. _____

f. _____

g. _____

h. _____

i. _____

j. _____

k. _____

l. _____

m._____

n. _____

o. _____

p. _____

q. _____

r. _____

s. _____

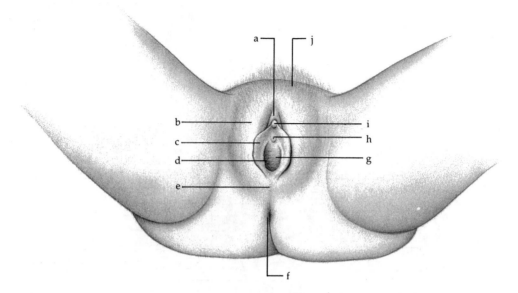

The Vulva

a. _____   f. _____

b. _____   g. _____

c. _____   h. _____

d. _____   i. _____

e. _____   j. _____

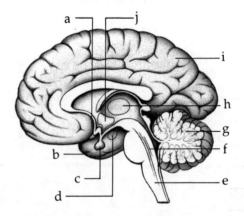

Side View of the Human Brain

a. _____   e. _____   i. _____

b. _____   f. _____   j. _____

c. _____   g. _____

d. _____   h. _____

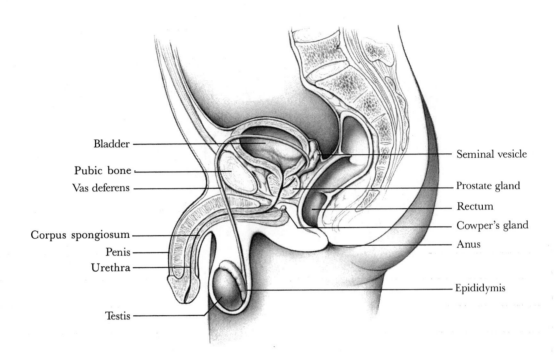

Bladder

Pubic bone

Vas deferens

Corpus spongiosum

Penis

Urethra

Testis

Seminal vesicle

Prostate gland

Rectum

Cowper's gland

Anus

Epididymis

The Male Genital System

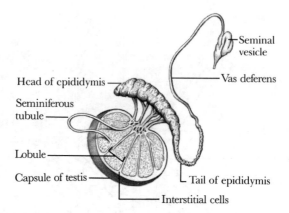

Head of epididymis

Seminiferous
tubule

Lobule

Capsule of testis

Seminal
vesicle

Vas deferens

Tail of epididymis

Interstitial cells

**Cross-Section of the Internal Structure
of a Testis**

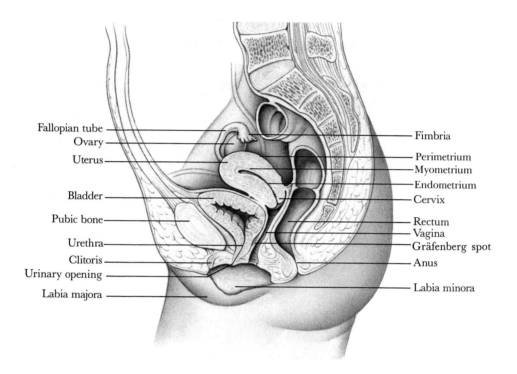

Fallopian tube

Ovary

Uterus

Bladder

Pubic bone

Urethra

Clitoris

Urinary opening

Labia majora

Fimbria

Perimetrium

Myometrium

Endometrium

Cervix

Rectum

Vagina

Gräfenberg spot

Anus

Labia minora

The Female Genital System

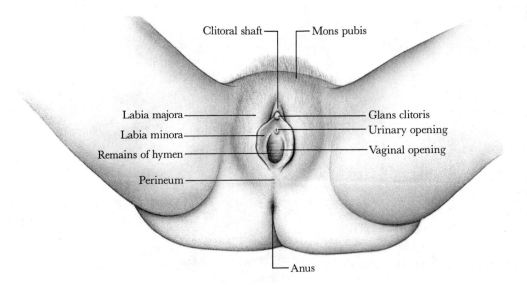

The Vulva

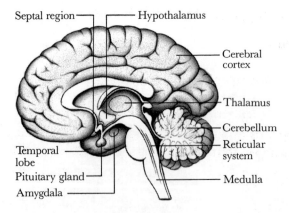

Side View of the Human Brain

Multiple-Choice Questions

1. Human sexual responses are a function of (p. 162):

    a. biological capacities.
    b. psychological processes.
    c. cultural experiences.
    *d. all of the above.

2. The specific objects and acts we find sexually arousing appear to be (p. 162):

    a. inborn.
    *b. conditioned by culture and experience.
    c. invariant over time.
    d. all of the above.

3. The capacity for sexual arousal is (p. 162):

    *a. innate.
    b. learned from peers.
    c. acquired by experience.
    d. acquired from one's specific culture.

4. Erotic attraction to specific stimuli is (p. 163):

    a. culturally conditioned.
    b. learned from peers.
    c. an example of classical and operant conditioning.
    *d. all of the above.

5 The _____ model explains how a neutral object can acquire sexual value simply by being paired with another object that already has sexual value (p. 164).

    *a. classical-conditioning
    b. operant-conditioning
    c. two-stage theory of emotions
    d. none of the above

6. You become aroused when you see a stranger driving a particular car because your dating partner drives the same car. Your response is best explained using the (p. 164):

    *a. classical-conditioning model.
    b. operant-conditioning model.
    c. two-stage model of emotion.
    d. none of the above.

7. You become aroused by someone who compliments you on your intelligence. Your response is best explained using the (p. 164):

    a. classical-conditioning model.
    *b. operant-conditioning model.
    c. two-stage model of emotion.
    d. James-Lange model.

8. Arousal acquired as a function of having behavior rewarded, ignored, or punished is best explained using the (p. 164):

    a. classical-conditioning model.
    *b. operant-conditioning model.
    c. two-stage model of emotion.
    d. altruistic model

9. You become aroused by those who punish you rather than those who reward you. Your response is best explained using the (p. 164):

    a. classical-conditioning model.
    b. operant-conditioning model.
    *c. two-stage model of emotion.
    d. none of the above.

10. According to the two-stage theory of emotion (p. 164):

    *a. we first experience physiological arousal and then search for an explanation.
    b. we first interpret an event and that interpretation leads to arousal.
    c. physiological arousal and the interpretation of that arousal occur simultaneously.
    d. whether we experience arousal before or after an event is interpreted depends on the environment.

11. According to Berscheid and Walster's (1974) two-stage model, any source of _____ can, under certain circumstances, increase the likelihood an individual will label his or her feelings as love or attraction (p. 164).

    a. relaxation
    *b. arousal
    c. alpha brain waves
    d. discrepancy

12. In the Dutton and Aron study conducted on the Capilano River in British Columbia, Canada, sexual attraction was greatest when the interviewer was (p. 165):

    a. male and the bridge was arousal inducing.
    b. male and the bridge was not arousal inducing.
    *c. female and the bridge was arousal inducing.
    d. female and the bridge was not arousal inducing.

13. The conclusion drawn from experiments testing the two-stage model of sexual arousal is that (p. 165):

    *a. arousal, regardless of its source, increases the likelihood that the aroused person will be attracted to another person.
    b. arousal is purely a matter of chance.
    c. males are more likely subsequently to seek out their female interviewers than are females to seek out their male interviewers.
    d. swaying bridges are more arousing to females than to males.

14. According to Berscheid and Walster, in appropriate circumstances, physiological arousal, regardless of its source, (p. 166):

    a. will increase the likelihood that a person will be attracted to an appropriate other if the other person is also aroused.
    *b. will increase the likelihood that a person will be attracted to an appropriate other.
    c. will decrease the likelihood that a person will be attracted to an appropriate other even if that other person is normally considered attractive.
    d. do none of the above.

15. Misattribution of arousal is more likely to occur when a male is experiencing (p. 166):

    a. low physiological arousal and does not know the source of arousal.
    b. loneliness and knows the source of arousal.
    c. hunger and knows the person nearby.
    *d. high physiological arousal but does not know the source of arousal.

16. During the initial stages of a relationship, the arousal from sexual attraction is likely to be accompanied by anxiety, which increases the level of the hormone (p. 166):

    *a. epinephrine.
    b. estrus.
    c. pheromone.
    d. estrogen.

17. As a relationship becomes more enduring, a diminishing of love might be perceived. This may result from (p. 166):

    a. becoming more aware of one's partner's faults.
    b. becoming tired of sexual arousal.
    *c. a lessening of anxiety, and thus a lessening of arousal.
    d. none of the above.

18. Human females differ from females of other species in that (p. 167):

    *a. the females of most nonhuman species are interested in sexual intercourse only when they are fertile.
    b. in human females the appearance of blood signals a time of fertility.
    c. human females are usually aroused by only one male.
    d. all of the above.

19. Which of the following is *not* true about sexual responding of human females (p. 167)?

   a. Human females are continuously capable of strong sexual arousal.
   *b. Human females are most receptive during estrus.
   c. Human females are sexually receptive only one-seventh of the time.
   d. Human females are sexually receptive even when they are not fertile.

20. _____ do not experience an estrus cycle (p. 167).

   a. Dogs
   b. Apes
   c. Cats
   *d. Humans

21. In complex species, sexual arousal has (p. 167):

   a. reproductive functions.
   b. nonreproductive functions.
   c. the potential to form the basis for a continuing bond.
   *d. all of the above.

22. Among human females, the discharge of blood from the uterus occurs at a time of (p. 167):

   *a. minimal fertility.
   b. maximal fertility.
   c. minimal sexual receptiveness.
   d. maximal sexual receptiveness.

23. Some parts of the body are more sensitive to touch than others. The most sensitive areas are called (p. 168):

   a. copula centers.
   b. erroneous zones.
   c. aphrodisiac areas.
   *d. erogenous zones.

24. The only type of stimulation that can produce a reflexive response in the body that is independent of higher brain centers is (p. 168):

   a. taste.
   *b. touch.
   c. sound.
   d. sights.

25. An example of a nonhuman organism that is most strongly affected by pheromones is the (p. 168):

   *a. moth.
   b. dog.
   c. cow.
   d. monkey.

26. In which of the following species do pheromones seem to have an irresistible and predictable effect on behavior (p. 168)?

    a. monkeys
    b. humans
    *c. insects
    d. all of the above

27. Which of the following statements about our sense of touch is *not* true (p. 168)?

    a. It is the only type of stimulation that can produce a reflexive response independent of higher brain centers.
    b. Receptors for touch and pressure are widely but unevenly distributed throughout the body.
    *c. Unlike sight and hearing, it isn't necessary for adequate human development until several years after birth.
    d. The areas where it is most highly concentrated are called the erogenous zones.

28. Bacteria that produce strong vaginal odors are best and most safely eliminated by (p. 169):

    a. vaginal deodorants.
    *b. regular bathing.
    c. use of perfumes.
    d. taking antibiotics.

29. The major objection to vaginal deodorants is that (p. 169):

    a. they are harmful to delicate genital tissue.
    b. they are unnecessary.
    *c. both a and b.
    d. none of the above; vaginal deodorants are recommended by most doctors.

30. Evidence suggests that human evaluation of bodily odors as pleasant or unpleasant is (p. 169):

    a. innate.
    *b. learned.
    c. similar to that of animals.
    d. an instinctive defense against harmful substances.

31. Which of the following is true about human response to bodily smells as unpleasant (p. 169)?

    a. This response seems to be consistent across cultures, so it is probably innate.
    *b. It is probably learned, given that young children do not appear to be troubled by the smell of bodily secretions.
    c. This response is consistent within families, so it is probably inherited.
    d. None of the above.

32. With respect to vision, which of the following is true (p. 169):

    *a. Across cultures, sight seems to play a more central role in evaluating attractiveness for women than for men.
    b. Humans have innate preferences for specific visual sights as erotic stimuli.
    c. Both a and b.
    d. The perception of physical beauty in others is probably determined by genetic factors in ourselves.

33. Which of the following senses probably affects sexual arousal less than others (p. 169)?

    a. touch
    *b. taste
    c. vision
    d. smell
    e. hearing

34. In their examination of what college students rate as important in judging male and female physical attractiveness, Franzoi and Herzog (1987) found generally that (p. 169):

    a. women stressed men's body functions related to sexuality.
    b. men stressed women's physical condition or endurance.
    *c. women stressed men's physical condition or endurance.
    d. both a and b.

35. Evolutionary theorists have suggested that (p. 169):

    a. human females place extreme emphasis on males' waist size.
    b. human females place comparatively strong importance on males' noses.
    c. human males are attracted by females' buttocks.
    *d. human males are attracted by females' complexions.

36. Generating sounds during sexual interaction (p. 169):

    a. is fairly rare for human males.
    *b. may facilitate orgasm.
    c. is fairly rare for primates.
    d. is common among human females and has been studied thoroughly.

37. In a study conducted about a quarter of a century ago, imagining each of 19 erotic themes led to _____ arousal among 42 married couples than did _____, especially for women (p. 170).

    *a. much greater; actual exposure to either erotic pictures or sexually stimulating stories
    b. somewhat greater; direct observation of a real couple having intercourse
    c. significantly less; direct observation of a real couple having intercourse
    d. significantly less; actual exposure to erotic pictures

38. Which of the following is true about erotic fantasies (p. 170)?

     a. A person's first erotic fantasies are usually about strangers.
     b. Sexual fantasies begin around age 8 in children.
     c. Erotic fantasies seldom affect the formation of actual sexual goals.
    *d. Erotic fantasies can be a major influence on sexual identity and orientation.

39. The sexual fantasies of late adolescents (p. 170):

     a. are rather vague, with unclear definitions of sexual activity.
    *b. are well-defined, specific erotic scripts.
     c. occur only when the person is alone.
     d. none of the above.

40. Freud and Reich believed that sexual fantasies (p. 170):

     a. were signs of emotional immaturity.
     b. were due to sexual frustration.
     c. were normal and indicative of psychological health.
    *d. both a and b.

41. Contemporary clinicians view sexual fantasy as (p. 171):

     a. a sign of emotional maladjustment.
     b. a sign of sexual frustration.
    *c. something that can enhance feelings of arousal and help one feel sexier.
     d. both a and b.

42. Males tend to report _____ than do females (p. 171).

    *a. more frequent sexual fantasies
     b. less frequent sexual fantasies
     c. fantasies that involve more emotional involvement
     d. more complex and vivid fantasies

43. In studying the relationship between engaging in sexual fantasies and sexual satisfaction, Cado and Leitenberg (1990) found that people who reported feeling (p. 171):

    *a. most guilty about having fantasies during intercourse were more sexually dissatisfied.
     b. guilty about having fantasies did not often have intercourse.
     c. least guilty about having fantasies during intercourse were more sexually dissatisfied.
     d. fortunate to have vivid fantasies were more sexually satisfied.

44. Sexual fantasies can be used to (p. 171):

     a. rehearse ways of approaching a person to whom we are attracted.
     b. consider the possible consequences of various behaviors.
     c. relive memories of previously rewarding sexual encounters.
    *d. all of the above.

45. Students receive their most accurate information about the reproductive aspects of sexuality from their (p. 173):

   a. mother.
   b. father.
   c. friends.
   *d. teachers.

46. Data suggest that people receive _____ of their information about sex from their parents (p. 173).

   *a. relatively little
   b. the vast majority
   c. about 50 percent
   d. none

47. The organ most often omitted from sex education materials is the (p. 173):

   a. penis.
   *b. clitoris.
   c. vagina.
   d. uterus.

48. One reason parents may not discuss the clitoris with their daughters is that (p. 173):

   a. they assume the term will be learned in school.
   b. they know little about the clitoris themselves.
   *c. it does not have a socially approved function.
   d. they hope that their daughters will learn about it through experience.

49. Which of the following statements concerning sexual development is true (p. 173)?

   a. Females begin to masturbate at a younger age than do males.
   b. Females experience orgasm at a younger age than do males.
   c. Females learn about their sexual response systems earlier than males.
   *d. Females develop sooner than males do physiologically.

50. In a study of family communication with 363 college students and their parents, Fisher found that (p. 175):

   a. males who had not discussed sex with their parents had more accurate sexual information than those who did.
   b. parents and students closely agreed as to how much sexual discussion actually took place between them.
   c. contraceptive use is more consistent among erotophilic students.
   *d. there was no relationship among responses to measures of parent-child communication and the sexual activity of the students.

51. A study of the relationship of parental attitudes toward sex, family communication, and adolescent sexual activity found that (p. 175):

    a. parents with restrictive attitudes more likely had adolescent females who were sexually active.

    b. parents with permissive attitudes more likely had adolescent females who were sexually active.

    c. males who discussed sex with their parents were more likely using contraceptives.

  *d. both b and c.

52. Studies have shown that in relation to communication about sex between parents and their offspring (p. 175):

    a. parents and their offspring give similar accounts as to the extent of communication that has taken place.

  *b. parents and their offspring give different accounts as to the extent of communication that has taken place.

    c. in comparison to offspring, parents overestimate the extent of communication that has taken place.

    d. all of the above.

53. _____ parents report giving less information about sex to their children than do _____ parents (p. 176).

    a. erotophilic; erotophobic

  *b. erotophobic; erotophilic

    c. authoritarian; permissive

    d. authoritative; authoritarian

54. Compared to erotophobic students, erotophilic students (pp. 176–177):

    a. are more likely to report contraceptive use.

    b. use contraception more consistently when they have sex.

    c. drew more details relevant to sexual anatomy.

  *d. all of the above.

55. Responding "yes" to the statement, "Erotica is filthy," on the Sexual Opinion Survey (SOS) is indicative of a respondent who is (p. 177):

  *a. erotophobic.

    b. erotophilic.

    c. pherophobic.

    d. misophilic.

56. Those high in sex guilt are likely to (p. 177):

    a. masturbate more frequently.
    b. enjoy their sexual desires.
   *c. perceive premarital sex as immoral.
    d. disapprove of childhood sex play.

57. Which of the following statements concerning sex guilt is correct (p. 177)?

   *a. It is assumed that individuals who feel guilty about sex were punished for sexual interest during their childhood.
    b. Teens high in sex guilt are more likely to use contraceptives regularly.
    c. Males score higher on measures of sex guilt than females do.
    d. Males who feel guilty about sex have orgasm more quickly.

58. Females in western cultures seem to score higher than males in measures of sex guilt because (p. 178):

    a. differences in guilt feelings reflect brain differences.
    b. they are more likely than males to contract STDs.
   *c. parents may be more restrictive in training their daughters.
    d. the sexual desires of females are lower than those of males.

59. Several studies have found that people high in sex guilt (p. 178):

    a. operate at higher levels of moral reasoning than do people with less sex guilt.
    b. are less likely to use effective contraceptives.
    c. operate at lower levels of moral reasoning than do people with less sex guilt.
   *d. both b and c.

60. Gerrard and Gibbons studied the relationship of sexual experience (not necessarily intercourse), sex guilt, and sexual moral reasoning. Their findings indicated that (p. 178):

    a. people high in sex guilt tend to seek out sexual experience.
   *b. experience is important in the development of sexual morality.
    c. sex guilt encourages women to use effective contraceptives.
    d. people high in sex guilt operate at higher levels of moral reasoning.

61. People who feel guilty about sex are *less* (p. 179):

    a. sexually active.
   *b. devout and constant in religious beliefs.
    c. offended by explicit sexual material.
    d. traditional in their beliefs about gender roles.

62. Compared to men, women are _____ capable of sexual arousal (p. 179).

    a. less
    b. more
   *c. equally
    d. less consistently

63. Gender differences in self-reported sexual arousal appear to stem primarily from the fact that (p. 179):

    a. men are more interested in sex than women are.
    b. women are more likely than men to attribute genital responses to sexual arousal.
    *c. women may underestimate their interest in erotica.
    d. none of the above.

64. Heiman found gender differences in response to erotic tape recordings in terms of (p. 180):

    a. heart rate.
    *b. self-report measures.
    c. sweating.
    d. pulse.

65. In Heiman's study of gender differences in response to erotic tape recordings, _____ reported _____ arousal than that measured by physiological recordings (p. 180):

    a. males; more.
    b. females; more.
    c. males; less.
    *d. females; less.

66. Self-report data have shown that, compared with males, females are _____ interested in and responsive to erotica, whereas physiological data have shown that, compared to males, females are _____ interested in and responsive to erotica (p. 180).

    a. more; less
    b. less; more
    *c. less; equally
    d. equally; less

67. Female error in self-reported arousal in Heiman's study was possibly due to cultural training and to (p. 180):

    a. sample bias—most participants were inexperienced sexually.
    *b. males' greater awareness than females of physical changes accompanying sexual arousal.
    c. the unreliability of self-report measures.
    d. all of the above.

68. Gender differences in self-reports of arousal to erotica probably result from (p. 180):

    a. self-report bias.
    b. the extent to which physical changes associated with sexual arousal are readily observable.
    c. actual gender differences in physiological arousal to erotica.
    *d. both a and b.
    e. all of the above.

69. Based on 900 hours of observations in bar settings, Perper (1985) concluded that _____ determine(s) the outcome of a casual contact in a singles' bar (p. 180).

    a. it is often men who
    *b. it is often women who
    c. both genders are equally likely to
    d. the amount of liquor consumed by a man and woman

70. Observations in singles' bar settings show initial interactions between men and women involving approach, (p. 180):

    *a. talk, turn, touch, and body synchronization.
    b. wink, offering a drink, asking to move to a private table.
    c. a man asking if a woman is alone, buying her a drink, asking her to come to his place.
    d. a woman asking if a man is alone, buying him a drink, asking him to come back to her place.

71. Based on observations Perper made in bar settings, which of the following is true about courtship (p. 181)?

    *a. Women tend to have a clearer understanding of courtship strategies than do men.
    b. In proceptive behavior, a man chooses a woman he is interested in. If the woman responds, a power transition may occur.
    c. In a parade behavior, a woman scans the room but does not make eye contact with anyone.
    d. In approach behavior, a man positions himself within two feet of a woman in order to initiate a conversation with her.

72. Proceptivity refers to (p. 181):

    a. a man's capacity to initiate and escalate a sexual interaction with a woman.
    *b. a woman's capacity to initiate and escalate a sexual interaction with a man.
    c. the week during a woman's menstrual cycle when she is most sexually responsive.
    d. none of the above.

73. In his study of courtship behavior, Perper found that (p. 181):

    *a. women engage in proceptive behavior, but men initiate sexual foreplay.
    b. men usually engage in proceptive behavior.
    c. women never engage in proceptive behavior.
    d. women always initiate sexual foreplay and men engage in proceptive behavior.

74. Moore (1985) investigated courtship behavior and found that (p. 181):

    a. men who signaled most often were most often approached by a woman.
    b. women who signaled least often were most often approached by a man.
    c. men who signaled least often were most often approached by another man.
    *d. women who signaled most often were most likely to be approached by a man.

75. Moore's observations of signaling by junior high school girls indicated that (p. 181):

    a. girls displayed more signals to boys than women did to men.
    *b. girls displayed fewer signals to men than women did to men.
    c. girls were more subtle and tentative in their signaling than were women.
    d. none of the above.

76. A study by Abbey on misperceptions of communication signals indicated that (p. 182):

    a. men are expected to be gatekeepers.
    b. more men than women report having had their friendliness misperceived as a sexual invitation.
    *c. neither men nor women perceived women's friendliness as indicating sexual intent.
    d. a signal of interest by a woman is more often a signal of a desire to have sex.

77. Muehlenhard and Cook's (1988) study concerned with participation in sexual intercourse and willingness to do so found that (p. 184):

    *a. more men than women reported engaging in sexual intercourse when not wishing to do so.
    b. more women than men reported engaging in sexual intercourse when not wishing to do so.
    c. men feel pressured to initiate sex.
    d. women seldom use the "token no."

78. The textbook's use of the phrase "token no" refers to (p. 184):

    a. men's unwillingness to accept the word "no" from women.
    *b. women saying "no" to sex when they really want to engage in it.
    c. men saying "no" to sex when they really want to engage in it.
    d. not agreeing as to whether to use birth control in a particular sexual encounter.

79. Three major reasons for the use of token no are (p. 184):

    a. practical, financial, and religious.
    b. financial, political, and inhibition related.
    c. political, manipulative, and aggression related.
    *d. practical, inhibition related and manipulative.

80. In reference to the use of token no, manipulative reasons include (p. 184):

    a. moral opinions.
    b. fear of getting pregnant.
    *c. the desire to be in control.
    d. fear of being promiscuous.

81. In reference to the use of token no, which of the following is *not* included in the category of inhibition-related reasons (p. 184)?

    a. religious feelings
    b. self-consciousness about one's body
    c. fear of physical discomfort
   *d. fear of contracting a sexually transmitted disease

82. Studies by Muehlenhard and colleagues that examined the use of token no found that (p. 184):

    a. men are seldom aware that women use the token no.
   *b. women who say no when they want to say yes at intermediate levels of traditionality in their sexual attitudes.
    c. women are culturally trained to initiate sex, no matter what.
    d. of the women who use the token no, very few indicated that practical reasons were important to their decision.

83. Which of the following is an issue to address in seeking to obtain informed consent for sexual intimacy with a potential partner (p. 185)?

    a. the level of relationship needed before becoming sexually intimate
    b. contraception will be dealt with
    c. one's beliefs about sexual exclusivity
   *d. all of the above

84. The textbook adheres to the ideal that success in handling "extrarelationship" attractions is best achieved by (p. 190):

    a. total monogamy.
    b. adultery.
    c. relative monogamy.
   *d. arriving at an agreement and then honoring it.

85. According to the textbook, after a couple has made a commitment to each other, they should engage in (p. 190):

    a. total monogamy.
    b. relative monogamy.
    c. open marriage.
   *d. attempts to honor whatever commitments or agreements they have made.

86. A couple has made a long-term commitment to one another. If either person feels attraction to a third person but does not want to act on it, the textbook authors recommend that the committed person do all of the following except (p. 190):

   *a. immediately telling the primary partner about this attraction to another.
    b. avoiding being alone with the third person until the attraction subsides.
    c. avoiding drinking much alcohol when the third person is around.
    d. thinking about ways of revitalizing the primary relationship.

Essay Questions

87. Your car skids on some ice as you and a good friend are returning from the library with books to work on a class project, but you get back to your apartment safely. As you begin to work on the project, you glance at each other and feel very attracted to each other for the first time. You begin to talk about your feelings for each other and end up getting little work done on the project that evening. Explain this sequence of events by the two-stage model of arousal (p. 164–167).

88. Describe the relationship of our senses and sexual arousal. How does our tactile (touch) sense differ from the other senses in its impact on sexual response (pp. 168–169)?

89. Why is kissing so potentially erotically powerful (p. 168)?

90. One of the functions of sexual arousal is to increase the likelihood of species reproduction. What are some other possible purposes of sexual arousal among humans (p. 167)?

91. Discuss fantasies and sexual arousal. What are some functions of fantasy? Are fantasies healthy or deviant (pp. 170–172)?

92. Discuss socialization for communicating about sex (pp. 173–174).

93. What are the differences between males and females in the process of communication of feelings (pp. 175–176)?

94. How are attitudes about sexuality (erotophilia versus erotophobia) and levels of sex guilt related to sexual behaviors and responses (pp. 176–178)?

95. Describe gender differences and similarities in response to erotic materials. Discuss the possible explanations for the differences (pp. 179–180).

96. Compare historical and contemporary views of the relationship between having sexual fantasies and psychological health (pp. 170–172).

97. How can interpersonal communications about personal and/or sexual feelings be enhanced (pp. 182–185)?

98. Assume that you have made a long-term commitment to your partner. After you have been involved for some time, you find yourself attracted to another person. Describe the textbook's suggestions for dealing with this situation. Then explain what you would do (pp. 188–190).

CHAPTER 7

Sexual Behavior

Multiple-Choice Questions

1. According to work by Kinsey, nocturnal orgasm, often accompanied by dreams, occurs (p. 196):

   a. only in males.
   b. primarily in females.
   c. primarily in people with sexual problems.
   *d. in both genders.

2. The Kinsey group found that males reported the highest frequency of nocturnal orgasm during their _____, but females reported the highest frequency of nocturnal orgasm during their _____ (p. 196).

   *a. late adolescence and early 20s; 40s
   b. early adolescence; early adolescence
   c. early 30s; early 20s
   d. early adolescence; late adolescence and early 20s

3. Wells (1986) found evidence that the percentage of young _____ reporting nocturnal orgasms may be _____ (p. 196).

   *a. women; increasing
   b. women; decreasing
   c. men; increasing
   d. men; decreasing

4. Masturbation is sometimes called (p. 197):

   *a. autoeroticism.
   b. cunnilingus.
   c. fellatio.
   d. analingus.

5. The function of nocturnal orgasm (p. 197):

   a. is to compensate for decreases in sexual outlets available when awake.
   b. is to parallel that of waking orgasm; as one increases, so does the other.
   *c. is not known at present.
   d. none of the above.

6. The most common form of sexual outlet reported by the majority of Americans is (p. 197):

   *a. masturbation.
    b. oral sex.
    c. nocturnal emission.
    d. coitus.

7. In the eighteenth century, Tissot theorized that semen was important for healthy bodily functioning and that (p. 197):

   *a. wasting it would weaken the body and produce illness.
    b. self-stimulation increased sperm production, resulting in better health.
    c. self-stimulation would cure impotency.
    d. none of the above.

8. Some nineteenth-century commentators considered people who masturbated to be (p. 198):

   *a. dangerous to society.
    b. normal.
    c. somewhat unusual.
    d. primarily single men.

9. Today the Roman Catholic church considers masturbation to be (p. 199):

   *a. a mortal sin.
    b. acceptable in moderation.
    c. acceptable for single people.
    a. undesirable but necessary.

10. Gagnon's study on contemporary parental views about masturbation found that _____ percent of the parents felt that their children's masturbation was acceptable, and _____ of them wanted their children to have a positive attitude toward masturbation (p. 199).

   *a. 60; one-third
    b. 90; most
    c. 5; one-third
    d. 20; one-quarter

11. Self-stimulation can function as (pp. 199–200):

    a. a reward for good behavior or solace after a difficult day.
    b. sexual release when a partner is unavailable or inappropriate.
    c. a source of self-knowledge about satisfying methods of stimulation.
   *d. all of the above.

12. At the start of ejaculation during masturbation, most men _____ penile stimulation, reporting that continued intense stimulation of the glans is _____ (p. 201).

   *a. decrease; unpleasant
    b. increase; pleasurable
    c. don't modify; desirable
    d. none of the above.

13. The average man reported to the Kinsey group that he ejaculated after stimulating himself for (p. 201):

    a. 30 to 60 seconds.
    *b. 2 to 3 minutes.
    c. 6 to 7 minutes.
    d. 10 to 12 minutes.

14. Masters and Johnson reported that most women in their research on masturbation preferred to (p. 202):

    *a. stimulate the entire mons area rather than concentrating exclusively on the clitoris.
    b. concentrate on the clitoris.
    c. stimulate the Gräfenberg spot.
    d. concentrate primarily on the breasts.
    e. reach orgasm through erotic fantasy with no direct stimulation of the genitals.

15. According to Masters and Johnson (1966), when women masturbate, vaginal penetration alone is _____ done (p. 202).

    a. almost always
    b. often
    *c. not frequently
    d. never

16. The average woman reported to the Kinsey group that she had an orgasm after stimulating herself for (p. 202):

    a. about 1 minute.
    *b. a little less than 4 minutes.
    c. a little more than 10 minutes.
    d. about 15 minutes.

17. In their survey of a wide variety of cultures, Ford and Beach (1951) found that kissing was mentioned in _____ cultures and accompanied sexual intercourse in _____ of them (p. 203).

    a. few; none
    *b. 21; 13
    c. 50; all
    d. most; all

18. Which of the following statements about kissing is true (p. 204)?

    *a. It can involve all the body senses.
    b. It is included among all societies in erotic interactions.
    c. It is not arousing because the lips, mouth, and tongue are not very sensitive.
    d. all of the above.

19. Kissing as an erotic activity is (p. 204):

    a. practiced in all known human cultures.
    b. in part a result of the pleasure of having all our senses stimulated.
    c. parallel to the sniffing and licking that many mammals practice upon meeting.
    *d. both b and c.
    e. none of the above.

20. Kissing may stimulate which of the following senses (p. 204)?

    a. smell
    b. taste
    c. hearing
    *d. all of the above

21. Historically, attitudes toward oral-genital sex have been negative. Today (p. 205):

    a. the incidence of oral sex is still low among adolescents.
    *b. acceptance of oral sex has increased significantly among married couples.
    c. the act is illegal only in Utah.
    d. it is more popular among black men than among white men.

22. Which of the following possibilities would tend *not* to be a common concern about oral-genital sex (p. 205)?

    *a. being arrested
    b. taking semen or vaginal secretions into the mouth
    c. exposure to excrement and germs
    d. odor and appearance of the genitals

23. Cunnilingus refers to (p. 205):

    *a. oral stimulation of the female's genitals.
    b. oral stimulation of the male's genitals.
    c. deep kissing.
    d. oral stimulation of the anus.

24. Fellatio refers to (p. 205):

    *a. oral stimulation of the male's genitals.
    b. oral stimulation of the female's genitals.
    c. deep kissing.
    d. oral stimulation of the anus.

25. The term *69* refers to (p. 205):

    *a. simultaneous oral stimulation by both partners of one another's genitals.
    b. the name of a book on sexual techniques.
    c. deep kissing.
    d. simultaneous manual stimulation.

26. In the 1940s, the Kinsey group found that most English-speaking couples in their sample reported relying primarily on the _____ coital position (p. 209).

    a. face-to-face, woman-above
  *b. face-to-face, man-above
    c. face-to-face, side-by-side
    d. rear-entry, side-by-side

27. A disadvantage of the face-to-face, man-above position is that (p. 209):

  *a. the man's hands are not free to stimulate his partner.
    b. the man has less control of body movement.
    c. the woman cannot adjust her position to increase contact of the clitoris.
    d. people tend to view this position as being less moral.

28. In research using a slide depicting a couple in the woman-above position and another slide depicting them in the man-above position, it was found that (p. 210):

    a. men rated the couple in the woman-above position as less moral and less normal.
  *b. women rated the couple in the woman-above position as less moral and less normal.
    c. women rated the couple in the man-above position as less clean.
    d. men rated the couple in the woman-above position as less clean.

29. Which of the following positions is particularly useful for overweight individuals and during late pregnancy (p. 210)?

  *a. face to face, side by side
    b. face to face, man above
    c. face to face, woman above
    d. standing up

30. The _____ position permits the greatest opportunity for both partners to control their body movements during coitus (p. 210).

  *a. face-to-face, side-by-side
    b. man-above
    c. woman-above
    a. double-S

31. Nonhuman species rely almost entirely on _____ as their main position during sexual interaction (p. 211).

    a. face to face, male above
    b. face to face, female above
    c. side entry
  *d. rear entry

32. Which of the following is true about anal sex (p. 213)?

    *a. Twenty-five percent of American women occasionally engage in receptive anal inter-
        course.
    b. The anus has very few nerve endings.
    c. Vaseline is the ideal lubricant for the anus.
    d. There has been a marked decline in anal sex in the United States in recent years.

33. Anal intercourse is best for couples attempting it if (p. 213):

    a. a lubricated condom is worn.
    b. afterward, the penis is not inserted into the mouth or vagina without washing it first.
    c. penile penetration is carried out gradually and gently.
    *d. all of the above.

34. Voeller (1991) reported that _____ percent of American women occasionally engage in
    receptive anal intercourse, and _____ percent do so regularly for pleasure (p. 213).

    a. 5; 1
    *b. 25; 10
    c. 50; 30
    d. 80; 5

35. Which of the following are more likely to engage in anal intercourse, according to the text-
    book (p. 213)?

    a. black males
    b. non-Hispanic white males
    c. Native American males
    *d. Hispanic males

36. Regarding the number of sexual partners since age 18, Smith found that (p. 214):

    a. women reported considerably more partners than did men.
    b. there were large ethnic differences in self-reported numbers of sexual partners.
    c. 50 percent of the men in the study had had 20 or more coital partners.
    *d. large gender differences were probably due primarily to men's overreporting and
        women's underreporting.

37. According to the textbook, an approach to orgasm that emphasizes _____ is probably
    the most satisfying one for many couples (p. 215).

    *a. ladies first
    b. gentlemen first
    c. simultaneous climax
    d. none of the above.

38. _____ was(were) the first scientist(s) to study human sexual response through systematic observation in a laboratory setting (p. 215).

   *a. Masters and Johnson
    b. Kinsey and colleagues
    c. Kaplan
    d. Westheimer

39. Masters and Johnson found that most bodily changes that occur in the sexual response cycle of men and women are due to (pp. 216–217):

    a. vasocongestion.
    b. myotonia.
    c. homeostasis.
   *d. both a and b.

40. _____ is the process by which various parts of the genitals become filled with blood during sexual excitement (pp. 216–217).

   *a. Vasocongestion
    b. Myotonia
    c. Erection
    d. Respiration

41. Production of vaginal lubricant in the female is the result of (p. 220).

   *a. vasocongestion.
    b. myotonia.
    c. the secretion of hormones by the vagina.
    d. all of the above.

42. _____ refers to contractions of muscles during sexual response (p. 217).

   *a. Myotonia
    b. Vasocongestion
    c. Propulsion
    d. Pulmonation

43. In the excitement phase, the penis becomes erect due to (pp. 216–217):

    a. water retention.
    b. muscle tension.
    c. pulmonation.
   *d. vasocongestion.

44. Masters and Johnson found only two major gender differences in sexual response systems. (p. 217):

    a. males could have orgasm more quickly, but females could have multiple orgasms.
    b. females could have more intense orgasms, but males could ejaculate.
   *c. males could ejaculate, but females could have multiple orgasms.
    d. males could have orgasm more quickly, but females could have more intense orgasms.

45. The phase in which sperm and fluid are expelled from the vas deferens, seminal vesicles, and prostate gland into the base of the urethra is called (p. 217):

    a. orgasm.
   *b. emission.
    c. ejaculation.
    d. expulsion.

46. The first stage of male orgasm is (p. 217):

   *a. emission.
    b. ejaculation.
    c. expulsion.
    d. refraction.

47. The second stage of male orgasm is (p. 217):

   *a. ejaculation.
    b. emission.
    c. erection.
    d. pulmonation.

48. For males, during the plateau phase of the sexual response cycle as conceptualized by Masters and Johnson (p. 217):

    a. a sex flush appears.
   *b. the testes increase as much as 50 percent in size.
    c. the testes return to normal size.
    d. none of the above.

49. A sweating reaction in 30 percent to 40 percent of males occurs in the _____ phase of the sexual response cycle (p. 216).

   *a. resolution
    b. excitement
    c. orgasm
    d. plateau

50. For males, the _____ stage of orgasm involves the contraction of the neck of the bladder (p. 217).

   *a. ejaculation
    b. myotonia
    c. erection
    d. micturation

51. Which of the following do men but not women experience (p. 218)?

    *a. refractory period
    b. resolution
    c. myotonia
    d. multiple orgasm

52. Masters and Johnson described the typical refractory period as lasting between (p. 218):

    a. 50 and 100 seconds.
    b. 5 and 7 minutes.
    *c. 30 and 90 minutes.
    d. 36 and 40 hours.

53. In terms of occurrence, which of the following is the correct order for the sexual response cycle identified by Masters and Johnson (p. 219)?

    *a. excitement, plateau, orgasm, resolution
    b. excitement, plateau, orgasm
    c. desire, orgasm, resolution
    d. initiation, orgasm, resolution, refractory period

54. A general loss of voluntary muscle or motor control in the male occurs during the _____ phase of the sexual response cycle (p. 219).

    a. excitement
    b. plateau
    *c. orgasm
    d. resolution

55. Retraction of the clitoris occurs until it is completely covered by the tissue of the clitoral hood during the _____ phase of the sexual response cycle (p. 219).

    a. excitement
    *b. plateau
    c. orgasm
    d. resolution

56. As the vaginal walls swell with blood, the inner two-thirds of the vagina widens and lengthens, in what is called the (p. 220):

    *a. tenting effect.
    b. vaginal swell.
    c. hypertensive reaction.
    d. orgasmic platform.

57. The constriction of the outer third of the vagina is called the (p. 220):

    *a. orgasmic platform.
    b. vaginal swell.
    c. tenting effect.
    d. engorgement phase.

58. Which of the following cycle patterns seems to occur in young or sexually inexperienced women (p. 221)?

    a. The female proceeds through the entire response cycle, having one or more multiple orgasms without interruption.
    *b. The female has gradual increases in arousal and a fluctuating plateau phase with small surges toward orgasm.
    c. The female has a single orgasm of extreme intensity with little time spent in the plateau phase.
    d. The female remains stuck in the excitement phase, unable to move into the next phase.

59. Which of the following is the correct order for the sexual response cycle identified by Kaplan (p. 222)?

    *a. sexual desire, excitement, orgasm
    b. arousal, orgasm, resolution
    c. arousal, sexual desire, plateau, excitement, orgasm
    d. sexual desire, plateau, excitement, orgasm, resolution

60. Which of the following statements concerning male and female sexual response patterns is true (p. 222)?

    a. Both males and females show little variability in sexual response patterns.
    b. Males show more variability than females in sexual response patterns.
    *c. Females show more variability than males in sexual response patterns.
    d. Both males and females show a great deal of variability in sexual response patterns.

61. A vulval orgasm is characterized by all of the following *except* (p. 223):

    a. inducement by either coital or noncoital stimulation.
    b. no refractory period afterward.
    c. involuntary rhythmic contractions of the orgasmic platform.
    *d. a gasping breath and involuntary breath holding.

62. Which of the following statements concerning male and female subjective experiences of orgasm has been found empirically (p. 223)?

    a. Although professionals can distinguish between male and female descriptions of orgasm, most people cannot.
    b. The subjective experience of orgasm is closely related to the physiological experience for both men and women.
    *c. Professionals are unable to distinguish between male and female written descriptions of orgasm.
    d. Generally women are unable to differentiate types of orgasms experienced at different times.
    e. Most adults cannot easily distinguish between their own orgasm and that of their partner.

63. The physiological recordings of Masters and Johnson indicated that (p. 223):

    *a. regardless of the site of stimulation, the same orgasmic response occurred.
    b. psychoanalysts were correct about their subjective analyses of orgasms.
    c. clitoral orgasms are distinct from vaginal orgasms.
    d. both b and c.

64. Which of the following conclusions was made by Masters and Johnson concerning subjective experiences of female orgasm (p. 223)?

    a. Women do not make subjective distinctions between masturbatory and coital orgasm, although some physiological distinctions were present.
    b. Women's subjective experiences of orgasm closely matched their physiological experiences.
    c. Women's subjective experiences of orgasm were in no way related to the measured physiological experiences.
    *d. None of the above. Masters and Johnson did not measure women's subjective experiences of orgasm.

65. Sherfey's argument on evolution and the female orgasm is that (p. 224):

    a. female orgasm is unique to humans.
    b. the primitive woman's weak sexual drive was very adaptive.
    c. female orgasm is found in only some mammals.
    *d. the absence or infrequency of orgasm in human females is the result of repression.
    e. both a and b.

66. Singer and Singer described _____ types of female orgasm (p. 225).

    a. 1
    b. 2
    *c. 3
    d. 5

67. According to Singer and Singer, a _____ orgasm is characterized by a gasping type of breath (p. 225).

    *a. uterine
    b. vulval
    c. blended
    d. clitoral

68. Singer and Singer described which of the following types of female orgasm (p. 225)?

    *a. vulval, uterine, and blended
    b. clitoral, uterine, and ovarian
    c. clitoral, vaginal, and uterine
    d. clitoral and vaginal

69. Some women have reported that stimulation of the anterior wall of the vagina (p. 225):

    *a. produces enlargement of the Gräfenberg spot.
    b. results in severe pain.
    c. produces profuse sweating.
    d. decreases the length of the resolution period.

70. Researchers report that some women ejaculate a fluid that has a high concentration of (p. 225):

    a. albumin.
    *b. prostatic acid phosphatase.
    c. progonadotropins.
    d. L-prostaglandins.

71. The findings on the consistency of female orgasm indicate that (p. 226):

    *a. women who had experienced orgasm (by any means) before marriage are more likely to experience orgasm after marriage.
    b. about 80 percent of women rarely or never have orgasms.
    c. most women have orgasm almost every time they have intercourse.
    d. most women can experience orgasm without direct clitoral stimulation.

72. The Kinsey group did not present detailed data on the consistency of male orgasm because they assumed (p. 226):

    *a. married men had orgasms almost 100 percent of the time.
    b. it was too difficult a topic to study scientifically.
    c. it was too controversial an issue.
    d. none of the above.

73. Masters and Johnson's research on multiple orgasms in females indicates (p. 227):

    *a. most women are capable of having multiple orgasms if adequately stimulated.
    b. most women prefer multiple to single orgasms.
    c. most women prefer clitoral to vaginal orgasms.
    d. most women prefer vaginal to clitoral orgasms.

74. The research on multiple orgasms in males indicates that (p. 227):

    a. some men can have orgasms and ejaculate repeatedly without a refractory period.
    b. some men can have orgasms repeatedly without ejaculating.
    *c. both of the above.
    d. none of the above.

Essay Questions

75. Describe the differences between males and females in the frequency of nocturnal orgasm as found by the Kinsey group. Have there been changes since that research was done? If so, what are they (pp. 196–197)?

76. Describe changes in historical views toward self-stimulation (pp. 197–200).

77. Summarize the research by Gagnon on parental views toward masturbation (p. 199).

78. How do males and females differ in their masturbatory patterns (pp. 200–202)?

79. Describe changes in attitudes and behavior toward oral-genital stimulation that have occurred between the time of the research by the Kinsey group and more recent research (pp. 204–206).

80. Identify the various coital positions, and describe the advantages and disadvantages of each (pp. 208–213).

81. Describe precautions that should be taken to avoid the risk factors associated with anal sex (pp. 212–213).

82. Describe some of the reasons that may make simultaneous orgasm less satisfying to partners than sequential orgasm (taking turns) (p. 215).

83. Compare and contrast the description of the phases of the sexual response cycle given by Masters and Johnson versus Kaplan (pp. 215–225).

84. Describe the physical reactions of males during the stages of the sexual response cycle identified by Masters and Johnson (pp. 216–218).

85. Describe the physical reactions of females during the stages of the sexual response cycle identified by Masters and Johnson (pp. 219–220).

86. To what extent are the subjective experiences of orgasm by males and females different (pp. 223–224)?

87. What are the different kinds of female orgasm that have been described by researchers (pp. 223–225)?

88. What is the current status of research conclusions on female ejaculation (pp. 225–226)?

89. What is the current status of research on male multiple orgasm (p. 226)?

Multiple-Choice Questions

1. Which of the following is a *psychological* factor that might lead to sexual dysfunction (p. 233)?

    a. endocrine disorder
    b. neurogenic disorder
    c. vascular disorder
    *d. none of the above

2. Most authorities believe that the majority of sexual dysfunctions are primarily due to (p. 233):

    a. sociological factors.
    b. organic factors.
    *c. psychosocial factors.
    d. physical factors.

3. Psychoanalytic theorists are most likely to explain sexual dysfunction in terms of (p. 233):

    *a. critical childhood experiences.
    b. communication problems.
    c. misinformation about sexuality.
    d. sociological factors.

4. Welch and Kartub (1978) found a positive correlation between the _____ of a culture and the incidence of difficulty in getting and maintaining an erection (pp. 233–234).

    *a. restrictiveness
    b. level of technological advancement
    c. permissiveness
    d. wealth

5. Which of the following is a current factor that can be involved in the development of sexual dysfunctions (p. 234)?

    a. communication difficulties
    b. sexual misinformation
    c. stress
    *d. all of the above

6. Concerning attitudes toward eroticism, research in North America has shown that (p. 234):

    a. learning to repress or despise sexual desire generally has no effect on sex in one's marriage.
    b. societal repressiveness tends to lead to increased interest in nonprocreative sex.
    c. the sexual restrictiveness of a cultural group rarely has an effect on attitudes toward eroticism.
    *d. people whose religion condemns sexual activity other than procreative coitus are at greater risk for sexual dysfunction.

7. According to recent research, which of the following statements is most likely to be true (p. 234)?

    a. Most sexual dysfunctions result from psychological factors alone.
    b. Freud's theory that critical childhood experiences explain sexual dysfunctions has much empirical support.
    c. Most sexual difficulties have biological causes.
    *d. Anxiety about sex and performance is probably the most important immediate cause of sexual dysfunction.

8. Masters and Johnson (1970) asserted that _____ is the most important immediate cause of sexual dysfunction (p. 234).

    a. excessive alcohol consumption
    b. fear of unwanted pregnancy
    *c. anxiety about sexual performance
    d. inhibitions about physical appearance

9. Spectating refers to (p. 234):

    a. watching erotic films but not becoming aroused.
    b. mentally removing oneself from therapy and observing the therapist instead.
    *c. monitoring one's own sexual activity rather than becoming immersed in the actual experience.
    d. viewing a videotape of oneself behaving sexually.

10. Couples experiencing sexual dysfunctions (pp. 236):

    a. are sometimes simply misinformed about sexual functioning.
    b. may feel inhibited about discussing their sexual feelings.
    c. need to give and receive information about sexual feelings.
    *d. all of the above.

11. In a series of studies by Barlow and colleagues, men who were functioning well sexually ("functional") were compared to men who had sexual difficulties ("dysfunctional"). It was found that _____ increased the arousal/sexual response of functional men but decreased the arousal/sexual response of dysfunctional men, whereas _____ decreased the arousal/sexual response of functional men but made little difference or increased it in dysfunctional men (p. 235).

    *a. performance demands; distraction
    b. stress; performance demands
    c. misinformation; stress
    d. hunger; misinformation

12. The majority of psychological factors associated with sexual dysfunction (p. 236):

    a. result from organic disorders.
    b. are not related to early childhood experiences.
    *c. can be related to the association of anxiety, fear, or anger with sexual functioning.
    d. result from misinformation about sexual functioning.

13. Until clinically sophisticated techniques were developed for distinguishing between the relative contributions of biological and psychosocial factors contributing to sexual dysfunction, it was assumed that _____ cases were the result of _____ factors (p. 237).

    a. most; biological
    b. most; both
    c. few; psychological
    *d. most; psychological

14. Abel and his coworkers (1982) found that approximately _____ percent of diabetics claiming erectile dysfunction appeared to suffer from psychological factors (p. 238).

    a. 5
    *b. 30
    c. 60
    d. 90

15. Wabrek and Burchell (1980) found a relationship between male sexual dysfunction and (pp. 238–239).

    a. fear and kidney failure.
    b. depression and circulatory problems.
    *c. stress and heart attacks.
    d. allergies and asthma.

16. The first time that psychosexual disorders were listed in the *Diagnostic and Statistical Manual,* which is used by mental health professionals, was in (p. 239):

    a. 1920.
    b. 1950.
    *c. 1980.
    d. 1995.

17. Individuals who do not experience desire for any kind of sexual activity are technically referred to as (p. 239):

   *a. hypoactive.
    b. hyperactive.
    c. oblative.
    d. homophobic.

18. Low sexual desire has been associated with (p. 240):

    a. religious orthodoxy.
    b. marital conflict.
    c. fear of closeness.
   *d. all of the above.

19. Women with inhibited sexual desire report _____ as many depressive episodes as women with normal sexual desire (p. 240).

   *a. twice
    b. five times
    c. seven times
    d. ten times

20. A _____ disorder reflects fear, disgust, or anxiety about sexual contact with a partner (p. 241).

   *a. sexual aversion
    b. pleasure personality
    c. hypoactive
    d. none of the above

21. A person with sexual aversion disorder may typically engage in _____ while avoiding _____ (p. 241).

   *a. masturbation and fantasy; interpersonal sexual behavior
    b. interpersonal sexual behavior; masturbation and fantasy
    c. violent sexual behavior; masturbation
    d. masturbation; fantasy

22. Excessive sexual desire is often associated with (p. 241):

    a. schizophrenia.
   *b. an obsessive-compulsive reaction.
    c. hostility toward one's parent(s).
    d. depression.

23. In _____, the individual becomes preoccupied with sexuality and masturbation, and/or sexual interaction with a partner may occur five or ten times per day (p. 241).

    a. sodomania
    b. manic depression
    *c. obsessive-compulsive states
    d. hypoactive disorders

24. A comparison of married women experiencing inhibited sexual desire with married women expressing normal sexual desire revealed (p. 242):

    a. significant differences in hormonal levels.
    b. more psychological disorders among women with inhibited desire.
    *c. greater dissatisfaction among the former group with their marital relationships.
    d. all of the above.

25. The major problem with the terms *impotency* and *frigidity* is that the terms (p. 242):

    *a. are degrading.
    b. represent dysfunctions that are very hard to diagnose.
    c. represent dysfunctions that are actually very rare.
    d. none of the above.

26. Frigidity and impotency are now referred to as _____ disorders (p. 242).

    *a. sexual arousal
    b. excessive sexual desire
    c. sexual aversion
    d. hypoactive sexual desire

27. Occasional nonresponsiveness during sexual interaction (p. 242):

    a. should be regarded with caution.
    *b. is normal.
    c. usually indicates that a dysfunction exists.
    d. usually indicates hostility toward one's partner.

28. _____ is diagnosed when a person has experienced sexual excitement in the past but is now nonresponsive (p. 242).

    *a. Secondary arousal disorder
    b. Primary arousal disorder
    c. Paraphilia
    d. Sexual aversion

29. During an average night, a male will have _____ during REM sleep (p. 242).

    a. one or two sexual dreams
    *b. three to five erections
    c. no erections
    d. one orgasm

30. The most common affliction seen among men who seek therapy is (p. 242).

    *a. erectile dysfunction.
    b. premature ejaculation.
    c. inhibited male orgasm.
    d. inhibited sexual desire.

31. _____ men who experience problems with erection after a period of normal responsiveness respond well to treatment. The prognosis is _____ for men who have never been able to attain or maintain an erection with a partner (p. 243).

    a. Most; just as good
    b. Some; much better
    c. Very few; also bleak
    *d. Most; not so good

32. A(n) _____ is a prolonged erection that is *not* linked to sexual arousal (p. 243).

    *a. priapism
    b. neuroticism
    c. operculum
    d. prosthesis

33. _____ involves continuous erection without continuous sexual arousal (p. 243).

    *a. Priapism
    b. Erectile dysfunction
    c. Hermaphroditism
    d. None of the above

34. Untreated, _____ can lead to destruction of the _____ of the penis (p. 243).

    *a. priapism; spongy tissue
    b. palpation; frenulum
    c. retrograde ejaculation; urethra
    d. anorgasmia; corpus spongiosum

35. Which of the following statements concerning orgasm is correct (p. 243)?

    a. Orgasm generally occurs simultaneously for most couples.
    b. If one partner responds with orgasm more quickly than the other, one of them is likely sexually dysfunctional.
    *c. There is an enormous amount of variation from one person to the next in the amount of stimulation enjoyed before orgasm occurs.
    d. Orgasmic dysfunctions are very rare.

36. Among the criteria used to determine and define premature ejaculation are (p. 243):

    a. number of times a man thrusts his penis into his partner before ejaculating.
    b. the amount of time between penetration and ejaculation.
    c. whether a man ejaculates before his partner has orgasm at least half the time.
    *d. all of the above.

37. Speed of ejaculation is associated with factors such as (p. 244):

    a. age.
    b. experience with intercourse.
    c. novelty of the sexual partner.
    *d. all of the above.

38. Control of ejaculation is (p. 244):

    a. inherited.
    *b. learned.
    c. both a and b.
    d. involuntary.

39. The best way to prevent premature ejaculation is to (p. 244):

    a. avoid sexual interaction.
    b. think of nonarousing thoughts during sexual interaction.
    *c. recognize signals that occur just before ejaculation.
    d. not try to control it at all.

40. The diagnosis of _____ is not appropriate unless the speed of a man's ejaculation becomes a regular, unwanted aspect of a couple's sexual activity (p. 244).

    *a. premature ejaculation
    b. priapism
    c. erectile dysfunction
    d. inhibited orgasm

41. Which of the following is false concerning inhibited orgasm in men (p. 244)?

    a. Many of these men say that they prefer masturbation over intercourse.
    b. The wives of the men with this problem often are multiorgasmic.
    c. Such men can sustain erections far beyond the ordinary range during coitus.
    *d. These men cannot typically continue to produce an erect penis for coitus with a partner.

42. In a physical condition known as _____, the neck of the bladder does not contract, allowing the semen to flow into the bladder rather than out through the urethral opening of the penis (p. 245).

    *a. retrograde ejaculation
    b. premature ejaculation
    c. inhibited male orgasm
    d. retarded ejaculation

43. One of the most common sexual complaints of women who seek treatment at sex therapy clinics is (p. 245):

    *a. difficulty with orgasm.
    b. inhibited sexual desire.
    c. vaginismus.
    d. dyspareunia.

44. _____ is associated with recurrent and persistent genital pain during sexual intercourse (p. 246).

    a. Vaginismus
    *b. Dyspareunia
    c. Priapism
    d. Genital herpes

45. Which of the following statements concerning dyspareunia is false (p. 246)?

    a. Repeated dyspareunia is likely to result in vaginismus.
    b. It is more common in women than in men.
    b. It is the technical term used for either a male or a female.
    *d. Most women suffer from it at some point in their lives.

46. The disorder associated with the involuntary contraction of the pubococcygeal muscle surrounding the outer third of the vagina is (p. 246):

    *a. vaginismus.
    b. functional dyspareunia.
    c. priapism.
    d. frigidity.

47. Recurrent or persistent genital pain in a male or a female before, during, or after sexual intercourse is called (p. 246):

    a. vaginismus.
    b. sexual arousal disorder.
    *c. dyspareunia.
    d. philophobia.

48. Among events that have been found to trigger vaginismus are (p. 247):

    a. rape.
    b. abortion.
    c. pelvic inflammatory disease.
    *d. all of the above.

49. Which of the following is false concerning vaginismus (p. 247)?

    a. Imagined rapes are associated with vaginismus in some women.
    b. Attempts at vaginal penetration produce pain and anxiety.
    c. Treatment appears to be highly effective in eliminating this dysfunction.
    *d. The contractions of vaginismus can be controlled by the woman on her own.

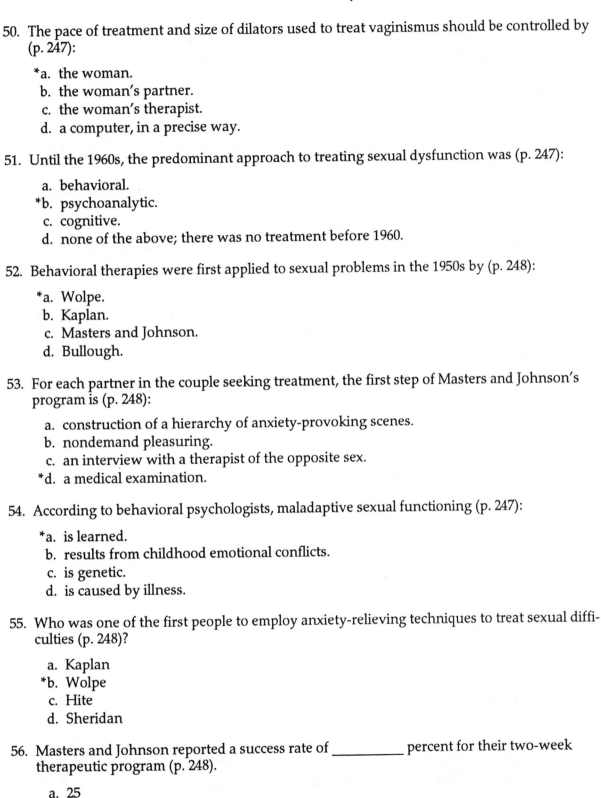

50. The pace of treatment and size of dilators used to treat vaginismus should be controlled by (p. 247):

   *a. the woman.
    b. the woman's partner.
    c. the woman's therapist.
    d. a computer, in a precise way.

51. Until the 1960s, the predominant approach to treating sexual dysfunction was (p. 247):

    a. behavioral.
   *b. psychoanalytic.
    c. cognitive.
    d. none of the above; there was no treatment before 1960.

52. Behavioral therapies were first applied to sexual problems in the 1950s by (p. 248):

   *a. Wolpe.
    b. Kaplan.
    c. Masters and Johnson.
    d. Bullough.

53. For each partner in the couple seeking treatment, the first step of Masters and Johnson's program is (p. 248):

    a. construction of a hierarchy of anxiety-provoking scenes.
    b. nondemand pleasuring.
    c. an interview with a therapist of the opposite sex.
   *d. a medical examination.

54. According to behavioral psychologists, maladaptive sexual functioning (p. 247):

   *a. is learned.
    b. results from childhood emotional conflicts.
    c. is genetic.
    d. is caused by illness.

55. Who was one of the first people to employ anxiety-relieving techniques to treat sexual difficulties (p. 248)?

    a. Kaplan
   *b. Wolpe
    c. Hite
    d. Sheridan

56. Masters and Johnson reported a success rate of _____ percent for their two-week therapeutic program (p. 248).

    a. 25
    b. 50
   *c. 80
    d. 95

57. Masters and Johnson recommended a treatment program involving (p. 248):

    a. only one of the relationship partners in the therapy.
    b. the use of sexual surrogates.
    *c. both a male and a female therapist for clients.
    d. only certified psychoanalysts as therapists.

58. Which of the following aspects of Masters and Johnson's therapy program may have led to high success rates, according to critics (p. 248)?

    a. There was greater cultural ignorance about sexuality when Masters and Johnson were reporting success rates.
    b. A "no treatment" group was not used.
    c. Most of their clients traveled to the clinic from other parts of the country, leaving daily routines behind.
    *d. All of the above.

59. The approach that attempts to help the client gain insight into the less conscious aspects of his or her personality is _____ therapy (p. 249).

    *a. psychosexual
    b. behavioral
    c. Rogerian
    d. implosive

60. Kaplan's approach to sexual therapy (p. 250):

    *a. uses behavioral methods first and then, if necessary, psychoanalytic methods.
    b. uses two therapists, as do Masters and Johnson.
    c. has reported success levels equal to those of Masters and Johnson.
    d. is initially geared to resolving unconscious conflicts.

61. Caird and Wincze (1977) have suggested that most behavioral treatments should include (p. 250):

    a. education.
    b. redirection of sexual behavior.
    c. graded sexual exposure.
    *d. all of the above.

62. Systematic desensitization (p. 251):

    a. is a technique used mostly by psychoanalytic therapists.
    b. is based on alternation between giving and receiving stimulation.
    *c. involves learning a series of muscle relaxation exercises.
    d. generally is ineffective for inhibited ejaculation.

63. The goal of _____ is to replace an anxiety-laden response to each member of a set of anxiety-provoking scenes with a relaxation response (p. 251).

    a. surrogate therapy
    *b. systematic desensitization
    c. implosive therapy
    d. sensate focus

64. In _____, the receiver concentrates on the sensations evoked by the giver's touch on various parts of the body (p. 252).

    *a. sensate focus
    b. systematic desensitization
    c. implosive therapy
    d. psychosexual therapy

65. Which of the following statements about nondemand sensate focus is false (pp. 252–254)?

    *a. One partner stays in the role of giver over the course of the treatment, while the other partner stays in the role of receiver.
    b. Over the course of treatment, the couple receives homework assignments to increase their range of sexual behaviors gradually.
    c. Partners take turns in the role of giver and receiver.
    d. During nondemand coitus, the woman-above position is recommended by Masters and Johnson.

66. Most programs for orgasmically inhibited women involve _____, particularly if the woman has never had an orgasm (p. 255).

    *a. masturbation training
    b. encounter groups
    c. drugs and medication
    d. psychoanalytic therapy to resolve unconscious conflicts

67. The squeeze technique was developed to aid men who (p. 255):

    a. have erectile dysfunction.
    *b. are premature ejaculators.
    c. suffer from retarded ejaculation.
    d. have urinary incontinence.

68. The most commonly employed treatment for premature ejaculators is (p. 255):

    a. the Semans start-stop technique.
    *b. the squeeze technique.
    c. masturbation training.
    d. systematic desensitization.

69. Based on information in the textbook about sexual surrogates, which statement is false (pp. 256–257)?

    a. The client and a partner, the surrogate, engage in private sexual activity.
   *b. Most professionals recommend sexual contact between clients and therapists.
    c. The use of sexual surrogates to treat sexual dysfunctions has been largely abandoned.
    d. No study has yet been conducted to compare the progress of clients treated by therapists employing surrogates with that of clients treated without surrogates.

70. Surgical procedures, including implants, have been used in the treatment of (p. 257):

   *a. erectile dysfunction.
    b. inhibited sexual desire.
    c. primary orgasmic dysfunction.
    d. premature ejaculation.

71. Which of the following statements is false about penile implants (p. 257)?

    a. Early bone implants resulted in a state of constant erection.
    b. Most men with implants are unable to experience ejaculation and orgasm.
    c. There are two basic types of plastic or silicone implants.
   *d. Follow-up studies of prosthesis recipients indicated that most were dissatisfied with the results of the surgery.

72. Hormones have been used for years to treat (p. 258):

    a. dyspareunia.
    b. excessive sexual desire.
   *c. erectile dysfunction.
    d. orgasmic dysfunction.

73. Of men with penile implants, _____ percent can have satisfactory sexual relations after the implant is functioning effectively (p. 257).

    a. 5 to 10
    b. 20 to 25
    c. 60 to 65
   *d. 90 to 95

74. _____ treatment for erectile dysfunction increases the risk of coronary thrombosis, atherosclerosis, and cancer of the prostate (p. 258).

   *a. Hormone
    b. Surgical
    c. Valium
    d. Megadose vitamin

75. _____ techniques bypass blocked arteries through grafts that allow for a greater blood supply to the penis (p. 258).

    *a. Microsurgery
    b. Drug-therapy
    c. Radiation
    d. None of the above

76. _____ can create pharmacological erection, which is especially useful for men with irreversible biological erectile dysfunction (p. 258).

    *a. Papavarine
    b. Librium
    c. Valium
    d. Testosterone

77. In the opinion of the authors, there are certain things that should *not* occur in the therapist's presence during sex therapy, including (p. 258):

    *a. overt sexual activities.
    b. explicit discussion of sexual acts.
    c. sexual role playing.
    d. discussion between the spouses.

78. One study indicated that _____ percent of clients who had been sexually intimate with their therapists reported some negative effects, such as feeling guilty or exploited (p. 259).

    a. 10
    b. 30
    c. 50
    *d. 90

Essay Questions

79. Discuss past experiences and current problems that can lead to sexual dysfunctions (pp. 232–239).

80. Discuss in detail the two types of sexual desire disorders (pp. 237–241).

81. Discuss sexual arousal disorders. What leads to the diagnosis of such a disorder (pp. 241–243)?

82. Describe problems associated with the use of the terms *frigid* and *impotent* (p. 242).

83. Identify and discuss the definitions of premature ejaculation. Which definition makes the most sense to you? Why (pp. 243–244)?

84. Discuss orgasm disorders of men and of women in detail (pp. 245–246).

85. Define and differentiate dyspareunia and vaginismus (pp. 246–247).

86. What are the similarities and differences between the sex therapy approaches of Kaplan versus Masters and Johnson? Which makes more sense to you, and why (pp. 247–256)?

87. Describe systematic desensitization and nondemand pleasuring (pp. 251–252).

88. Describe masturbation training and the squeeze technique (pp. 255–256).

89. What is involved in the use of sexual surrogates? What do the critics say about this practice (pp. 256–257)?

90. Discuss the three ethical and emotional problems mentioned in the textbook that can arise with therapist-client sexual intimacy (pp. 258–259).

CHAPTER 9

Pregnancy and Birth

Multiple-Choice Questions

1. Human sperm are capable of fertilizing an ovum for _____ after ejaculation into the vagina (p. 264).

    a. 1 month
    b. 2 weeks
    c. 1 week
    *d. a few days

2. To maximize the chances of conception, a couple should have intercourse (p. 264):

    a. a few days before ovulation.
    *b. during ovulation.
    c. a few days after ovulation.
    d. a few days before the a menstrual period begins.

3. Which coital position maximizes the chances of conception (p. 264)?

    *a. face to face, man above
    b. face to face, woman above
    c. rear entry
    d. side entry

4. How long should a woman remain on her back after the man has ejaculated into her vagina when attempting to maximize the chances of conception (p. 264)?

    a. 1 minute
    *b. 20 minutes
    c. 1 hour
    d. 90 minutes

5. Little scientific work on gender selection in humans had been done until _____ and his colleagues began to publish the results of their work on the subject in the _____ (p. 264).

    a. Shettles; early 1920s
    *b. Shettles; late 1960s
    c. King; early 1920s
    d. King; late 1980s

6. In the process of studying the differences between sperm carrying X chromosomes and those carrying Y chromosomes for purposes of gender-selection techniques, it was found that (p. 264):

   *a. Y-bearing sperm have greater motility and die more quickly than X-bearing sperm.
   b. X-bearing sperm have greater motility and die more quickly than Y-bearing sperm.
   c. Y-bearing sperm are almost twice as large as X-bearing sperm.
   d. X-bearing sperm are more coiled in shape.

7. Shettles suggested that couples wanting to improve their chances of conceiving a female should have sexual intercourse _____ ovulation and should use an _____ douche (p. 264).

   *a. before; acidic
   b. before; alkaline
   c. the day of; acidic
   d. the day of; alkaline

8. _____ methods are useful only for couples desiring boys (p. 265).

   a. Sperm-coding
   b. Chorionic villi sampling
   c. Prenatal diagnostic
   *d. Sperm-separation

9. Which of the following statements regarding preferences for the gender of a baby is true (p. 265)?

   a. The status of women in the United States has declined over the past few years, making a daughter less preferable.
   *b. The preference for sons over daughters has been declining.
   c. In the United States, people are increasingly more positive in their attitudes toward gender-selection methods.
   d. The preference for girls has remained about the same.

10. For most women, the first real indication of pregnancy is (p. 265):

   a. a fullness of the abdomen.
   b. a frequent need to urinate.
   c. nipple irritation.
   *d. absence of menstruation.

11. Urine tests for the presence of HCG, which indicates pregnancy, are highly accurate as early as _____ the expected (but missing) menstrual period (p. 268).

   a. 4 days before
   *b. the first day of
   c. 18 to 21 days after
   d. 30 to 40 days after

12. The expected delivery date is normally calculated by subtracting _____ from the first day of the last menstrual period and then adding _____ to that figure (p. 268).

    *a. 3 months; 53 weeks
    b. 15 days; 9 months
    c. 2 months; 12 months
    d. 45 days; 7 months

13. Pregnancy is conventionally divided into _____ trimesters (p. 268).

    a. two
    *b. three
    c. six
    d. nine

14. Most babies are born an average of _____ after conception (p. 268).

    a. 200 days
    *b. 266 days
    c. 310 days
    d. 90 weeks

15. About a month after the first missed menstrual period due to pregnancy, the cervix feels relatively (p. 269):

    a. hard and resilient.
    b. slippery due to mucus.
    c. rigid, like the end of the nose.
    *d. soft and malleable.

16. Which of the following feelings are common during the first trimester of pregnancy (p. 269)?

    *a. fatigue, irritability, and dependency
    b. high energy and happiness
    c. fatigue, happiness, and calmness
    d. well-being and pleasure

17. Quickening is typically noticed during the (p. 270):

    a. first trimester.
    *b. second trimester.
    c. third trimester.
    d. time of birth.

18. _____ is the first awareness of fetal movement by the pregnant woman (p. 270).

    a. Dopplering
    b. Bonding
    *c. Quickening
    d. Myocardia

19. The fetal heartbeat can first be detected around the (p. 272):

     a. end of the second month.
     b. beginning of the third trimester.
     c. beginning of the third week.
 *d. middle of the second trimester.

20. The average woman gains _____ pounds by the end of her pregnancy (p. 273).

     a. 15 to 19
     b. 20 to 24
 *c. 25 to 30
     d. 31 to 36

21. The average weight for a full-term baby is _____ pounds (p. 273).

     a. 4.3
     b. 5.2
 *c. 7.5
     d. 9.1

22. In the _____ culture intercourse ceases for most couples as soon as the woman knows that she is pregnant (p. 274).

 *a. So
     b. Azande
     c. Mika
     d. Darantos

23. In North America, frequency of sexual expression during pregnancy tends to follow two patterns. In one pattern, _____, and in the other, _____ (p. 274).

 *a. frequency of intercourse declines with each trimester; intercourse decreases during the first trimester but increases during the second trimester
     b. frequency of intercourse increases with each trimester; intercourse increases during the first trimester but levels off during the second and third
     c. frequency of intercourse declines with each trimester; intercourse ceases entirely
     d. frequency of intercourse peaks in the second trimester; intercourse peaks in the third trimester

24. During the final month of pregnancy in North America, it is typical to have _____ in sexual intercourse (p. 274).

 *a. a sharp decrease
     b. a gradual decrease
     c. a sharp increase
     d. no change

25. The major reason given by women surveyed in North America for the reduction of coitus during pregnancy was (p. 275).

    a. fear for the fetus.
    b. the complete loss of sexual desire.
    c. feeling sexually unattractive.
    *d. physical discomfort.

26. Which of the following is *false* about intercourse during pregnancy (p. 276)?

    a. If a woman in her third trimester is uncomfortable with coitus, she and her partner can engage in noncoital forms of sexual intimacy.
    b. The couple's fears notwithstanding, there is no reason to limit sexual activity in a healthy pregnancy.
    *c. Frequent coitus is likely to produce premature delivery.
    d. Blowing air into the vagina of a pregnant woman should be avoided.

27. A pregnant woman should avoid (p. 276):

    a. coitus.
    b. exercising.
    c. wearing makeup.
    *d. sexual contact with a partner who has a sexually transmitted disease.

28. _____ during pregnancy can cause fetal and maternal death (p. 276).

    *a. Blowing air into the vagina
    b. Cunnilingus
    c. Anal intercourse
    d. Vaginal use of spermicide

29. Labor for the average woman lasts (p. 277):

    a. 2 hours.
    b. 4 hours.
    *c. 15 hours.
    d. 30 hours.

30. Anesthesia was not used for childbirth until 1847, at least in part because (p. 279):

    a. anesthetics were too costly.
    b. there is a definite danger to the fetus.
    c. there were no anesthetics before that time.
    *d. the Bible held that children should be brought forth in pain and sorrow.

31. In 1932 the physician _____ questioned the use of _____ (p. 279).

    *a. Dick-Read; anesthetics during labor
    b. Lamaze; anesthetics during labor
    c. Spock; enemas before labor
    d. Williams; episiotomies during birth

32. One technique introduced by Lamaze, called _____, consists of light, circular stroking of the abdomen with the fingertips (p. 279).

    *a. effleurage
    b. coaching
    c. Swedish massage
    d. flexing

33. After observing women in Russia undergoing labor with little pain, _____ began to train pregnant women and their husbands in muscle-relaxation methods and breathing techniques (p. 279).

    a. Dick-Read
    b. Santos
    c. Pavlov
    *d. Lamaze

34. The intensity of contractions can be reduced by (p. 279):

    a. relaxing one's muscles.
    b. breathing exercises.
    c. focusing the eyes on a specific object.
    *d. all of the above.

35. Mothers using prepared childbirth often have (p. 279):

    *a. higher self-esteem and a greater sense of self-control.
    b. more guilt and conservative attitudes.
    c. more episiotomies.
    d. strong religious beliefs and healthier babies.

36. Braxton-Hicks contractions (p. 279):

    a. may reduce a woman's discomfort.
    b. may result in miscarriage.
    *c. are irregular and are often mistaken for the onset of labor.
    d. none of the above.

37. Which of the following statements concerning the onset of labor is correct (p. 280)?

    *a. Most women are instructed to call their doctors or midwives when the contractions occur at 5-minute intervals.
    b. The amniotic sac always breaks during labor.
    c. Scientists have no clue as to why labor beings.
    d. All of the above.

38. Compared with more traditional approaches to childbirth, mothers using prepared childbirth have (p. 280):

    a. fewer birth complications.
    b. shorter labor.
    c. less use of anesthesia.
    *d. all of the above.

39. It has been speculated that labor begins when the (p. 280):

    *a. adrenal glands of the fetus produce hormones that are secreted into the placenta and uterus.
    b. fetus rotates into a position with the head at the bottom of the uterus.
    c. brain of the fetus produces electroencephalogram patterns called delta waves.
    d. uterine fluid becomes excessively acidic.

40. The watery discharge that occurs near the onset of labor contractions (p. 280):

    a. results from the placenta's being expelled from the uterus.
    b. results from the release of the mucus plug in the cervix.
    *c. results from the rupturing of the amniotic sac.
    d. is a signal that the baby will be born breech.

41. The first symptom of labor for many women is (p. 280):

    a. a discharge of watery fluid.
    *b. gradual awareness of contractions.
    c. frequent headaches and fatigue.
    d. a low fever and sweating reaction.

42. Contractions are (p. 280):

    a. irregular from onset until birth.
    b. fairly regular from onset until birth.
    *c. irregular at first but become more regular over time.
    d. regular at first but become irregular just before birth.

43. Which of the following statements concerning location of birth is correct (p. 280)?

    *a. Most American babies are born in hospitals or birthing centers.
    b. Most American babies are delivered by midwives.
    c. In Holland, increases in home delivery have been accompanied by increased mortality rates.
    d. American babies born at home are found to experience more distress during birth than those born in hospitals.

44. Most women are instructed to call their doctor when contractions occur at (p. 280):

    a. 2-hour intervals.
    b. 30-minute intervals.
    *c. 5-minute intervals.
    d. 1-minute intervals.

45. During the second stage of labor (p. 281):

    *a. birth occurs.
    b. the cervix begins to open gradually to permit the baby to pass through.
    c. the placenta is expelled from the uterus.
    d. all of the above.

46. Labor is divided into _____ stages (p. 281).

    a. two
    *b. three
    c. four
    d. five

47. During the first stage of labor (p. 281):

    *a. the cervix gradually opens.
    b. the placenta is expelled.
    c. the umbilical cord is cut.
    d. birth occurs.

48. The movement of the head of the fetus into a lower position in the abdominal cavity past the mother's pelvic bone structure is called (p. 281):

    *a. engagement.
    b. effacement.
    c. effleurage.
    d. transition.

49. The flattening and thinning of the cervix that occurs before and during childbirth is called (p. 281):

    a. engagement.
    b. effleurage.
    c. transition.
    *d. effacement.

50. The necessity of which of the following practices has recently been questioned (p. 282)?

    a. washing the vulva, thighs, and stomach with an antiseptic solution to reduce the chances of transmitting infection to the baby during birth
    b. the giving of an enema
    c. the shaving of pubic hair
    *d. both b and c
    e. all of the above

51. After the cervix has dilated about _____, the pituitary gland secretes oxytocin, and the frequency and intensity of the contractions _____ considerably (p. 282).

    *a. 2 inches; increase
     b. 1/2 inch; increase
     c. 1 inch; decrease
     d. 5 inches; increase

52. The end of first-stage labor is signaled by a relatively _____ period of intense contractions known as _____ (p. 282).

     a. long; episiotomy
     b. short; effacement
     c. long; effleurage
    *d. short; transition

53. The surgical cut from the bottom of the entrance to the vagina down toward the anus is called an (p. 282):

    *a. episiotomy.
     b. epidural.
     c. effleurage.
     d. effacement.

54. The episiotomy is (p. 282):

     a. rarely performed.
    *b. unnecessary unless the baby is very large or the woman's vaginal opening is very small.
     c. reduces rates of vaginal tearing.
     d. all of above.

55. Transition refers to the time when (p. 282).

     a. labor contractions first begin.
     b. the placenta is expelled through the uterus.
    *c. the dilation of the cervix is completed so that the baby's head can pass through it.
     d. the baby's head first passes the pelvic bone.

56. Which of the following is *false* concerning the expulsion of the placenta (p. 285)?

     a. After the baby is born, a woman continues to have a few contractions that aid her in expelling the placenta.
     b. The placenta is also called the afterbirth.
     c. The woman's vital signs are monitored for an hour or so to ensure that blood vessels close properly after the placenta is expelled.
    *d. The placenta is expelled shortly before the child is born.

57. Which of the following is *false* concerning the time soon after giving birth (p. 285)?

     a. The baby is bathed and antibiotic is placed in his or her eyes.
    *b. New mothers are encouraged to stay in bed for 24 hours.
     c. The woman's vital signs are monitored for about an hour.
     d. Women are given a meal if they are hungry.

58. A doctor may ask a woman to control the urge to bear down (p. 285):

     a. so that the baby will not be injured.
     b. to decrease discomfort.
    *c. to decrease the likelihood of vaginal tearing.
     d. to decrease her heavy panting.

59. The umbilical cord is cut (p. 285):

     a. immediately after birth.
     b. after all tests on the baby have been concluded.
     c. after the baby opens its eyes.
    *d. after the cord stops pulsating and the baby is able to rely on his or her own lungs for oxygen.

60. The cutting of the umbilical cord is (p. 285):

    *a. painless for both mother and baby.
     b. painless for mother but not baby.
     c. painless for baby but not mother.
     d. painful for both mother and baby.

61. The process of childbirth entailing the greatest risk for the mother is the (p. 285):

     a. episiotomy.
     b. transition period.
    *c. expulsion of the placenta.
     d. "bearing-down" period.

62. A solution of antibiotic is placed in the newborn's eyes to (p. 285):

     a. test how the baby's responds to light.
    *b. minimize the chance of infection.
     c. test the baby's depth perception.
     d. eliminate the waxy film covering the eyes.

63. Which of the following is an advantage of breast-feeding over commercial formulas or cow's milk (p. 286)?

     a. protection from some infections and diseases
     b. healthier teeth
     c. less trouble with diarrhea or constipation
    *d. all of the above

64. The first liquid refreshment provided by the nipples to the newborn is a thin, yellowish fluid called (p. 285):

    a. oxytocin.
  *b. colostrum.
    c. prolactin.
    d. pitocin.

65. _____ aids in milk production, and _____ stimulates contractions of cells to eject milk into the duct so that a baby can easily obtain milk by sucking (p. 285):

    a. Oxytocin; testosterone
    b. Prolactin; androgens
  *c. Prolactin; oxytocin
    d. Testosterone; oxytocin

66. Nipple tenderness during breast-feeding can be reduced by (p. 286):

    a. taking drugs.
    b. taking a warm shower.
    c. packing the breasts in ice.
  *d. allowing the breast milk to dry on the nipples.

67. _____ has a stimulating effect on the smooth muscles of the uterus, helping it to return to its normal size (p. 286).

  *a. Oxytocin
    b. Sayman
    c. Lochia
    d. Estrogen

68. Which of the following statements about breast-feeding is *false* (pp. 285–286)?

    a. During the early twentieth century, the popularity of breast-feeding declined throughout the world.
  *b. Colostrum from the nipples is replaced by milk about 1 month after giving birth.
    c. Secretion of prolactin aids in milk production.
    d. The American Pediatric Society recommends breast milk as the optimal food for the first 4 to 6 months of life.

69. Which of the following statements concerning circumcision is correct (p. 286)?

    a. It reduces the chance of cervical cancer in men's partners.
    b. It is legally required in the United States.
    c. It leads to increased penis sensitivity.
  *d. None of the above.

70. Which of the following is true about male circumcision (p. 287)?

    a. A child who has been circumcised is more likely to masturbate.
    *b. Circumcision is usually done with anesthesia.
    c. The complication rate for circumcision is about 20 percent.
    d. The proportion of newborn U.S. boys who are circumcised has been increasing.

71. More than about _____ male babies are circumcised each year in the United States (p. 287).

    a. 500,000
    b. 800,000
    *c. 1 million
    d. 2 million

72. The six weeks following childbirth are inherently stressful because (p. 289):

    a. there is a rapid increase in levels of estrogen and progesterone in the female.
    b. the opportunity for uninterrupted conversation or lovemaking is sharply curtailed.
    c. parents experience a loss of freedom as they attend to the infant's needs.
    *d. both b and c.
    e. all of the above.

73. Which of the following statements concerning postpartum depression is correct (p. 289)?

    a. Postpartum blues and postpartum depression refer to exactly the same phenomenon.
    b. It is more common for third- or fourth-time mothers than first- or second-time mothers.
    c. It is entirely due to dramatic changes in hormone levels following birth.
    *d. Severe symptoms of depression affect about 1 or 2 women per 1,000 births.

74. A discharge consisting of a small amount of red or brown blood that may continue for two to four weeks or more following birth is called (p. 290):

    *a. lochia.
    b. colostrum.
    c. prolactin.
    d. resumption of menstruation.

75. After birth, sexual intercourse (p. 290):

    a. should definitely not be resumed for 6 months.
    *b. is resumed during the fifth week for the majority of women.
    c. is enjoyed most during the first month because it is almost impossible to get pregnant during this period.
    d. none of the above.

76. Henderson instructed a group of new mothers to _____ and found that they had greater muscle tone at their first postpartum checkup than did a control group of women (p. 290).

   *a. perform Kegel exercises
    b. sleep at least 9 hours per day
    c. eat raw vegetables and whole grains
    d. swim daily for at least 20 minutes

77. _____ means something that causes birth defects (p. 292).

   *a. Teratogenic
    b. Hellenogenic
    c. Ultracentic
    d. Serpentic

78. Symptoms of fetal alcohol syndrome in humans include all but the following (p. 292).

   *a. large, hook-type nose
    b. short eyeslits
    c. missing or minimal ridges between the nose and mouth
    d. retarded physical growth

79. Which of the following is true about the use of drugs during pregnancy (p. 292)?

    a. The tranquilizer thalidomide does not cross the placental barrier.
    b. The liver of a newborn human begins functioning immediately after birth and is capable of breaking drugs down as efficiently as an adult's liver.
   *c. Heavy alcohol consumption during pregnancy is the leading environmental cause of mental retardation in infants.
    d. All of the above.

80. Which of the following is true about maternal infections (p. 292)?

    a. A woman infected with an initial case of genital herpes during the first 20 weeks of gestation is more likely to have a spontaneous abortion.
    b. Women who have chlamydia during the first trimester of pregnancy have a greater incidence of premature births.
    c. Transmission of HIV to the baby is usually through the placenta, breast-feeding, or infusion of contaminated blood.
   *d. All of the above.

81. In the first trimester, the principal threat to the life of a pregnant woman is (p. 293):

   *a. ectopic pregnancy.
    b. eclampsia.
    c. chlamydia.
    d. use of thalidomide.

82. Signs of impending _____ are vaginal bleeding, abdominal cramping, and lower back-ache (p. 293).

    a. eclampsia
    *b. miscarriage
    c. toxemia
    d. breech birth

83. Signs of _____ include the retention of toxic body wastes, high blood pressure, protein in the urine, swelling, and fluid retention (p. 293).

    a. miscarriage
    *b. preeclampsia
    c. spontaneous abortion
    d. ectopic pregnancy

84. Which of the following is true about a tubal pregnancy (p. 293)?

    a. When it is diagnosed, a cesarean section is normally performed immediately.
    *b. It can occur when a woman has scar tissue in her fallopian tubes.
    c. A tubal pregnancy rarely aborts spontaneously.
    d. Experiencing one means the woman will probably never be able to get pregnant in the future.

85. Approximately _____ percent of babies are born _____ (p. 295).

    *a. 90; head first
    b. 75; buttocks first
    c. 50; shoulder first
    d. 20; head first

86. _____ twins carry the same genetic information and are sometimes called identical twins (p. 296).

    *a. Monozygotic
    b. Dizygotic
    c. Surrealistic
    d. Allelic

87. Multiple births usually occur after a _____ gestation period than is characteristic of single births, and the infants typically weigh significantly _____ than usual (p. 296).

    *a. shorter; less
    b. shorter; more
    c. longer; less
    d. longer; more

Essay Questions

88. Assume that you and your partner are trying to have a baby. Describe the steps you can take to increase your chances of conception (pp. 263–265).

89. How would you and your partner try to increase your chances of conceiving a girl? Of conceiving a boy (pp. 263–265)?

90. What are the pros and cons of gender selection? Would you consider using gender selection techniques if you wanted to have a baby of a certain gender (p. 265)?

91. In which trimester of pregnancy is a woman likely to be most comfortable, and why? What happens in that trimester (pp. 268–270)?

92. Compare and contrast, in terms of benefits, the use of anesthesia for childbirth versus the use of prepared childbirth training (pp. 277–279).

93. Discuss the issues of routine use of shaving the vulva, giving enemas, and the episiotomy. Under what conditions should each be used (pp. 281–282)?

94. Describe in detail what happens during the third stage of labor (p. 285).

95. Compare and contrast the advantages and disadvantages of breast-feeding and bottle feeding (pp. 285–286).

96. Compare and contrast the advantages and disadvantages of the circumcision of male infants (pp. 286–289).

97. Describe the conditions that mothers face during the first few months after having a baby (pp. 289–292).

98. Discuss some issues that arise with postpartum sexual expression (pp. 290–292).

99. Compare and contrast the use of amniocentesis, chorionic villi sampling, and ultrasonography. What information do these tests yield (pp. 295–297)?

100. What are the major environmental threats to fetal development (pp. 297–298)?

101. What are the problems associated with prematurity, low birth weight, and delayed birth (pp. 297–298)?

102. Discuss some of the dangers faced by pregnant women (pp. 293–298).

103. Discuss complications that can arise during the birth process (pp. 295–298).

104. Discuss fetal alcohol syndrome (p. 292).

CHAPTER 10

Contraception

Multiple-Choice Questions

1. In Europe, large segments of the population began to use birth control in the (p. 304):

    a. early tenth century.
    b. early twelfth century.
    c. middle of the fifteenth century.
    *d. latter part of the eighteenth century.

2. With each passing minute, more than _____ babies will have been added to our population (p. 304).

    a. 100
    b. 130
    *c. 175
    d. 225

3. The contraceptive pill was first marketed in (p. 304):

    a. 1915.
    b. 1950.
    *c. 1960.
    d. 1972.

4. The world's population now surpasses _____, and it is expected to hit _____ by the year 2000 (p. 304).

    a. 2 billion; 3 billion
    *b. 5 billion; 6 billion
    c. 8 billion; 10 billion
    d. 50 billion; 51 billion

5. The National Birth Control League was founded in the United States in 1914 by (p. 304):

    a. Alfred Kinsey.
    b. Anna Freud.
    c. Maria Calderone.
    *d. Margaret Sanger.

6. In _____, the U.S. Supreme Court overturned state laws prohibiting the dissemination of contraceptive information and devices (p. 305).

    *a. 1965
    b. 1970
    c. 1975
    d. 1980

7. The financial and scientific investment in developing female contraceptive methods
_____ that for male methods (p. 305).

    a. is far less than
    b. is about the same as
   *c. is far greater than
    d. none of the above; no such comparison has been made.

8. Greater investment in female than in male contraceptive methods probably occurs because (p. 305):

    a. women are fertile for only a few days each month.
    b. men are always fertile.
    c. of assumptions that women are more motivated than men to use contraceptives.
   *d. all of the above.

9. The number of conceptions that occur when a contraceptive method is used correctly is known as the _____ failure rate (p. 305).

    a. actual
   *b. theoretical
    c. methodological
    d. effective

10. For a birth-control method, _____ is calculated by determining the number of sexually active women out of 100 who become pregnant in the course of a year while relying on a particular method (p. 305).

   *a. probability of failure
    b. theoretical failure rate
    c. absolute effectiveness
    d. actual failure rate

11. The effectiveness of contraceptives is evaluated by determining their (p. 305):

    a. success rate.
   *b. probability of failure.
    c. side effects.
    d. financial cost.

12. The _____ is the total number of pregnancies that occur as a result of failure of a particular birth control method or failure to use the method correctly (p. 305).

   *a. actual failure rate
    b. probability of failure
    c. absolute effectiveness
    d. theoretical failure rate

13. Comparatively more women die each year from which of the following (pp. 306–307)?

    *a. complications of pregnancy and childbirth
    b. side effects of IUDs
    c. side effects of oral contraceptives
    d. side effects of barrier methods of contraceptives

14. The majority of Americans (p. 307):

    a. use reliable contraceptive methods.
    b. remain virgins until about the age of 20.
    *c. become sexually active before the age of 20.
    d. use contraceptives at the time they become sexually active.

15. Of teenagers who had first intercourse at age 16 or younger, fewer than _____ had received sexual and contraceptive education in school (p. 308).

    a. one-sixteenth
    b. one-eighth
    c. one-quarter
    *d. one-half

16. Approximately _____ percent of American females have engaged in premarital intercourse by the time they reach their eighteenth birthday (p. 308).

    a. 4
    b. 26
    *c. 53
    d. 79

17. Nearly _____ of sexually active adolescent females have at least _____ premarital pregnancy (p. 308).

    a. one-sixteenth; one
    b. one-eighth; one
    *c. one-third; one
    d. 60 percent; one

18. More than _____ teenagers in the United States become pregnant each year (p. 308).

    a. 600
    b. 5,000
    *c. 1 million
    d. 2 million

19. About two decades ago, Furstenberg attributed the lack of contraceptive education in the United States to the fact that (p. 310):

     *a. the general approach to social problems in American society was reactive rather than preventive.
     b. the majority of Americans were against birth control services for sexually active teens.
     c. the majority of Americans were opposed to sex education in the schools.
     d. sex education caused unwanted pregnancies, sexually transmitted diseases, and the moral decline of America.

20. Comparisons among 37 developed countries showed that _____ had the highest pregnancy rate and was _____ open about sex, compared with most other countries (pp. 309–310).

     a. Sweden; very
     *b. the United States; far less
     c. France; very
     d. the United States; very

21. In the extensive study carried out at junior and senior high schools in Baltimore, it was found that exposure to contraceptive education and services over the three-year period resulted in (pp. 311–312):

     *a. an increase in the accuracy of students' knowledge about sexuality and a delay in the average age of first intercourse.
     b. a boycott of the schools by concerned parents.
     c. more pregnancies in that three-year period than at any other time in the history of those schools.
     d. more treatment of stress-related disorders in students by school counselors.

22. In the extensive study carried out at junior and senior high schools in Baltimore, it was found that after twenty-eight months, the pregnancy rate _____ in the program schools and _____ in the control-group schools (p. 312).

     *a. declined; increased
     b. declined; declined
     c. increased; declined
     d. increased; increased

23. The use of reliable contraceptives the first time they have sex is greatest among (p. 312):

     a. people having a "one night stand."
     b. people who are promiscuous.
     c. couples who are in love.
     *d. couples who are planning to marry.

24. Studies of the relationship between contraceptive use and promiscuity have found that (p. 313):

    a. college women who are just beginning to use the pill have fewer sexual partners than do those who have been taking the pill for 12 months.
   *b. reliable contraceptive use is associated with strong commitment to one's partner.
    c. greater promiscuity is related to greater contraceptive use.
    d. none of the above.

25. Of the following factors for unmarried women, which is related to using reliable contraceptives consistently (p. 313)?

    a. number of sexual partners
    b. church attendance
   *c. accuracy of knowledge about birth control
    d. all of the above

26. The conscientious contraceptive user, compared to the less conscientious user, tends to be (p. 313):

    a. less sexually active.
   *b. of higher socioeconomic status.
    c. a regular church attendee.
    d. both a and c.

27. The _____ of teenage women who consistently use contraception tends to be _____ than that of women who are less conscientious (p. 314):

    a. religious beliefs; stronger
   *b. socioeconomic status; higher
    c. number of sexual partners; higher
    d. IQ; higher

28. Women who _____ when they first have intercourse are more likely to use birth control (p. 314).

   *a. are older
    b. have higher grades in school
    c. own automobiles
    d. are church members

29. Consistent contraceptive use is more likely among women (p. 314):

    a. with positive attitudes about sex.
    b. with low levels of sex guilt.
    c. who are less traditional in their gender-role identification.
   *d. all of the above.

30. High-sex-guilt females (p. 314):

    a. start intercourse at a later age.
    *b. take longer to begin using a reliable contraceptive.
    c. are likely to receive contraceptive help from members of their families.
    d. are likely to carry condoms in case their partner does not have one.

31. The conscientious female contraceptive user is (p. 314):

    *a. less concerned with conforming to the "nice girl" image.
    b. more traditional in her gender-role identification.
    c. more likely to believe what happens to her is based on chance.
    d. all of the above.

32. The greatest mortality risk for sexually active young women is (p. 316):

    *a. unprotected sexual intercourse.
    b. using a barrier method of contraception.
    c. a first-trimester abortion.
    d. using birth-control pills.

33. The only birth control method, other than celibacy, permitted by the Catholic church is (p. 317):

    a. oral contraceptives.
    *b. rhythm.
    c. the IUD.
    d. condoms.

34. Which method of birth control involves abstaining from coitus for at least a week around the time of ovulation (p. 317)?

    a. the pill
    *b. rhythm
    c. the IUD
    d. the cap

35. The average menstrual cycle is about _____ days long, with ovulation occurring on average _____ days prior to the onset of the menstrual period (p. 317).

    a. 35; 18
    *b. 28; 14
    c. 25; 11
    d. 21; 6

36. To detect variations in basal body temperature, a woman must take her temperature (p. 317):

    *a. each morning before getting out of bed.
    b. each evening before falling asleep.
    c. each day at noon.
    d. every other day after 9:00 P.M.

37. The basal body temperature is lowest (p. 317):

    a. just after menstruation.
  *b. during ovulation.
    c. just after ovulation.
    d. just before menstruation.

38. Which of the following methods of charting menstrual cycles is least reliable (p. 317)?

  *a. the calendar method
    b. thermometer to measure basal body temperature
    c. monitoring of cervical mucus
    d. Barclay technique

39. Checking the stretchability of cervical mucus is associated with which method of contraception (p. 318)?

    a. vaginal suppositories
  *b. sympto-thermal
    c. spermicide
    d. Orbach

40. _____, the cervical mucus stretches and resembles unbeaten raw egg whites in consistency (p. 318).

    a. Just after menstrual bleeding has stopped
    b. A week before ovulation
  *c. During ovulation
    d. Just before menstruation

41. When using the sympto-thermal birth control method, a woman should abstain from coitus for _____ days prior to ovulation and for _____ day(s) following ovulation (p. 318).

    a. 10; 8
  *b. 5; 3
    c. 4; 2
    d. 2; 1

42. Which of the following birth control methods may be obtained only by prescription from a clinic or physician (p. 319)?

  *a. diaphragm
    b. condom
    c. foam
    d. contraceptive sponge

43. The first widely available birth control method for women was (p. 319):

    a. IUD.
    *b. diaphragm.
    c. cervical cap.
    d. aerosol foam.

44. Which of the following is true about the diaphragm (p. 319)?

    a. They are sold over the counter.
    b. About 25 percent of women currently use it as a contraceptive device.
    *c. It should be refitted after weight increases or deceases of 10 pounds or more.
    d. Use of spermicide with it is optional.

45. The diaphragm should be removed (p. 320):

    a. immediately after intercourse.
    b. 2 to 4 hours after intercourse.
    *c. 6 to 8 hours after intercourse.
    d. no sooner than 12 hours after intercourse.

46. The diaphragm should be inserted (p. 320):

    a. about 10 hours before intercourse.
    b. about 6 hours before intercourse.
    *c. no more than 2 hours before intercourse.
    d. none of the above; it is equally effective when inserted anytime before intercourse.

47. After it has been inserted in the vagina and positioned against the cervix, the contraceptive sponge absorbs and kills sperm for at least _____ hours (p. 322).

    a. 8
    b. 12
    *c. 24
    d. 36

48. The contraceptive sponge is easily removed by (p. 322):

    *a. pulling on a small loop attached to the sponge.
    b. a physician or nurse.
    c. a hook-type device that comes with it.
    d. none of the above; it does not need to be removed because it disintegrates.

49. The contraceptive sponge is (p. 322):

    a. available without a prescription.
    b. generally more expensive to use than the diaphragm.
    c. discarded after each use.
    *d. all of the above.

50. Which of the following is true about condoms (p. 323)?

    *a. A cecum condom is more costly than a latex one and provides less protection from sexually transmitted diseases.
    b. Couples who receive instructions designed to make condom use more erotic become more positive in their attitudes toward condoms and report more sexual pleasure than couples who do not receive such instruction.
    c. The intravaginal female condom has never been approved for use by the Food and Drug Administration.
    d. For added lubrication with a condom, the use of petroleum jelly, such as Vaseline, is recommended.

51. Use of a _____, which is pressed onto the cervix, was approved by the Food and Drug Administration in 1988 (p. 323).

    *a. cervical cap
    b. diaphragm
    c. contraceptive sponge
    d. progestin ring

52. The _____ works by preventing sperm from entering the vagina (p. 323).

    *a. condom
    b. diaphragm
    c. contraceptive sponge
    d. cervical cap

53. Condoms (p. 324):

    *a. should be stored away from heat.
    b. can be purchased only by prescription.
    c. have decreased in use since 1986.
    d. were designed to be reused.

54. The failure rate of condoms can be decreased by (p. 325):

    a. putting the condom on prior to any penetration.
    b. holding on to the rim of it when withdrawing.
    c. using petroleum jelly as a lubricant.
    *d. both a and b.
    e. all of the above.

55. For additional lubrication when using condoms, a couple can use (p. 325):

    a. types that are prelubricated.
    b. surgical (K-Y) jelly.
    c. petroleum jelly.
    *d. both a and b.
    e. all of the above.

56. Cecum condoms are made from (p. 326):

    *a. the intestinal tissue of lambs.
    b. latex rubber.
    c. nonoxynol-9.
    d. polyurethane.

57. Latex and cecum condoms differ in terms of (p. 326):

    a. cost.
    b. the amount of sensation experienced by the male.
    c. the manufacturing material.
    *d. all of the above.

58. A contraceptive suppository must be placed in the vagina at least _____ and no more than _____ before ejaculation of semen into the vagina (p. 327).

    *a. 10 minutes; 2 hours
    b. 3 minutes; 1 hour
    c. 20 minutes; 1 hour
    d. 30 minutes; 90 minutes

59. Contraceptive foam (p. 327):

    a. can be purchased without a prescription.
    b. should be stored in a cool place.
    c. must be shaken before placed in an applicator.
    *d. all of the above.

60. The major disadvantage(s) associated with using foam alone as a birth control method is(are) that (p. 327):

    a. the failure rate is high.
    b. it should remain in the vagina for six to eight hours after ejaculation.
    c. more foam must be inserted if a couple has intercourse for a second time during the same lovemaking session.
    *d. all of the above.

61. The progestin in birth control pills (p. 328):

    a. prevents ovulation in conjunction with estrogen.
    b. interferes with the development of the lining of the uterus.
    c. thickens the cervical mucus.
    *d. all of the above.

62. To use most oral contraceptives, a woman takes one pill each day for _____ days, stops for _____ days to permit menstrual bleeding, and then begins a new cycle (p. 327).

    a. 15; 13
    *b. 21; 7
    c. 23; 5
    d. 28; 9

63. Of all the oral contraceptives, the _____ pill is most effective (p. 328).

    a. placebo
    *b. combination
    c. mini
    d. progestin-alone

64. Which of the following methods is least disruptive when it comes to interrupting lovemaking (p. 329)?

    *a. oral contraceptives
    b. male condom
    c. foams and suppository
    d. female condom

65. Persistent breakthrough bleeding in females using oral contraceptives indicates that (p. 329):

    *a. the dosage is too low.
    b. the woman is allergic to the pill.
    c. the pill should not be used as a contraceptive.
    d. the dosage is too high.

66. Which of the following minor side effects is associated with using the pill (p. 329)?

    a. weight loss
    b. increased menstrual blood flow
    *c. slight breast enlargement
    d. hemorrhoids

67. Women who take the pill should not (p. 330):

    a. consume dairy products.
    b. take antibiotics.
    c. drink alcohol.
    *d. smoke cigarettes.

68. Pill use has been linked to heart disease from clotting for women (p. 330):

    a. under age 25.
    b. aged 25 to 39.
    c. who smoke cigarettes.
    *d. aged 25 to 39 who smoke cigarettes.
    e. none of the above.

69. Use of low-dosage birth control pills is associated with some reduced risk of _____ cancer (p. 330).

    a. cervical
    b. endometrial
    c. ovarian
    *d. all of the above

70. _____ is an implant that releases a synthetic hormone over a five-year period (pp. 331–332).

    a. Progestasert
    b. Copper T
    *c. Norplant
    d. Depo-Provera

71. Which of the following women are advised not to take the pill (p. 331)?

    a. smokers
    b. those with high blood pressure
    c. those with diabetes
    d. those with cystic fibrosis
    *e. all of the above

72. The intrauterine device (IUD) is (p. 332):

    a. swallowed.
    *b. placed inside the uterus.
    c. placed on the penis.
    d. pressed on the cervix.

73. By 1986, all but one type of _____ had been withdrawn from the market by manufacturers (p. 333).

    a. diaphragm
    *b. IUD
    c. contraceptive foam
    d. cervical cap

74. Which of the following is a slow-release contraceptive that consists of thin, flexible capsules inserted under the skin of a woman's upper arm (p. 331)?

    a. Progestasert
    b. Copper T
    *c. Norplant
    d. Dalkon

75. The Copper T and Progestasert are two highly effective types of (p. 333):

    a. diaphragm.
    *b. IUD.
    c. douche.
    d. condom.

76. It is thought that the IUD works primarily by (p. 333):

    *a. reducing the likelihood of a fertilized egg's implantation in the uterine lining.
    b. increasing the thickness of cervical mucus.
    c. increasing acidity of the vagina.
    d. both b and c.

77. Which of the following birth control methods is *least* effective (p. 333)?

    a. oral contraceptives
    *b. withdrawal
    c. condom
    d. diaphragm

78. The withdrawal method of contraception is problematic because (p. 333):

    a. a man is not always successful in removing the penis from the vagina prior to ejaculation.
    b. the Cowper's glands secrete fluid that sometimes contains sperm.
    c. its failure rate is high.
    *d. all of the above.

79. What do withdrawal, postcoital douching, and breast-feeding have in common (p. 333)?

    *a. They are unreliable forms of birth control.
    b. They appear to decrease the incidence of cervical cancer.
    c. They are more effective birth control measures than the condom.
    d. They are all recommended by the AMA.

80. Studies indicate that (p. 334):

    a. in the United States, the act of breast-feeding causes a delay in subsequent conception.
    b. postcoital douching is effective if an acidic douche is used.
    *c. frequent nursing can sometimes delay ovulation.
    d. breast-feeding is a reliable form of contraception for North Americans.

81. Which of the following is true concerning sterilization (p. 335)?

    a. Hormone production and the menstrual cycle are affected by tubal ligation.
    b. Tubal ligation is less complicated and less expensive than vasectomy.
    c. A vasectomy is usually performed under general anesthesia in a hospital.
    *d. Vasectomized men should use another contraceptive technique until two successive semen analyses have confirmed the absence of sperm.

82. The leading method of contraception for couples throughout the world today is (p. 334):

    a. oral contraceptives.
    b. the condom.
    c. the diaphragm.
    *d. sterilization.

83. Vasectomy involves (p. 335):

    a. altering hormones so that semen is not produced.
    b. killing sperm so that they do not leave the epididymis.
    *c. cutting the vas deferens.
    d. removing the epididymis.

84. Tubal ligation involves (p. 336):

    a. altering the production of hormones.
    b. removing the fallopian tubes.
    c. blockage of the passageway between the uterus and the fallopian tubes.
    *d. cutting the fallopian tubes.

85. In a "band-aid" sterilization procedure (pp. 336–337):

    a. a vasectomy is reversed.
    b. a tubal ligation is reversed.
    c. general anesthesia is not used.
    *d. a laparoscope is inserted through an incision near the naval.

Essay Questions

86. Describe the political and social issues related to the development of modern contraceptives (pp. 304–305).

87. Describe the technological and medical issues associated with the development of currently used contraceptives (pp. 305–307).

88. Discuss the topic of adolescents and contraceptive use (pp. 307–310).

89. Some critics have claimed that providing sexual and contraceptive education stimulates young people to have sexual intercourse. Evaluate that conclusion in the light of recent research on the topic (pp. 309–313).

90. Discuss the topic of birth control education (pp. 310–312).

91. Compare and contrast the advantages and disadvantages of the following methods of contraception: sympto-thermal method, diaphragm and spermicide, contraceptive sponge, condom, foams and suppositories, oral contraceptives, hormone implants, and IUDs (pp. 317–333).

92. How are sexual attitudes related to contraceptive use? Refer to relevant studies that have been conducted (pp. 313–314).

93. Describe the methods of birth control that involve identification of time of ovulation, including the pros and cons of each method (pp. 317–319).

94. Describe how the diaphragm/spermicide method of birth control is used and how it works (pp. 319–321).

95. Describe three relatively ineffective methods of contraception and explain why they have low levels of effectiveness (pp. 333–334).

96. What are the advantages and disadvantages of vasectomy, and how reversible is it (pp. 334–336)?

97. What are the advantages and disadvantages of tubal ligation, and how reversible is it (pp. 336–337)?

98. Describe the methods of male contraception that are currently under study. Which, if any, of them show promise of being an effective method, lacking serious side effects (pp. 337–338)?

99. Describe the methods of female contraception that are currently under study (p. 338).

100. Compare and contrast a vasectomy to a tubal ligation (pp. 334–337).

CHAPTER 11

Resolving Unwanted Pregnancy

Multiple-Choice Questions

1. The most frequent decision for resolving unwanted pregnancy is to (p. 334):

    *a. obtain an abortion.
    b. put the baby up for adoption.
    c. keep the baby.
    d. none of the above.

2. _____ of all brides and _____ of those under 20 are pregnant on their wedding day (p. 334).

    a. One-quarter; one-third
    b. One-eighth; one-quarter
    *c. One-third; half
    d. One-sixteenth; the majority

3. During the past decade, slightly under _____ of all pregnant American women obtained abortions each year (p. 334).

    a. one-sixteenth
    b. one-eighth
    *c. one-third
    d. one-half

4. Abortion has been practiced since (p. 334):

    a. the Civil War.
    b. the Middle Ages.
    c. the year 1000 A.D.
    *d. well before the time of Christ.

5. The majority of abortions in the United States during the past decade were performed on _____ women (p. 334).

    *a. young, white, unmarried
    b. middle-aged, black, married
    c. young, black, unmarried
    d. middle-aged, Hispanic, unmarried

6. The majority of abortions in the United States during the past decade were performed in the first _____ weeks of pregnancy (p. 334).

   a. 4
   *b. 8
   c. 11
   d. 14

7. An estimated _____ million abortions are performed every year throughout the world (p. 334).

   a. 5 to 6
   b. 15 to 24
   *c. 36 to 53
   d. 80 to 97

8. Strictly speaking, which of the following birth control methods is actually an early abortion method (p. 334)?

   a. diaphragm
   b. oral contraceptive
   *c. intrauterine device
   d. contraceptive sponge

9. Historically, the Catholic church (p. 334):

   a. has always condemned abortion.
   *b. permitted early abortion until the middle of the nineteenth century.
   c. has permitted abortions only when the mother's life is threatened.
   d. has always permitted abortion in the case of rape.

10. Many countries that have legalized abortion have done it for which of the following reasons (p. 334)?

   a. Legal abortion helps to limit population growth.
   *b. Illegal abortion poses a threat to public health.
   c. Legal abortion helps to increase the mother's standard of living.
   d. Legal abortion helps to decrease the number of mentally deficient babies.

11. Which of the following is true about attitudes toward abortion in the United States (p. 334)?

   a. People with high levels of sex guilt are less accepting of abortion than are those with lower levels of sex guilt.
   b. Catholics and Mormons feel more negatively about legalized abortion than do Protestants.
   c. College-educated Americans, as well as those with higher incomes, are more supportive of legalized abortion than are their less-educated and less-affluent counterparts.
   *d. All of the above.

12. _____ of the world's people live in countries where abortion is legal at least for health reasons, and more than half of these reside in areas where abortion can be obtained on request for any reason (p. 344).

     a. Nine-tenths
    *b. Three-quarters
     c. One-eighth
     d. One-sixteenth

13. People are more likely to be opposed to abortion if (p. 350):

     a. they have high sex guilt.
     b. they are Catholic or Mormon.
     c. they do not have a college education.
    *d. all of the above.

14. In a study in which college students were asked to evaluate a series of fictitious case histories to find out more about people's decision making when judging the appropriateness of abortion, it was found that the students (pp. 348–350):

     a. advocated abortion only in the case of genetic defects in the fetus.
     b. tended to advocate "punishing" conscientious women by refusing them abortions.
     c. did not approve of abortion even in the case of use of a reliable contraceptive that failed.
    *d. supported abortion for women who had become pregnant with a steady partner rather than during a casual sexual encounter.

15. _____ hold more negative attitudes about abortion than do _____ (p. 350).

    *a. Catholics and Mormons; Protestants and agnostics
     b. Baptists; Catholics
     c. Lutherans and Methodists; Catholics and Mormons
     d. Episcopalians; Baptists

16. People with _____ are less accepting of abortion for women who desire abortion than are those with _____ (p. 350).

    *a. higher levels of sex guilt; lower levels of sex guilt
     b. college education; less education
     c. higher incomes; lower incomes
     d. fewer children; more children

17. Which of the following groups holds relatively more negative attitudes toward abortion (p. 350)?

     a. college educated
     b. whites
     c. unmarried women
    *d. Catholics

18. According to Tietze and Jain, data from nations with a history of legal abortion longer than ours suggest that the percentage of repeat abortions _____ for a few years following legalization and then _____ (p. 354).

   *a. increases; levels off
   b. increases; continues to increase
   c. decreases; increases
   d. increases; drops off radically

19. Essentially two early-abortion methods are available to North American women who wish to terminate a potential pregnancy immediately. They are (p. 354):

   *a. hormone administration and menstrual extraction.
   b. hysterotomy and calumny.
   c. cervicectomy and hormone administration.
   d. menstrual extraction and Rhogam treatment.

20. DES, the "morning-after" pill, is capable of terminating pregnancy after unprotected intercourse if used within (p. 355):

   *a. 72 hours.
   b. 1 month.
   c. the first trimester.
   d. 4 months.

21. In general, DES is recommended for the termination of pregnancy only (p. 355):

   a. for women in the second trimester of pregnancy.
   b. for women who have irregular menstrual cycles.
   *c. in emergencies such as rape.
   d. if one is allergic to copper IUDs that could be inserted to terminate pregnancy.

22. Of the following abortion methods, which is the least expensive (p. 355)?

   a. suction
   b. postcoital IUD
   *c. DES
   d. menstrual extraction

23. Use of DES as an early-abortion method (p. 355):

   a. may produce nausea, vomiting, and headaches as side effects.
   b. is very effective.
   c. is very expensive.
   *d. both a and b.
   e. all of the above.

24. A hormonal abortion procedure developed in France is called (p. 355):

    a. Projestesert.
    b. Nonpreg–38.
    c. Filme le Port.
    *d. RU-486.

25. The advantages of _____ are that it is less expensive than a suction abortion, requires less dilation of the cervix than most other methods, and can be performed before a woman knows whether she is pregnant (p. 355).

    *a. menstrual extraction
    b. vacuum aspiration
    c. dilation and curettage
    d. none of the above.

26. More than 90 percent of abortions are performed (p. 356):

    a. within 24 hours of a missed period.
    *b. in the first trimester.
    c. in the second trimester
    d. in the third trimester.

27. After a suction abortion, a woman (p. 356):

    a. can resume douching in a couple days.
    b. can resume intercourse in a few days.
    *c. should use sanitary napkins rather than tampons to absorb the bleeding that continues for several days.
    d. can engage in unprotected intercourse for up to 3 months after the procedure because it takes that long for ovulation to resume.

28. Which is the safest abortion procedure (p. 356)?

    a. dilation and curettage (D&C)
    b. dilation and evacuation (D&E)
    *c. suction abortion
    d. intra-amniotic injection

29. For _____ compared to _____, the time required for the procedure is shorter, recovery is quicker, and complications are fewer (p. 356).

    *a. suction abortion; D&C
    b. D&C; suction abortion
    c. D&E, suction abortion
    d. hysterotomy; D&C

30. The most serious complication associated with suction abortion is (p. 357):

    a. hemorrhage.
    *b. uterine perforation.
    c. infection.
    d. constricted blood flow.
    e. all of the above.

31. Suction abortions (p. 357):

    a. generally take longer than D&C abortion.
    b. are preferred to D&C abortions when the pregnancy is close to the end of the first trimester.
    *c. are less risky than D&C abortions.
    d. are more expensive than D&C abortions.

32. Which of the following is true about second-trimester abortions compared to those obtained during the first trimester (p. 357)?

    a. Most American women who seek abortions do so during the second trimester.
    b. The psychological reactions of the pregnant woman tend to be less complicated.
    *c. The maternal mortality rate is greater.
    d. All of the above.

33. An abortion method often performed under general anesthesia is (p. 358):

    a. saline abortion.
    b. menstrual extraction.
    c. suction method.
    *d. D&C.

34. Women may seek a second trimester abortion because of (p. 358):

    a. exposure to diseases or drugs that can cause fetal deformities.
    b. unexpected financial hardship.
    c. changes in relationships, such as divorce.
    *d. all of the above.

35. The _____ method of abortion involves withdrawal of some amniotic fluid and replacing it with about a cup of saline solution (p. 358).

    a. suction abortion
    b. D&C
    c. D&E
    *d. intra-amniotic injection

36. A complication of intra-amniotic injections is (p. 358):

    a. accidental injection of the saline into a blood vessel.
    b. accidental injection of the saline into the uterine muscle.
    c. infection.
    d. hemorrhage.
    *e. all of the above.

37. An abortion method that should not be used with asthmatic women is (p. 358):

    a. suction.
    b. D&C.
    c. D&E.
    *d. prostaglandin technique.

38. Hysterotomies are performed (p. 359):

    *a. only under emergency conditions.
    b. during the first trimester only.
    c. only in Europe.
    d. none of the above.

39. An emergency abortion method in which the fetus is removed through an incision in the abdomen is called (p. 359):

    a. calumny.
    b. cervicectomy.
    c. D&E.
    *d. hysterotomy.

40. In interviews with women who were deciding whether to terminate an unwanted pregnancy, Belenky and Gilligan (1979) identified three groups of women, which they referred to as the _____ groups (p. 359).

    *a. Gain, Stable, and Loss
    b. Humanitarian, Egalitarian, and Control
    c. Conflict, Anxiety, and Loss
    d. none of the above

41. Studies have found that after an abortion, most women primarily feel (p. 359):

    a. resentment and regret.
    b. guilt and anger.
    c. sorrow.
    *d. mixed emotions, with positive feelings predominating over negative ones.

42. Which of the following is true for most women who experience abortion (p. 359)?

     a. They primarily experience resentment afterward.
     b. The greatest distress occurs after the abortion rather than before it.
    *c. The more support and encouragement they receive, the more positive they are about their ability to cope with the abortion.
     d. Being hassled by individuals picketing the abortion clinic they are going to has almost no effect on the women.

43. Interested in exploring the male role in abortion, Lees interviewed men who accompanied their unmarried partners to a Detroit abortion clinic and found that (p. 361):

    *a. the more emotional involvement the men reported with their partners, the greater was their anxiety during the pregnancy termination.
     b. most of the men experienced long-term negative reactions.
     c. most of the men were not supportive of the abortion decision.
     d. most were embarrassed and angry.

44. Pfuhl (1978) found that among men involved in unintended pregnancies (p. 361):

    *a. many did not disclose the conception to their families.
     b. most viewed themselves as sexual exploiters.
     c. most regarded the conception as a moral mistake.
     d. none of the above.

45. _____ for the pregnant adolescents has been increasing (p. 364).

     a. Conception-induced marriage
     b. Giving the child up for adoption
    *c. Maintaining pregnancy but not marrying
     d. None of the above

46. Two variables are strongly associated with the development and life experiences of adolescent mothers and their offspring. They are the single parent's (p. 364):

     a. education level and the geographic location in which the single-parent family resides.
    *b. economic level and the social support received by the single-parent family.
     c. ethnic background and the number of children in the family.
     d. economic level and the religion of the family.

47. In comparison to children who were wanted, unwanted children as a group (p. 366):

     a. had recovered psychosocially by the time of young adulthood.
    *b. were less well adjusted by the start of adolescence.
     c. were similar to those who were wanted in terms of adult relationships.
     d. tended to be embarrassed and angry toward teachers.

Essay Questions

48. Compare and contrast the terms *unplanned pregnancy* and *unwanted pregnancy*. Describe some of the problems associated with attempting to get an accurate estimate of the unwanted pregnancy rate (pp. 344–345).

49. Abortion is one of the most controversial issues of our time. Assume that you are a member of a right-to-life group, and prepare the best justification that you can for passing a constitutional amendment banning abortion. Now assume that you are a member of a pro-choice group, and prepare the best justification that you can supporting the legal right of women to choose to terminate pregnancy (pp. 345–348).

50. In 1973, in *Roe* v. *Wade*, the U.S. Supreme Court ruled on the issue of abortion. What was the ruling, and on what constitutional ground was it based? What has happened in the legal system of the United States to change the status of abortion since *Roe* v. *Wade* (pp. 345–348)?

51. What is likely to happen if legal abortion becomes unavailable (pp. 352–353)?

52. Discuss the "abortion as birth control" hypothesis (p. 354).

53. Compare and contrast first-trimester abortion methods with second-trimester methods (pp. 354–358).

54. Under what conditions is each of the following abortion methods most appropriate for a woman who chooses to terminate pregnancy: DES; RU-486; suction abortion; D&C; D&E; intra-amniotic injection of saline; intra-amniotic injection of prostaglandins; and hysterotomy (pp. 354–360)?

55. Discuss the issue of men's rights regarding women's desire to maintain or terminate an unwanted pregnancy. How are the reactions of men who are dealing with an unwanted pregnancy related to their partners' psychological well-being (pp. 361–362)?

56. Describe how motherhood affects the lives of adolescent mothers compared to those of older mothers. In addition, two variables are strongly related to the development and life experiences of adolescent mothers and their offspring. What are they, and what do you think accounts for the relationships (pp. 362–365)?

57. To study the reactions of men whose unmarried partners maintained an unplanned pregnancy, Pfuhl published an ad soliciting interviews with single fathers. Single fathers are sometimes stereotyped as heartless sexual exploiters. What did Pfuhl find from the interviews with the 140 men who answered his ad? Did his findings support or refute the stereotype (pp. 365–367)?

58. Based on research findings in Chapter 10 on contraceptive behavior and in Chapter 11 on unwanted pregnancy, indicate how you would raise your own children to try to reduce the likelihood that they will face an unwanted pregnancy.

59. Assume that you are a member of your local school board. Based on research findings in Chapter 10 on contraceptives and in Chapter 11 on unwanted pregnancy, what kind of curriculum might you recommend to try to reduce the likelihood that adolescent students would experience an unwanted pregnancy? At what grade would you begin to introduce it, and why?

Gender and Sexuality in Childhood and Adolescence

1. Which is true about research on childhood sexuality (p. 372)?

    a. Many studies have been done, but the findings are inconsistent.
    b. Most of the research indicates that infants show no sexuality.
  *c. Only a few studies have been done on childhood sexuality because this remains a relatively forbidden area of research.
    d. Most of this research has been done in America rather than Europe because Americans are less opposed to such research.

2. A person very much opposed to research on childhood sexuality is (p. 373):

    a. Mary Calderone.
    b. Freud.
    c. Erik Erikson.
  *d. none of the above.

3. Who is a leading proponent of sex education in North America, as cited in your textbook (p. 373)?

    a. Margaret Mahler
    b. Erik Erikson
  *c. Mary Calderone
    d. Leo Buscaglia

4. Freud theorized that after a sexually active first five years, children enter a period of repressed sexual interest and activity, which lasts until about age 11, called (p. 373):

    a. autonomy.
  *b. latency.
    c. fixation.
    d. role confusion.

5. According to Freud, the _____ complex involves the idea that _____ compete with the parent of the same gender for a sexual relationship with the parent of the other gender (p. 373).

    a. Oedipus; girls
    b. evolutionary; boys
    c. castration anxiety; boys
  *d. Electra; girls

6. Erikson described _____ stages of life, each of which involves a crisis for the individual (p. 374).

    a. 2
    b. 4
   *c. 8
    d. 12

7. According to Erikson, the newborn's first crisis is (p. 374):

    a. autonomy versus doubt.
   *b. trust versus mistrust.
    c. industry versus inferiority.
    d. initiative versus guilt.

8. According to _____, successful resolution of life crises enables us to become more healthy, well developed, integrated, and mature human beings (p. 374).

   *a. Erikson
    b. Bandura
    c. Skinner
    d. Calderone

9. _____ theorists assume that gender differences emerged over time and stem from the reproductive success of individuals with adaptive traits (p. 375).

   *a. Evolutionary
    b. Social-learning
    c. Learning
    d. Cognitive

10. Evolutionary theorists argue that _____ favored the evolution of _____ assets in males (p. 375).

   *a. selective pressure; hunting
    b. genetic transfer; farming
    c. attachment bonds; business
    d. none of the above.

11. Evolutionary theorists argue that the offspring of our female ancestors lacking the attributes of _____ would have been less likely to survive (p. 375).

   *a. sociability and interpersonal sensitivity
    b. aggressiveness and resourcefulness
    c. assertiveness and good gross motor skills
    d. long legs and good spatial skills

12. _____ theorists believe that sexual attitudes and behavior are influenced throughout the life span by rewards, expectations, and punishments associated with sexual activities, as well as by observations of these activities (p. 375).

    a. Evolutionary
  *b. Social-learning
    c. Cognitive
    d. Humanistic

13. According to Erikson, if, in the first months after birth, caretakers are unloving or react inconsistently to the infant's needs, the child (p. 375):

  *a. may form an attitude of generalized mistrust.
    b. is unlikely to realize it because of cognitive limitations.
    c. will probably have low self-esteem as a school-age child.
    d. will become future oriented.

14. Unlearned responses displayed by mothers toward their infants that probably strengthen the bond between them include (p. 377):

    a. the secretion of oxytocin, which makes nipples erect for nursing when the infant cries.
    b. cradling of infants in the left arm, enabling the infant to be soothed by the mother's heartbeat.
    c. a type of speech that elongates the vowels.
  *d. all of the above.

15. Which of the following statements about father-child attachments is correct (p. 377)?

    a. The relationship of fathers to their offspring has been extensively studied.
    b. In most cultures, father have traditionally taken many responsibilities in raising children.
  *c. Recently, many fathers in our culture have begun to take a much more active role in caring for their infants.
    d. all of the above.

16. Parke and Sawin (1976) studied parental feeding skills and found that _____ were more skilled at responding to infant's cues than were _____ (p. 378).

    a. mothers; fathers
    b. fathers; mothers
    c. grandparents; parents
  *d. neither a nor b; both were equally skilled

17. Initially, the contribution of fathers tends to involve physical assistance of the infant, but fathers usually do not become heavily invested in the parenting role until the child (p. 378):

  *a. begins to walk and talk, at about age 1.
    b. starts school, at about age 5.
    c. enters adolescence, at about age 12.
    d. completes toilet training, at about age 2.

18. Fathers tend to emphasize _____ with their infants, whereas mothers are more likely to _____ (p. 378).

    *a. physical games; engage in verbal games
    b. verbal games; engage in physical games
    c. musical games; encourage cleanliness
    d. musical games; encourage talking

19. Even among monkeys, _____ is the primary mode of interaction between fathers and their offspring (p. 378).

    *a. physical play
    b. making vocal noises
    c. making noises with objects
    d. caretaking

20. For a brief time after birth, almost all infants show several signs associated with (p. 379):

    *a. reproductive maturity.
    b. adrenarche.
    c. osteopathy.
    d. extremely high IQ.

21. Penile erections have been observed in males from _____ on (p. 379).

    *a. birth
    b. the age of 6 months
    c. the age of 2 or 3 years
    d. the age of about 12

22. After fluctuation in testosterone levels early in a male's life, testosterone levels remain fairly similar to those in female infants from the _____ month until _____ (p. 379).

    *a. third; puberty
    b. ninth; age 6
    c. twelfth; age 9
    d. twenty-fourth; age 15

23. From birth on (p. 379):

    a. male babies are capable of erection.
    b. female babies are capable of vaginal lubrication.
    c. both males and females are capable of orgasm.
    *d. both a and b.

24. Parental reactions to early childhood sexuality (p. 380):

    a. are negative in almost all societies.
    b. should, in most cases, be negative so as to discourage autoerotic play, according to the textbook authors.
    *c. may play an important role in whether the child will be able to give and receive erotic pleasure in adulthood.
    d. accurately reflect the extent of pleasure the parents derive from their own sexual relationship.

25. Erik Erikson maintains that during the second year of life, children face the conflict of (p. 381):

    a. industry versus inferiority.
    b. trust versus mistrust.
    c. identity versus role confusion.
    *d. autonomy versus shame and doubt.

26. According to Erikson, it is best for parents to (p. 381):

    a. be overprotective of the child so that he or she won't get hurt.
    b. let the child explore as much as he or she wants.
    *c. offer a moderate amount of protection to the child.
    d. none of the above; it does not really matter how protective parents are at this time.

27. The association between dirt and genitals is likely to be more intense, long lasting, and sexually inhibiting for females than males because (p. 382):

    a. the quality of dirtiness is traditionally a more serious offense for girls than for boys.
    b. after urination, males are not taught to wipe their sexual organ whereas females are taught to wipe their genitals.
    c. urination and defecation are more erotically stimulating for girls than for boys.
    *d. both a and b.
    e. none of the above.

28. Ability to apply the appropriate gender label to oneself is gender _____; understanding that gender does not change over time is gender _____ (p. 383).

    *a. identity; constancy
    b. identity; permanence
    c. constancy; androgyny
    d. role identification; androgyny

29. As toddlers, children generally rely on _____ to distinguish girls from boys (p. 383).

    *a. external cues such as clothing or haircuts
    b. the absence or presence of a penis
    c. neither a nor b; they cannot distinguish boys from girls
    d. information from parents

30. According to Erikson, what conflict occurs about the same time as the Oedipal conflict described by Freud (p. 384)?

    a. autonomy versus shame
    b. trust versus mistrust
    c. industry versus inferiority
    *d. initiative versus guilt

31. Which of the following is true about gender differences (p. 384)?

    a. Both parents usually engage in differentiation based on the gender of their offspring, but distinctions made by fathers are more pronounced than those made by mothers.
    b. The specific traits and behaviors that are expected of males and of females vary from one culture to the next.
    c. The gender stereotype that females are less aroused by explicit sexual material has not been supported by contemporary research.
    *d. All of the above.

32. According to Erikson, the stage in which children begin to incorporate criticism and punishment into their self-images is (p. 384):

    *a. initiative versus guilt.
    b. trust versus mistrust.
    c. autonomy versus doubt.
    d. industry versus inferiority.

33. Barry, Bacon, and Child (1957) found that 82 percent of the cultures they surveyed encouraged _____ in girls more than in boys and _____ more in the training of boys than in the training of girls (p. 384).

    a. lying; rough-and-tumble play
    b. self-reliance; morality
    *c. nurturance; achievement
    d. initiative; socialization

34. According to _____, boys internalize moral values more completely than do girls (p. 385).

    *a. Sigmund Freud
    b. Erik Erikson
    c. social-learning theory
    d. the Goldmans

35. _____ assume more of a role in socializing children to play according to traditional gender roles than do _____ (p. 385).

    *a. Fathers; mothers
    b. Siblings; fathers
    c. Mothers; fathers
    d. Peers; mothers

36. Which of the following is true about sexual learning (p. 386)?

    a. As much is known about childhood sexuality for females as is known for males.
    b. Discouraging and punishing a child's sexual exploration will not affect the child's attitudes toward sex.
    *c. Through acting out roles in fantasy play, children learn to practice roles they will assume as they grow older.
    d. The capacity for self-stimulation and orgasm seems to be potentially available to very few children.

37. Which of these statements about children's awareness of gender is correct (p. 386)?

    a. Most children cannot accurately label their own gender until the age of 4.
    b. Most children cannot identify the gender of another unless the person is nude.
    *c. Children can generally apply the correct gender label to themselves by the time they are 2 or 2 1/2.
    d. Young girls are much better able to identify gender than are young boys.
    e. None of the above.

38. The primal scene refers to (p. 387):

    a. the male child's apparent realization that he might be castrated if he doesn't give up his love for his mother.
    b. the first time a male child recognizes that he has a penis whereas his mother does not.
    *c. a child's witnessing of parental lovemaking.
    d. a child observing an animal engaged in coitus.

39. Lewis and Janda (1988) found that (p. 387):

    *a. the sexual adjustment of college students was unrelated to either the extent of their childhood memories of parental nudity or to exposure to nudity in general.
    b. early childhood sex play led to more guilt for a female when she reached adulthood.
    c. among males, occasionally sleeping in the parental bed as a child was a source of guilt and anxiety once they reached adulthood.
    d. none of the above.

40. The Goldmans found that most children in English-speaking countries could not give an accurate answer when asked how to tell a newborn boy from a newborn girl until they were _____ years old (p. 388).

    a. 3
    b. 6
    *c. 9
    d. 12

41. If a child has been raised in a less restrictive atmosphere and happens to observe his or her parents having sex, the authors suggest that the child should be (p. 389):

    a. sent out of the room with no explanation.
    b. given a vague explanation of what was observed.
    c. given some information on sex education.
    *d. told that her or his parents are cuddling.

42. The Goldmans' research on the sexual knowledge of children found _____ children to be most knowledgeable (p. 389).

    a. American
    b. Canadian
    *c. Swedish
    d. Australian

43. Sweden differs from English-speaking countries in that in Sweden (p. 390):

    a. sex education is mandatory from kindergarten on.
    b. gender-role egalitarianism is emphasized in its education system.
    c. children take coed physical education classes and share coed locker rooms.
    d. all of the above.
    *e. both a and b.

44. Children judge physical attractiveness (p. 391):

    a. using the same attributes that adults do.
    b. beginning at a very young age.
    *c. both a and b.
    d. none of the above.

45. The earliest time at which children tend to differentiate between attractive and unattractive female faces, according to Langlois et al., is (p. 392):

    a. around the age of 6.
    b. around the age of 10.
    *c. as early as 2 months of age.
    d. as early as 4 years of age.

46. According to Erikson, when children reach the age at which they first enter school, they face the _____ crisis (p. 392).

    a. trust versus mistrust
    *b. industry versus inferiority
    c. autonomy versus doubt
    d. simplicity versus complexity

47. Money (1976) suggests that sexual play among children is (p. 392):

    *a. a natural developmental stage.
    b. an early sign of mental illness.
    c. related to sexual orientation in adulthood.
    d. none of the above.

48. Homosociality usually begins around age _____ and peaks at about ages _____ (p. 393).

    a. 4; 6 to 8
    *b. 8; 10 to 13
    c. 12; 14 to 16
    d. 15; 16 to 19

49. A 9-year-old girl who says, "Boys are dirty, mess, noisy creatures. I just don't like them," would be exhibiting (p. 394):

    a. gender reciprocity.
    *b. homosociality.
    c. gender identity.
    d. latent homosexuality.

50. During the homosocial phase (p. 394):

    a. children in North America feel considerable distaste for children of the opposite gender.
    b. homosexual behavior is fairly common.
    c. children have experiences that are important in determining orientation toward same-gender sexual partners later in life.
    *d. both a and b.
    e. all of the above.

51. Children's conceptions of the association between sexual intercourse and pregnancy (p. 396):

    a. tend to be well formulated, although incorrect, by the age of 8.
    b. are learned mostly from parents and school teachers.
    *c. are often inaccurate and vague, involving other parts of the anatomy such as the anus and the digestive tract.
    d. none of the above.

52. Various studies have shown that the majority of respondents would choose to get their sex education from (p. 396):

    *a. parents.
    b. books.
    c. school.
    d. peers.

53. Research has shown that when parents accept their children's interest in sex and discuss sexuality with them, the children (p. 396):

    a. tend to have sexual intercourse at earlier ages.
  *b. tend to delay their initial sexual intercourse.
    c. feel guilty about sex.
    d. tend to have many sex partners in adolescence.

54. Which of the following is true about sexuality education programs in the United States (p. 398)?

    a. Given the results of preliminary testing of the effect of abstinence-only programs, it has been speculated by Roosa and Christopher that such approaches may stimulate rebellion rather than responsibility.
    b. Opponents of sex education sometimes cite Freud's latency hypothesis—the idea that late childhood is a time during which sexual interest and activity are repressed, not to emerge again until the onset of puberty.
    c. The Howard and McCabe (1990) and Kirby et al. (1991) studies showed that boys and girls who were not yet sexually active at the time they received sex and contraceptive education were more likely to postpone sexual activity than were those who did not receive such education.
  *d. All of the above.

55. Comparisons of abstinence-only programs with postponement and contraceptive protection programs suggest that the latter are _____ in encouraging young people to _____ (p. 398).

    a. more effective; be rebellious and do the opposite of the information provided
    b. no different; postpone sexual activity
    c. less effective; use contraceptives
  *d. more effective; postpone sexual activity and to use contraceptives when they do become sexually active.

56. According to Erikson, the challenge of adolescence involves the crisis of (p. 402):

    a. realization versus ignorance.
    b. generativity versus stagnation.
    c. intimacy versus isolation.
  *d. identity versus role confusion.

57. Erikson suggests that it is most desirable for the adolescent psychologically if the parents (p. 402):

    a. allow the adolescent as much freedom as possible.
    b. significantly curtail the adolescent's freedom.
    c. completely avoid discussions of a sexual nature.
  *d. allow moderate levels of freedom.

58. Freud called the last step in psychosexual development the _____ stage (p. 402):

    *a. genital
    b. identity versus role confusion
    c. phallic
    d. anal

59. Girls tend to learn about masturbation from (p. 403):

    a. parents.
    b. peers.
    *c. accidental self-discovery.
    d. sex-education classes.

60. According to Gagnon and Simon (p. 403):

    a. the development goal of adolescence is identity versus stagnation.
    *b. basic sexual roles and scripts emerge gradually during adolescence.
    c. the biological changes of puberty are most important in determining sexual identity.
    d. adolescents experience renewed sexual interest in the parent of the opposite gender.

61. In Bem's scoring system, people who describe themselves as having masculine and feminine traits and behaviors in equal measure are called _____, whereas those who endorse characteristics traditionally associated with their genetic sex are called _____ (p. 404).

    *a. androgynous; gender typed
    b. assertive; rigid
    c. latent; genital
    d. individualed; profluent

62. Carl Jung wrote extensively about androgyny and characterized masculine traits and impulses in a woman as _____, and feminine traits and impulses in a man as _____ (p. 404).

    a. estrus; testrus
    *b. animus; anima
    c. healthy; undesirable
    d. sex typed; yeoman typed

63. Kinsey et al. (1948, 1953) found that _____ percent of females and _____ percent of the males recalled having masturbated to orgasm by the time they were 12 (p. 405).

    a. 38; 72
    b. 4; 60
    c. 3; 49
    *d. 12; 21

64. Boys tend to learn about masturbation from (p. 405):

    a. parents.
    *b. peers.
    c. accidental self-discovery.
    d. sex-education classes.
    e. television.

65. Data collected by Hunt (1974) indicated that _____ than they did when the Kinsey group conducted its work (p. 405).

    a. girls appear to engage in masturbation at a later age
    b. boys and girls begin masturbating at a later age
    c. boys and girls experience more anxiety and guilt about masturbation
    *d. boys and girls begin masturbating at a younger age

66. Tanner found that in Western Europe, menarche occurred at the average age of _____ in the year 1840 and that menarchal age is now at about ages _____ (p. 406).

    *a. 17; 12 or 13
    b. 8; 13 or 14
    c. 12; 13 or 14
    d. 13; 10 or 11

67. Vern Bullough found problems with Tanner's analysis of menarche. Examination of cross-cultural data now shows that the average age of menarche varies between _____ for most of the world, and _____ (p. 406).

    a. 9 and 10; the range was from between 16 to 18 prior to the Middles Ages.
    b. 10 and 11; the range used to be higher in the past
    *c. 12.5 and 14.5; this is about the same range as has been reported throughout most of recorded history.
    d. 14 and 15; the range was lower at the beginning of the twentieth-century.

68. The secular decline hypothesis states that (p. 406):

    a. changes in mood are caused by fluctuations in hormones associated with phases of the menstrual cycle.
    b. menstrual cycles of women living in close proximity to one another become synchronized.
    *c. the age of first menstruation has been declining dramatically over the past 140 years.
    d. changes in mental ability are caused by fluctuations in hormones associated with phases of the menstrual cycle.

69. A strong relationship between educational level and sexual repertoire was found by the Kinsey group, with college-educated people engaging in a greater range of sexual activities than less-educated people. Research conducted by DeLamater and MacCorquodale (1979) indicates that this relationship (p. 407):

    a. continues to exist.
    b. has grown stronger.
    *c. no longer exists.
    d. none of the above.

70. Which of the following is true about the first dating experiences in adolescence (p. 407)?

    *a. Dating typically starts around the age of 12 or 13.
    b. Kissing is rarely done.
    c. Genital fondling is attempted.
    d. Exclusive relationships are the norm.

71. Over the past few generations (pp. 407–408):

    a. men's acceptance of premarital sexual expression has increased more than women's acceptance.
    *b. women's acceptance of premarital sexual expression has increased more than men's.
    c. both men's and women's acceptance of premarital sexual expression has remained unchanged.
    d. the majority of young people believe that women, more than men, should initiate sexual expression.

72. The double standard still exists with respect to the acceptability of (pp. 407–409):

    a. premarital intercourse for males versus females.
    *b. female versus male initiation of sexual interaction.
    c. female versus male paying for dating expenses.
    d. female versus male orgasm.

73. When presented with strategies to seek sexual intimacy or to avoid sexual intimacy, young men and women rated strategies to (p. 409):

    *a. seek sexual intimacy as primarily employed by men rather than women.
    b. avoid having sexual intimacy as primarily employed by men rather than women.
    c. seek sexual intimacy as equally likely to be employed by men and women.
    d. avoid having sexual intimacy as equally likely to be employed by men and women.

74. The majority of contemporary adolescents describe their first sexual partner as a (p. 410):

    a. prostitute.
    b. person with whom they had a casual relationship.
    *c. person with whom they felt emotional attachment or love.
    d. person to whom they were engaged to be married.

Essay Questions

75. Describe Freud's theory of psychosexual development from birth to puberty (pp. 373–374).

76. Compare Freud's perspective on the development of sexual behavior with those of the evolutionary and social-learning theorists (pp. 373–376).

77. Compare Freud's view with Erikson's in terms of the importance of the early years of life in personality development (pp. 373–376).

78. Describe Erikson's theory of psychosocial development (p. 374).

79. The association between the dirtiness of human waste products and the genitals may account for some of the differences between the sexual attitudes and behavior of boys and girls. Discuss this statement (pp. 381–382).

80. Discuss the process of gender-role socialization (pp. 384–385).

81. What is the difference between gender differences and gender stereotypes? Why is it important to understand the difference between them (pp. 385–386)?

82. Pretend that your 4-year-old child wakes up from her nap and wanders into your bedroom while you and your mate are making love. Based on suggestions from the text, how would you respond to this situation (pp. 387–388)?

83. Discuss sex education, considering both schools and parents as sources of information. Based on the available research, what effects does sex education have on students' permissiveness (pp. 395–397)?

84. Discuss the history of abstinence-only sex education programs (pp. 397–399).

85. Compare and contrast abstinence-only sex education programs with postponement and protection sex education programs (pp. 397–402).

86. Discuss the notion of androgyny, including the ideas of Constantinople, Bem, and Jung (pp. 403–404).

87. What is the secular decline hypothesis? Based on evidence, present an argument against it (pp. 406–408).

88. What is the sexual double standard, and to what extent does it still exist today between males and females (pp. 407–408)?

89. Discuss the affective responses of women to their first coital experience. What factors are associated with women's positive or negative feelings about first intercourse (p. 411)?

CHAPTER 13

Gender and Sexuality in Adulthood

Multiple-Choice Questions

1. According to Erikson, the critical challenge of young adulthood is (p. 416):

    a. trust versus mistrust.
    *b. intimacy versus isolation.
    c. autonomy versus doubt.
    d. industry versus inferiority.

2. When Roche (1986) asked subjects what they considered to be proper sexual behavior dur-ing the five stages of a dating relationship, he found that (p. 416):

    a. there were strong gender differences in the last two stages.
    *b. during the first three stages, men condoned greater permissiveness than women.
    c. the majority of men and women indicated oral sex was appropriate at stage 2.
    d. few women reported engaging in sexual intercourse during stages 4 and 5.

3. In the Roche dating study, the only gender difference to emerge for the later stages of a dating relationship involved (p. 417):

    *a. oral-genital sex.
    b. sexual interactions with another person.
    c. heavy petting and intercourse.
    d. having fantasies about strangers.

4. A large majority of students in the Roche study thought that (p. 417):

    a. women should not initiate sex with a man, even if they are in love.
    b. oral-genital sex is not appropriate until after marriage.
    *c. sexual intercourse was acceptable for a couple who were in love and dating each other exclusively.
    d. none of the above.

5. Which of the following is true about nonmarital sexual intimacy (p. 417)?

    a. Contemporary attitudes about it are almost the same in North America as in the rest of the world.
    *b. The longitudinal research needed to answer questions about the role of early emo-tional and sexual intimacy in nonmarital relationships is lacking.
    c. Research has shown that, in general, men today do not respect women with whom they have nonmarital coitus.
    d. None of the above.

6. Traditionally, women were taught to use sexual intimacy (p. 417):

    a. for their own enjoyment and to improve their self-esteem.
    *b. as a tool for obtaining a marriage proposal.
    c. to become sexually experienced in preparation for married life.
    d. none of the above.

7. Traditional assumptions about differences between male and female sexuality include beliefs that (p. 417):

    a. the purpose of marriage is to have sex.
    b. men want sex more than women do.
    c. women who engage in nonmarital intercourse are not respected by men.
    *d. all of the above.

8. None of the _____ dating college couples in Peplau et al.'s. (1977) longitudinal study had divorced in the 15-year follow-up period (p. 418).

    *a. traditional
    b. moderate
    c. liberal
    d. moderate or liberal

9. In the Peplau et al. (1977) study (p. 417):

    a. more couples in the later-coitus group, compared to the early-coitus group, gave low estimates of the probability of marrying their partner.
    b. a higher proportion of the couples in the early-coitus group reported being in love.
    *c. about half of the couples reported having had sexual intercourse within a month of their first date.
    d. none of the above.

10. As identified by Peplau et al. (1977), which of the following is true (p. 418)?

    a. Compare with those who were sexually intimate, the couples who abstained from intercourse were less likely to report being in love.
    b. Men's reported sexual satisfaction with their partners did not differ as a function of the time of first coitus together.
    c. Women in the early-coitus group reported greater sexual satisfaction with their partners than did women in the later-coitus group.
    *d. All of the above.

11. At the end of the study, Peplau et al. (1977) found that after two years, there was _____ between the pattern of sexual behavior (coitus within a month, later coitus, or abstention) and the outcome of relationships (marriage, still dating, or separation) (p. 418).

    *a. no association
    b. a strong positive correlation
    c. a weak positive correlation
    d. a weak negative correlation

12. In the longitudinal research by Peplau et al. (1977), compared to couples who had coitus within a month, couples who chose to wait longer before having coitus (p. 417):

   a. reported feeling closer to their partner and knowing him or her better.
   b. were more likely to report being in love.
   c. gave higher estimates of the probability of marrying their partner.
   *d. all of the above.

13. In a 15-year follow-up of the couples in the original study by Peplau et al. (1977), it was found that (p. 418):

   *a. gender-role attitudes assessed while the volunteers were in college were largely unrelated to the general patterns of marriage and childbearing for either gender.
   b. traditional women were unlikely to have married their college sweetheart.
   c. all of the traditional women had divorced.
   d. the divorce rate among the couples who married their college partner was high.

14. In a survey of students enrolled in sex education courses from 1975 through 1984, Story (1985) found (p. 418):

   a. less and less concern with sexually transmitted diseases.
   b. a decrease in the proportion of college students who said they were in love over that time span.
   c. results similar to those found by Peplau et al. (1977).
   *d. increases in conservative sexual attitudes and behaviors over time.

15. About _____ percent of Americans marry, and about _____ percent of them return to single status through separation or divorce (p. 418).

   a. 75; 40
   *b. 90; 64
   c. 50; 25
   d. 65; 50

16. The number of households containing only one person (p. 419):

   a. is almost one out of four.
   b. is rapidly increasing.
   c. is rapidly declining.
   *d. both a and b.
   e. both a and c.

17. Which of the following statements about premarital sex is true (p. 420)?

   a. AIDS has reduced the likelihood of premarital coitus.
   b. The likelihood of engaging in fellatio and cunnilingus has declined in the past 20 years.
   *c. The trend toward more conservative attitudes about premarital sex does not appear to be reflected in the actual behavior of adolescents.
   d. both a and b.

18. Women with a _____ of education are less likely to marry (p. 420).

    a. substantial amount (graduate-school training)
    b. moderate amount (completed bachelor's degree)
    c. small amount (less than total of five years in school)
    d. both a and b.
  *e. both a and c.

19. According to Bumpass et al. (1991) (p. 421):

  *a. most cohabitors report that their lives would be about the same if they were married
    b. a larger percentage of cohabitors report that they are more sexually satisfied than married couples.
    c. cohabitation as a replacement for early marriage is most frequent for those who have completed college.
    d. cohabitation is more common in rural areas.

20. Which of the following is true about cohabitors (p. 421)?

    a. Cohabitors report less sexual satisfaction than do noncohabitors.
    b. Most cohabitors plan to marry the person with whom they are living.
    c. For most couples, cohabitation appears to be an alternative to marriage.
  *d. Marriages that are preceded by cohabitation have higher dissolution rates than marriages without previous cohabitation.

21. Concerning romantic relationships, the textbook states that men are more likely than women to (p. 422):

  *a. readily fall in love.
    b. end a relationship that seems ill-fated.
    c. weigh a relationship against various alternatives.
    d. all of the above.

22. The average age of first marriage (p. 422):

    a. has been declining steadily for the past decade.
  *b. has been rising steadily for the past three decades.
    c. has remained constant for the past half-century.
    d. none of the above.

23. As of 1992, the average age of first marriage was _____ for women and _____ for men (p. 422).

    a. 19.2; 21.1
    b. 21.5; 22.0
  *c. 24.4; 26.5
    d. 25.5; 20.1

24. Which of these statements about research comparing mothers who idealized motherhood with those who acknowledged mixed feelings about is correct (p. 423)?

    *a. Women who idealized motherhood displayed more discomfort in their mothering behavior.
    b. Children of women who idealized motherhood were more dependent on their mothers.
    c. Women who idealized motherhood felt that it made them a "real woman."
    d. Women with mixed feelings had more children with neurotic disorders.

25. Which of the following is true about families with children (p. 424)?

    a. When a married woman returns to work after having given birth, the couple typically divides up household chores evenly.
    b. Few new mothers take a maternity leave before returning to their occupations.
    c. By 1991, 10 percent of mothers with children under 1 year old were employed outside the home.
    *d. The length of time women remain at home after giving birth has decreased in recent years.

26. Which of the following is true concerning sex for couples (p. 426)?

    *a. Married couples typically engage in intercourse two or three times a week during the early years, with frequency of intercourse declining over time.
    b. Parenthood is unrelated to frequency of sexual intercourse.
    c. A drop in sexual activity does not tend to occur for cohabiting couples.
    d. None of the above.

27. There tends to be a drop in sexual activity over the duration of a relationship for couples who are (p. 426):

    a. married.
    b. gay.
    c. cohabiting.
    *d. all of the above.

28. Which of these statements about marriage and sexual intimacy is correct (p. 426)?

    a. Couples make love less frequently early on in marriage.
    b. Couples with large families like sex more than couples with fewer children.
    *c. The arrival of babies is usually followed by a decrease in the frequency of coitus.
    d. True marital intimacy has a destructive impact on the couple's sexual relationship.

29. In nineteenth-century America, marriage lasted an average of _____ years before one of the partners died (p. 426).

    a. 8
    *b. 12
    c. 20
    d. 33

30. The most important quality for marital sexual happiness in Hunt's study was (p. 427):

    a. frequency of sex.
    b. absence of sexual dysfunction.
    *c. similarity of the couple's sexual desires.
    d. the amount of variation in sexual activity.

31. According to Troll and Smith (1976), over a period of time in marriages, there are likely to be (p. 427):

    *a. decreases in attraction and increases in attachment.
    b. increases in attraction and decreases in attachment.
    c. decreases in intimacy and decreases in attachment.
    d. increases in conflict and decreases in security.

32. In a number of mammalian species, a male who copulates and ejaculates several times with one female and then stops will become aroused again when confronted with a different female. This has been labeled the (p. 428):

    a. generativity theory.
    b. promiscuity principle.
    c. hen-peck hypothesis.
    *d. Coolidge effect.

33. Which of the following is supported by data (p. 429)?

    a. Three-quarters of Americans disapprove of extramarital sex under any conditions.
    b. The trend toward extramarital sex has begun to decline.
    c. Attitudes towards extramarital sex are more negative in the United States than in Western Europe.
    *d. All of the above.

34. Regarding extramarital sex (p. 429):

    a. most Americans disapprove of it and don't do it.
    *b. most Americans disapprove of it, but about half have had extramarital relations.
    c. most Americans expect monogamy when first married and become even less tolerant of extramarital sex over the course of the marriage.
    d. Western Europeans are less likely to approve of it than are Americans.

35. Which of the following statements is supported by data (p. 429)?

    a. Individuals who rated their marriages as happy were less likely to approve of extramarital sex than those who rated their marriages as less happy.
    b. Men and women often begin affairs to seek a reaffirmation of sexual attractiveness.
    c. Marital imbalances sometimes lead a spouse to seek an extramarital relationship.
    *d. All of the above.

36. Research conducted in an airport by Glass and Wright (1992) on extramarital sex found that (p. 432):

    *a. men were more likely to endorse sex as a justification for extramarital involvement.
    b. women were more likely to perceive such affairs as destructive.
    c. men and women were equally likely to be involved in extramarital affairs.
    d. men were more likely to endorse love as a justification for extramarital involvement.

37. As identified by Walster et al., equity is (p. 432):

    a. basic agreement with marriage partners on political and religious issues.
    *b. a perceived balance between the benefits that a relationship provides and the personal investment it requires.
    c. the difference between the expectations and realities of marriage.
    d. another term for extramarital sex.

38. In a *Psychology Today* survey, Berscheid et al. (1972, 1973) found that the frequency of extramarital relationships varied according to (p. 432):

    a. gender.
    b. length of the primary relationship.
    *c. perceptions of equity of the primary relationship.
    d. both a and b.

39. In a study of married Dutch persons who had been involved in extramarital affairs, Prins, Buunk, and Van Yperen (1993) found that (p. 432):

    a. women reported stronger desires than men to engage in extramarital sex.
    b. more men than women reported involvement in extramarital affairs.
    c. men who felt deprived in their marital relationships were more likely to have extramarital relations than men who reported equity in their marriages.
    *d. women who felt deprived or advantaged in their marital relationships were more likely to have extramarital relations than women who reported equity in their marriages.

40. In a series of studies, Gilmartin (1974) found that, compared to nonswingers, swingers (p. 433):

    *a. reported less gratifying relationships with their parents during childhood and adolescence.
    b. had less happy marriages.
    c. were more likely to have been in therapy.
    d. were more likely to have problems with alcohol.
    e. all of the above.

41. Gilmartin's (1974) research on swingers suggests that (p. 433):

    *a. they often rate their marriage as happy or very happy.
    b. their education level is often lower than that of the general public.
    c. they are very liberal in their political and social attitudes.
    d. none of the above.

42. From the standpoint of marital longevity, it is best to marry at which age (p. 434)?

    a. in the early 20s for men and women
    b. between ages 25 and 27 for women and in the late 30s for men
    *c. after age 30 for women
    d. after age 40 for both men and women

43. Which of the following statements is true about divorce (p. 434)?

    a. Individuals with less education are less likely to divorce.
    b. Divorce is usually a result of difficulties with in-laws.
    c. The proportion of divorces is highest at around the seventh year of marriage in most societies that have been studied.
    *d. Divorce peaks between the ages of 20 to 24 for both genders in the United States.

44. A survey of 160 societies indicated that _____ was the *most* common reason given for divorce (p. 434).

    a. cruelty by the husband
    *b. infidelity, particularly by the wife,
    c. financial difficulty
    d. gender-role disagreement

45. Which of the following statements about adjustment to divorce is true (p. 435)?

    a. The problems women face after divorce affect only a minority, whereas the majority of divorced men have adjustment problems.
    *b. Men are more likely to experience severe depression.
    c. Women are more likely to experience illnesses requiring hospitalization.
    d. Postdivorce adjustment is more related to gender than to the extent to which the couple want the divorce.

46. After divorce (p. 435):

    *a. men and women usually do not become celibate.
    b. men are less sexually active than women.
    c. older divorced people are more sexually active than younger divorced people.
    d. none of the above.

47. Which of the following statements concerning life expectancy is correct (p. 436)?

    *a. Old age is a relatively new phenomenon.
    b. Men live longer than women.
    c. Life expectancy increased up to the year 1970 but has since begun to decline.
    d. Most women are able to reproduce until they die.

48. The textbook authors attribute the double standard of aging to (p. 437):

    a. the media's portrayal of male and female sexuality.
    b. increased life expectancy beyond reproductive capacity.
    c. gender differences in the speed of termination of reproductive capacity.
    *d. all of the above.

49. Erikson's developmental crisis of the midlife years involves (p. 438):

    a. integrity versus despair.
    b. sexuality versus money.
    c. identify versus role confusion.
   *d. generativity versus stagnation.

50. Menopause (pp. 438–439):

    a. is the gradual cessation of ovulation and menstruation.
    b. can occur between the ages of 35 and 55 but for the average woman occurs at age 51.
    c. involves instability between the cardiovascular and muscular system.
   *d. all of the above.

51. Research by Cutler, Garcia, and McCoy (1987) on menopause (p. 439):

    a. substantiated the general belief that menopausal women show a sharp decline in vaginal lubrication.
    b. substantiated the general belief that menopausal women show a sharp decline in sexual response.
   *c. contradicted the general belief that menopausal women's decrease in estrogen secretion produces decreases in vaginal lubrication.
    d. both a and b.

52. Recent research with menopausal women found little reduction in their sexual arousal and vaginal lubrication. The researchers concluded that the findings may be due to (p. 439):

    a. the women's use of postmenopausal estrogen therapy.
   *b. an interaction of social class with sexual responsiveness and menopause.
    c. the recent remarriages of the women in the sample.
    d. the use of large doses of vitamin E by women in their sample.

53. Research with both young women and menopausal women by Cutler et al. (1987) indicates that (p. 439):

    a. low levels of sexual activity are the result of low levels of estrogen.
    b. low levels of sexual activity cause low levels of estrogen.
   *c. low levels of sexual activity are somehow related to unusually low levels of estrogen.
    d. menopause per se automatically brings sexual responsiveness to an end.

54. A review of the male menopause literature by Fetherstone and Hepworth (1985) found that (p. 439):

    a. males with strong masculine images are less psychologically troubled at this time.
    b. psychological difficulties in middle age appear to stem from hormonal changes.
   *c. psychological difficulties in middle age appear to stem from cultural and lifestyle changes.
    d. both b and c.

55. Hunt attributed the increase in the frequency of marital coitus for couples aged 46 to 60 (compared to frequency reported for this age group by the Kinsey group) to (p. 440):

    a. more liberal attitudes toward sexuality and the middle-aged.
    b. increased awareness of the variety of coital techniques.
    c. widespread advice by physicians that sexual activity will prolong life.
    *d. both a and b.

56. Midlife reassessment tends to be easier for (p. 439):

    a. men with strong masculine images.
    *b. men who take on androgynous values and behaviors.
    c. women who are passive.
    d. women with strong feminine images.

57. Which of these physiological changes occur in males as they reach old age (p. 440)?

    *a. The prostate gland often enlarges.
    b. The ability to have orgasm is lost.
    c. Sperm production stops.
    d. The length of the refractory period decreases.

58. Which of these physiological changes occur in females as they age (p. 441)?

    *a. Estrogen production usually declines between ages 40 and 60.
    b. The ability to have orgasms is lost.
    c. The vaginal walls thicken.
    d. The vagina becomes more acidic.

59. Which of the following is true about aging in women (p. 441)?

    a. The prostate gland often enlarges.
    b. There is a reduction in testosterone secretion.
    c. Fibrous tissue in the breasts is replaced by glandular material.
    *d. Breast tissue atrophies.

60. When males reach their 70s and 80s, the size of the _____ decreases (p. 440).

    a. prostate
    b. scrotum
    *c. testes
    d. all of the above

61. Research done by Murnen and Allgeier (1985) to try to explain the finding that college students perceive their parents as less sexually active than a normative sample of adults found that students (p. 443):

   a. get anxious at the thought of their parents having sex because of incest fears.
   *b. whose parents communicated more with them about sex had higher estimates of their parents' frequency of sexual activity.
   c. are generally disgusted by the idea of their parents' having sex.
   d. none of the above.

62. Pocs and Godow (1976) found that college students tended to underestimate (p. 443):

   *a. their parents' sexual activities.
   b. the negative effects of aging on sexual desire.
   c. the effect of diabetes on sexual desire.
   d. the number of women who are widows.

63. The Kinsey group found no other factor for men that affected the frequency of total sexual outlet as much as (p. 443):

   a. number of partners.
   b. marital happiness.
   c. religious values.
   *d. age.

64. According to Brecher's (1984) *Consumer Reports* study, _____ 70 years old or older still engage in sexual intercourse (p. 443).

   a. a small minority of men and women
   b. many men and a small minority of women
   *c. the majority of men and women
   d. all of those interviewed who were

65. The largest survey to date on sexuality and the elderly was published in (p. 443):

   a. the *Journal of Experimental Psychology*.
   *b. *Consumer Reports*.
   c. the *Hite Report*.
   d. *Gerontology Today*.

66. A difficulty with using cross-sectional research to study possible changes in frequency of sexual activity as people age is that (p. 444):

   *a. observed differences may be a function of the time periods in which the age groups received their sexual socialization and values.
   b. people who are over 70 have been unwilling to admit engaging in sexual activity.
   c. this approach cannot take into account physical infirmities that may eliminate the capacity to engage in sexual activity.
   d. this approach violates the principle of informed consent.

67. Among the elderly, in addition to physiological capability, sexual performance appears to be associated with which factor(s) (p. 444)?

    a. past sexual activity
    b. opportunity
    c. number of children
    d. number of previous marriages
    *e. both a and b

68. Both men and women married to younger spouses tend to live longer than those married to older spouses because (p. 444):

    a. healthier, more vigorous people choose younger spouses.
    b. younger (versus older) women are more likely to choose healthy, more vigorous men.
    c. marriage to younger women causes older men to take better care of themselves.
    *d. none of the above; the cause of this relationship is unknown.

69. Studies of the effect of retirement on marriage have centered primarily on (p. 446):

    *a. gender-role differentiation.
    b. the ability to enjoy sexual interaction.
    c. the frequency of sexual interaction.
    d. the role of physical health and sexuality.

70. Which of these statements about widowhood is correct (p. 446)?

    a. There are more widowed men than widowed women.
    b. Women experience greater trauma than men when marriages terminate due to death.
    *c. Older women are becoming more open to masturbation as a means of sexual outlet.
    d. Widowed men have greater difficulty finding a sexual partner than do widowed women.

71. Research on institutionalization of the aged indicates that (p. 447):

    *a. many nursing home residents retain sexual interests and activity.
    b. many residents and staff are quite knowledgeable about sexuality.
    c. institutional design and planning is specially geared to the sexual needs of the elderly.
    d. most young adults recognize the importance of the sexuality of the elderly.

72. Provision of gender-integrated living arrangements in one New York City nursing home was associated with (p. 448):

    a. increased sexual contact.
    b. improved self-care.
    c. a more cheerful atmosphere.
    *d. all of the above.

Essay Questions

73. Discuss the five stages of a dating relationship as described by Roche (1986). What did Roche's subjects consider to be proper sexual behavior during these stages? Refer to gender differences (p. 417).

74. Discuss the research on sexual behavior and emotional intimacy conducted by Peplau et al. (p. 417).

75. Describe the results of the longitudinal research by Peplau et al. (1977) in terms of the association between timing of first coitus and the outcome of a relationship (p. 417).

76. Discuss the misconceptions associated with single lifestyles. Who is more likely to remain single? What are some difficulties associated with this lifestyle? What are some advantages (pp. 418–420)?

77. Various studies indicate that a number of people cohabit with a romantic partner for some period of time in their lives. How do cohabitors differ from those who do not cohabit (pp. 420–421)?

78. What advice is given regarding the negotiation of relationship contracts in the textbook? What advice is given for all couples who decide to live together, whether or not they want to draw up a contract (pp. 421–422)?

79. Discuss the contrast between the dream and the reality of most American marriages. Include a discussion of multiple roles and the allocation of household and parenting tasks both before and after the birth of a child. Also mention the expansion hypothesis (pp. 422–423).

80. Most Americans disapprove of extramarital sex, yet about 50 percent report they engage in it. Explain this discrepancy (pp. 428–432).

81. What is unique about consensual extramarital sex? Who engages in it? Based on the research, is it successful (pp. 433–434)?

82. Discuss postdivorce adjustment, noting gender differences in response to separation and divorce. What variables correlate with positive adjustment to divorce (pp. 434–435)?

83. Describe the double standard of aging and several factors that may be associated with it (pp. 436–437).

84. Discuss menopause and the various related studies. Mention specific hormones. How does menopause affect the sexuality of most women (pp. 438–439)?

85. Describe the factors that may be associated with decreasing sexual activity among the elderly (pp. 440–444).

86. Describe the physiological changes in the reproductive system of the male and of the female (pp. 440–443).

87. Discuss long-term relationships and sexual satisfaction (pp. 440–443).

CHAPTER 14

Enhancing Sexual Health

Multiple-Choice Questions

1. Which of the following is *not* a factor evaluated by the Sexual Self-Concept Scale (p. 455)?

   a. sexual preoccupation
   b. sexual depression
   *c. sexual maturity
   d. sexual esteem

2. Using the Sexuality Scale in research with college students, Snell and Papini (1989) found that for _____, scores on sexual esteem and sexual depression were _____ correlated (p. 455).

   *a. both genders; negatively
   b. women only; negatively
   c. both genders; positively
   d. men only; positively

3. Using the Sexuality Scale in research with college students, Snell and Papini (1989) found that for _____, sexual preoccupation was positively correlated with sexual _____ (p. 455).

   a. men; esteem
   b. women; depression
   c. both genders; depression
   *d. women; esteem

4. High-school and college students who scored high on the Sexual Self-Concept Scale (Winter, 1988) were more likely to (p. 455):

   *a. use contraception.
   b. have been in trouble with the law.
   c. have lower grades.
   d. be under 20 years old.

5. White, Case, McWhirter, and Mattison (1990) assessed the relationship of exercise, physical fitness, and sexuality among middle-aged men and found that (p. 457):

   a. performing aerobic exercise had no relationship to risk for coronary heart disease.
   *b. sexual activity increased more for the exercisers than for the control group.
   c. within the exercising group, there were fewer orgasms.
   d. within the control group, there was comparatively more masturbation.

6. Comparing both genders, at normal body weight, _____ are _____ as likely to regard themselves as overweight (p. 457).

   a. women; four times
   b. men; twice
   *c. women; twice
   d. men; just as likely

7. Freedman (1986) maintains that female beauty as personified by slimness has been an ideal in Western culture for _____ of the past 600 years (p. 458).

   a. 20
   *b. 60
   c. 100
   d. 400

8. People with _____ tend to fall within 10 pounds of their normal weight range and follow a binge-purge cycle to control their weight (p. 457).

   *a. bulimia
   b. anorexia nervosa
   c. Reye's syndrome
   d. premenstrual syndrome

9. A study of male anorexics and bulimics by Herzog, Norman, Gordon, and Pepose (1984) found a high prevalence of _____ in the male sample and that the males were _____ likely to have had sexual relations than a comparison group of females with eating disorders (p. 459).

   a. blacks; less
   b. sexually transmitted diseases; more
   c. bisexuality; more
   *d. homosexuality; less

10. A series of studies with girls from fifth through the twelfth grades showed that (p. 462):

    a. expectations may be important in experiences of menstruation.
    b. younger girls expected less severe menstrual distress than did older volunteers.
    c. older girls were less likely to discuss menstruation.
    *d. both a and b.

11. Which of the following statements is true about premenstrual days (pp. 460–461)?

    a. Women using the pill report more mood swings than women not taking oral contraceptives.
    *b. The days of the week were found to be more closely related to mood than was a woman's menstrual phase.
    c. About 22 percent of women experience severe premenstrual symptoms.
    d. Women on the pill have been found to experience more anxiety about pregnancy during the premenstrual period.

12. Recent research with menopausal women found that the range and invasiveness of side effects associated with menopause may be due to (p. 464):

    a. the women's use of postmenopausal androgen therapy.
    *b. an interaction with social and cultural variables.
    c. the recent remarriages of the women in the sample.
    d. the use of large dosages of vitamin E by women in the sample.

13. Hormone-replacement therapy (HRT) is sometimes used for (p. 464):

    *a. postmenopausal women.
    b. women with premenstrual syndrome.
    c. menstrual cramps.
    d. all of the above.

14. The use of supplementary estrogen by postmenopausal women (p. 464):

    a. is ill advised, as it may contribute to osteoporosis.
    b. is recommended by the National Institutes of Health.
    c. should be combined with daily calcium and weight-bearing exercise.
    *d. both b and c.

15. Which of the following is true about estrogen therapy (p. 464)?

    a. The risks of long-term HRT outweigh the benefits.
    *b. It appears to increase the risk of endometrial cancer.
    c. It is correlated with increased risk of heart disease.
    d. It is correlated with increased risk of osteoporosis.

16. Approximately _____ percent of people of childbearing age in the United States experience infertility (p. 465).

    a. 5
    b. 10
    *c. 15
    d. 25

17. If a couple engages in intercourse without contraception on a regular basis for a year without conceiving a child, it is assumed that they are (p. 465):

    *a. infertile.
    b. sexually dysfunctional.
    c. both a and b.
    d. none of the above.

18. Of the couples who go through an infertility analysis, about _____ percent of the time the woman's reproductive system is the source of the infertility, and about _____ percent of the time infertility is attributed to the man (p. 465).

   *a. 40; 30
    b. 80; 10
    c. 98; 2
    d. 20; 20

19. Several general conditions, including anemia, vitamin deficiencies, malnutrition, and environmental or psychological stress, are associated with (p. 465):

   *a. the absence of ovulation.
    b. blocked fallopian tubes.
    c. very thick cervical mucus.
    d. none of the above.

20. Infertility in women may be caused by (pp. 465–467):

    a. endometriosis.
    b. blocked fallopian tubes.
    c. genetic and chromosomal disorders.
   *d. all of the above.

21. When women are given drugs to correct hormonal imbalances or to stimulate ovulation, there is a related possibility of (p. 466):

   *a. multiple births.
    b. heart disease.
    c. emphysema.
    d. birth defects.

22. The process of in vitro fertilization/embryo transfer involves (p. 466):

    a. removal of scar tissue from the fallopian tubes.
   *b. removal of egg cells from the ovary so that they can be fertilized in the lab and then transferred to the uterus.
    c. removal of a mature egg from the ovary and placement of it in a portion of the fallopian tube below a blockage point.
    d. the placement of donor sperm in the uterus for cases in which the woman's partner is sterile.

23. Gamete transfer involves (p. 466):

   *a. removing a mature egg from a woman's ovary and placing the egg and sperm in her functioning fallopian tube.
    b. moving a mature egg from one woman to another.
    c. placing donated sperm in the uterus of a woman who is allergic to her partner's semen.
    d. transplantation of an ovary from one woman to another.

24. The gamete transfer procedure to remedy infertility requires (p. 466):

   *a. at least one intact fallopian tube.
   b. conception outside the woman's body.
   c. use of maternal blood transfusions.
   d. waiting until the woman is at least 35 years old.

25. _____ is a condition in which cells from the lining of the uterus grow in places other than the uterus (p. 467).

   *a. Endometriosis
   b. Exogenesis
   c. Postpartum
   d. Alveoli

26. Infertility rates _____ age (p. 467).

   *a. increase with
   b. decrease with
   c. generally stay the same with
   d. are not related to

27. _____ is treated through surgical removal of abnormally located cell growths or by administration of danazol, a synthetic hormone (p. 467).

   *a. Endometriosis
   b. Gamete transfer
   c. IVF/ET
   d. Failure to ovulate

28. A _____ is an enlarged or damaged vein in the testes or vas deferens (p. 468).

   *a. varicocele
   b. mycoplasma
   c. rhomboid
   d. plage

29. Infertility in men may be caused by (p. 468):

   a. undescended testes.
   b. varicoceles.
   c. environmental pollutants.
   *d. all of the above.

30. For couples in which the woman produces antibodies against the man's sperm, _____ is recommended (p. 468).

   a. in vitro fertilization
   b. the Estes operation
   c. adoption
   *d. the use of condoms

31. A review of studies published worldwide from 1940 to 1990 indicated which of the following about male fertility (p. 468)?

    *a. Average sperm density in men fell by almost 50 percent.
    b. Most infertility is caused by emotional problems.
    c. It is possible for a woman to develop antibodies against sperm but not possible for men to develop antibodies to their own sperm.
    d. All of the above.

32. Concerning research on people with visual impairments and their sexuality, it has been found that (p. 470):

    a. few studies have been conducted on the sexuality of visually impaired people.
    b. gender-role acquisition is relatively unimpeded among blind children.
    c. when sexual information has been taught from the beginning of school, blind children are as informed as their sighted peers.
    *d. all of the above.

33. Which of the following is a movie about the challenges faced by a young deaf woman in attempting to develop her professional skills and personal relationships (p. 471)?

    a. *Shirley Valentine*
    b. *In the Name of the Father*
    c. *Coming Home*
    *d. *Children of a Lesser God*

34. Spinal-cord injuries (p. 473):

    *a. do not prevent women from giving birth.
    b. invariably eliminate men's ability to respond sexually.
    c. do not disrupt men's sexual response if the injury is confined to the lower part of the spinal cord.
    d. both a and c.

35. Individuals with spinal cord injuries (p. 473):

    a. are often incapable of erection and ejaculation.
    b. are sometimes capable of reproducing.
    c. can often receive sexual stimulation and pleasure.
    d. both a and b.
    *e. all of the above.

36. A substance that is believed to heighten sexual arousal or enhance the pleasure of sexual stimulation and orgasm is called a(n) (p. 474):

    a. pheromone.
    *b. aphrodisiac.
    c. stimulant.
    d. opiate.

37. Which of the following substances has been found to be a true aphrodisiac (p. 476)?

    a. bees' wings
    b. Spanish fly
    c. powdered rhinoceros horn
    d. bull testes
   *e. none of the above.

38. Which of the following is true about yohimbine (p. 476)?

   *a. There is not sufficient evidence to classify it as an aphrodisiac.
    b. It is effective in treating human males for impotence.
    c. It is available through pharmacies.
    d. It can be poisonous in large dosages.

39. Alcoholism is associated with (p. 477):

    a. erectile failure.
    b. decreased vaginal lubrication.
    c. atrophy of the testes.
    d. breast enlargement in males.
   *e. all of the above.

40. Alcohol is best characterized as (p. 477):

    a. a stimulant that enhances all reflexes, including sexual ones.
   *b. a depressant.
    c. a substance that was used in Victorian times as an anaphrodisiac.
    d. none of the above.

41. Which of the following is true about cocaine and sexual functioning (p. 478)?

    a. Cocaine inflames and irritates the urinary tract and dilates genital blood vessels.
    b. Those who regularly use cocaine over long periods of time tend to experience increased sexual response.
   *c. Heavy use generally leads to decline in sexual interest.
    d. both a and b.

42. Amyl nitrate is (p. 478):

    a. a central nervous system depressant.
    b. a hallucinogen.
   *c. an amphetamine.
    d. an anabolic steroid.

43. Opiates such as heroine and morphine (p. 478):

    a. have an effect on sexual arousal similar to that of marijuana; that is, stimulating for some, depressing for others.
   *b. depress sexual interest and activity.
    c. have no effect on sexual arousal.
    d. have been shown to increase sexual activity in laboratory rats.

44. Anaphrodisiacs have been sought at least since the Victorian era to (p. 479):

    a. curb masturbation.
    b. treat sexual offenders.
    c. increase fertility.
    d. increase sexual desire.
  *e. both a and b.

45. Which of the following substances has been found to be a true anaphrodisiac (p. 479)?

    a. saltpeter
    b. testosterone for men
    c. yohimbine
    d. androgens for females
  *e. estrogens for men

Essay Questions

46. What are some factors that can influence the potential impact of a health problem on a person's sexuality (pp. 454–457)?

47. Discuss sexual self-esteem, referring to both the Sexuality Scale and the Sexual Self-Concept Scale (p. 455).

48. Discuss body image as it relates to sexuality. Include a discussion of eating disorders (p. 456).

49. Discuss the risks and benefits of hormone-replacement therapy for postmenopausal women. Why does the National Institutes of Health recommend that postmenopausal women also consume 1,000 milligrams of calcium daily (p. 464)?

50. Discuss the ethical and legal implications of artificial insemination and surrogate motherhood. Do you think surrogate motherhood should be banned? Explain your answer (p. 469).

51. Discuss the relationship of sensory impairments to sexuality (p. 470).

52. How can developmental disabilities influence a person's sexuality? What approaches to contraceptive protection for developmentally disabled people were mentioned in the textbook? What are the pros and cons of these approaches (pp. 471–474)?

53. Define the terms *aphrodisiac* and *anaphrodisiac* and summarize our current knowledge about them. Are there any true aphrodisiacs or anaphrodisiacs? If so, what are they (pp. 474–480)?

54. What substances have been mistakenly thought to be aphrodisiacs? What substances have been thought to be anaphrodisiacs (pp. 474–480)?

55. Describe the effects of alcohol, barbiturates, amphetamines, and psychedelic drugs on sexual arousal and functioning (pp. 474–480).

CHAPTER 15

Sexual Orientation

Multiple-Choice Questions

1. Sexual orientation refers to (p. 486):

    a. fear of homosexuality.
    b. desire to change one's gender to that of the opposite sex.
    *c. erotic attraction toward people of the same gender, the other gender, or both genders.
    d. a tendency toward transvestism.
    e. none of the above.

2. Kinsey et al. (1948) found that _____ percent of males and _____ percent of females in their sample had had at least one homosexual encounter (p. 486).

    a. 12; 4
    b. 25; 15
    *c. 37; 13
    d. 50; 9

3. In classifying sexual orientation, Kinsey emphasized (p. 487):

    a. biological factors.
    b. early childhood influences.
    *c. behavioral criteria.
    d. fantasy.
    e. orgasm.

4. Anna Freud's definition of homosexuality involves (p. 487):

    a. the frequency with which an individual engages in same-gender (as opposed to other-gender) sex.
    *b. the kind of fantasies an individual experiences while engaging in sexual activity.
    c. the age at which same-gender sexual activity begins.
    d. the degree of Oedipal repression that an individual has experienced.

5. To measure sexual orientation, Kinsey used a (p. 487):

    a. two-point scale—heterosexual, homosexual.
    b. three-point scale—heterosexual, homosexual, bisexual.
    *c. seven-point scale, ranging from exclusively heterosexual to exclusively homosexual.
    d. nine-point Likert scale.

6. When female-female mounting occurs among mammals, the receiver is usually in the _____ stage of the estrus cycle (p. 487).

    a. preovulatory
    b. ovulatory
    c. postovulatory
    *d. peak

7. Male-male mountings are more likely to occur when (p. 487):

    a. both males display "masculine" behavior.
    b. both males display "feminine" behavior.
    *c. one male displays "masculine" behavior and the other displays "feminine" behavior.
    d. none of the above.

8. Beach proposed an explanation of homosexual behavior in other species based on an expression of (p. 488):

    a. sexual desire.
    b. least effort.
    c. ethnocentric behavior.
    *d. dominance.

9. Beach maintained that the more frequent occurrence of heterosexual behavior than homosexual behavior among mammals stems from differences in (p. 488):

    *a. male-female gonadal secretion of hormones.
    b. anatomy.
    c. the limbic system.
    d. all of the above.

10. The assertion that homosexuality is "biologically normal" is (p. 488):

    a. supported by empirical evidence.
    b. refuted by empirical evidence.
    c. limited to explaining such behavior in humans alone.
    *d. neither supported nor refuted by empirical evidence.
    e. both b and c.

11. Information about homosexual expression in other cultures is primarily based on observations by (p. 488):

    *a. anthropologists.
    b. philosophers.
    c. psychologists.
    d. historians.

12. The Sambia of New Guinea believe that young males (p. 488):

    a. who are discovered engaging in homosexual contact should be put to death.
    b. should practice homosexual behavior in order to learn how to become better lovers for their future wives.
    *c. need to ingest semen in order to reach maturity.
    d. who masturbate are likely to be transvestites.

13. Which of the following is supported by research in England and the United States (p. 488)?

    a. Most homosexual men are attracted to effeminate partners.
    b. Most lesbian women are attracted to "butch" partners.
    *c. A substantial portion of male homosexuals express both masculine and feminine roles.
    d. Most British homosexuals think their U.S. cohorts are too masculine.
    e. None of the above.

14. According to the textbook, there is no stigma attached to the active (inserter) participant in homosexual encounters in (p. 490):

    a. India and Pakistan.
    *b. Mexico, Brazil, Greece, and Turkey.
    c. New Zealand, Australia, and Fiji.
    d. East African nations.

15. Evidence from Reiss (1986) indicates that the greater the rigidity of the male gender role in male-dominant societies (p. 490):

    a. the lower the likelihood of male homosexual behavior.
    *b. the higher the likelihood of male homosexual behavior.
    c. the higher the likelihood of female homosexual behavior.
    d. the higher the likelihood of male homosexual behavior in adolescence and the lower is the likelihood of male homosexual behavior in adulthood.

16. In 1974, members of the American Psychiatric Association ratified a resolution that (p. 490):

    *a. removed homosexuality from the list of official mental disorders.
    b. made it possible for homosexuals to become members of the association.
    c. categorized homosexuality under neurotic disorders.
    d. concluded that homosexuals suffer from impaired judgment and need psychotherapy.
    e. both c and d.

17. The American Psychiatric Association currently takes the position that homosexuality in itself (p. 490):

    *a. does not imply impaired judgment or instability.
    b. is a genetic illness.
    c. can be cured with hormone injections.
    d. is learned in a triangular family system.

18. _____ refers to "unnatural" sex acts, which can involve anal sex, oral sex, and/or sex with animals (p. 492).

    a. Tribadism
    b. Allogamy
    c. Dosimetry
 *d. Sodomy

19. The laws under which homosexuals have most often been prosecuted are _____ laws (p. 492):

    a. pornography
 *b. sodomy
    c. homosexuality
    d. fornication

20. In 1986, the Supreme Court ruled that (p. 492):

    a. an individual can be charged with sodomy only if he or she is under age 21.
    b. sodomy laws are unconstitutional.
 *c. decriminalization of sodomy laws is an issue to be decided by state legislatures.
    d. homosexuality is a moral rather than a legal issue.
    e. both b and d.

21. As of 1994 in the United States, sodomy was (p. 492):

    a. considered punishable by death in Massachusetts.
 *b. no longer considered a crime in more than half the states.
    c. changed by the Supreme Court to the name of "buggery."
    d. legal in all of the states.

22. Which of the following is true about sexuality in Mexico (p. 490)?

    a. Overall, fellatio is more common in Mexico than in the United States.
    b. There is greater variation in sexual expression among both heterosexuals and homosexuals in Mexico as compared to the United States.
 *c. Homosexual Mexican males are expected to achieve sexual satisfaction through anal intercourse rather than fellatio.
    d. Heterosexual Mexicans are expected to prefer fellatio more than sexual intercourse.

23. In Canada, sodomy (p. 492):

    a. is known as buggery.
    b. includes having sex with animals.
    c. is punishable only if a participant is under 21.
    d. is punishable only if the act takes place in public or involves an animal.
 *e. all of the above.

24. In the United States, the beginning of the gay liberation movement dates back to _____, when the police raided the _____ (p. 492).

    a. the 1920s; Paramount Speakeasy
    b. the World War II era; Bronx Hilton
    *c. the late 1960s; Stonewall Inn
    d. the onset of the AIDS epidemic; Marshfield Bar

25. The National Gay Task Force (now the National Gay and Lesbian Task Force) was created in (p. 492):

    a. 1951.
    b. 1961.
    *c. 1973.
    d. 1992.

26. There is evidence from Boxer and Cohler (1989) that young _____ identify themselves as gay at _____ if they are able to _____ (p. 494).

    a. European females; an earlier age; meet openly with gay women in a supportive environment
    b. European males; an earlier age; discuss the topic with their parents
    c. women; a later age; marry first and have children
    *d. men; earlier age; meet openly with gay men in a supportive environment

27. According to Diamond (1993) and Le Vay (1993), the best estimate seems to be that about _____ percent of men and _____ percent of women are predominantly homosexual for a large part of their lives (p. 494).

    a. 1 to 3; 10 to 12
    *b. 4 to 6; 2 to 4
    c. 15 to 20; 16 to 18
    d. 7 to 9; 15 to 17

28. One study of 1,000 gay people indicated that homosexual feelings occurred typically at age _____ among males and about age _____ among females (p. 494).

    a. 6; 8
    *b. 14; 16
    c. 18; 10
    d. 20; 19

29. Research on gay males indicates that (p. 494):

    a. the acquisition of a gay identity is a sudden process.
    b. most engage in a homosexual love relationship within a few months after they realize they are gay.
    *c. after they have experienced homosexual feelings, most do not engage in a homosexual love relationship for several years or more.
    d. most are in their late 20s before they realize they are gay.

30. "Coming out" refers to a homosexual individual's (p. 495):

    a. first experience of homosexual feelings.
    b. first homosexual encounter leading to orgasm.
    *c. acknowledging his or her homosexual identity to others.
    d. participation in political rallies for homosexuality.

31. Most males "come out" at about age (p. 494):

    a. 12 or 13.
    *b. 19 or 20.
    c. 26 or 27.
    d. 34 or 35.

32. Most females "come out" (p. 495):

    a. in preadolescence.
    b. in their early teens.
    *c. in their early 20s.
    d. in their early 40s.

33. For _____, the homosexual feelings arose _____ before they made genital contact with a person of the same gender (p. 494).

    *a. both males and females; at least 2 years
    b. females only; about 1 month
    c. males only; about 4 years
    d. males only; about 6 years

34. Of students observing videotaped interviews of heterosexual and homosexual males and females, about _____ percent were unable to identify accurately the sexual orientation of those in the videotape beyond chance expectations (p. 495).

    a. 10
    b. 20
    c. 30
    *d. 80

35. In Bell and Weinberg's (1978) study, more than _____ percent of the gay males and approximately _____ percent of the gay females were involved in a steady relationship at that time (p. 496).

    a. 10; 90
    b. 20; 80
    *c. 50; 70
    d. 80; 40

36. Cruising often involves going to (p. 496):

   a. gay bars.
   b. private parties.
   c. public parks.
   *d. all of the above.

37. Homosexuals use the same methods of sexual expression as heterosexuals, with the exception of (p. 496):

   *a. coitus.
   b. fellatio.
   c. analingus.
   d. cunnilingus.

38. _____ refers to one woman's lying on top of the other and making rhythmic thrusting movements to stimulate their clitorises (p. 496).

   a. Fellatio
   *b. Tribadism
   c. Whisking
   d. Cunnilingus

39. The most common methods of sexual stimulation among lesbian women involve (p. 496):

   *a. tribadism.
   b. interfemoral intercourse.
   c. analingus.
   d. the use of dildoes.
   e. all of the above.

40. _____ refers to stimulation of the anal area with the tongue (p. 496).

   a. Tribadism
   b. Dowering
   c. Cunnilingus
   *d. Analingus

41. _____ involves rubbing the penis between the partner's legs until orgasm is reached (p. 496).

   a. Packing
   b. Mutual masturbation
   *c. Interfemoral intercourse
   d. Assuaging

42. Which of the following concerning gay lifestyles is correct (pp. 496–497)?

    a. The lowest incidence of cruising occurs in public restrooms and movie theaters.
    b. Homosexuals search for most of the same things that heterosexuals do.
    c. Almost all homosexuals have been involved in a relatively steady relationship with a same-gender person during part of their life.
    *d. All of the above.
    e. None of the above.

43. Gay men most frequently engage in (p. 496):

    a. pecking.
    b. anal intercourse.
    *c. fellatio.
    d. tribadism.

44. Masters and Johnson found that gay people are more _____ than heterosexuals during their sexual interactions (p. 497).

    a. performance oriented
    b. demanding
    *c. communicative
    d. aggressive

45. In contrast to Masters and Johnson's conclusions, Jay and Young (1979) reported that 42 percent of the 1,000 lesbians in their study (p. 497):

    a. no longer had sex with their partners, although they continued to live together.
    b. were slower and less demanding in their approach to sex.
    c. were goal oriented.
    *d. complained of frequent difficulty in sexual communication with their partners.

46. In a series of studies, Peplau and her colleagues found that gay individuals differed from heterosexuals in that the gay individuals (p. 497):

    a. were more committed to their relationships.
    b. were more satisfied with their relationships.
    *c. attached less importance to sexual exclusivity in a relationship.
    d. had a more romantic view of love.

47. Gender differences that have been found among homosexuals include which of the following (p. 498)?

    a. Lesbian love affairs are longer lasting than male homosexual love affairs.
    b. Public cruising is less frequent among lesbians than among male homosexuals.
    c. Lesbians value emotional expressiveness in a relationship more than male homosexuals do.
    *d. All of the above.

48. Almost half the white male homosexuals in the Bell and Weinberg (1978) study said that they had had at least _____ different sexual partners during their lives; _____ of the gay females in the study reported having had this many partners (p. 498).

    a. 4; 40 percent
    b. 10; 25 percent
    c. 30; 10 percent
    *d. 50; none

49. Bell and Weinberg (1978) found that _____ percent of lesbians, black and white, had actively sought sexual encounters during the year previous to the research and that cruising was almost entirely limited to _____ (p. 498).

    a. 8; shopping malls
    *b. 17; bars and private parties
    c. 22; beaches
    d. 34; bars

50. About _____ percent of black and white male homosexuals reported cruising about once a month in a study by Bell and Weinberg (1978) (p. 498).

    a. 24
    b. 40
    *c. 85
    d. 97

51. According to Peplau (1979), _____ ranked emotional expressiveness and equality in their love relationships as more important than did _____ (p. 498).

    a. lesbians; gay men
    *b. all women; gay and straight men
    c. heterosexual women; lesbians
    d. gay men; lesbians

52. _____ asserted that lesbian and gay male sexual behavior represents a pure form of female and male sexuality, respectively (p. 498).

    a. Masters and Johnson
    *b. Symons
    c. Bell and Weinberg
    d. Peplau

53. According to the Bell and Weinberg (1978) study, _____ percent of homosexual white males claimed having 1,000 or more partners (p. 498).

    a. 12
    *b. 28
    c. 37
    d. 50

54. Symons (1979) suggests that (p. 498):

    a. gays never fantasize about heterosexual encounters.
    b. homosexuals are completely different from heterosexuals in their ideas about what is important in relationships.
    *c. males and females in heterosexual relationships are forced to compromise their true sexual natures.
    d. homosexuals should elect to have sex-change surgery if they can afford to.

55. There is some evidence to support which of the following statements (p. 498)?

    a. Compared to heterosexuals, younger gays tend to have better self-concepts than older gays.
    *b. Homosexuals do not experience midlife crises to the same degree that heterosexuals do.
    c. Attraction of same-gender people results from some pathological condition that becomes more intensified with age.
    d. Many older gay men turn to young children for sexual gratification.

56. Weinberg and Williams (1975) found that _____ were less anxious about growing old than were _____ (p. 499).

    a. homosexual males; heterosexual males
    b. heterosexual females; homosexual males
    c. heterosexual females; homosexual females
    *d. homosexual females; homosexual males

57. Which of the following is true of the people who engage in same-gender relations in prison (p. 499)?

    a. Most had already engaged in homosexual acts before they arrived.
    b. Most continue same-gender relations after leaving.
    c. Very few inmates engage in homosexual acts.
    d. Both a and b.
    *e. None of the above.

58. In Clemmer's (1958) study of prison life, about _____ percent of the convict population was found to have engaged in homosexual activity (p. 499).

    a. 20
    *b. 40
    c. 60
    d. 80

59. Among prison inmates who engage in situational homosexual behavior (p. 500):

    a. most male relationships involve coercion.
    b. most female relationships do not involve coercion.
    c. most return to heterosexual behaviors upon their release.
    *d. all of the above.

60. A commonality of hereditary, hormone, and harmful family pattern theories is that they (p. 500):

    a. explain both homosexuality and heterosexuality.
    *b. assume that attraction to same-gender people results from some pathological condition.
    c. are all well supported by research.
    d. all of the above.

61. Flaws in Kallmann's (1952) research on the influence of heredity on sexual orientation include the fact(s) that (p. 500):

    *a. many of the men in his study came from prisons and psychiatric institutions.
    b. he did not use a longitudinal design.
    c. the findings were not statistically significant.
    d. both b and c.

62. From Kallmann's (1952) research on heredity and homosexuality, it can be safely concluded that (p. 501):

    a. concordance rates prove that homosexuality is genetic.
    b. high correlations suggest a relationship between genetics and homosexuality.
    c. when genes lack certain information, homosexuality is the result.
    *d. none of the above; methodological flaws prevent conclusions from being made.

63. When Le Vay (1991) compared the INAH regions of the brains of deceased homosexual men, heterosexual men, and heterosexual women, he found that (p. 502):

    *a. there were highly significant differences in the volume of INAH-3 among the groups.
    b. heterosexual men had the lowest volume in that region of the hypothalamus, compared to the other two groups.
    c. homosexual men had the highest volume in the INAH-3 region.
    d. there were no differences among them.

64. Research on androgens indicates that they affect sexual (p. 502):

    a. orientation in males or females with hypogonadal conditions.
    b. orientation only if decreased through surgical castration or chemical means.
    c. orientation in males but not females.
    *d. interest but not sexual orientation in both males and females.
    e. desire in males but not females.

65. Findings from endocrine research on homosexuals are difficult to interpret because (p. 502):

    a. of nonrepresentative samples.
    b. of failure to specify criteria for sexual orientation.
    *c. hormone levels can fluctuate widely in a 24-hour period.
    d. all of the above.

66. The vast majority of homosexual males have testosterone levels _____ found among heterosexual males (p. 503):

    a. higher than those
  *b. within the normal range
    c. lower than those
    d. none of the above; testosterone levels of homosexual males have not been measured.

67. Bieber's (1962) theory concerning the triangular system in the family has been questioned because (p. 503):

    a. his results are based only on people in therapy.
    b. many homosexuals did not come from a triangular family system.
    c. many heterosexuals come from a triangular family system.
  *d. all of the above.

68. Whitam (1977) found that homosexual men were more likely than heterosexual men to characterize their childhoods as having involved (p. 503):

    a. interest in toys stereotypic for girls.
    b. preference for the company of women.
    c. cross-dressing.
  *d. all of the above.

69. Weinrich et al. (1992) found out which of the following about adult gay men (p. 504)?

  *a. Those who have a strong preference for receptive anal intercourse have the strongest recollections of gender-role nonconformity in childhood.
    b. Those who engage in cross-dressing started doing so as an adult.
    c. Most are actually bisexual.
    d. They tend to have extremely accurate childhood memories.

70. In a study of more than 11,000 people, intense sexual experiences and feelings of _____ associated with early experiences were the strongest correlate(s) of adult sexual orientation (p. 504).

    a. discomfort
    b. pleasure
    c. arousal
  *d. all of the above

71. Gallup and Suarez (1983) describe the development of sexual orientation from a(n) _____ viewpoint (p. 505).

  *a. evolutionary
    b. cognitive
    c. psychoanalytic
    d. behavioral

72. Sexual orientation appears to be fairly well established in males by age _____ and in females by age _____ (p. 505).

    *a. 18; 21
    b. 18; 35
    c. 21; 16
    d. 29; 18

73. Research by Bell and Weinberg has indicated that prior to identifying themselves as homosexuals, _____ engaged in heterosexual intercourse (p. 505).

    a. a large majority of gay men and a small percentage of lesbian women
    *b. a large majority of lesbian women and a small percentage of gay men
    c. the majority of both gay men and women
    d. a small minority of both gay men and gay women

74. A problem with many earlier studies on the adjustment of homosexuals is that (p. 506):

    a. the investigators tended to assume that homosexuals were maladjusted.
    b. the homosexuals used in the research were in therapy.
    c. control groups of heterosexuals were not in therapy.
    *d. all of the above.

75. Which of the following statements concerning therapy for changing sexual orientation is correct (p. 506)?

    a. The use of therapy for this purpose is on the rise.
    b. Psychoanalysis and behavior therapy have been very effective.
    *c. These theories assume that a homosexual orientation is pathological.
    d. Long-term follow-up of treated individuals indicates that this type of therapy is highly effective.

76. A problem with Masters and Johnson's claim that 67 percent of the gay men and 60 percent of the lesbian women in their treatment program had "achieved" heterosexual behavior is that (p. 506):

    a. approximately a quarter of the applicants were denied admission to the program for various reasons, including insufficient motivation.
    b. half the clients in the program were in heterosexual marriages.
    c. only a small percentage of the clients were predominantly or exclusively homosexual.
    *d. all of the above.

77. Many therapists now concentrate on helping their homosexual clients (p. 507):

    a. accept their sexual orientation.
    b. develop the potential to survive in a homophobic society.
    c. convert to heterosexuality.
    *d. both a and b.

78. According to the textbook, which of the following is true about contemporary attitudes toward homosexuals (pp. 508–509)?

    a. It is rare for Americans to believe the myth that homosexuals are abusers of young children.
    b. A poor predictor of heterosexuals' attitudes toward gay men is personal contact with a gay man or lesbian woman.
    *c. There has been a gradual decrease in antigay prejudice over the past few decades.
    d. Only a minority of Americans believe that homosexual relations are wrong today.

79. According to a national survey in 1984, _____ percent believed that homosexual relations between adults were always or almost always wrong; in 1988, _____ did (p. 509).

    a. 11; even less
    b. 24; the same percentage
    c. 57; more
    *d. 78; a lesser percentage

80. _____ attitudes toward homosexuals are more prevalent among _____ (p. 509).

    a. Positive; males
    *b. Negative; males
    c. Negative; females
    d. Ambivalent; males

81. Compared to people who are tolerant of others' sexual orientation, people who are very antihomosexual (p. 509):

    *a. view sex as primarily for procreation purposes.
    b. are from urban areas.
    c. seldom attend church.
    d. are more liberal in their political views.

82. Compared with people who are tolerant of others' sexual orientation, antihomosexuals (p. 509):

    a. tend to display greater gender-role rigidity.
    b. come from rural areas.
    c. are more likely to be affiliated with fundamentalist religions.
    *d. all of the above.

83. Which of the following is supported by research (p. 509)?

    a. Most child molesting is done by homosexual rather than heterosexual men.
    b. At least one parent of most homosexuals is also homosexual.
    c. Most teenagers have their first homosexual experience with an adult rather than a peer.
    *d. None of the above.

84. _____ refers to the ability to respond erotically to both genders (p. 510).

    a. Transsexuality
    b. Homosexuality
    *c. Bisexuality
    d. Transvestism

85. Bisexual women (pp. 512–513):

    a. tend to marry at an early age.
    b. are more likely than bisexual men to become aware of their homosexual feelings after they wed.
    c. terminate their marriages early because of conflicts arising from their bisexuality and sexual dissatisfaction.
    *d. all of the above.

86. Blumstein and Schwartz (1976) found which of these themes to be prevalent among bisexuals whom they interviewed (p. 511)?

    a. sexual experimentation in the context of friendship
    b. interaction in group sex
    c. belief systems in which bisexuality is seen as a natural state
    *d. all of the above
    e. none of the above

87. According to work by Lever et al. (1992), men who labeled themselves as bisexuals, compared to heterosexual men, report _____ likelihood to _____ (p. 512).

    *a. more; have more adolescent homosexual experiences
    b. less; participate in fellatio
    c. less; engage in anal sex
    d. none of the above

Essay Questions

88. Discuss the legal status of homosexual behavior in the United States and Canada (pp. 490–492).

89. Discuss the context within which the gay liberation movement emerged. Discuss its roots and its current focus (p. 492).

90. Discuss gay lifestyles. Include a discussion of lifestyle in general, sexual expression, gender differences, and aging for gay people (pp. 496–498).

91. Discuss situational homosexuality, including in your essay the context of male prisons, female prisons, and the military (pp. 499–500).

92. Discuss Kallmann's (1952) study of sexual orientation in twins. Be sure to present his results, and discuss any methodological errors (pp. 500–502).

93. Describe and evaluate the evidence relevant to the following theories that attempt to explain the development of homosexual orientation: genetic, atypical hormone exposure, and atypical family patterns (pp. 500–506).

94. Discuss evidence that indicates that one path to becoming a homosexual in adulthood is nonconformity to societal expectations for one's gender in early childhood (pp. 504–505).

95. Discuss how early sexual experience can influence one's sexual orientation as an adult. Be sure to contrast Van Wyk and Gerst's view of boys' and girls' early experiences with the view of Gallup and Suarez (p. 505).

96. Discuss the various therapeutic procedures used with homosexual clients. Be sure to refer to psychoanalytic therapy, behavior therapy, and the current focus of therapy for homosexuals (pp. 506–508).

97. Discuss homophobia. Address its definition, the verbal and physical abuse of gays, the characteristics of antihomosexuals, and some of the myths regarding homosexuality (pp. 508–510).

98. Should therapists attempt to "cure" homosexuality? Explain your answer (pp. 508–510).

99. Discuss the three themes that Blumstein and Schwartz (1976) found to be prevalent among bisexuals in their study (pp. 510–513).

Multiple-Choice Questions

1. _____ is sexual material that is suggestive but not explicit in portraying the genitals or sex acts (p. 518).

    a. Pornography
    b. Obscenity
    c. Hard-core erotica
    *d. Soft-core erotica

2. The term _____ generally refers to sexually oriented material that is acceptable to the viewer (p. 518).

    a. soft-core pornography
    *b. erotica
    c. hard-core pornography
    d. erotophilia

3. _____ became the first mass-market magazine to display pubic hair on its models (p. 518).

    *a. *Penthouse*
    b. *Playboy*
    c. *Club International*
    d. *Hustler*

4. The peak circulation of such magazines as *Playboy* and *Penthouse* came in the (p. 518):

    a. 1950s.
    b. 1960s.
    *c. 1970s.
    d. 1980s.

5. For products that are _____ to sexuality, research indicates that overt sexual content in advertisements is _____ effective than nonsexual content (p. 518).

    a. related; less
    *b. unrelated; less
    c. unrelated; more
    d. none of the above

6. A person who is _____ would be likely to say, "Erotica is obviously filthy, and people should not try to describe it as anything else" (p. 519).

    a. erotophilic
    b. pornophilic
  *c. erotophobic
    d. pornophobic

7. Despite the frequent references to intercourse on television, depictions of sexuality rarely deal with (p. 520):

    a. sexually transmitted diseases.
    b. contraception.
    c. love.
  *d. both a and b.
    e. all of the above.

8. Regarding television's portrayal of sexual relationships, groups such as Planned Parenthood have suggested that (p. 520):

    a. erotic activity on TV should be censored.
    b. erotic activity should be shown on TV only after 8:00 P.M.
    c. sexually transmitted diseases should not be discussed on TV.
  *d. when sexual activity is portrayed, the possible unwanted consequences should also be presented.
    e. none of the above.

9. _____ was the first X-rated movie to be given wide publicity and shown in regular theaters instead of "adult" cinemas (p. 520).

    a. *Valley of the Dolls*
    b. *The Sterile Cuckoo*
    c. *Last Tango in Paris*
  *d. *I Am Curious (Yellow)*

10. The U.S. public's interest in hard-core films appears to be _____, and the number of X-rated theaters is _____ (p. 521).

  *a. increasing; decreasing
    b. decreasing; increasing
    c. increasing; increasing
    d. decreasing; decreasing

11. Historically, most erotica has been aimed at arousing _____ fantasies (p. 522).

    a. adolescent female
    b. adolescent male
    c. adult female
  *d. adult male

12. Hard-core and X-rated movies generally contain _____ than R-rated films (p. 522).

    *a. less violence
    b. more sadistic sex
    c. more rape depictions
    d. more murders

13. Reiss (1986) pointed out that the typical X-rated film depicts a situation in which women (p. 522):

    a. have no negotiating power.
    b. are sexually insatiable.
    *c. both a and b.
    d. none of the above.

14. Erotic themes designed to appeal to females are depicted in (p. 523):

    a. X-rated films.
    b. X-rated magazines.
    *c. romance novels.
    d. hard-core films.

15. Based on surveys conducted by the National Opinion Research Center, a person is more likely to have attended an X-rated movie in the past year if he or she is (p. 524):

    a. between the ages of 40 and 60.
    b. over age 60.
    *c. well educated.
    d. living in the South.

16. Patrons of an "adult" movie theater who responded to questionnaires had (p. 524):

    a. more negative attitudes toward women than did the general population.
    b. high ratings on the scale designed to measure deviance.
    c. relatively low levels of education.
    *d. more positive attitudes toward women in general than did college men and women.

17. Strippers (p. 525):

    a. tend to believe that society views them in a negative light.
    b. in most American cities can strip down only to G-strings.
    c. have traditionally been women, but men increasingly are entering the occupation.
    *d. all of the above.

18. According to the textbook authors, the failure to find a cure for AIDS will likely serve to _____ erotica (p. 527).

    a. increase the role of organized crime associated with
    b. eliminate the demand for
    c. decrease the demand for
    *d. increase the demand for

19. In American law, _____ refers to sexual media that are illegal (p. 527).

   *a. obscenity
   b. pornography
   c. soft-core erotica
   d. hard-core erotica

20. The _____ made the mailing of obscene, lascivious, or lewd material a felony as of 1873 (p. 527).

   a. Decree of Vice
   *b. Comstock Act
   c. Sanger statutes
   d. Anthony Act

21. The doctrine of _____ states that obscenity must be determined based on the work as a whole (p. 528).

   a. erotic content
   b. diminished arousal
   *c. dominant effect
   d. totality

22. The Supreme Court in _____ stated that in order for material to be considered obscene, it must meet three essential criteria (p. 528).

   *a. *Roth* v. *United States*
   b. *Roe* v. *Wade*
   c. *Barrymore* v. *Arizona*
   d. *Miller* v. *Adams*

23. Which is *not* one of the essential criteria for obscenity as defined by the Supreme Court (p. 528)?

   a. It must be offensive to contemporary community standards.
   b. The dominant theme of the work must appeal to prurient interest in sex.
   *c. It must not explicitly show sexual penetration.
   d. It must be devoid of serious literary, artistic, political, or scientific value.

24. The Allgeier et al. (1984) study in which students rated photos on the basis of their offensiveness suggested that (p. 528):

   a. most people agree as to what constitutes obscenity.
   b. men and women gave similar ratings to the most of the photos.
   *c. establishing a community standard of obscenity would be very difficult.
   d. none of the above.

25. A 1987 Supreme Court decision ruled that some sexually explicit works (p. 528):

    *a. are not obscene if a "reasonable" person finds value in the work as a whole.
    b. are obscene if most people in a given community think the work has no value.
    c. should be judged by state governments to determine whether they are obscene.
    d. should be banned locally if a petition of 3,000 or more signatures is presented to a city council.

26. Most social pressure to censor erotic material comes from (p. 528):

    a. political conservatives.
    b. religious fundamentalists.
    c. feminists.
    *d. both a and b.

27. In the 1970s, some feminists distinguished between erotica and pornography on the basis of whether (p. 528):

    *a. women are portrayed as subordinate and degraded.
    b. complete nudity is shown.
    c. explicit intercourse is shown.
    d. there was a plot.

28. Cowan and Dunn's (1994) study using clips from X-rated films found that (p. 528):

    a. most women rated films containing degrading themes toward men as more arousing than those perceived as nondegrading.
    b. there are negative side effects from short-term exposure to nonviolent, sexual materials.
    c. most men rated films containing degrading themes toward women as more arousing than those perceived as nondegrading.
    *d. perceptions of the degradation of women vary as a function of whether the viewers are men or women.

29. Among the findings of the U.S. Commission on Obscenity and Pornography (1970) were all of the following *except* which one (p. 528)?

    a. Depictions of conventional sexual behavior are generally more stimulating than depictions of less conventional sexual activity.
    *b. Sex offenders have had more adolescent experience with erotica than have other adults.
    c. Exposure to erotic stimuli produces a substantial degree of sexual arousal in men and women.
    d. Evidence shows that increased availability of erotic material in Denmark is associated with a decrease in the rate of sex crimes.

30. The 1970 Commission on Obscenity and Pornography concluded that exposure to explicit sexual materials results in (p. 533):

    *a. no harm to the average citizen.
    b. moderate harm to the average citizen.
    c. increased crime in a community.
    d. an increased rate of emotional disturbance among males in a community.

31. The British Commission on Obscenity and Film Censorship drew conclusions (p. 533):

    *a. that were similar to those of President Johnson's 1970 U.S. Commission on Obscenity and Pornography.
    b. that contradicted those of President Johnson's 1970 U.S. Commission on Obscenity and Pornography.
    c. that led to government legislation to restrict access to erotica in all counties immediately.
    d. none of the above.

32. The 1985 Meese Commission claimed to have found a causal relationship between sexual violence and erotica that featured (p. 534):

    a. total nudity.
    b. children.
    c. violence.
    *d. both b and c.
    e. all of the above.

33. The 1985 Meese Commission has been criticized because (p. 534):

    *a. the conclusions were not warranted by the data its members reviewed.
    b. the members neglected to make recommendations to halt the spread of erotica.
    c. the members were too liberal.
    d. the members consisted solely of males over 65 years of age.

34. Research by Donnerstein on the connection between violent erotica and rape found that of the male volunteers who had been angered prior to watching the movie (p. 534):

    a. the version of the film did not affect the aggression toward the male confederate.
    b. those who viewed a film where the victim had a negative reaction to forced sex gave high levels of electric shock to the female confederate.
    c. those who viewed a film where the victim had a positive reaction to forced sex gave high levels of electric shock to the female confederate.
    *d. all of the above.

35. Research by Malamuth (1981) found that _____ male volunteers reported having more arousal fantasies after exposure to the rape version than after exposure to the mutual-consent version (p. 535).

    *a. force-oriented
    b. nonforce-oriented
    c. schizophrenic
    d. both b and c

36. In an investigation of the effect of violent pornography on women's arousal, Stock (1982) found that (p. 536):

    a. women generally are not aroused by rape when it is described in a realistic manner.
    *b. women generally are aroused by eroticized depictions of rape in which the victim does not suffer and no harm is done.
    c. rape victims are secretly aroused during the rape process.
    d. most of the women in his study refused to complete the experiment.

37. Research on women's reactions to violent erotica (p. 536):

    a. indicates that many women actually want to be raped.
    b. is inconclusive because equal numbers of women were aroused or disgusted by it.
    c. has yet to be published or studied.
    d. found that a large percentage of women found accurate rape depictions quite erotic.
    *e. none of the above.

38. A consistent finding among college students is that sexual arousal in response to coercive sex is associated with (p. 537):

    *a. a callous attitude toward rape and rape victims.
    b. a student's major area of study.
    c. gun ownership.
    d. IQ.

39. Abel and his colleagues (1977, 1978) found that convicted rapists were as aroused by portrayals of _____ as they were by portrayals of _____. In comparison, nonrapists were more aroused by portrayals of _____ than by portrayals of _____ (p. 537).

    a. rape; war; war; rape
    b. rape; war; food; rape
    *c. rape; consensual sex; consensual sex; rape
    d. defecation; rape; consensual sex; rape

40. The Zillmann and Bryant studies demonstrated that long-term exposure to nonviolent erotica _____ aggressive attitudes and _____ aggressive behaviors (p. 537).

    *a. increased; had no effect on
    b. increased; increased
    c. had no effect on; increased
    d. had no effect on; had no effect on
    e. decreased; decreased

41. Kelley and Musialowski (1986) found that viewing nonviolent erotic movies every day for four days (p. 537):

    a. decreased sexual arousal.
    b. decreased desires to see the same films again.
    c. increased acceptance of force in sexual encounters.
   *d. both a and b.
    e. all of the above.

42. Malamuth and Check (1984) found that after debriefing subjects who participated in studies on short-term exposure to nonviolent erotica, the significant differences in attitudes toward women (p. 538):

    a. became stronger.
    b. remained the same.
    c. decreased slightly.
   *d. disappeared.

43. In Japan, laws ban the public display of _____ in magazines and on television (p. 538).

   *a. pubic hair and adult genitals
    b. bare breasts
    c. bondage
    d. rape

44. Japan has (p. 538):

    a. public TV shows that are less sexually explicit than those in the United States.
   *b. one of the lowest reported rates of sexual assault in the industrialized countries.
    c. few depictions of rape in novels and films.
    d. all of the above.

45. Most children and adolescents involved in erotica also participate in (p. 539):

   *a. prostitution or other sexual activities with adults.
    b. drug rings.
    c. movies with PG or G ratings.
    d. all of the above.

46. The textbook authors argue that adults who employ children in the production of pornography should be prosecuted under child abuse laws rather than obscenity laws because (p. 539):

    a. obscenity laws at times violate First Amendment guarantees of freedom of expression.
    b. it is difficult to determine whether erotic material is obscene.
    c. children, whether clothed or nude, are not obscene.
   *d. all of the above.

47. In _____ states of the United States, publishers and sellers of child erotica may be prosecuted without the need to prove the material is obscene (p. 539).

    a. 3
    b. 25
    c. 37
    *d. all

48. Regarding the potential damage from exposure to certain types of media, the textbook authors agree with Donnerstein and Linz (1986) that the basic issue involves (p. 540):

    a. sexual explicitness.
    b. the amount of nudity.
    *c. how violent the material is.
    d. how erotic the material is.

49. The word *prostitute* comes from a Latin verb that means (p. 540):

    a. "to sell."
    b. "to be alone."
    *c. "to expose."
    d. "to be illegal."

50. The phenomenon of prostitution (p. 540):

    a. appears to have been practiced since the beginning of recorded history.
    b. began during the Industrial Revolution.
    c. flourished during the Victorian era.
    d. has always been illegal in Europe and North America.
    *e. both a and c.

51. Which word developed from the ancient Roman practice of prostitutes' taking patrons to the arches beneath public buildings for sex (p. 540)?

    a. *sodomy*
    b. *copulation*
    c. *intercourse*
    *d. *fornication*

52. Which of the following events is related to the decline in the legal toleration of prostitution in the sixteenth century (p. 541)?

    a. lack of interest in sex outside marriage, and the spread of gonorrhea
    b. lack of women willing to be prostitutes and the Reformation
    *c. the spread of syphilis and the Reformation
    d. economic trends in Europe and the spread of influenza

53. Red-light districts refer to areas containing (p. 541):

    *a. houses of prostitution.
    b. abortion clinics.
    c. contraception clinics.
    d. none of the above.

54. Prostitution is currently legal in (p. 541):

    a. San Francisco.
    b. Taiwan.
    *c. some counties in Nevada.
    d. some provinces in Canada.

55. _____ are on the lowest rung of the ladder in the hierarchy of prostitution (p. 541).

    a. Call girls
    *b. Streetwalkers
    c. Hotel and bar prostitutes
    d. Topless dancers

56. _____ are most likely to work for a pimp (p. 542).

    a. Call girls
    *b. Streetwalkers
    c. Hotel and bar prostitutes
    d. Women who work for escort services

57. _____ frequently find themselves in competition with amateurs (p. 542).

    a. Call girls
    b. Streetwalkers
    *c. Hotel and bar prostitutes
    d. Women in massage parlors

58. The most frequent sexual activity provided by massage parlors is (p. 542):

    *a. massage and masturbation.
    b. oral sex and intercourse.
    c. bondage.
    d. bondage and intercourse.

59. The highest rung on the ladder in the hierarchy of prostitution is the (p. 542):

    a. streetwalker.
    *b. call girl.
    c. bar and hotel prostitute.
    d. woman in a massage parlor.

60. A male homosexual prostitute is sometimes called a (p. 543):

    a. hustler.
    b. boy.
    c. gigolo.
    d. all of the above.
    *e. both a and b.

61. Which of the following is the most common way to refer to a male who is paid to be a woman's escort and provide her with sexual services (p. 543)?

    *a. gigolo
    b. hustler
    c. bath boy
    d. pimp

62. Recent studies on prostitution have found that (p. 544):

    a. almost all prostitutes hate men.
    b. adolescent prostitutes have a more positive attitude toward men than older prostitutes do.
    *c. most prostitutes consider themselves to be heterosexual or bisexual.
    d. male prostitutes have been found to seldom use illegal drugs.

63. A study of streetwalkers in Philadelphia found that (p. 544):

    a. less than 1 percent reported having orgasms with clients.
    *b. the greater was the sexual enjoyment in their private life, the higher was the erotic pleasure in their professional realm.
    c. less than half enjoyed receiving oral sex in their private lives.
    d. less than one-third enjoyed performing oral sex as part of their job.

64. Silbert (1986) reported that prostitutes who are (p. 544):

    a. females are increasingly engaging in anal sex.
    b. females seldom use condoms with their clients.
    *c. juvenile females have a growing concern about AIDS.
    d. males typically think of themselves as being heterosexual.

65. Which of the following statements about prostitution is correct (p. 546)?

    a. Prostitution is an easy activity to define or categorize.
    b. Prostitution is a relatively recent phenomenon that began within the last 500 years.
    *c. Every state in the United States has laws regulating prostitution.
    d. The majority of prostitutes have long and happy careers.
    e. All of the above.

66. A disproportionate number of people prosecuted for prostitution are (p. 546):

    a. male.
    *b. black.
    c. over age 40.
    d. none of the above.

67. Prostitution is the only crime for which (p. 546):

    *a. women are prosecuted more often than men.
    b. fines are given but arrests are not made.
    c. the buyer and the seller of illegal "goods" are held equally responsible by the law.
    d. women under age 18 are not arrested.

68. Which of the following concerning prostitution and the law is correct (p. 546)?

    a. Patronizing a prostitute is illegal everywhere in the United States.
    b. Enforcement of the laws is fairly consistent from one locality to the next.
    *c. Prostitutes tend to be given short jail sentences.
    d. The customer is usually implicated for his or her contribution to prostitution.

69. Which of the following statements concerning pimping is true (p. 546)?

    a. The punishment for pimping is less severe than that for prostitution.
    *b. Few pimps are arrested.
    c. Pimping is legal.
    d. Another name for a pimp is a john.

70. Which of the following groups lobby for decriminalization and legalization of prostitution (p. 546)?

    *a. COYOTE and Scapegoat
    b. LAP and Flag
    c. FREE and Easy
    d. PRESSURE and Talk

71. _____ is known for her efforts to lobby for the decriminalization of prostitution (p. 546).

    a. Naomi McCormick
    *b. Margo St. James
    c. Marcia Kelly
    d. Lori Shaffer

72. According to the textbook, decriminalization of prostitution could (p. 546):

    a. reduce the influence of pimps and organized crime in prostitution.
    b. allow for the licensing and taxing of prostitutes.
    c. include a requirement for regular screening of prostitutes for sexually transmitted diseases.
    *d. all of the above.

73. For females, becoming a prostitute is associated with (p. 547):

    a. poverty.
    b. physical and sexual abuse.
    c. nymphomania.
    *d. both a and b.

74. The average span of a prostitute's career is (p. 548):

    a. 6 months.
    b. 2 years.
    *c. 5 years.
    d. 9 years.

75. Studies of massage-parlor patrons on the West Coast and in Illinois found that the typical customer (p. 548):

    a. was a "loser" who couldn't attract a sexual partner without paying for sex.
    *b. was indistinguishable from the average American male.
    c. usually didn't have an ongoing personal relationship with a woman other than the prostitute.
    d. didn't bother with the usual courtship behaviors prior to seeing a prostitute, such as showering, dressing fashionably, and using cologne.
    e. was over 50 years old.

Essay Questions

76. How is sex used in various magazines and newspapers? Does the use of sexual content in an advertisement enhance the likelihood that consumers will purchase a particular item (pp. 518–520)?

77. Describe what happened to the market for X-rated films in theaters versus home videos during the 1980s (pp. 520–524).

78. Trace the history of laws regulating erotic material in the United States. Summarize the current legal stance regarding erotic materials. What are the ambiguities in the laws? What makes defining obscenity so problematic (pp. 527–532)?

79. What effects of short-term and long-term exposure to erotica have been discovered through experimental research (pp. 532–537)?

80. Summarize the studies on the effect of exposure to violent pornography. Include a discussion of romanticized versus realistic depictions of rape (pp. 534–537).

81. Describe the differences in types of erotica and attitudes toward erotica in the United States and Japan. Include a comparison of sexual assault rates in both countries. Why do you think these differences exist (pp. 538–539)?

82. Discuss the topic of children in pornography. The textbook authors take the position that the use of children in erotic materials should be prosecuted under child abuse laws. Describe the three reasons they put forth for that position (p. 539).

83. Compare and contrast the types of female prostitutes in contemporary society. Include a discussion of male prostitutes, in which you compare them with female prostitutes (pp. 540–547).

84. Discuss the issue regarding prostitution and the law, describing law enforcement practices toward pimps, prostitutes, and johns. How is each person typically punished (pp. 545–547)?

85. Discuss the advantages and disadvantages of decriminalizing prostitution (p. 546).

86. What kinds of people seek the services of prostitutes (pp. 548–549)?

CHAPTER 17

Sexually Transmitted Diseases

Multiple-Choice Questions

1. Students of today, from first-year in high school through graduate school, are more knowledgeable about _____ than about other sexually transmitted diseases (STDs) (p. 555).

    *a. AIDS
    b. syphilis
    c. herpes
    d. chlamydia

2. Regarding knowledge that college students have about STDs, Benton et al. (1993) found that (p. 555):

    *a. more education is needed with regard to the modes of HIV transmission.
    b. students who were accepting of homosexual behavior were more knowledge about AIDS than those who were relatively intolerant of homosexual behavior.
    c. most college students learn about STDs from their parents.
    d. minority students are especially well informed about the preventive effectiveness of condom use.

3. In a study in San Francisco to assess awareness that condom use could reduce the risk of transmitting HIV, Di Clemente et al. (1988) concluded that _____ were particularly ill informed.

    a. high school teachers
    b. grade school teachers
    *c. minority high school students
    d. Anglo college students

4. A national survey of college students revealed that _____ of the homosexual respondents reported multiple sexual partners and that approximately 60 percent used condoms _____ when they engage in sexual intercourse.

    a. 80 percent; more than half the time
    *b. 50 percent; less than half the time
    c. 30 percent; the majority of the time
    d. 10 percent; less than a quarter of the time

5. Minority adolescents appear to be (p. 555):

    a. more likely than their white counterparts to engage in safer-sex practices.
    *b. less likely than their white counterparts to engage in safer-sex practices.
    c. just as likely as their white counterparts to engage in safer-sex practices.
    d. less susceptible to AIDS.

6. Surveys of adolescents indicate that (p. 556):

   *a. those who viewed their peers as supporting condom use were more likely to report using condoms themselves.
   b. minority adolescents regarded themselves as more susceptible to AIDS.
   c. a perception of susceptibility to HIV infection had no relationship to engaging in high-risk behaviors.
   d. all of the above.

7. Darrow, a research sociologist at the Centers for Disease Control, made which of the following major points concerning STDs in your textbook (p. 557)?

   a. The failure to educate youngsters in schools can only lead to a higher incidence of STDs.
   b. More money must be made available to study the causes of STDs.
   *c. Physicians have been negligent in their efforts to control STDs.
   d. Abstinence is the best method for preventing STDs.

8. Darrow (1981) believes that physicians should pay closer attention (p. 557):

   a. diagnosing STDs accurately.
   b. completely reporting each case of an STD.
   c. screening people who are susceptible to STDs.
   *d. all of the above.

9. A random sample of 72 public restrooms (p. 559):

   a. found gonorrhea bacteria on 10 percent of the toilet seats.
   *b. yielded no gonorrhea bacteria on the toilet seats.
   c. found herpes II virus on 20 percent of the toilet seats.
   d. none of the above; no such study has been conducted.

10. Which of the following is relatively easy to cure (p. 560)?

   *a. gonorrhea
   b. herpes II
   c. genital warts
   d. hepatitis B

11. Which of the following is true about gonorrhea (p. 560)?

   a. Gonorrhea is caused by a virus.
   b. Of women who contract gonorrhea, 10 percent have mild symptoms or no symptoms at all.
   *c. Symptoms usually appear within 2 to 10 days after intimate contact with an infected person.
   d. Gonorrhea is typically treated with streptomycin.

12. Which of the following is the most likely cause of acute pelvic inflammatory disease (PID) (p. 560)?

    a. syphilis
   *b. gonorrhea
    c. herpes II
    d. genital warts

13. Gonorrhea (p. 561):

    a. is usually detected with a blood test.
   *b. can pass to a baby during childbirth, possibly causing blindness.
    c. is suspected in men who have a rash on the inner thighs and a fever.
    d. is screened for as part of an annual PAP smear.

14. Untreated gonorrhea can lead to (p. 560):

    a. infertility.
    b. ectopic pregnancy.
    c. acute PID.
   *d. all of the above.

15. This STD is transmitted through contact with hard but painless chancres (p. 561).

    a. gonorrhea
   *b. syphilis
    c. chlamydia
    d. herpes II

16. The probability of one's becoming infected with syphilis from a single contact with a syphilis carrier is about _____ percent (p. 561).

    a. 3–5
    b. 10–15
   *c. 20–30
    d. 60–70

17. Secondary syphilis is characterized by a generalized body rash, sometimes accompanied by (p. 562):

    a. fever.
    b. headache.
    c. indigestion.
   *d. all of the above.

18. Syphilis is highly contagious during (p. 562):

    a. the primary stage alone.
    b. the secondary stage alone.
   *c. the primary and secondary stages and the first year of the latent stage.
    d. the third stage.

19. The incidence of chlamydia among female college students ranges from _____ percent (p. 562).

    *a. 6 to 10
    b. 21 to 25
    c. 40 to 44
    d. 61 to 65

20. The number of new cases of _____ each year has increased markedly since the mid-1970s, and it appears to be the most prevalent bacterial STD in the United States (p. 562).

    a. shigellosis
    b. syphilis
    *c. chlamydia
    d. herpes

21. Chlamydia can be transmitted (p. 563):

    a. through sexual or nonsexual contact with an infected person.
    b. from contact with the feces of an infected person.
    c. through contact with the fingers of an infected person.
    *d. all of the above.

22. Chlamydia is (p. 563):

    a. caused by a virus.
    b. an infection affecting only women.
    c. transmittable only by sexual contact.
    *d. none of the above.

23. Although most women are asymptomatic for _____, when symptoms of this STD do appear, they include mild irritation in the genitals, itching and burning during urination, and some cervical swelling (p. 563).

    a. gonorrhea
    b. syphilis
    *c. chlamydia
    d. herpes II

24. Because most women have no symptoms of _____ infection in its early stages, they are unlikely to seek treatment and diagnosis until their reproductive organs are badly damaged (p. 563).

    a. cystitis
    b. syphilis
    *c. chlamydia
    d. herpes II

25. Symptoms of _____ in men include a thin, relatively clear, whitish discharge from the urethra (p. 563).

   a. shigellosis
   *b. chlamydia
   c. syphilis
   d. herpes II

26. Which of the following is true about chlamydia (p. 563)?

   *a. It can be effectively treated with tetracycline.
   b. Symptoms generally appear 4 to 6 weeks after contact with the infection.
   c. A blood test is used to detect it.
   d. Pregnant women with untreated chlamydia rarely pass it on to the infant.

27. Complications of untreated chlamydia include (p. 563):

   a. PID.
   b. infertility in men.
   c. premature birth, blindness, or pneumonia of the offspring of infected women.
   *d. all of the above.

28. Which of the following is recognized as the greatest cause of preventable blindness in the world (p. 563)?

   *a. chlamydia
   b. syphilis
   c. herpes
   d. genital warts

29. Which of the following may be caused by frequent or vigorous intercourse (p. 564)?

   a. chlamydia
   *b. cystitis
   c. gonorrhea
   d. none of the above

30. _____ is found only in men (p. 564).

   a. Chlamydia
   b. Herpes II
   *c. Prostatitis
   d. Cystitis
   e. None of the above

31. Cystitis (p. 564):

   a. is characterized by urinary problems.
   b. is more common among women.
   c. can result from wiping from the anus toward the urethra.
   *d. all of the above.

32. _____ produces a thin leukorrhea that ranges in color from gray to greenish-yellow and has an unpleasant odor (p. 564).

    *a. Gardnerella
    b. Syphilis
    c. Herpes II
    d. Scabies
    e. A genital wart

33. Which of the following, diagnosed by culturing a stool specimen, can be transmitted through oral stimulation of the anus of an individual with shigellosis (p. 564)?

    a. chancroid
    b. chlamydia
    *c. shigellosis
    d. candidiasis

34. Symptoms of shigellosis include which of the following (p. 564)?

    a. fever
    b. diarrhea
    c. inflammation of the mucous membranes of the large intestine
    *d. all of the above

35. Which of the following may be treated with ampicillin or tetracycline but rapidly develop resistance to antibiotics (p. 564)?

    a. *Escherichia coli*
    *b. *Shigella bacteria*
    c. *Chlamydia trachomatis*
    d. *Treponema pallidum*

36. Women with acute PID (p. 565):

    a. may show symptoms within weeks after contracting the STD that caused the PID.
    b. can experience intense lower abdominal pain.
    c. experience pain from movement of the cervix from side to side.
    *d. all of the above.

37. Pelvic inflammatory disease is (p. 565):

    a. the most common serious complication of untreated gonorrhea, chlamydia, and other genital infections in females.
    b. a cause of ectopic pregnancy and sterility.
    c. often mistaken for appendicitis.
    *d. all of the above.

38. Which of the following is true about PID (p. 565)?

     a. Sexually active women who use oral contraceptives are less likely to be hospitalized than sexually active women who do not use oral contraceptives.
     b. Smoking cigarettes and douching are associated with an increased risk of catching PID.
     c. The vast majority of patients respond quickly to treatment with penicillin, ampicillin, or tetracycline.
    *d. All of the above.

39. PID occurs when infection develops in the (p. 565):

     a. labia.
     b. fallopian tubes.
     c. uterus.
    *d. both b and c.

40. Who is the first Westerner known to have died of AIDS (p. 567)?

    *a. Dr. Grethe Rask
     b. Abraham Mahler
     c. Roberta Jones
     d. Daniel Hudson

41. Evidence indicates that AIDS can be contracted (p. 568):

     a. from mice.
     b. from mosquitoes.
     c. from pigs.
    *d. none of the above.

42. The HIV virus (p. 568):

     a. is self-diagnosed in most cases.
     b. directly attacks the nervous system, causing slow deterioration and death.
    *c. disables the body's immune system, leaving patients vulnerable to opportunistic infections.
     d. causes the patient's immune system to malfunction, causing death immediately.

43. Percentage-wise, AIDS is more prevalent (p. 568):

     a. among elderly gay males than young gay males.
     b. in northern states than southern states.
     c. among lesbian than heterosexual females.
    *d. in large urban centers than in rural areas.

44. Through September 1993, more than half of U.S. AIDS patients were _____. Now there is a higher percentage of HIV-infected _____ (p. 568).

     a. heterosexual drug users; homosexual males
     b. homosexual females; homosexual males
    *c. homosexual males; heterosexuals
     d. residents of Atlanta; residents of Minneapolis

45. Those people at the highest risk to contract the AIDS virus include (p. 568):

    a. homosexual and bisexual males.
    b. intravenous drug users.
    c. those having sexual contact with homosexual males, bisexual males, intravenous drug users, and prostitutes.
    d. sexually active heterosexuals.
  *e. all of the above.

46. The _____ percent of AIDS cases in the United States occur among intravenous drug users (p. 568).

    a. 13
  *b. 24
    c. 33
    d. 41

47. With respect to transmission of AIDS in Haiti and Africa, which of the following is true (p. 569)?

  *a. AIDS is far more prevalent among heterosexuals than among homosexual men.
    b. The percentage of Haitian victims of AIDS who were female dropped between 1983 and 1985.
    c. AIDS is primarily transmitted by means of carrier mosquitoes.
    d. HIV antibodies were found more often among African prostitutes of higher socioeconomic status.

48. Of individuals diagnosed with AIDS before 1993, _____ percent had died (p. 569).

    a. 18
    b. 31
  *c. 53
    d. 87

49. The average survival time of an AIDS victim from the date of initial diagnosis is about (p. 570):

    a. 7 to 17 months.
  *b. 18 to 36 months.
    c. 3 to 4 years.
    d. 5 to 6 years.

50. HIV is (p. 570):

    a. the antibody whose presence in a person's blood shows infection with AIDS.
    b. an acronym for the two groups most at risk for contracting AIDS: homosexuals and intravenous drug users.
  *c. the retrovirus that causes AIDS.
    d. a drug that slows but does not halt the course of AIDS infection.

51. Which is the least likely of the following to be a place where HIV would be found (p. 571)?

    *a. saliva
    b. blood
    c. semen
    d. vaginal secretions

52. The AIDS virus has been found to be most prevalent in those who engage in (p. 572):

    a. receptive fisting.
    b. receptive anal coitus.
    c. receptive fellatio.
    *d. all of the above.

53. Which of the following statements about the spread of AIDS is *not* true (p. 573)?

    a. It is more likely to occur among people with a history of other STDs.
    b. The risk of contracting AIDS rises dramatically with the number of sexual partners one has.
    *c. Some instances are known of the disease's being contracted in the process of donating blood.
    d. Pregnant women can transmit the virus to their fetuses.

54. Symptoms of AIDS can resemble those of (p. 573):

    a. the flu.
    b. psychological stress.
    c. the common cold.
    *d. all of the above.

55. Which of the following is a blood test for AIDS (p. 573)?

    a. LIZA
    b. MARI
    *c. ELISA
    d. none of the above

56. Of the following, the opportunistic infection *most* commonly suffered by AIDS victims is (p. 573):

    a. Kaposi's sarcoma.
    *b. pneumocystis carinii pneumonia.
    c. dysentery.
    d. pertussis.

57. _____ is *not* an early sign of AIDS infection (p. 573).

    a. Lymphadenopathy
    *b. Weight gain
    c. Persistent fever and night sweats
    d. Skin rashes and easy bruising

58. Which of the following is true concerning treatment of AIDS (p. 575)?

     a. HIV vaccine research is performed on animals.
     b. HIV does not become resistant to AZT.
     c. AZT has no side effects and can reduce the severity of the illness.
    *d. There is no cure for AIDS.

59. Which of the following is true about testing positive for HIV (p. 574)?

     a. People who text positive for HIV are not at risk to spread the disease until they develop symptoms.
     b. A large percentage of those with HIV antibodies eventually experience symptoms of AIDS.
     c. The currently available blood tests for HIV are 100 percent reliable.
    *d. There may be as long as a 6-month period between infection and testing positive for HIV.

60. Kaposi's sarcoma is (p. 575):

    *a. a rare form of cancer of the skin and connective tissues.
     b. a drug that has shown some success in slowing the progress of AIDS infections.
     c. a lung infection leading to the form of pneumonia from which many AIDS patients die.
     d. an often fatal side effect of some efforts to treat AIDS.

61. Which of the following cancers has been on the increase in HIV infected bisexual men and gay males (p. 576)?

     a. prostate cancer
    *b. Kaposi's sarcoma
     c. testicular cancer
     d. cervical cancer

62. Which of the following is the most common opportunistic disease associated with AIDS (p. 575)?

     a. leukemia
     b. testicular cancer
    *c. pneumocystis carinii pneumonia
     d. Kaposi's sarcoma

63. One of the most promising drugs that slows the effects of the AIDS virus to some extent is (p. 576):

     a. tetracycline.
     b. penicillin.
     c. sulfisoxazole.
    *d. AZT.

64. One of the potential side effects of using AZT is (p. 574):

    *a. anemia.
    b. herpes II.
    c. prostate cancer.
    d. high numbers of white blood cells.

65. A major obstacle to experimentation with AIDS vaccines is that (p. 575):

    a. there are ethical problems.
    b. research must be conducted with humans.
    c. no good animal model for the disease exists.
    *d. all of the above.

66. Cytomegalovirus infections (p. 576):

    a. result in seizures and spasms.
    b. are also referred to as AIDS dementia complex.
    c. lead to symptoms including discharge from the penis.
    *d. are caused by a group of herpes viruses.

67. How many babies born to mothers with HIV become infected with the virus (p. 576)?

    a. 5 percent
    *b. 33 percent
    c. 70 percent
    d. 90 percent

68. A baby is at risk of becoming infected with HIV from his or her mother if the mother develops AIDS (p. 576):

    a. before or during pregnancy.
    b. and breast-feeds the child.
    c. after the baby is born.
    *d. both a and b.

69. According to the results of studies involving hundreds of men, how has popular awareness of AIDS affected contemporary sexual practices (p. 577)?

    a. There has been no impact on the number of sex partners men report having.
    *b. The proportion of people engaging in unprotected anal intercourse has declined.
    c. Modification toward safer-sex practices has been more prevalent among heterosexual than homosexual couples.
    d. Both a and c.

70. As of 1994, _____ was still incurable (p. 580).

    a. gonorrhea
    b. syphilis
    c. chlamydia
    *d. herpes II

71. The time needed to heal from which virus can be reduced by an ointment (acyclovir/Zovirax) (p. 580)?

    *a. herpes II
    b. hepatitis B
    c. genital warts
    d. viral gynococcal genitalis

72. The symptoms of herpes II (p. 581):

    a. include an overall body rash.
    b. consist of painless, hard sores.
    c. are worsened by the use of any contraceptive method that contains spermicides.
    *d. appear at the site of the infection 3 to 7 days after infection.

73. _____ is linked to cancer in women and can cause fetal malformations in the offspring of women who have it (p. 581).

    a. Chlamydia
    *b. Herpes II
    c. Gonorrhea
    d. Hepatitis B

74. Among the greatest risks associated with herpes II are those that may be incurred by _____, such as _____ (p. 581).

    a. women; PID
    b. men; prostate cancer
    *c. fetuses; severe neurological difficulties
    d. none of the above

75. Primary herpes infections can cause (p. 581):

    a. fetal malformations.
    b. abortions.
    c. premature labor.
    *d. all of the above.

76. Which reduce the risk of transmitting or contracting genital herpes (p. 581)?

    a. oral contraceptives.
    b. Norplants.
    *c. spermicides containing nonoxynol-9.
    d. all of the above.

77. Most male partners of women with genital warts or human papilloma virus (HPV) (p. 582):

    *a. have no visible genital warts.
    b. develop prostate cancer.
    c. develop herpes I.
    d. develop herpes II.

78. Genital warts (p. 582):

    a. are contracted through direct contact with the warts.
    b. may be contracted through nonsexual contact.
    c. can be diagnosed with a screening test in people without visible warts.
  *d. both a and b.

79. Which of the following is *not* true of hepatitis B (p. 582)?

    a. The first symptom is a hard chancre on the genitals.
    b. Infection usually begins within 2 days after exposure to an infectious carrier.
  *c. No vaccination exists to prevent it.
    d. The virus attacks the pancreas.

80. Hepatitis B (p. 582):

    a. is now curable.
  *b. risk can be eliminated by vaccination.
    c. is a bacterial infection.
    d. attacks the cardiovascular system.
    e. all of the above.

81. Hepatitis B virus infection is diagnosed by a (p. 582):

    a. CAT scan.
    b. physical examination.
    c. tissue biopsy.
  *d. blood test.

82. This yeastlike infection produces a thick, white discharge resembling the curd of cottage cheese, with an unpleasant odor, and causing severe itching and inflammation of the vagina (p. 583).

  *a. candidiasis
    b. chlamydia
    c. syphilis
    d. scabies

83. Candidiasis can result in infection if a woman (p. 583):

    a. uses an IUD.
    b. douches frequently.
    c. is taking antibiotics.
  *d. both b and c.

84. Which of the following about trichomoniasis is correct (p. 583)?

    a. It is diagnosed through visual inspection without the need for a microscope.
    *b. Most people who have it are asymptomatic.
    c. It has severe consequences for the fetus of infected women during labor.
    d. The incubation period ranges from 1 to 2 days.
    e. Both a and c.

85. Pediculosis pubis (crabs) (p. 584):

    a. is a bacterial infection.
    *b. grows in warm, hairy body areas.
    c. cannot be transmitted sexually.
    d. is killed with antibiotics.

86. Pediculosis pubis is a _____ infection (p. 584).

    a. bacterial
    b. viral
    c. vaginal
    *d. parasitic

87. Scabies is (p. 584):

    a. not very contagious.
    b. a bacterial infection.
    *c. caused by infestation with parasitic mites.
    d. treated with penicillin.

88. Among the safer-sex practices that reduce the risk of contracting AIDS or other STDs are all of the following *except* (pp. 585–586):

    a. using condoms.
    b. using spermicides.
    c. limiting the number of sexual contacts.
    *d. douching.

89. Which of the following reduces the risk of contracting an STD (p. 585)?

    a. taking a shower or bath before being sexually intimate
    b. urinating after sex
    c. using condoms and spermicides during intercourse
    *d. all of the above

90. Use of the _____ has(have) been found to reduce the risk of HIV transmission when used properly (p. 586).

    a. condom
    b. diaphragm with spermicide
    c. pill
    *d. both a and b.

Essay Questions

91. Why is it important for anyone diagnosed with an STD to make sure that his or her partner(s) is(are) informed (p. 554)?

92. What are some attitudinal factors that influence educational attempts to reduce transmission of AIDS? Include a discussion of attitudes toward STD patients in general (pp. 555–558).

93. What are the symptoms of gonorrhea? What are the possible complications of untreated gonorrhea (pp. 559–560)?

94. What are the symptoms of syphilis? Describe each stage (pp. 561–562).

95. The annual incidence of chlamydia is higher than that for any other STD. What are its symptoms and potential complications (pp. 562–563)?

96. What is cystitis? How is it transmitted? What is prostatitis? What causes it (p. 564)?

97. What is pelvic inflammatory disease? How is it treated? How is it related to IUD use (p. 565)?

98. List the viral STDs. Briefly discuss each, and indicate the extent to which each can be cured (pp. 565–582).

99. Discuss AIDS. What are the symptoms? What causes it? Describe the risk factors for contracting it (pp. 565–580).

100. Discuss the responses of the government and scientific community to AIDS. How has AIDS been changing sexual practices among heterosexuals and homosexuals (pp. 565–580)?

101. List and describe the opportunistic infections that attack AIDS patients (pp. 575–580).

102. Describe herpes simplex type II (pp. 580–581).

103. What are genital warts? What risks do they pose (p. 582)?

104. Describe hepatitis B. Include a discussion of how it affects the body and how it is transmitted (pp. 582–583).

105. Describe the various parasitic infections mentioned in the textbook (pp. 583–584).

106. A number of ways of reducing the risk of contracting STDs were described in the textbook. Identify and discuss five of these (pp. 584–587).

Multiple-Choice Questions

1. Technically, rape is in a category of sexual encounter that is called (p. 591):

   a. problematic consent.
   *b. sexual assault.
   c. negotiation.
   d. harassment.

2. Our knowledge of sexual assault may be biased because (p. 592):

   a. most research on sexual assault has involved convicted assailants.
   b. many victims do not report assault to the authorities.
   c. police sometimes dismiss reports of assault as unfounded.
   *d. all of the above.

3. About _____ percent of reported sexual assaults in 1992 resulted in the arrest of alleged assailants (p. 592).

   a. 10
   *b. 33
   c. 65
   d. 90

4. The idea that a victim is responsible, at least partially, for sexual assault is called (p. 592):

   *a. victim precipitation.
   b. oblivious coercion.
   c. premeditated attack.
   d. diffused responsibility.

5. The largest proportion of arrests for sexual assault are (p. 592):

   a. homosexual men aged 26–35.
   b. adolescent boys.
   *c. heterosexual men aged 18–24.
   d. men aged 30–50.

6. Which of the following is false (p. 593)?

   a. The largest proportion of unidentified rapists are teenagers and males in early adulthood.
   b. The majority of convicted rapists use weapons to coerce their victims.
   c. The majority of offenders are either drinking or drunk at the time of the sexual assault.
   *d. In the United States, a woman has never been convicted of rape.

7. Tactics used by unidentified rapists most often include (p. 593):

    a. the use of weapons.
    b. physical restraint.
    c. threats.
    *d. both b and c.

8. Which of the following is characteristic of convicted rapists (p. 593)?

    a. Many have lacked self-confidence from an early age.
    b. A high proportion were themselves victims of assault, violence, and neglect during childhood and adolescence.
    c. Many report having victimized others during childhood and adolescence.
    *d. All of the above.

9. Men who voluntarily but anonymously report that they have engaged in coercive sex (p. 594):

    *a. rarely have been arrested for sexual offenses.
    b. have, in the majority of cases, been arrested for some crime other than rape.
    c. rarely hold white-collar jobs or diplomas.
    d. all of the above.

10. Which of the following is characteristic of unidentified (unreported) rapists (p. 594)?

    a. These men differ from nonrapists in their race, social class, or places of residence.
    *b. Adolescent rapists are often alienated from families and schools.
    c. These men tend to want to dominate their more passive friends.
    d. These rapists recognize that they have victimized women unjustly and show some remorse.

11. Which of the following is true about rapists (p. 595)?

    *a. Many rapists are guilt-ridden individuals.
    b. Rapists tend to score high on measures of responsibility and socialization.
    c. Rapists report less disgust, anger, shame, and fear about rape than do nonrapists.
    d. There is no difference between rapists and nonrapists on attitudes toward sexual aggression.

12. According to Groth and Burgess (1977), who conducted interviews with men convicted of sexual assault, it is very common for convicted rapists to (p. 596):

    a. have problems with premature ejaculation.
    *b. experience problems maintaining erection during an assault.
    c. experience significant sexual dysfunction in relationships with consenting partners.
    d. none of the above.

13. The relationship between a strong sexual appetite and the likelihood to commit a sexually aggressive act is (p. 596):

    a. stronger for convicted rapists.
   *b. stronger for unidentified rapists.
    c. equal for both groups.
    d. none of the above; research has not been done in this area.

14. Research by Mahoney et al. (1986) found that, of the following, the strongest predictor of coercive behavior by college men was (p. 596):

    a. grade-point average.
    b. state in which the student lived.
   *c. the lifetime number of sexual partners.
    d. whether the student was married.

15. According to the textbook, the most common sexual problem of convicted rapists tends to be (p. 596):

    a. lack of a refractory period.
    b. retrograde ejaculation.
    c. premature ejaculation.
   *d. retarded ejaculation.

16. Women raped by _____ are the most likely to report the incident (p. 597).

    a. steady boyfriends
    b. casual acquaintances
    c. spouses
   *d. strangers

17. Many states define crimes involving male rape victims as (p. 598):

    a. statutory rape.
    b. battery but not rape.
   *c. sodomy.
    d. harassment.

18. Research by Groth and Burgess (1980) focusing on convicted male rapists who had raped men found that three-quarters of the male victims were (p. 598):

   *a. total strangers.
    b. casual acquaintances.
    c. coworkers.
    d. fellow prison inmates.

19. In a study of Los Angeles households conducted by Sorenson, Stein, Siegel, Golding, and Burnam (1987), it was found that of the 1,480 men interviewed (p. 597):

    a. none reported ever having been pressured into sexual contact by a male.
    b. for 10 percent, some form of anal intercourse had occurred.
    c. the majority said that they had been raped by men in prison settings.
    *d. the majority of those who reported having been forced into sexual contact said that the female had been the perpetrator.

20. Which of the following is *not* a style of attack in which men are raped by other men, according to Groth and Burgess (p. 598)?

    a. physical force
    b. intimidation
    *c. projection
    d. entrapment

21. When Aizenman and Kelley (1988) questioned 800 college students about sexual violence in dating relationships, it was found that female victims were more likely to report _____, but that male victims were more likely to report _____ (p. 598).

    *a. physical restraint; psychological force
    b. intimidation; entrapment
    c. projection; use of a weapon
    d. entrapment; physical restraint

22. In 1992, _____ U.S. women reported being sexually assaulted (p. 599).

    a. 31,000
    b. 54,000
    *c. 109,000
    d. 220,000

23. _____ are most at risk of being sexually assaulted (p. 600).

    a. Women aged 25 to 30
    b. Men in their early 20s
    c. Women aged 35 to 45
    *d. Women in their teens and early 20s

24. Acquaintance rape first received attention when _____ (1977) surveyed college women regarding their experience with offensive sexual aggression (p. 600).

    *a. Kirkpatrick and Kanin
    b. Black and Hall
    c. Rutherford and McMurphy
    d. Sowl and Santos

25. Women from lower social classes tend to predominate in statistics of reported rapes, probably because these women tend to (p. 600):

  a. be on the street more often.
  b. date men who view sex as aggression.
  c. have a large number of sexual partners.
  *d. be less able to seek treatment from private sources.
  e. all of the above.

26. Most studies have shown that anywhere from _____ percent of various samples of college _____ report being victims of sexual aggression (p. 600).

  a. 10 to 25; women
  *b. 40 to 80; women
  c. 70 to 95; women
  d. 30 to 50; men

27. Rape by a(n) _____ is the type more likely to involve either a weapon or physical injury (p. 601).

  a. acquaintance
  *b. stranger
  c. steady boyfriend
  d. spouse

28. According to the textbook, acquaintance assault is less likely to be (p. 601):

  a. experienced by college women.
  b. perpetrated by college men.
  *c. one involving a weapon or physical injury.
  d. one including verbal threats.

29. Mynatt and Allgeier (1990) found that women with relatively assertive personalities _____ than relatively nonassertive women (p. 601).

  a. are more likely to be sexually assaulted in the first place
  b. engage in more self-hatred as a result of the assault
  c. report more fear following the assault
  *d. engage in less self-blame for the assault

30. The first state to eliminate the spousal exception clause was _____, in the late 1970s (p. 602).

  a. New York
  b. Florida
  *c. Oregon
  d. California
  e. none of the above; the spousal exception clause in rape laws still exists in all states.

31. Feild and Bienen (1980) found that of the Americans they sampled, about _____ believed that "women provoke rape by their appearance or behavior" (p. 602).

   *a. two-thirds
    b. one-third
    c. one-eighth
    d. only men

32. Studies show that a woman _____ is likely to be perceived as indicating sexual interest (p. 602).

    a. hitchhiking
    b. wearing tight clothing
    c. accepting an invitation to a man's apartment
   *d. all of the above

33. Which of the following is true (p. 603)?

    a. A woman cannot be raped against her will.
    b. Many cases of rape involve a woman who willfully participates in sex and later claims rape.
    c. People who endorse traditional roles for women are less likely to blame rape victims.
   *d. People who see rape as an act of aggression are less likely to blame victims of rape.

34. The notion that rape is related to aggression rather than sexual interest is supported by findings that (p. 603):

    a. legalized prostitution does not appear to reduce the incidence of rape.
    b. many rapists have consenting sexual partners available to them.
    c. times of war, societal upheaval, and economic instability are associated with increased incidence of rape.
   *d. all of the above.

35. About _____ percent of the citizens in Feild and Bienen's research thought that rapists were motivated by sexual desire (p. 603).

    a. 20
   *b. 50
    c. 75
    d. 90

36. Kanin (1985) found that the male assailants in his study perceived themselves to be (p. 604):

    a. studs, although according to women they had previously dated, they weren't.
    b. angrier than most other people, although according to reports from their parents they were mild mannered in childhood.
    c. less than handsome, although according to reports by objective judges of their photographs, they weren't.
   *d. sexually deprived, although the average number of monthly sexual outlets they reported exceeded the norm.

37. People who view women in the traditional gender role are likely to see rape as (p. 604):

    a. the woman's fault.
    b. motivated by a man's need for sex.
    c. resulting in the raped woman's losing something very valuable.
    *d. all of the above.

38. According to work by McCormick (1994), rapists tend to (p. 605):

    a. be strong believers in the double standard.
    b. feel extremely guilty for their actions.
    c. place great value on a woman's virginity.
    *d. both a and c.

39. Concerning the aftermath of sexual assault (p. 605):

    a. the anguish of the assault doesn't usually extend beyond the actual incident.
    b. most victims go through a series of ten stages after the assault occurs.
    *c. rape by an acquaintance may be as traumatic as rape by a stranger.
    d. none of the above.

40. The specific emotional and behavioral responses of a victim who has been raped is called (p. 605):

    a. expressive reaction.
    *b. rape-trauma syndrome.
    c. silent rape reaction.
    d. situational anxiety syndrome.

41. Which of the following is *not* a term used in the textbook to describe what happens in the aftermath of sexual assault (p. 606)?

    a. numbing
    *b. dull phase
    c. reorganization phase
    d. intrusive imagery

42. Reactions characteristic of posttraumatic stress disorder (PTSD) that are typically suffered by rape victims include all of the following *except* (p. 606):

    *a. urinary system impairment.
    b. disturbance in sleep patterns.
    c. an impairment of memory and/or powers of concentration.
    d. exaggerated startle response.

43. A rape victim who says, "I see his face on every man, all the time," is most likely experiencing (p. 607):

    *a. intrusive imagery.
    b. numbing.
    c. symbolic guilt.
    d. all of the above.

44. In response to a sexual assault, it is recommended that a rape victim *not* (p. 609):

   *a. change clothes and bathe before reporting the assault.
   b. receive medical treatment as soon as possible.
   c. report the assault to the police.
   d. use a rape crisis center for counseling and support.

45. Victims often do not report sexual assault to the police because they (p. 609):

   a. feel guilty and responsible for the attack.
   b. fear rejection by their families and friends.
   c. doubt that the rapist will be arrested or convicted.
   *d. all of the above.

46. Which of the following is the only legitimate reason the police should use for declaring a report of sexual assault unfounded (p. 609)?

   a. The victim is a prostitute or drug abuser and probably initiated the attack.
   *b. The victim's account of the assault contains obvious discrepancies.
   c. The victim may have provoked the attack through dress or behavior.
   d. The assailant is unlikely to be convicted.

47. Research suggests that a rapist's chances of being arrested, charged, and convicted are approximately (p. 610):

   *a. 4 in 100.
   b. 15 in 100.
   c. 26 in 100.
   d. 58 in 100.

48. Studies by McCahill's group (1979) show that _____ is most related to police acceptance of a rape report (p. 610).

   *a. the presence of another woman while the victim is giving her report
   b. the woman's ability to describe the rapist precisely
   c. reported use of a weapon during the sexual assault
   d. a relatively low conviction rate in the area where the rape took place

49. Which of the following is *not* a goal of the reform of sexual assault laws (p. 610)?

   a. to increase the likelihood of reporting an assault
   b. to make the legal standards for sexual assault consistent with those for other crimes
   *c. to increase the likelihood of victim precipitation
   d. to sensitize and educate society about the status and rights of women

50. The Rape Victim's Privacy Act of 1979 (p. 612):

   a. banned the media from the courtroom during a rape trial.
   b. allowed rape cases to be heard by judges rather than juries, thereby minimizing the number of people who hear the evidence.
   c. allowed the victim's name to be withheld from the public during the legal proceedings.
   *d. limited the extent to which evidence of the victim's previous sexual experience with those other than the defendant could be introduced in court.

51. A victim's _____ can be used in courts in most states as evidence of consent to a sexual assault (p. 612).

    a. use of a rape crisis center
    b. report of having been assaulted one or more times prior to the present attack
   *c. passive submission to the assault
    d. all of the above

52. Of the following, _____ are most at risk for sexual assault (p. 613).

   *a. single women
    b. older women
    c. married women
    d. young, divorced men

53. A woman's chances of suffering sexual assault appear to increase sharply if she (p. 613):

    a. is single.
    b. is sexually active.
    c. identifies with a delinquent peer group.
   *d. all of the above.

54. Based on research cited in the textbook, which of the following is false (p. 613)?

    a. If a young woman is part of a peer group that is sexually active, the male who rapes her may assume that she is interested in sex.
   *b. Victims of sexual assault were more likely than nonvictims to report that they believed that their first intercourse experience would lead to marriage.
    c. Victims of assault are likely to report that they felt pressured or obligated during their first sexual experiences.
    d. Adolescent women who are alienated from parents and teachers and who engage in delinquent acts are more likely than other adolescents to become rape victims.

55. _____ is useful as a strategy to reduce the risk of sexual assault (p. 614).

    a. Determining the circumstances under which you would find sexual intimacy acceptable
    b. Avoid becoming intoxicated if you are with a person with whom you do not wish to become intimate
    c. Making your feelings known, both verbally and nonverbally, if someone tries to force you to have sex
   *d. All of the above.

56. Studies show that _____ is a strong deterrent when one is sexually assaulted (p. 614).

    a. talking to the assailant
    b. submitting but threatening to report the attack to police
   *c. screaming
    d. silence

57. Comparisons of women who successfully resisted rape on one occasion but were raped on another occasion suggest that the most successful way to escape rape is to (p. 614):

    a. try to talk the assailant out of assault.
    b. struggle against the assault.
    c. scream.
    d. fight or run from the assailant.
    *e. use as many of these strategies as possible.

58. Males attempting assault tend to cite which of the following reasons for failed attempts (p. 615)?

    a. their own guilt
    b. their own fright
    c. victim resistance
    *d. all of the above

59. Sexual harassment that occurs in work, educational, and therapeutic settings is specifically characterized by (p. 616):

    a. complicity.
    b. secrecy.
    *c. abuse of power.
    d. promises that are broken.

60. Sexual harassment can readily occur in _____ settings (p. 616).

    a. employment
    b. school
    c. therapeutic
    *d. all of the above

61. A 1980 ruling that broadened the definition of sexual harassment was made by the (p. 616):

    *a. Equal Employment Opportunity Commission.
    b. Civil Rights Commission.
    c. Occupational Safety and Health Administration.
    d. Supreme Court.

62. Sexual harassment was not clearly perceived as a social problem before the mid- (p. 616):

    a. 1920s.
    b. 1950s.
    *c. 1970s.
    d. 1980s.

63. A study of sexual harassment by Grieco (1987) reported that over one-third of the nurses surveyed had experienced (p. 617):

    a. no sexual harassment at all.
    b. lewd comments only.
    *c. grossly inappropriate sexual comments or brief, minor touching.
    d. attempted or actual rape.

64. Grieco (1987) found that the greatest proportion of harassers of nurses were (p. 617):

   a. doctors.
   *b. patients.
   c. coworkers.
   d. administrators.

65. The majority of women in Loy and Stewart's 1984 sample said that they had reacted to sexual harassment by (p. 617):

   *a. ignoring the harassment or confronting the harasser.
   b. quitting their jobs or seeking a transfer.
   c. seeking legal action.
   d. approaching a grievance committee.

66. Which of the following is false (p. 618)?

   a. The greater is the organizational power of the harasser over the harassed, the greater is the seriousness of the harassment.
   b. Those who sexually harass their employees or coworkers appear to have a great need for dominance and power.
   c. Except in the rarest cases, it is likely that sexual harassment victims do not cause their own victimization.
   *d. All sexual intimacy, even between coworkers who are mutually consenting, constitutes sexual harassment.

67. In testimony before a Senate subcommittee, _____ claimed that "sexual harassment on the job is not a problem for the virtuous woman, except in the rarest of cases" (p. 618).

   a. Anita Bryant
   b. Susan Brownmiller
   *c. Phyllis Schlafly
   d. Abigail Moore

68. Harassment of students differs from harassment in the workplace in that (p. 618):

   a. students may have more options than employees for finding other people with whom they can work if a particular faculty member attempts to harass them.
   b. students are in school for a specific period of time, whereas an employee may feel forced to remain in his or her job for economic reasons.
   c. students may be more naive and vulnerable to harassment than employees.
   *d. all of the above.

69. Studies of college students and sexual harassment have found that (p. 618):

   a. between 13 percent and 33 percent of students reported experiencing this problem.
   b. the majority of harassed students knew that campus policy prohibited sexual harassment.
   c. 25 percent of male faculty members reported having sexual encounters with students.
   *d. all of the above.

70. Sexual harassment is most common among female graduate students who are (p. 619):

    *a. younger and single.
    b. older and single.
    c. younger and married.
    d. older and divorced.

71. According to the authors, the best first response to make if you are harassed in an educational setting is probably to (p. 619):

    a. change courses so that you avoid the harassing professor.
    b. report the incident to the police.
    *c. report the incident to authorities on campus.
    d. warn as many other students as possible.

72. Students may be reluctant to report harassment by a professor to campus authorities for fear that they will be flunked or the professor will be fired. Students should be aware that (p. 620):

    a. if there have been no other harassment reports, the professor is generally watched closely, and if there are no other reports, no career damage will result.
    b. professors who harass typically do so to a number of students.
    c. current affirmative action regulations protect people who file harassment from grade discrimination.
    *d. all of the above.

73. Vinson (1984) found that in California, therapist-client sexual contacts accounted for _____ percent of the disciplinary actions taken by the licensing board for psychologists (p. 621).

    a. 3
    b. 11
    c. 34
    *d. 56

74. Which of the following is false (p. 621)?

    a. Feelings of attraction occasionally develop between clients and professionals who are not sexual harassers.
    b. Most therapists who have sex with their clients do so with numerous clients.
    c. Most professionals see client-professional sexual relationships as highly unethical.
    *d. Sexual intimacy between clients and professionals is typically followed by clients' reporting positive consequences.

75. Doctors, psychologists, teachers, and health professionals who work with children are legally required to (p. 622):

    a. gather convincing evidence before reporting cases of suspected child sexual abuse.
    *b. report all suspected cases of child sexual abuse to legal authorities.
    c. treat most reports of sexual encounters made by children with skepticism.
    d. question all suspected child abusers who have been named by two or more children.

76. Sexual activity between relatives is called (p. 622):

    a. pedophilia.
    b. statutory rape.
    *c. incest.
    d. sexual abuse.

77. Adult-child sexual contact is (p. 623):

    a. commonplace outside North America.
    *b. permitted in a only small number of cultures.
    c. unheard of in non-Western cultures.
    d. none of the above.

78. According to the textbook, a probable reason that the number of reported child abuse cases reported annually to the American Humane Association's national data collection system increased dramatically during the period from 1976 to 1982 is (p. 624):

    a. a sudden epidemic in the incidence of the sexual abuse of children.
    b. increased media attention to child sexual abuse.
    c. enforcement of state laws regarding child sexual abuse.
    *d. both b and c.
    e. all of the above.

79. In the Finkelhor et al. (1990) study on sexual contact during childhood, it was found that (p. 624):

    *a. reports of incestuous sexual contact with mothers were extremely rare.
    b. almost no one in Sweden reported having been sexually abused as a child.
    c. a much larger percentage of women reported having been sexually approached in childhood by adults compared to what was found in the Kinsey group's study of the 1950s.
    d. all of the above.

80. Which of these is *not* given as a risk factor for a female child for sexual abuse during childhood (p. 624)?

    a. an unhappy family life
    b. living without a biological parent
    c. inadequate sex education
    *d. living with middle- or upper-class parents

81. Which of the following statements is false (p. 626)?

    a. Heterosexual men are the perpetrators of most cases of sexual abuse of girls.
    *b. Homosexual men are the perpetrators of most cases of sexual abuse of boys.
    c. Sexual abusers are not generally violent.
    d. Children, like women, are more likely to be sexually abused by acquaintances than by strangers.

82. Most commonly, perpetrators of sexual abuse, assault, and harassment are (p. 626):

    a. heterosexual women.
    *b. heterosexual men.
    c. homosexual men.
    d. men and women in equal numbers.

83. Based on research, which of the following statements is false (p. 626)?

    a. Being reared by a "sex-punitive mother" was correlated with experiencing sexual abuse.
    *b. When sexually abusing children, most perpetrators use physical force rather than tricks or bribes to initiate sex.
    c. For male children, the main risk factor for being abused is living with their fathers alone.
    d. Child abuse has been found to occur in all social strata.

84. A small group in the United States that advocates both child-child and child-adult sex is the (p. 626):

    a. Ethical Sexuality Society.
    b. the Pederasty Cult.
    c. Sexual Socialization Society.
    *d. René Guyon Society.

85. Many mental health professionals believe that the key factor in determining the effect of sexual abuse on children is (p. 627):

    a. the extent of sexual activity involved.
    b. the age of the child.
    *c. the reaction of parents, relatives, and adult authorities.
    d. the child's relationship with the abuser.

86. _____ is a child's most common reaction to a forced sexual interaction with an adult (p. 627).

    a. Anger
    b. Disgust
    c. Confusion
    *d. Fear

87. Adults may not report a child's account of sexual abuse because they (p. 627):

    a. do not believe the child.
    b. fear that an offending family member will be removed from the home.
    c. fear that the child will be removed from the home.
    *d. all of the above.

88. An important response to incest involving a young person is to (p. 627):
   a. provide detailed information about normal sexual functioning.
   b. reinforce incest taboos as forcefully as possible.
   *c. talk and provide support as the victim discusses the experience.
   d. all of the above.

89. Kilpatrick (1992) found that in a survey of 501 predominantly middle-class women (p. 627):
   a. a minority reported having had some sexual experience with peers during adulthood.
   b. a minority reported having had some sexual experience with adults during adulthood.
   *c. the presence or absence of sexual contact during childhood was unrelated to depression in adulthood.
   d. sexual contact during childhood typically led to low self-esteem in adulthood.

90. Hrabowy and Allgeier (1987) found that among the women who had unwanted childhood sexual experiences (p. 627):
   a. most had grown up in rural areas.
   b. the majority had problems with marital satisfaction as adults.
   c. the level of invasiveness of childhood sexual experiences was significantly related to general measures of psychological adjustment in adulthood.
   *d. the more invasive the act, the more troubled the women were by it.

Essay Questions

91. Describe the socialization, personality, and sexual characteristics of unidentified rapist (pp. 592–596).

92. Describe and evaluate the extent of support for the major attempts to explain the phenomenon of sexual assault, including victim precipitation, uncontrolled lust, uncontrolled aggression, and exaggerated gender-role identity (pp. 602–605).

93. Following sexual assault, victims tend to experience what is known as the rape-trauma syndrome. Describe the phases and variations of this response pattern (pp. 605–609).

94. Describe the changes that have been occurring during the past decade in state laws regarding sexual assault (pp. 609–612).

95. Women in adolescence and their early 20s are most at risk of sexual assault. What other factors are associated with the risk of assault, and what steps can women take to reduce their vulnerability to sexual assault (pp. 613–616)?

96. If a college student experiences sexual harassment by a professor, what steps should the student take (pp. 618–620)?

97. In what ways does the principle of informed consent govern our values regarding child-adult sexual relations (pp. 624–626)?

98. Assume that you have a 10-year-old cousin who tells you about having been molested by a family friend or relative. What can you do to be most helpful to your cousin (pp. 629–630)?

99. Finkelhor and Russell have described eight hypotheses to account for the greater likelihood of males' than females' sexually abusing children. Describe four of these, and indicate the extent to which these four are supported by evidence (pp. 631–632).

HAPTER 19

typical Sexual Activity

ultiple-Choice Questions

1. The currently preferred term for the love of unusual or atypical sexual activity is (p. 637):

    a. perversion.
    *b. paraphilia.
    c. fetishism.
    d. sexual deviance.

2. In recent years, clinicians have labeled an atypical pattern of sexual behavior as a(n) (p. 638):

    *a. variation.
    b. deviation.
    c. illness.
    d. subversive activity.

3. Data on the frequency of paraphilic behaviors are difficult to obtain because (p. 638):

    a. the American Psychiatric Association has censored the information.
    b. most people with paraphilias are not willing to cooperate with researchers.
    *c. most data come from people who are in therapy or jail.
    d. all of the above.

4. Which of the following is true concerning paraphilias (p. 638)?

    *a. Males are far more likely to engage in them than are females.
    b. Primarily psychologists are interested in evaluating such behavior.
    c. The majority of people who engage in such behavior are in prison.
    d. None of the above.

5. The word *fetish* is derived from the Portuguese word meaning (p. 639):

    *a. "obsessive fascination."
    b. "disinhibition."
    c. "desensitization."
    d. "orgasm."

6. Fetishism is thought to be primarily a (p. 639):

    *a. male characteristic.
    b. female characteristic.
    c. characteristic shared equally by men and women.
    d. typical stage of psychological development.

7. Most frequently, fetish objects are (p. 639):

    a. used only by psychologically disordered people.
    b. dirty, smelly objects.
  *c. used in connection with fantasy and masturbation.
    d. used in connection with sexual assault.

8. One of the most common phallic symbols used in a variety of cultures are (p. 639):

    a. hands.
  *b. feet.
    c. fingers.
    d. arms.

9. In the Slovene language, the penis is referred to by a term that translates into _____ in English (p. 639).

  *a. "third foot"
    b. "little finger"
    c. "rubber boot"
    d. "coat of arms"

10. The feet participate reflexively in orgasm in what are called (p. 640):

    a. vestibular vortexes.
    b. arch twitches.
    c. alveoli cramps.
  *d. carpopedal spasms.

11. What type of approach to explaining fetishes would stress the association between the fetishistic object and sexual arousal (p. 640)?

  *a. behavioral
    b. psychoanalytic
    c. Freudian
    d. social learning

12. Fetishism is most likely to be (p. 640):

    a. a fascination involving the hands.
  *b. learned early in life.
    c. seen in women.
    d. innate.

13. A person who is sexually stimulated or gratified by wearing the clothes of the other gender is a (p. 640):

    a. homosexual.
  *b. transvestite.
    c. transsexual.
    d. bisexual.

14. The transvestite wears clothing stereotypic of the other gender (p. 640):

    a. because he or she desires to change his or her biological gender to the other gender.

    b. for the purpose of attracting a partner.

    *c. for the purpose of arousing himself or herself.

    d. as a fashion statement.

15. Transvestism (p. 640):

    a. is practiced almost exclusively by homosexuals.

    b. is participated in by only about one thousand heterosexual males in the United States.

    c. is primarily seen as men who want to undergo sex-reassignment surgery.

    *d. has been reported in Greek legend and among Roman emperors.

16. In a survey of subscribers to *Transvestia*, it was found that most reported (p. 641):

    *a. having been married.

    b. a homosexual experience.

    c. being treated as girls, not boys, during childhood.

    d. had a strong desire to be the other gender.

    e. all of the above.

17. Research with transvestite has indicated that (p. 641):

    *a. they felt like women when dressed like women but like men when nude.

    b. they began cross-dressing around age 18.

    c. very few were married.

    d. when exposed to motion pictures of nude females, transvestites' sexual arousal was far less than that of heterosexual males.

18. Based on the results of personality tests administered to transvestites (p. 641):

    a. they revealed a high degree of involvement with other people.

    *b. they scored higher on scales of femininity than did control groups.

    c. most were anxious to be cured.

    d. it was found that transvestism is associated with major psychiatric symptoms.

19. The fear most children of transvestites express is that (p. 642):

    a. their fathers might influence them to be transvestites.

    b. their parents will get divorced.

    *c. other children might tease them about their father.

    d. they might experience gender-role identity problems at some time.

20. The evidence indicates that transvestism is related to (p. 642):

    a. genetic factors.

    b. deficient testosterone levels.

    c. living in a society with restrictive norms.

    d. both a and b.

    *e. none of the above.

21. It is unlikely that extreme gender differences in the incidence of transvestism are the result of differences in restrictiveness of norms regarding clothing styles because (p. 642):

    a. females don't appear to derive the sexual satisfaction characteristic of males when they cross-dress.
    b. transvestism appears in cultures with relaxed rather than restrictive gender-role norms.
    *c. both of the above.
    d. none of the above.

22. In a review of cross-cultural research, Robert Munroe and his colleagues found a tendency for transvestism to be more prevalent in cultures with (p. 643):

    a. relaxed gender-role norms.
    b. greater pressure on the male than the female to ensure the family's economic survival.
    c. more homosexuality.
    *d. both a and b.
    e. all of the above.

23. The term *transsexualism* was first used in _____ by _____ (p. 644).

    *a. 1910; Hirschfeld
    b. 1850; Swetland
    c. 1788; Michaelson
    d. 1602; Felswirth

24. It is estimated that 1 in every _____ individuals over the age of 15 is likely to be a _____ (p. 644).

    a. 100,000; transsexual
    *b. 50,000; transsexual
    c. 200,000; transvestite
    d. 500,000; voyeur

25. For most male-to-female transsexuals, preference for girl's clothing typically begins (p. 644):

    *a. at an early age.
    b. in midlife.
    c. late in life.
    d. none of the above; there is no observed pattern.

26. Male-to-female transsexuals' behavior when compared to the behavior of biological females has been found to be (p. 644):

    *a. more stereotypically feminine than the behavior of biological females.
    b. very different from the behavior of biological females.
    c. similar to the behavior of female-to-male transsexuals.
    d. similar to the behavior of homosexual males.

27. Male-to-female transsexuals (p. 645):

    a. almost always follow through with sex-reassignment surgery.
    b. are frequently arrested and end up in prison.
    c. view themselves as men if they should happen to have anal intercourse with men.
    *d. who marry women tend to visualize themselves as women during coitus with their wives.

28. Sex-reassignment surgery is (p. 646):

    *a. frequently more successful for male-to-female transsexuals than for female-to-male transsexuals.
    b. fairly inexpensive in industrial nations.
    c. performed immediately on people who desire it without any psychological screening first.
    d. less expensive for a female-to-male operation than for a male-to-female operation.

29. Most female-to-male transsexuals report (p. 646):

    *a. cross-identification's first occurring at about 3 or 4 years of age.
    b. a preference for girls as close friends in childhood.
    c. intense interest in handling and being around babies.
    d. find menarche to be a source of pleasure.

30. Applicants for female-to-male sex-reassignment surgery are asked to go through (p. 646):

    a. psychological screening.
    b. a 3-month to 1-year period of living as a male.
    c. a process of taking androgenic compounds.
    *d. all of the above.

31. Which of the following motives fit the definition of a transsexual (p. 647)?

    a. homosexuals who hope to comply with a heterosexually oriented society
    b. people punishing themselves for "sins"
    c. disturbed, aging people trying to prolong life
    *d. none of the above

32. The definite cause of transsexualism has been (p. 650):

    a. found in early family experiences.
    b. explained by prenatal exposure to high levels of inappropriate hormones.
    c. found in the study of brain wave patterns.
    *d. elusive to researchers.

33. Concerning sex-reassignment surgery (p. 650):

    a. most transsexuals claim it probably wouldn't make them any happier to go through the procedure than to stay the way they are.
    *b. afterward, female-to-male transsexuals more often have stable relationships and appear more socially adjusted than male-to-female transsexuals do.
    c. there were no differences in psychological adjustment in postsurgical transsexuals compared to presurgical ones.
    d. it rarely alleviates the emotional distress associated with feeling that one is of a different gender than one's anatomy indicates.

34. The intentional infliction of physical or psychological pain on a consenting person in order to excite oneself sexually is called sexual (p. 651):

    *a. sadism.
    b. masochism.
    c. assault.
    d. all of the above.

35. Individuals who are sexually masochistic experience _____ as sexually arousing (p. 651).

    a. all pain
    b. all pain inflicted by other people
    *c. only pain inflicted in specific situations and to specific body areas
    d. only pain inflicted by someone of the opposite gender

36. Questionnaire studies that have been conducted with individuals located through sadomasochistic magazines and clubs found that (p. 652):

    a. women are significantly more likely to be masochistic, whereas males are significantly more likely to sadistic.
    *b. more than half of the respondents report playing both dominant and submissive roles.
    c. females become interested in such activities at a younger age than do males.
    d. females discover sadomasochism on their own, whereas males are introduced to it by a sexual partner.

37. Which of the following is a popular sadomasochist activity (p. 652)?

    a. spanking
    b. a master-slave relationship
    c. torture and use of excrement
    *d. both a and b

38. Which of the following statements is true (p. 653)?

    a. The most popular sadomasochistic sexual activities include spanking and master-slave relationships.
    b. The syndrome of masochism was named for Leopold von Sacher-Masoch.
    c. The "House of Torture" in New Jersey specialized in sadomasochistic services.
    *d. All of the above.

39. John Money claims to have identified (p. 655):

    *a. about 40 paraphilias.
    b. a biological cause of sadomasochism.
    c. a new type of voyeurism.
    d. none of the above.

40. The hypothesis that males have a greater sensitivity to visual sexual stimuli is associated with (p. 656):

    a. psychoanalysis.
    b. visual kinesics.
    c. social learning theory.
    *d. evolutionary theory.

41. Interest in watching beauty contests, female models in men's magazines, and bikini-clad women at a beach are all instances of (p. 656):

    a. voyeurism.
    b. scoptophilia.
    c. coprophilia.
    *d. culturally sanctioned gazing.

42. Which of the following is most appropriately called voyeurism (p. 656)?

    a. observing beauty contestants
    b. looking at nude models in men's magazines
    *c. observing a neighbor undressing at a window who is unaware of being watched
    d. watching a waitress in a topless bar

43. In most states, a man caught observing nude or partially nude people without their consent is prosecuted under (p. 656):

    a. laws against voyeurism.
    b. antiloitering laws.
    c. disorderly conduct laws.
    *d. both b and c.
    e. all of the above.

44. Cross-cultural studies show that (p. 656):

    a. no group studied allowed women to expose their genitals except under restricted circumstances.
    b. prohibitions against female nudity may be due to beliefs that this will protect females from unwanted sexual advances by males.
    c. girls are clothed before boys are.
    d. both a and c.
    *e. all of the above.

45. Voyeurs tend to (p. 657):

    *a. be young and male.
    b. have serious mental disorders.
    c. be young and female.
    d. be older males.

46. A person traditionally described as a "peeping tom" is called a(n) (p. 657):

    a. paraphile.
    b. exhibitionist.
    *c. voyeur.
    d. masochist.

47. Voyeurs probably do not overflow nudist camps or strip shows because (p. 657):

    a. these places are hard to locate.
    *b. most voyeurs are excited by secrecy and risk taking.
    c. voyeurs tend to be homosexual men.
    d. all of the above.

48. Most voyeurs (p. 657):

    a. have serious mental disorders.
    b. have alcohol and/or drug problems.
    *c. are sexually aroused by the idea that they are violating the privacy of their victims.
    d. both a and b.
    e. all of the above.

49. Gebhard and his associates (1965) found that voyeurs (p. 657):

    a. rarely had serious mental disorders.
    b. were seldom using alcohol or drugs when "peeping."
    c. are able to interact sexually with consenting partners with no evidence of dysfunction.
    *d. all of the above.

50. The cause of voyeurism is (p. 657):

    *a. unknown.
    b. the accidental association of sexual arousal with peeping.
    c. observing the primal scene during childhood.
    d. peer encouragement and reinforcement.

51. The act of exposing one's genitals to obtain erotic gratification is (p. 657):

    a. indecent exposure.
    b. against the law.
    c. called exhibitionism.
    *d. all of the above.

52. There are laws against _____ in every state (p. 657).

    a. voyeurism
    *b. exhibitionism
    c. stripteasing
    d. all of the above

53. Exhibitionism occurs primarily (p. 657):

    a. during warm weather.
    b. in the middle of the week.
    c. between 3:00 P.M. and 6:00 P.M. in public settings.
    *d. all of the above.

54. The exhibitionist seems to derive gratification from (p. 658):

    *a. the startled or frightened response of the target.
    b. sexual advances toward the exhibitionist by the target.
    c. being ignored by the target.
    d. being dominated by the target.

55. Based on arrest records _____ is the most common sexual offense (p. 658).

    a. voyeurism
    *b. exhibitionism
    c. tourism
    d. frotteurism

56. An exhibitionist derives little gratification from his behavior if the woman (p. 658):

    a. pays no attention to him.
    b. tells him that he is foolish or disturbed.
    c. approaches rather than flees from him.
    *d. all of the above.

57. Many exhibitionists expose themselves (p. 658):

    a. and use the episode as a source of fantasy for later masturbation.
    b. and want the viewer to be impressed by the size of their penises.
    c. repeatedly in the same place and at the same time of day.
    *d. all of the above.

58. A good response to an obscene phone call is to (p. 659):

    a. stay on the line until the caller eventually hangs up.
    b. try to counsel the caller.
    *c. hang up.
    d. let the caller know that you're upset.

59. Obtaining sexual arousal by touching or rubbing one's body against the body of an unsuspecting person is (p. 660):

    *a. frotteurism.
    b. voyeurism.
    c. troilism.
    d. necrophilism.

60. Sexual contact between an adult and a child is called (p. 660):

    a. frotteurism
    b. harassment.
    c. rape.
    *d. pedophilia.

61. Which of the following is characteristic of convicted pedophiles (p. 660)?

    a. They tend to be younger than other convicted sex offenders.
    b. Most are mentally retarded.
    *c. Many display shyness and low self-esteem.
    d. They tend to be less moralistic and less religious than the population at large.

62. Which of the following statements is *false* about adults who have sex with children (p. 661)?

    a. The incidence of coitus between children and child sexual abusers is low.
    *b. The pattern of sexual activities of pedophiles is much like that of exhibitionists.
    c. Many convicted child abusers were abused themselves as children.
    d. Most child sex abusers are not pedophiles.

63. The conclusions of Gebhard et al. (1965) and others based on research with convicted pedophiles suggest that (p. 661):

    a. the average age of first conviction is 18.
    b. although they have sex with children, they rarely have sex with adult women.
    *c. sexual interest in children is a specific deviant psychological state affecting a small group of men who have had traumatizing developmental experiences.
    d. all of the above.

64. Sexual interaction between a human and a member of another species is called (p. 661):

    a. myopia.
    b. frotteurism.
    *c. zoophilia.
    d. coprophilia.

65. Which of the following statements is false (p. 662)?

    a. References to sexual contact between animals and humans appear throughout recorded history.
    *b. The majority of animal contacts reported by Kinsey's group were by adolescent males.
    c. Modern pornography sometimes contains depictions of sexual relations between women and animals.
    d. Research shows that substantial numbers of people are aroused by observing animals having coitus.

66. Having sexual relations with a corpse is called (p. 663):

    a. mortalism.
    b. coprophagia.
    *c. necrophilia.
    d. klebsiella.

67. The following practice involves decreasing oxygen supply to the brain to produce a state of euphoria and often leads to accidental death (p. 663).

    *a. asphyxiophilia
    b. coprophagia
    c. denitrification
    d. klebsiella

68. Sexual addiction is marked by preoccupation with sex and also by (p. 663):

    a. ritualization.
    b. compulsive sexual behavior.
    c. despair.
    *d. all of the above.

69. The concept of sexual addiction (p. 664):

    a. applies to women but not men.
    b. applies to men but not women.
    *c. is highly controversial.
    d. has been thoroughly researched.

70. Modifying paraphilias by conventional counseling or psychotherapy has (p. 664):

    a. been extremely successful in leading to long-term change.
    b. been extremely successful in leading to short-term change.
    *c. not been very effective.
    d. been highly effective with females but not males.

71. _____ is correlated with the development of paraphilias (p. 664).

    *a. Physical abuse in childhood
    b. A particular genetic pattern
    c. The inability to find a consenting sexual partner
    d. All of the above

72. The rationale for using castration as a treatment for sex offenders is (p. 665):

    a. that the sex offender has an abnormally weak sex drive.
    b. that punishment is preferable to treatment.
    *c. an inaccurate belief that the testes are necessary for sexual behavior in males.
    d. that the tendency to engage in sexual offenses is inherited.

73. A problem with the use of estrogen as a chemical treatment for sex offenders is that this chemical (p. 666):

    a. promotes secretion of testosterone.
    b. enhances rather than inhibits sex drive.
    *c. can have feminizing effects on males, including enlargement of breasts.
    d. all of the above.

74. A fairly rare approach to treating sexual offenders is _____, which involves destruction of part of the hypothalamus (p. 666).

    a. topectomy
    b. moxibustion
    c. androgen therapy
    *d. psychosurgery

75. Psychosurgery to control or eliminate sexual behavior has been practiced on (p. 666):

    a. aggressive sex offenders.
    b. exhibitionists.
    c. "hypersexual" men.
    d. homosexuals.
    *e. all of the above.

76. _____ has shown potential in treating several of the problems associated with paraphilias without producing negative side effects (p. 667).

    a. Psychosurgery
    b. Chemical aversion therapy
    c. Surgical castration
    *d. Covert sensitization

77. Therapy that attempts to modify or eliminate undesirable behavior by pairing it with an imagined unpleasant event is called (p. 667):

    a. electric aversion therapy.
    *b. covert sensitization.
    c. olfactory aversion therapy.
    d. sexual fantasy alteration.

78. Determining the success of various therapies for sex offenders is difficult because (p. 667):

    a. relatively few controlled investigations have been carried out.
    b. most reports involve techniques used by only one therapist with a few clients.
    c. therapy is typically conducted while offenders are imprisoned.
   *d. all of the above.

Essay Questions

79. Define paraphilia. What is the current view of paraphilia taken by most clinicians (p. 638)?

80. What does fetishism refer to? What are the more common fetish objects? List some cross-cultural practices involving these objects (pp. 638–640).

81. What does a transvestite do? How is transvestism different from transsexualism? In general, what was found by the research that questioned the readers of *Transvestia* and the members of the Seahorse Club? What are some explanations of transvestism (pp. 640–644)?

82. Assume that you and your mate discover your adolescent son cross-dressing. How would you respond to his behavior, and why? Similarly, assume that you are a woman and discover your husband cross-dressing. How would you respond in that case (pp. 640–644)?

83. Describe the general characteristics (gender identity, family background, marital status, sexual orientation, and so forth) of nonclinical samples of transvestites (pp. 640–644).

84. Discuss transsexualism in general. Include a discussion of the procedures followed when sex-reassignment surgery is elected (pp. 644–651).

85. Discuss the behavioral characteristics of female-to-male transsexuals compared with those of male-to-female transsexuals (pp. 644–651).

86. What is involved in sexual sadism? How is it different from sexual masochism? What are the more popular sadomasochistic activities (pp. 651–655)?

87. Some psychoanalytic theorists have seen sadism as primarily a male activity and masochism as primarily a female activity. Evaluate those hypotheses in the light of contemporary evidence (pp. 653–655).

88. What is voyeurism? Include some common characteristics of voyeurs. What gender differences have been observed? What are some explanations for those differences (pp. 655–657)?

89. What is exhibitionism? What are the characteristics of exhibitionists? A common belief is that exhibitionists are unlikely to engage in any other sex offense. To what extent do current data support that belief (pp. 657–659)?

90. What are the similarities and differences between the erotic enjoyment of watching another person versus voyeurism, and stripteasing and nude modeling versus exhibitionism (pp. 655–659)?

91. Define pedophilia. What are the characteristics of pedophiles? Finkelhor (1984) suggested that four factors must be present for a person to become a pedophile. What are they (pp. 660–661)?

92. Define zoophilia. How prevalent is it? What are the common characteristics of the people who practice it (pp. 661–662)?

93. According to Carnes (1983), what is sexual addiction? How does he propose to treat sexual addiction? In what ways does Money (1988) disagree with Carnes (pp. 663–664)?

94. Assume that a relative of yours, convicted as a sex offender, has been offered a reduced prison term providing that he complete a treatment program. Of the currently available programs, which would you recommend, and why? What is involved in the treatment, and what negative side effects (if any) might he expect from it (pp. 664–667)?

95. How is surgical castration used? What belief is it based on? Is it an effective technique? How is chemical treatment of sex offenders different from castration? Are there side effects of chemical treatment? If so, what are they (pp. 665–666)?

CHAPTER 20

Loving Sexual Interactions

Multiple-Choice Questions

1. Maslow's term for an experience that gives one feelings of ecstasy, peace, and unity with the universe is (p. 671):

    *a. peak experience.
    b. multiple orgasm.
    c. self-actualization.
    d. sheer happiness.

2. _____ is clearly associated with personal, social, and sexual maladjustment during adulthood (p. 672).

    a. Parental divorce
    b. Sibling rivalry
    *c. Physical and/or emotional abuse
    d. All of the above.

3. When allowed to choose between two surrogate mothers, monkeys raised without their real mothers spent more time clinging to the (p. 672):

    a. terry-cloth covered "mother" only when she provided milk.
    b. wire "mother," who provided milk.
    *c. terry-cloth covered "mother," whether or not she provided milk.
    d. bars of the cage than to either of the surrogates.

4. Research shows that monkeys (p. 672):

    a. raised in isolation become social misfits.
    b. raised in isolation are unable to mate.
    c. require parental attention in infancy if they are to develop normally.
    *d. all of the above.

5. Harlow's experiments with primates established that (p. 673):

    a. monkeys raised in isolation for at least six months irreversibly become adult social and sexual misfits.
    b. monkeys' and humans' needs for nurturing as infants are fundamentally different.
    *c. controlled interactions with younger "normal" monkeys can restore isolated monkeys' ability to function sexuality and socially.
    d. none of the above.

6. The studies involving rhesus monkeys described in the textbook suggest that (p. 673):

    a. monkey infants and human infants have very little in common.
   *b. early care of infants may have a profound effect on later adult behavior.
    c. monkeys' and humans' needs for nurturing as infants are fundamentally different.
    d. both a and c.

7. Growing up in institutions where contact with adults is brief and hurried is associated with (p. 673):

   *a. major disturbances in interpersonal relationships.
    b. greater independence and imagination.
    c. no significant differences in social functioning.
    d. production of a trusting, loving person.

8. Based on what was mentioned in the textbook, _____ are most related to childhood deprivation that is associated with social problems later in life (p. 674).

    a. large families with many children
   *b. institutions without enough staff
    c. single-parent families
    d. families with only one child

9. Recent research shows that children's occasional expression of the desire to marry one or both parents probably stems from (p. 676):

    a. their love of their parents.
    b. their observation of the pleasure that their parents take in their marriage.
    c. copulatory urges.
   *d. both a and b.
    e. all of the above.

10. Cross-cultural studies show that those cultures in which (p. 676):

   *a. infants are shown much physical affection tend to display little physical violence.
    b. infants are shown little physical affection tend to function as well-adjusted adults.
    c. premarital sex is acceptable are often extremely violent.
    d. affection is valued also value aggressive behavior.

11. Which of the following statements is false (p. 677)?

   *a. Self-esteem and selfishness are similar feelings.
    b. People who don't like themselves tend to direct energies toward protecting and helping themselves rather than others.
    c. Insecure people who are ashamed of their bodies tend to hide and protect their bodies.
    d. Love for oneself is intricately connected with love for any other being.

12. The authors suggest that self-love is (p. 677):

    a. the same as selfishness and is a negative characteristic.
    b. not typically related to how a person treats others.
    *c. different from selfishness and may help people be more loving with others.
    d. none of the above.

13. Cancian (1986) proposed that many scales employed to measure love have resulted in the _____ of love (p. 678).

    a. instrumentalization
    *b. feminization
    c. sterilization
    d. possessiveness

14. Cancian (1986) argues for a more _____ conception of love (p. 678).

    *a. androgynous
    b. expressive
    c. romantic
    d. scientific

15. Which of the following statements is false (p. 679)?

    a. Males are more likely than females to view love as a game to be played out with a number of partners.
    b. Females are more likely to merge love and friendship than are males.
    c. Women emphasize "love planning" more than men.
    *d. Men have been socialized to view sex as a precious commodity that must be guarded.

16. According to Sternberg, the emotional component of love is (p. 679):

    a. passion.
    *b. intimacy.
    c. commitment.
    d. romance.

17. According to Sternberg, passion is the _____ component of love (p. 679).

    a. emotional
    b. cognitive
    *c. motivational
    d. affective

18. A form of friendship in which we are as concerned with the well-being of our friend as we are with our own well-being is called (p. 680):

    a. intimacy.
    b. cognitive love.
    *c. platonic love.
    d. limerence.

19. Friendship (p. 680):

    a. involves a bond between people who are "equal" to one another.
    b. until recently has been seen as unlikely or impossible between a male and a female.
    c. according to Sternberg, involves intimacy without passion or commitment.
    *d. all of the above.

20. A *Psychology Today* survey found that friendships between men and women were perceived as different from same-gender friendships because males and females (p. 681):

    a. may have their friendships complicated by potential sexual tensions.
    b. have less social support for their friendships.
    c. are believed to have less in common than same-gender friends.
    *d. all of the above.
    e. both a and b.

21. Sternberg calls love involving only passion (p. 681):

    a. consummate love.
    *b. infatuation.
    c. empty love.
    d. romantic love.

22. According to Tennov, limerence is characterized by (p. 681):

    a. preoccupation with the limerent object.
    b. unintentional thinking about the limerent object.
    c. desire exclusively for the limerent object.
    *d. all of the above.

23. Tennov proposes that limerence develops in stages, the first being (p. 681):

    a. awareness of sexual attraction.
    *b. admiration for another person who possesses valued qualities and for whom one feels a basic liking.
    c. belief that initial interest might be reciprocated.
    d. a focus on the good qualities of the other person while ignoring the bad qualities.

24. Tennov proposes that limerence is likely to end due to (p. 681):

    a. the development of a deeper relationship with the person.
    b. abandonment as a result of a lack of reciprocity on the part of the other person.
    c. transfer of attention to a different person.
    *d. all of the above.

25. In Sternberg's model, romantic love involves (p. 682):

    a. intimacy.
    b. commitment.
    c. passion.
    *d. both a and c.
    e. both a and b.

26. Which of the following is false (p. 682)?

    *a. During a lifetime, it is impossible to form a romantic bond with more than one person.
    b. Some researchers maintain that romantic love does not differ from infatuation.
    c. People are more likely to like those who reward them than those who do not.
    d. Unrequited love involves very intense feelings for another person.

27. In their two-stage model of love, Berscheid and Walster agree that we are more likely to like someone who rewards us but contend that this relationship may be less applicable to romantic love because people are sometimes more infatuated with someone who (p. 683):

    a. is nonrewarding or even punishing than someone who rewards us.
    b. is not the least interested in us (unrequited love).
    c. elicits jealousy in us, although jealousy is not a pleasant emotion.
    d. both b and c.
    *e. all of the above.

28. According to Sternberg, _____ involves commitment without intimacy or passion and is sometimes seen in long relationships that have become stagnant (p. 683).

    *a. empty love
    b. fatuous love
    c. companionate love
    d. consummate love

29. According to Sternberg, passion and commitment without intimacy is sometimes seen in whirlwind courtships, and is called (p. 683):

    a. empty love.
    *b. fatuous love.
    c. companionate love.
    d. consummate love.

30. When all three components of Sternberg's love triangle are present in a relationship, _____ love exists (p. 684).

    a. companionate
    b. romantic
    *c. consummate
    d. fatuous

31. Consummate love includes (p. 684):

    a. passion.
    b. intimacy.
    c. commitment.
    *d. all of the above.

32. People who view the events affecting them as largely under their own control (internals), compared to people who view events affecting them as controlled by external forces (externals), are (p. 686):

    a. more likely to report that they have been in love.
    b. less likely to report that they have been in love.
    c. less likely to perceive romantic love as mysterious and volatile.
    *d. both b and c.

33. One likely explanation for an unhappy woman's tolerating a pattern of physical or emotional abuse from her partner is (p. 687):

    a. companionate love.
    b. fatuous love.
    c. lust.
    *d. dependency.

34. Jealousy appears to be less common among cultures practicing (p. 688):

    a. capitalism.
    *b. polygamy.
    c. monogamy.
    d. serial monogamy.

35. Feelings of jealousy are probably (p. 688):

    a. similar in all cultures.
    b. similar in both men and women in Western culture.
    *c. associated with feelings of inadequacy.
    d. associated with aggressive tendencies.

36. According to White (1981) _____ are more likely to experience jealousy when they are feeling inadequate, whereas _____ are more likely to become aware of jealousy first and then begin to feel inadequate (p. 690).

    *a. women; men
    b. men; women
    c. neither a nor b; both experience jealousy in the same order.
    d. adolescents; adults

37. Jealousy is most common among (p. 691):

    a. older people.
    b. more educated people.
    *c. people who report overall dissatisfaction with their lives.
    d. people in long-term relationships.

38. According to the authors, the most effective way of dealing with the painful feeling of jealousy is that of (p. 691):

     a. attacking one's partner for specific behaviors.
     b. withdrawing from one's partner.
     c. demanding a change in the behavior of one's partner.
    *d. acknowledging one's feelings and describing their source.

39. Sexual dysfunction is less likely among couples who (p. 693):

     a. view sex as a responsibility to be fitted into a busy schedule.
    *b. look forward to sex for reassurance and support.
     c. view sex as a measure of their sexual prowess.
     d. think of sex as one of many duties.

Essay Questions

40. Based on research with primates, observations of institutionalized infants, and cross-cultural studies, what child-rearing advice would you give to new parents, and why (pp. 672–677)?

41. Compare and contrast the characteristics of cultures in which infants are given a high degree of physical affection with cultures in which infants are either neglected or subjected to physical pain. Be as specific as you can (pp. 676–677).

42. Describe Sternberg's model of the components of love. Include a discussion of the eight triangles that he employs (pp. 679–684).

43. Define limerence, and describe the characteristics of a person in a limerent state (pp. 681–682).

44. What are some potential problems associated with confusing lust with love (pp. 684–686)?

45. Some people experience "love" as an intense form of dependency on another person. Discuss dependency and the idea of emotional attachment as addiction (pp. 686–688).

46. What is the source of jealousy? What are some of the characteristics of people who more commonly experience jealousy? What is a productive way to deal with feelings of jealousy (pp. 688–691)?

47. How can a couple keep vitality in a long-term relationship? What are some of the traps to avoid that were mentioned in the textbook (pp. 693–694)?